HERESY TRIALS IN THE DIOCESE OF NORWICH, 1428–31

edited for the Royal Historical Society
from
Westminster Diocesan Archives MS. B.2
by

NORMAN P. TANNER

CAMDEN FOURTH SERIES
Volume 20

LONDON
OFFICES OF THE ROYAL HISTORICAL SOCIETY
UNIVERSITY COLLEGE LONDON, GOWER STREET
LONDON WC1E 6BT
1977

ISBN 0 901050 39 3

Printed in Great Britain by Butler & Tanner Ltd
Frome and London

ACKNOWLEDGEMENTS

I thank the Archbishop of Westminster for permission to publish the present manuscript. The matter contained in the Appendix, which is a transcript of Crown-copyright records in the Public Record Office, appears by permission of the Controller of Her Majesty's Stationery Office.

Of many other people to whom I am indebted, I wish to thank especially Dr A. Hudson, for so generously giving me the benefit of her great knowledge of Lollardy; Miss E. Poyser, Archivist of the Westminster Diocesan Archives, for the trouble she has taken in putting the manuscript at my disposal; and Mrs D. M. Owen, for her help on a number of points.

Campion Hall,
Oxford

NORMAN TANNER

CONTENTS

ABBREVIATIONS

Bale, *Scriptorum Catalogus*	J. Bale, *Scriptorum Illustrium Maioris Brytannie Catalogus* (Basle, 1557).
Blomefield, *Norfolk*	F. Blomefield and C. Parkin, *An Essay towards a Topographical History of the County of Norfolk* (11 vols., London, 1805–10).
DNB	*Dictionary of National Biography*, ed. L. Stephen and S. Lee (63 vols., London, 1885–1900).
Emden, *BRUC*	A. B. Emden, *A Biographical Register of the University of Cambridge to 1500* (Cambridge, 1963).
Emden, *BRUO*	A. B. Emden, *A Biographical Register of the University of Oxford to A.D. 1500* (3 vols., Oxford, 1957–9).
Foxe, *Acts* (ed. Pratt)	J. Foxe, *The Acts and Monuments* (ed. J. Pratt, 4th edn., 8 vols., London, 1877).
Hudson, 'A Lollard Compilation'	A. Hudson, 'A Lollard Compilation and the Dissemination of Wycliffite Thought', *Journal of Theological Studies*, new series, xxiii (1972), 65–81.
Hudson, 'Examination of Lollards'	A. Hudson, 'The Examination of Lollards', *Bulletin of the Institute of Historical Research*, xlvi (1973), 145–59.
McFarlane, *Wycliffe*	K. B. McFarlane, *John Wycliffe and the Beginnings of English Nonconformity* (London, 1952).
REG	Norfolk and Norwich Record Office, Norwich Diocesan Archives, REG (Bishops' Registers).
Reg. Chichele, ed. Jacob	*The Register of Henry Chichele, Archbishop of Canterbury, 1414–43*, ed. E. F. Jacob (4 vols., Oxford, 1938–47).
Thomson, 'John Foxe'	J. A. F. Thomson, 'John Foxe and some Sources for Lollard History: Notes for a Critical Appraisal', *Studies in Church History*, ii (ed. G. J. Cuming, London: Edinburgh, 1965), 251–7.
Thomson, *Later Lollards*	J. A. F. Thomson, *The Later Lollards 1414–1520* (Oxford, 1965).
Trialogus	J. Wycliffe, *Trialogus et Supplementum Trialogi* (ed. G. Lechler, Oxford, 1869).

INTRODUCTION

The manuscript here edited records proceedings against sixty men and women who were prosecuted for heresy in the diocese of Norwich between 1428 and 1431. It is perhaps the most important record of heresy trials in the British Isles before the Reformation. Other such trials, or groups of trials, involved roughly as many defendants,[1] or even considerably more in the case of the trials of Oldcastle's followers in 1414.[2] But of the former, only Bishop Blyth's proceedings against suspected heretics in the diocese of Coventry and Lichfield in 1511–12[3] and those of Archbishop Warham in Kent in 1511[4] survive in anything like the detail of the present manuscript; and the extant records of the proceedings against Oldcastle's followers are concerned with treason more than with heresy.[5] Neither the proceedings of Bishop Blyth nor those of Archbishop Warham have been published; nor has the present manuscript, though several historians have recently drawn attention to its importance.[6] The manuscript is also of local interest because it is by far the most important record of Lollardy in East Anglia. It shows the extent of heresy at an early date in the area, which produced few participants in Oldcastle's revolt and few known Lollards either before the revolt or after 1431.[7] Thus it offsets East Anglia's reputation as an exceptionally 'High Church' area in the late Middle Ages and helps to explain why it later became a Puritan stronghold.

As a record compiled by and for ecclesiastical authorities, the manuscript reveals much about their attitude towards heresy. It shows how they proceeded against suspects, what views they regarded as heretical and what punishments they inflicted. But

---

[1] See Thomson, *Later Lollards*, pp. 237–8.

[2] McFarlane, *Wycliffe*, p. 176.

[3] Discussed in J. Fines, 'Heresy Trials in the Diocese of Coventry and Lichfield, 1511–12', *Journal of Ecclesiastical History*, xiv (1963), 160–74; I. Luxton, 'The Lichfield Court Book: a Postscript', *Bulletin of the Institute of Historical Research*, xliv (1971), 120–5.

[4] Discussed in Thomson, *Later Lollards*, pp. 187–90.

[5] McFarlane, *Wycliffe*, pp. 171–80.

[6] E. Welch, 'Some Suffolk Lollards', *Proceedings of the Suffolk Institute of Archaeology*, xxix (1962), 154–65; Thomson, *Later Lollards*, pp. 120–31, 223–4 and 231–2; Thomson, 'John Foxe', 251–7; *English Historical Documents, 1327–1485*, ed. A. R. Myers (London, 1969), pp. 864–8; Hudson, 'Examination of Lollards', 151–2; N. P. Tanner, 'Popular Religion in Norwich with special Reference to the Evidence of Wills, 1370–1532' (unpublished Oxford D.Phil. thesis, 1973), pp. 305–6 and 309–10.

[7] McFarlane, *Wycliffe*, pp. 150 and 172–3; Thomson, *Later Lollards*, pp. 117 and 131–7; and see R. A. Houlbrooke, 'Persecution of Heresy and Protestantism in the Diocese of Norwich under Henry VIII', *Norfolk Archaeology*, xxxv (1973), 309–12 and 319–21.

indirectly it reveals much about Lollardy from the standpoint of Lollards. It contains information about their beliefs as well as about the practice of Lollardy—an aspect that has been receiving increasing attention from Dr Hudson[8] and other historians. Thus it provides glimpses of how Lollards put their beliefs into practice, and gives some idea of how the movement was organized and how it spread.

The sections of the manuscript in English are also of interest as examples of the language from East Anglia, and because they give some indication of the importance of the vernacular in the Lollard movement.

i. *The Manuscript and its Contents*

The manuscript forms pages 205–362 of Westminster Diocesan Archives MS. B.2. The pagination was written on to the manuscript in 1881 when it was bound to several other manuscripts, with whose contents it is not connected, to form the 'volume' MS. B.2.[9] However, its leaves are also numbered according to folios. This is the enumeration to which Archbishop Ussher (1581–1656) referred when he made his notes which survive as folios 119r–122v of MS. D.3.4 of Trinity College, Dublin, and it may well date back to the writing of the manuscript. Several page and folio numbers are duplicated, some folio numbers are missing, some folios are blank and others are missing.[10] Neither the whereabouts nor the contents of the missing folios are known, though the folios may have been the additional material to which Foxe had access.[11]

The order in which the folios appear in the manuscript follows neither the chronological order of their subject-matter nor any other apparent scheme. As will be argued shortly, the only explanation seems to be that the manuscript is not the original minutes of the trials but consists of copies of original documents. Since a chronological order seems much more preferable, the contents of the manuscript have been rearranged in this edition so that, as far as is possible, all the matter relating to the trial of a particular person has been put together, and then the trials have been arranged chronologically, according to the date of the first proceedings in the cases of trials that lasted more than one day.[12]

---

[8] See the articles cited below in the Introduction and in the footnotes to the text, and her edition of selected Wycliffite writings to be published by the Cambridge University Press in 1977.

[9] See note on fly-leaf at beginning of MS. B.2.

[10] See Table 1 (p. 3).

[11] See p. 8, n. 47.

[12] See Contents pages (pp. iv–v) and Table 1 (p. 3).

Table 1

Pagination in the MS.		Foliation in the MS.		Sections in this Edition
205–6		no folio numbers		1
207		no folio number		3
208		no folio number		9
209–13		16r–18r		13
214	blank	18v	blank	
215–17		19r–20r		2
218	blank	20v	blank	
219–28		20r–24v		4–6
229–33		35r–37r		31
234		37v		12
235–6		38r–v		42
237–43		40r–43r ⎫		36–7
242		43v ⎭		
243–7		44r–46r		35
248–9		46v–47r		43
250–8		47v–51v		46–54
259–60		52r–v		45
261		53r		44
262		53v		55
263–4	blank	55r–v	blank	
265–8		56r–57v		7–8
269		58r		11
270–2	blank	58v–59v	blank	
273–8		60r–62v		4
279–81	blank	63r–64r	blank	
282		64v		10
283–4	blank	65r–v	blank	
285–6		66r–v		12
287–8		67r–v		38–40
289–91		68r–69r		17
292	blank	69v	blank	
293–4		70r–v		15
295		71r		21
296–316		⎰ 71v–76v ⎱ ⎱ 79r–83v ⎰		18–20, 22–5
317–22		84r–86v		29
323–7		87r–89r		32
328		89v		41
329–32		90r–91v		14
333–40		92r–95v		26–7
341–5		96r–98r		16
346		98v		34
347–51		99r–101r		30
352–7		101v–104r		28
358	blank	104v	blank	
359–62		105r–106v		33

All the pages of the manuscript are of paper. The contents of most of them are fairly easy to read. The most important exception is the first page, the bottom part of which is almost entirely illegible even under ultra-violet rays. In addition some words have disappeared, especially towards the end of the manuscript, as the outside edges of pages have worn away.

It is not known for certain who wrote the manuscript. A few of the marginal notes are additions by unidentifiable later hands. They are mentioned in the footnotes. The rest is written in one or more hands of the first half of the fifteenth century, presumably by scribes from the scriptorium of the bishopric of Norwich. Very probably the sole writer was John Excestr, who is mentioned in the text as the writer of many of the original documents[13] of which the manuscript in question is a copy: the writing of the manuscript, albeit of varying styles and varying degrees of neatness, is strikingly similar to the script of those parts of the registers of the bishops of Norwich which were identified by Professor Jacob as having been written by him.[14] A notary public and a cleric of the diocese of Exeter, he served as registrar to several bishops of Norwich, dying quite a wealthy widower sometime between 1445 and 1447.[15] Once he is styled Master,[16] but there is no other evidence that he was a university graduate.

Classifying the manuscript presents several difficulties. Its almost exclusive subject-matter is the trials for heresy which were conducted in the diocese of Norwich between 1428 and 1431.[17] Yet it does not form part of an episcopal register, where proceedings against heretics are usually found. Indeed, it is noticeable that neither the trials nor the manuscript are mentioned in the registers of the bishops of Norwich. It is perhaps best described as a court-book. As a court-book dealing almost exclusively with heresy, it is a rare document for medieval England. The only other one of a similar nature that is more or less complete and known to survive is the rather briefer record of Bishop Blyth's proceedings against suspected heretics in the diocese of Coventry and Lichfield in 1511–12, now classified as Lichfield Episcopal Archives MS. B.C.13; though it is clear that others, including those of bishops Fitzjames and Tunstal

---

[13] See pp. 32 and 174 and elsewhere.

[14] E. F. Jacob, 'Thomas Brouns, Bishop of Norwich, 1436–1445', *Essays in British History presented to Sir Keith Feiling*, ed. H. R. Trevor-Roper (London, 1964), p. 70, where he is called John Exeter.

[15] Ibid., p. 70; see below, p. 207; Norfolk and Norwich Record Office, Probate Records, Registered copies of wills proved in the Norwich Consistory Court, Register Wylbey, fos. 107r–108r.

[16] See p. 40.

[17] The only exception consists of the record of the penance which six men and women did 'pro aliis causis' (i.e., not for reasons of heresy); see p. 195.

of London (1506–22 and 1522–30) and Longland of Lincoln (1521–47), once existed.[18] The manuscript is not, however, the original minutes of the trials. Its lack of chronological order; the fact that the records of the abjurations are not indentures, as were the originals;[19] the absence of notarial marks and the repetition of fo. 103v on fo. 104r,[20] which is inexplicable on the assumption that the folios are the original minutes but which can readily be explained as a copyist's error, show that most of the manuscript consists of copies. Presumably they are copies of the original documents, made—if what has been said about the writer of the manuscript is correct—shortly after the events they describe. A few parts of the manuscript may, however, be rough drafts and not copies. For example, the two documents concerning Thomas Wade's penance[21] may well be drafts of a letter which the bishop of Norwich sent to Thomas's parish priest. At all events, none of the originals that may once have existed, nor any copies other than the manuscript in question, are known to survive.

Dr Thomson thought the manuscript was written in answer to the request which Archbishop Chichele made to his suffragans in 1428 that they inform him of any actions they might take against heretics.[22] Certainly this hypothesis could explain why Lambeth Palace was the first place known to have housed the manuscript.[23] But the lack of order and of neatness in the manuscript, as well as the incompleteness with which it records many of the trials, suggest that it would have been of much use only to somebody who had witnessed the trials. So it is more likely that the bishop of Norwich had it written for his own reference; the general dispersion of ecclesiastical records during the Civil War and Interregnum could explain how it reached Lambeth Palace. There is no further trace of the manuscript at Lambeth Palace.[24] Nor is it known how it reached the

[18] J. Fines, 'Heresy Trials', op. cit., p. 161; 'The Post-Mortem for Heresy of Richard Hunne', English Historical Review, lxxviii (1963), 528–9.

[19] See pp. 59 and 82 and elsewhere.

[20] See pp. 142–4.

[21] See pp. 35–8.

[22] Thomson, Later Lollards, p. 223; Thomson, 'John Foxe', 252, n. 6.

[23] Archbishop Ussher noted that it was there when he saw it (Trinity College, Dublin, MS. D.3.4, fo. 119r). It is not known when he consulted it. Foxe, Acts, Book 6 (ed. Pratt, iii, pp. 580 and 597, n. 1) simply described the manuscript as (part of) a register of the diocese of Norwich, without saying where it was housed.

[24] The manuscript does not appear in the catalogue of Lambeth Palace Library compiled after Archbishop Abbot's death in 1633 (Library Record 6). Nor was it part of the collection transferred to Cambridge in 1647 and restored to Lambeth in 1664 (E. G. W. Bill, A Catalogue of Manuscripts in Lambeth Palace Library, Mss. 1222–1860 (Oxford, 1972), pp. 1–51). Nor does it appear in the catalogue of the material in the archbishop's study (Bodleian Library, Tanner MS. 88, fos. 20r–69v). I am indebted to Dr Bill, Librarian of Lambeth Palace, for most of the information in this footnote.

Westminster Diocesan Archives, where it was by 1881[25] and where it has remained ever since.

Although the amount of information that the manuscript provides about a particular person's trial varies considerably, the information appears in forms that are repeated and to a considerable extent stereotyped. The account of the trial usually begins with its date and place, and the names of the people involved in it.[26] Sometimes there is a brief description of the arrest and imprisonment of the suspect.[27] A list of the charges and the defendant's plea to them normally follow. Most of the defendants pleaded guilty to all the charges brought against them: in these cases the judge reminded the man that he was guilty of heresy, and the latter stated his desire to abjure.[28] Sometimes the judge fixed another day for the abjuration, but more often the man abjured there and then. If he abjured immediately, there usually followed one or more oaths to the effect that in future he would neither hold any heretical opinions nor help other heretics, that he would inform the appropriate ecclesiastical authorities of any heretics whom he might come to know of, and that he would perform the penances which were about to be enjoined upon him. Then the record usually states that the judge absolved the man from the excommunication which he had incurred by his heresy, and describes the penances which the judge ordered him to perform.[29] Sometimes it also mentions that the judge warned him that, if he relapsed into heresy, he would be in danger of being handed over to the secular arm to be burnt.[30] Occasionally the details of the penances are followed immediately or elsewhere in the manuscript by a note stating that the penances had, or had not, been performed.[31] Regarding the defendants who admitted some of the charges but denied others, the records proceed in a similar way to those of the defendants who pleaded guilty to all the charges, except that they seem to have been punished only for the offences which they admitted, and that sometimes the reasons why they denied particular charges are given.[32] However, with those who denied all the charges brought against them, reasons why they denied them are not given. In these cases the judge ordered the defendant to purge himself, usually on another day and usually after the judge had inquired among the neighbours of the defendant who were present at the trial, and had found nothing incriminating against him. There follow descriptions of the purgations, in all of which the defendants vindicated themselves.[33]

---

[25] Westminster Diocesan Archives, MS. B.2, title page and fly-leaf at beginning of volume.

[26] e.g., p. 125.   [27] e.g., pp. 51–2 and 211.   [28] e.g., pp. 60–2.

[29] e.g., p. 132.   [30] e.g., pp. 190–1 and 197.   [31] See p. 25.

[32] e.g., pp. 91–2.   [33] e.g., pp. 39–40 and 210.

Quite often the records of a trial include a copy of the whole of the defendant's indentured abjuration, and not just the statement that he abjured. Robert Cavell, who was a priest, read his own abjuration.[34] But the other abjurations are preceded by statements to the effect that the defendant, unable to read because he was a layman or because his sight was poor, appointed a cleric to read it for him. While Cavell's abjuration appears in Latin, the others are in English, and they make up almost all of the manuscript that is in the vernacular. The abjurations appear as the first-person statements of the defendants. As regards content, they contain little that has not already been mentioned: basically they consist of a list of the offences, the defendant's admission of his guilt, his oath renouncing his heresies and oaths concerning his good conduct in the future.[35]

This, then, is the information most commonly found in the manuscript. Of the remainder, two types of records need to be mentioned: depositions of witnesses[36] and letters from the bishop of Norwich to the parish priests of men found guilty of heresy, instructing them to see that the men performed their penances.[37]

In addition to the manuscript, the relevant sections of the records of a delivery of the gaol in Norwich Castle are included as an appendix. The records, which were hitherto unknown and which are the only records of gaol deliveries involving the defendants mentioned in the manuscript that are known to survive, throw interesting light on the arrests and earlier activities of several of the accused.

i. *The Trials*

In the spring of 1428 Bishop Fleming of Lincoln had what were supposed to be Wycliffe's bones dug up and burnt, and the ashes cast into a nearby stream.[38] Indeed, the year 1428 saw the beginning of what seems to have been a concerted persecution of Lollardy all over the province of Canterbury,[39] led by the archbishop himself, who is reported to have ridden for several days and nights hunting down suspects.[40] As well as a response to the internal problem of heresy in England, which the Convocation of Canterbury province meeting in London in July 1428 had declared to be 'more than usually growing in strength',[41] the persecution was no doubt

---

[34] See p. 94. [35] e.g., pp. 115–17.
[36] See pp. 43–51 and 72–6.
[37] See pp. 35–8 and 83–4.
[38] McFarlane, *Wycliffe*, p. 120.
[39] Thomson, *Later Lollards*, pp. 28–30, 57–61, 120–31, 144–8, 174–7 and 223–4; see below, pp. 29–30.
[40] *Reg. Chichele*, ed. Jacob, i, p. cxxxvii.
[41] Ibid., iii, p. 185.

stimulated by the English bishops' desire to show the forthcoming[42] Council of Basle that they were tackling heresy.

The diocese of Norwich was one area where the persecution took place, from 1428 to 1431. Though the present manuscript is by far the most important record of the persecution in the diocese, it is not the only one. There are the records printed in the Appendix: the manuscript does not refer to the trial of William White which took place in Norwich on 13 September 1428, and which is recorded in *Fasciculi Zizaniorum*;[43] nor to those of John (or William)[44] Waddon and Hugh Pye, who were burnt with White for heresy in Norwich in the same year;[45] nor is there any reference to the brief investigations which the bishop conducted into heresy in Bury St Edmunds, also in 1428.[46] Indeed Foxe, who evidently had access to yet more material,[47] put the number of people who were examined for heresy during the persecution in the diocese as high as about a hundred and twenty.[48]

The manuscript covers the trials of sixty men and women. The first was on 2 September 1428 and the last was in March 1431, probably on 23 March. However, they were not spread evenly through the two and a half years: there were several intervals of between three and five months without any trials; half of them took place in the final eight months; and on days when they did take place, the number of people arraigned varied between one and at least seven. Why the trials came to an end in March 1431 is not clear. However, it is noticeable that in the last ones recorded by the manuscript, most of the defendants denied all the charges brought against them and successfully purged themselves.[49] So it may have been the resistance of these men, many of whom came from the same village,[50] that persuaded the bishop to cease further prosecutions.

[42] C. J. Hefele and H. Leclerq, *Histoire des Conciles* (Paris, 1907–16), vii, pp. 638–9.
[43] *Fasciculi Zizaniorum*, ed. W. W. Shirley (Rolls Series, London, 1858), pp. 417–32.
[44] See p. 45, n. 45.
[45] *Annales Monasterii Sancti Albani a Johanne Amundesham conscripti*, ed. H. T. Riley (Rolls Series, London, 1870–1), i, p. 29; *The Records of the City of Norwich*, ed. W. Hudson and J. Tingey (Norwich, 1906–10), ii, p. 66.
[46] REG/5, Book 9, fos. 108r–109v. And see: J. Gage, 'Letters . . . for the Suppression of the Lollards', *Archaeologia*, xxiii (1831), 339–43; J. A. F. Thomson, 'A Lollard Rising in Kent: 1431 or 1438?', *Bulletin of the Institute of Historical Research*, xxxvii (1964), 100–2.
[47] See Foxe, *Acts*, Book 6 (ed. Pratt, iii, pp. 584–600). The principal record used by Foxe in his account of the persecution in the diocese is the manuscript here edited. The manuscript shows that there are many errors in his account. So it is difficult to know how reliable is his handling of this additional material. Some of the inaccuracies are discussed in Thomson, 'John Foxe', 251–7.
[48] Foxe, *Acts*, Book 6 (ed. Pratt, iii, p. 587).
[49] See pp. 210–16.   [50] Earsham, south-east Norfolk.

Most of the trials were held in the Bishop's Palace in Norwich, usually in the chapel. A few were held elsewhere in the city: one in St Stephen's parish church, one in the secular college of St Mary in the Fields and one in the house of John Excestr. Half a dozen took place in the bishop's manor-house at Thorpe, just outside the city boundaries. Part of one seems to have been held in a 'claustrum' leading to an unspecified wine-cellar![51] One took place in the hall of the bishop's manor-house at Thornage in Norfolk, another in the parish church of St James within the abbey of Bury St Edmunds.

John Excestr seems to have conducted parts of two of the trials.[52] But in all the other instances for which the relevant information is given, Bishop Alnwick or his vicar general, William Bernham, presided or acted as judge: in almost every case before October 1430 it was the bishop, and in every case after it was his vicar general. Present, too, or explicitly described as assisting, were usually at least three or four and quite frequently a dozen or more clerics and notaries. In all some sixty attended at least once. John Excestr, the writer of the *acta* of the trials, was almost invariably present. Other frequent attenders were William Worstede, prior of Norwich Cathedral Priory, and William Ascogh, who later became bishop of Salisbury and was murdered in June 1450. The Franciscan Robert Ryngman, who, as 'episcopus Gradensis', acted as suffragan to Alnwick and other bishops of Norwich, attended one trial. Several other friars, including the Carmelite writers John Thorp, John Kenynghale and Peter de Sancta Fide, and the Franciscan writer Robert Colman, attended others. It is noticeable, however, that Thomas Netter of Walden, the well-known opponent of Lollardy, who was prior provincial of the English Carmelites until his death in November 1430, is never mentioned as present; he had attended the trial of William White and appears to have been in England until April 1430.[53] As mentioned, neighbours of the defendants attended at least some trials. But apart from Robert Goverton, rector of Earsham, no parish priest, rural dean or archdeacon is mentioned as attending the trial of a person subject to his jurisdiction. Their absence underlines the fact that the initiative in the persecution seems to have come at the diocesan rather than at more local levels.

The known records of the persecutions which began all over the province of Canterbury in 1428 give the impression that they were conducted very largely by the ecclesiastical authorities.[54]. The

[51] See p. 75. [52] See pp. 75 and 89.
[53] Emden, *BRUO*, ii, pp. 1343–4.
[54] See Thomson, *Later Lollards*, pp. 28–30, 57–61, 120–31, 144–8, 174–7 and 223–4.

manuscript here edited supports this impression for the diocese of Norwich. As mentioned, it records that several defendants were warned that if they relapsed they would be handed over to the secular arm to be burnt. It also records that John Skylly was delivered from gaol to the bishop on the orders of three justices of the peace.[55] But otherwise the secular authorities are not mentioned. The records printed in the Appendix are important because they correct this impression. The secular authorities are shown to have cooperated with the Church and to have taken the initiative; they arrested and imprisoned at least some of the suspects; they conducted a preliminary inquiry into their heretical beliefs and activities; and they handed them over to the bishop. In all this they were following the statute against Lollards passed by the Leicester Parliament of April 1414,[56] which the authorities themselves cite.[57]

iii. *The Beliefs of the Defendants*

Specific beliefs, as distinct from general accusations of heresy, were mentioned in forty-five of the sixty trials which the manuscript covers.[58]

In comparison with other trials of Lollards,[59] beliefs concerning the sacraments seem to have been considered unusually important— at least by the prosecution. Thus charges concerning Baptism, Confession, the Eucharist, Confirmation and Matrimony were among those most frequently mentioned, and usually came in a bunch at the beginning of the list of charges. In most cases the charge contained not only an attack on the sacrament as then administered by the Church, but also a more positive doctrine. The latter was implied by the qualification, 'if the parents of the child are Christians', which frequently followed denials of the value of Baptism and Confirmation.[60] It was also expressed by more direct statements as to why the two sacraments were considered worthless. Baptism was said to be so because Christ's people were sufficiently baptized in his blood or in his passion;[61] or because a child's soul was infused with the grace of the Holy Spirit as soon as it became united to a body in the womb of its mother.[62] Confirmation was declared worthless

---

[55] See pp. 51–2.
[56] *The Statutes of the Realm* (London, 1810–28), ii, pp. 181–4.
[57] See p. 219.
[58] See Table 2 (p. 11).
[59] See Thomson, *Later Lollards*, ch. 12; A. K. McHardy, 'Bishop Buckingham and the Lollards of Lincoln Diocese', *Studies in Church History*, ix (ed. D. Baker, Cambridge, 1972), 138–45.
[60] e.g., p. 198.
[61] e.g., pp. 153 and 179.
[62] See pp. 94–5.

Table 2[1]

Sacraments		fasting and abstinence	32
Baptism[2]	29	keeping Sundays and	
Confession[3]	37	feast-days holy	25
Eucharist[4]	35	tithes, oblations and	
Confirmation[5]	23	mortuary fees[17]	32
Matrimony[6]	28	precepts of the Church[18]	13
Orders[7]	13	censures of the Church[19]	17
Extreme Unction[8]	6	Clergy and Religious Orders	
sacraments in general	10	celibacy of priests and nuns	10
Saints and Prayer		temporal goods of the	
praying to saints[9]	23	Church[20]	2
Our Father as the only		pope and others as	
prayer[10]	3	Antichrist[21]	14
images[11]	37	Contacts with Heresy	
relics[11]	2	meeting heretics	25
pilgrimages[11]	34	attending heretical schools	10
St Thomas of Canterbury	6	through books	6
Sts Augustine, Ambrose,		Nature of the Church[22]	4
Gregory and Jerome	1	Trinity	1
Morality and Canon Law		Heaven, Hell and Purgatory	4
swearing[12]	22	Indulgences[23]	1
pleading[13]	5	Holy Water and Blessed Bread	8
lying[14]	1	Churches as Holy Places	6
fighting[15]	5	Church Bells	6
killing[16]	8		

---

[1] The numerals indicate the number of trials in which a particular topic was mentioned. The footnotes refer to possible sources in Wycliffe's works of the views which the defendants allegedly held on the topics, though frequently their alleged views were more extreme than anything that Wycliffe is known to have said or written. Exhaustive references would take up far too much space, and Wycliffe changed his mind on many matters. Therefore the *Trialogus*, which best represents Wycliffe's mature thought on a wide range of questions, has been taken as the basic work of reference. Only where no references can be found in it are other works referred to. References to these other works are from the Wyclif Society editions (1883-1921); for the edition of the *Trialogus* used, see above, p.vi.

[2] *Trialogus*, iv. 11 (p. 282).
[3] Ibid., iv. 23 (pp. 326-8).
[4] Ibid., iv. 4 (pp. 255-8).
[5] Ibid., iv. 14 (p. 294).
[6] Ibid., iv. 22 (p. 323).
[7] Ibid., iv. 11 (pp. 280-1).
[8] Ibid., iv. 26 (pp. 335-6).
[9] Ibid., iii. 30 (pp. 234-5).
[10] Ibid., iv. 38 (p. 380).
[11] *De Ecclesia*, xix (pp. 465-6); *Sermones* (ii, pp. 164-5).
[12] *Opus Evangelicum*, i. 49-51 (i, pp. 177-89).
[13] *De Civili Dominio*, ii. 16 and 18 (ii, pp. 209-33 and 264-5).
[14] Ibid., ii. 16 (ii, p. 228).
[15] Ibid., ii. 17-18 (ii, pp. 233-75).
[16] Ibid., ii. 18 (ii, pp. 264-5).
[17] *Trialogus*, Supplementum, iii (pp. 417-23)
[18] *De Civili Dominio*, i. 17 (i, pp. 118-24).
[19] Ibid., i. 38 and 43 (i, pp. 279-85 and 374-5); *Dialogus*, 27 (pp. 56-7).
[20] *Trialogus*, iv. 19 and 38 (pp. 311-14 and 382).
[21] Ibid., iv. 32 and Supplementum, ix (pp. 357-60 and 448-52).
[22] Ibid., iv. 22 (pp. 324-5).
[23] Ibid., iv. 32 (pp. 357-60).

because a child was sufficiently confirmed (by the Holy Spirit) when it came to the age of discretion and could (and wanted to) understand the word of God.[63]. Oral confession to a priest was said to be of no value (unless the penitent was at the point of death[64]) because God alone could forgive and remit sins;[65] though two defendants were accused of not confessing at the prescribed times,[66] and others of wanting to replace the penance enjoined by the priest with abstention from 'lying, backbiting and evil doing'.[67] Having his mind on God was considered an adequate substitute for Extreme Unction for a man at the point of death.[68] And the consent (of love in Jesus Christ) of the two partners (together with the agreement of their friends) was regarded as sufficient for marriage and therefore made a ceremony in a church unnecessary;[69] though one defendant had wanted marriage to be abolished altogether for some time![70] In the case of Orders, the charge was almost invariably that the defendant believed in the 'priesthood of all believers': namely that every good or faithful Christian, or every man living in charity, was a priest.[71] But, of course, the sacrament was also attacked by denials of transubstantiation and of the value of confessing to a priest; the frequency of these indirect attacks may explain why direct attacks on the sacrament were not more common. Regarding the Eucharist, the charge was almost always that the defendant denied transubstantiation;[72] though two people were charged with not fulfilling their obligations to communicate.[73] The Eucharist was, therefore, the only sacrament to which no alternative was suggested.[74]

The charges relating to the sacraments revealed a striking concern to bypass intermediary persons and things in order to reach God directly. A similar concern was shown by a group of charges which centred around devotion to the saints. It was expressed most directly in those concerned with praying to the saints. Thus one reason invariably given for not praying to them was that all prayers should be directed to God.[75] Two other reasons were mentioned: that all saints were made by ordinances of popes and other ecclesiastics;[76] and it was doubtful whether the saints which 'these singemesse' ordered to be worshipped and prayed to were in heaven.[77] In

---

[63] e.g., pp. 140 and 153.
[64] See p. 173.
[65] e.g., p. 95.
[66] See pp. 103 and 173.
[67] e.g., p. 141.
[68] e.g., p. 141.
[69] e.g., pp. 86 and 111.
[70] See p. 91.
[71] e.g., pp. 57 and 142.
[72] e.g., p. 111.
[73] See pp. 103 and 174.

[74] But for the alternative of *panis sanctificatus* mentioned in the records printed in the Appendix, see p. 218. For alternatives to transubstantiation mentioned in other trials, see p. 33, n. 14, and Thomson, *Later Lollards*, pp. 246–7.

[75] e.g., p. 108.   [76] See p. 154.   [77] See p. 142.

addition, three defendants were accused of believing that the Our Father was the only prayer that should be said.[78]

Another devotion to the saints that was frequently attacked, as it was by Lollards everywhere,[79] was venerating their images. For two reasons it seems that the images rather than the saints were the principal targets. The first is that often the defendant was simply accused of denying the value of honouring images, without any indication as to whose images were involved.[80] The second is that when the attacks were specified as being on the images of saints and of Our Lady, they were usually accompanied by attacks on the veneration of crucifixes or the wood of the true cross (it is not always clear which),[81] yet the value of Christ's death on the cross was never questioned. Usually reasons why the defendants objected to images being venerated were not given, but those that were varied considerably. Some objected on the grounds that images were man-made idols—one added that only men were images of God and therefore only they should be revered[82]—and some included in their attacks those who made them.[83] Margery Baxter was accused of saying that the devils who fell from heaven with Lucifer entered the images in churches, and have continued to dwell in them, so that people who adored them were committing idolatry.[84] Some were accused of believing the crucifix or the sign of the cross was the sign of Antichrist,[85] others that crucifixes were no holier than the gallows upon which thieves were hanged.[86] When asked to help pay for the painting of the images in his parish church, William Colyn had said he would rather pay for images to be burnt,[87] while Richard Fleccher had wanted them all to be done away with.[88] But the only evidence of images actually being destroyed is contained in the Appendix.[89]

The belief that earthly objects were not made holier by being associated with heavenly persons was implied in the attacks on images. Evidently the belief was also held by the two men who denied that relics of saints should be honoured, for both pointed out that such relics were merely the flesh and bones of dead men.[90] Presumably it was also a principal reason for the attacks on pilgrimages.

[78] See pp. 69, 72 and 81.

[79] W. R. Jones, 'Lollards and Images: The Defense of Religious Art in Later Medieval England', *Journal of the History of Ideas*, xxxiv (1973), 31.

[80] e.g., p. 207. [81] e.g., pp. 154 and 158.

[82] See p. 142. [83] e.g., pp. 148 and 160.

[84] See p. 49. [85] e.g., pp. 154 and 166.

[86] e.g., pp. 44 and 179.

[87] See p. 91.

[88] See p. 86.

[89] See p. 218. For the destruction of an image of St Mary at Exeter in 1421, see R. Foreville, 'Manifestations de Lollardisme à Exeter en 1421?', *Le Moyen Age*, lxix (1963), 705.

[90] See pp. 53 and 95.

The attacks were very numerous, as in other trials of Lollards,[91] and usually contained one of two qualifications: either that only pilgrimages to poor people were justified,[92] or that the expenses of pilgrimages should be given to the poor.[93] William Masse only allowed pilgrimages that were made at the pilgrim's own expense,[94] and very material reasons for not making them were given by Hawisia Mone. She confessed to believing that 'all pilgrimage goyng servyth to nothyng but oonly to yeve prestes good that be to riche and to make gay tap[s]ters and proude ostelers'.[95] Three shrines were singled out for criticism: Our Lady of Walsingham, Our Lady of Woolpit and St Thomas of Canterbury—sometimes punned as 'the Lefdy of Falsyngham, the Lefdy of Foulpette and Thomme of Cankerbury'.[96] The holiness of St Thomas's death was questioned by several defendants.[97] Margery Baxter was alleged to have given as a reason that, far from awaiting death patiently at the altar, he had fled like a false traitor and had been killed at the door of the cathedral. She was also alleged to have said that St Thomas was in hell because he had harmfully endowed the Church with possessions, and had initiated and supported in the Church many heresies that seduced the common people.[98] Saints Augustine, Ambrose, Gregory and Jerome and their teaching, which 'Cristis puple calleth doctours draght', were also singled out for attack;[99] though Wycliffe had praised them[100] as well as St Thomas of Canterbury.[101] Another indication of inconsistency was the alleged remark of Margery Baxter: that she prayed to William White, the priest who had been burnt for heresy, in order that he might intercede with God on her behalf;[102] for such prayers would have clashed with the view of many defendants that prayers should not be directed to saints.

Morality and Canon Law were the concern of a third group of charges. Some issues were seen as exclusively questions of morality: that is to say as involving actions which were right or wrong in themselves, or because God permitted or prohibited them, and not

[91] Thomson, *Later Lollards*, pp. 245–6; and see J. Sumption, *Pilgrimage* (London, 1975), pp. 71, 196, 258–9, 270, 272–4 and 300.

[92] e.g., pp. 71 and 81.

[93] e.g., p. 122.   [94] See p. 205.

[95] See p. 142.   [96] See pp. 47, 74 and 148.

[97] See pp. 45, 53 and 96. For the attitude of Lollards to St Thomas, see J. F. Davis, 'Lollards, Reformers and St Thomas of Canterbury', *University of Birmingham Historical Journal*, ix (1963), 1–15.

[98] See p. 45.

[99] See p. 148. For other attacks on the four men, see Thomson, *Later Lollards*, pp. 66 and 122.

[100] *Trialogus*, Supplementum, ii (p. 413).

[101] J. Wycliffe, *De Ecclesia*, ix and xiv (ed. J. Loserth, Wyclif Society, London, 1885–6, pp. 199 and 310).   [102] See p. 47.

because the Church commanded or forbade them. Much the most frequently mentioned issue of this type was swearing. The defendants were usually charged with maintaining that swearing was wrong in all circumstances.[103] However, one defendant allowed oaths 'ad servandam famam' before a judge,[104] and another allowed them when they involved a man's life.[105] Five defendants were accused of believing a person should never plead (before a judge[106]). Only once, however, was a reason given: namely, that those who do so 'amittunt caritatem'.[107] Richard Fleccher was accused of holding what seems an orthodox Christian view, that it was never lawful to lie.[108] As for fighting, one defendant thought it was wrong in all circumstances:[109] the others were accused of maintaining that fighting for a country or for an inheritance was wrong, the only reason given being, again, that those who do so 'amittunt caritatem'.[110] All the charges about killing began by accusing the defendant of believing that nobody may kill another man. Most added that he also thought it was wrong to condemn to death by means of the law men convicted of various crimes—theft, homicide and treason were the ones mentioned. The only reason given was that men should remit vengeance to God.[111] These, then, were the issues apparently regarded by all the participants in the trials as questions about the intrinsic morality of various acts. It is noticeable, however, that many of them were connected with the processes of the law.

Several other issues were regarded by some as questions of morality and by others as questions of Canon Law: namely, fasting and abstinence; keeping Sundays and feast-days holy; and paying tithes, oblations and mortuary fees. Regarding the first, most defendants were charged with believing that nobody was obliged to fast or to abstain from meat on Fridays and other days appointed by the Church. Some, however, were accused of not fasting or abstaining on certain days.[112] Occasionally reasons for the opposition to fasting and abstinence were mentioned: either that God did not institute them[113]—in one case a Pope Sylvester was named as the inventor of Lent[114]—or, in the case of Margery Baxter, the practical consideration that it was more economical to eat on Friday the scraps of meat left over from the preceding day than to go to the market and buy fish![115] The argument that the precept was of man and not of God, and therefore was invalid, also seems to have been the basic objection to keeping Sundays and feast-days holy. Thus, most defendants

---

[103] e.g., p. 153.
[104] See p. 42.
[105] See p. 74.
[106] See pp. 53 and 58.
[107] See p. 96.
[108] See p. 87.
[109] See p. 71.
[110] e.g., p. 158.
[111] e.g., pp. 71 and 142.
[112] e.g., pp. 49–51, 75–6 and 165.
[113] e.g., p. 57.
[114] See p. 46.
[115] See p. 46.

were charged with believing it was lawful to perform corporal works on these days, or that there was no need to 'sanctify' them or to go to church on them.[116] Sometimes, however, the point was made more explicitly by distinguishing between Sundays, which ought to be kept holy because God commanded them to be, and other feast-days, which need not be because the Church created them.[117] (The division of opinion about Sunday reveals another area of disagreement among the defendants). The same point was implied by the qualification that, although a man might work on Sundays and feast-days, he must abstain from sin on them[118]—a qualification that was also mentioned in connection with fast-days.[119] One other reason for not keeping the days holy was mentioned: namely, priests had established them out of greed, so as to collect tithes and oblations from the people.[120] Regarding the payment of tithes and oblations,[121] which was also, of course, an issue much discussed outside Lollard circles, most defendants were accused of holding that a man had a right not to pay them to a church or its curate.[122] A few were accused of believing it was better or more meritorious, or even a duty, not to pay them[123] (at least to an ecclesiastic in mortal sin[124]). The reasons given varied from largely negative considerations to positive alternatives: they made priests proud and lecherous;[125] God had no part in them and a man was bound to 'decimare animam suam tantum Deo';[126] and the money should be given instead to the poor.[127] Thomas Ploman was the only person accused of not paying them. His case is interesting, too, because it suggests uncertainty existed among the laity about the Church's teaching on the matter. Accused of not paying them to any churches or curates for at least seven years, he admitted he had not paid any tithes, but said he had given the money to the poor, as he thought was lawful.[128] Of other points of Canon Law disputed by Lollards, the one most noticeably missing from the trials was whether preachers needed to be licensed by the appropriate ecclesiastical authorities.[129] However, at least some defendants seem to have denied outright the authority of the Church: some denied that breaking the precepts of the Church was sinful:[130] while others denied that ecclesiastical censures, such as excommunications, suspensions and interdicts, had any force.[131]

[116] e.g., pp. 86 and 177.
[117] e.g., pp. 74 and 165.
[118] e.g., pp. 61 and 127.
[119] See pp. 69 and 154.
[120] See p. 153.
[121] Mortuary fees were only mentioned once (see p. 86).
[122] e.g., pp. 116 and 199.
[123] e.g., pp. 141 and 183.
[124] See pp. 100–1.
[125] e.g., pp. 77 and 153.
[126] See p. 74.
[127] e.g., p. 61.
[128] See p. 103.
[129] Hudson, 'Examination of Lollards', 151.
[130] e.g., p. 135.
[131] e.g., p. 158.

Anticlericalism was a marked characteristic of Lollards generally,[132] though it was by no means confined to them. It has featured in several topics already discussed. It appeared in three other issues: the celibacy of priests and nuns, the temporal possessions of the Church, and the identification of the pope and other ecclesiastics with Antichrist and his disciples. Regarding the first, all the defendants in question were charged with holding, in one way or another, that it was more meritorious for priests and nuns to marry 'and bring forth fruit of their bodies' than to remain celibate, or that it was lawful for them to do so.[133] (It is interesting that one of the accused seems to have thought that in 'various remote parts' it was the custom for priests to marry.[134]) However, it is noticeable that the repudiation in principle of private religion,[135] about which suspected Lollards were usually questioned,[136] did not appear in the charges.[137] Despite its importance for Wycliffe,[138] the second issue appeared in only two charges. Both accused defendants of believing that 'temporal lords and temporal men' were bound, under pain of mortal sin, to confiscate the temporal possessions of ecclesiastics and to give them to the poor. One charge added, and to 'compelle thaym to sustene thaymself with labour of here owyn handes'.[139] The third issue was developed along lines which closely resembled views that Oldcastle expressed at his trial before Archbishop Arundel in September 1413.[140] Sometimes Antichrist was identified with the dragon 'mentioned in Holy Scripture', presumably the dragon of the Book of Revelation.[141] The pope was described as the head of the dragon, the bishops and other prelates as its body and the friars as its tail.[142] At other times it was argued that the pope, being Antichrist, had no power on earth to bind or to loose.[143] This point was sometimes refined by an implied distinction between the office of pope and its holders, the argument being that the pope had not the power which Christ gave to Peter unless he lived as Peter had lived.[144] Others were accused of believing that the man called pope was Antichrist, and the holiest person on earth was the real pope.[145] A local note was introduced by the condemnation that Margery Baxter was

---

[132] Thomson, *Later Lollards*, pp. 244–50.
[133] e.g., pp. 61 and 166.   [134] See p. 73.
[135] i.e., living in a religious Order.
[136] Hudson, 'Examination of Lollards', 146 and 151.
[137] But see: Margery Baxter's alleged advice to a friar (p. 48); and Batild Burell's alleged remark about friars destroying the world (p. 75).
[138] McFarlane, *Wycliffe*, pp. 59–62 and 92–3.
[139] See pp. 141 and 147.
[140] *Concilia Magnae Britanniae et Hiberniae*, ed. D. Wilkins (London, 1733–7), iii, p. 356.
[141] chs. 12–14.
[142] e.g., p. 61.   [143] e.g., p. 53.
[144] e.g., pp. 135 and 147   [145] e.g., pp. 141 and 147.

alleged to have pronounced on the bishop of Norwich, that 'Caiaphas', and those 'devils', his ministers.[146] Despite differences of
emphasis, a common line of thought is clearly discernible: a hierarchy in the Church may have been justifiable in principle but its
members could forfeit their authority by their evil living, as the
present members had done.

The sacraments, devotion to the saints and prayer, morality and
Canon Law, the clergy and religious Orders: these, then, together
with the ways in which contact was made with heresy,[147] were the
main topics of the charges. Of the others, the views about the nature
of the Church in many ways summed up the alleged beliefs of all the
defendants, inasmuch as they stressed the invisible nature of the
Church as the communion of the saved, at the expense of its visible
and institutional aspects. One defendant confessed to believing the
Church was the 'congregacio solum salvandorum',[148] another that
the Church was the soul of every good Christian,[149] and a third that
'ther is no Churche but oonly hevene'.[150] A fourth, Margery Baxter,
confessed to believing that only those who kept God's precepts were
Christians here on earth,[151] and she was later accused of saying that
the Church existed only in the homes of those who belonged to her
sect.[152] The interesting Trinitarian doctrine which William Colyn
was accused of holding[153] had no parallel in these or, so far as is
known, any other trials of Lollards.[154] Heaven, hell and purgatory
were the concern of four charges. Two accused defendants of maintaining that no purgatory other than this life existed, and therefore
everybody would go straight to heaven or hell when they died—
and therefore masses and prayers for the dead were useless, added
one charge.[155] The third was connected with the doctrine of the
priesthood of all believers: Margery Baxter was accused of believing
that every good man was a priest, and only priests would enter
heaven.[156] The fourth accused William Colyn of maintaining that no
soul had entered heaven since Christ's incarnation; a rather strange
belief, which he denied holding.[157] Somewhat surprisingly, indulgences appeared only once.[158] Several were charged with holding
that bread and water could not be made holier by being blessed by
priests.[159] Attacks on the sanctity of churches usually took the form
of saying they were mere synagogues, and prayers said in them were

[146] See pp. 45–7.   [147] Discussed below, pp. 20–30.
[148] See p. 61.   [149] See pp. 73 and 77.
[150] See p. 154.   [151] See p. 42.
[152] See p. 49.   [153] See pp. 90–1.
[154] Thomson, *Later Lollards*, p. 130.
[155] See pp. 74, 78 and 148.
[156] See p. 42.   [157] See p. 91.
[158] See p. 46.   [159] e.g., pp. 86 and 154.

no better than those said in fields.[160] But in one case the point at issue was the value of being buried in a church or cemetery.[161] Finally, several were accused of hostility to church bells, the reasons mentioned being that they were Antichrist's horns or that the only purpose of ringing them was to enable priests to collect money.[162]

The significance of the charges depends to a large extent on how far they represented the stereotyped questions of the prosecutors and how far the beliefs of the accused. It is difficult, however, to assess where the balance lay between the two. On the one hand Dr Hudson has shown that the charges were based on a set of questions, though it is not known to survive. Only on this assumption is it possible to explain why the charges relating to a particular topic, as well as the orders in which the charges appeared, were so similar. And the existence of similar questionnaires in the register of Bishop Polton of Worcester and elsewhere shows it was the practice to use one. Clearly the questions asked determined, to a considerable extent, the picture of the defendants' beliefs. Thus, it cannot be assumed they did not hold unorthodox views about such topics as private religion and unauthorized preaching simply because the charges did not mention them. The omissions might well be because they were not asked about them.[163] Furthermore, the large majority of defendants pleaded guilty to all the charges mentioned; very few expanded their thoughts on the charges, for example by distinguishing between what they did and what they did not accept in them. So in most cases information about a defendant's beliefs is limited to a blanket confession to a list of charges which were to a considerable extent stereotyped.

On the other hand the number of charges mentioned in a trial varied considerably. And some, such as those concerning the sacraments, appeared much more frequently than others. So where a blanket confession to the charges appeared, it might well be that the defendant was asked all the questions in the questionnaire, but only the charges which he admitted were recorded. In so far as this was the case—and clearly the argument should not be pressed since it is largely *ex silentio*—an indication may be had of which charges a defendant denied as well as of those which he admitted. Another way in which the charges revealed the beliefs of the defendants, and not just the questions of the prosecutors, was the remarkably generous way in which the allegedly heretical views were recorded. This is evident from what has been said about how the charges frequently mentioned positive alternatives to doctrines that defendants were

---

[160] e.g., pp. 44 and 67.   [161] See pp. 108 and 112.
[162] e.g., pp. 49, 61 and 81.
[163] Hudson, 'Examination of Lollards', 146–7 and 150–1.

alleged to have attacked, as well as varied and serious reasons in support of their views.[164] Such variety and generosity was unlikely to have stemmed exclusively from the prosecutors. Finally, the views and personalities of a few defendants were revealed in a particularly individual way. Those of Robert Berte and William Colyn, both of whom argued with their interrogators, and John Burell and Margery Baxter, who were the central figures in the two fullest sets of depositions, were the most obvious examples.[165]

No doubt the questionnaire on which the charges were based has made the defendants' beliefs appear more uniform than they were. And a few of the accused, including Margery Baxter, may have been on the lunatic fringe of Lollardy. But the defendants, taken together, accord neither with Professor Knowles's description of Lollardy as 'an ill-defined . . . body of sentiment', nor with Professor Chadwick's description of it as 'a few ignorant groups'.[166] Clearly there was a considerable measure of agreement on a number of topics, notably the sacraments. Here, as has been argued, the agreement was both about denying the value of the sacraments as they were then administered by the Church and about a positive alternative to them. The heart of the alternative was the belief that man could reach God directly and that he might therefore bypass intermediary things and persons, particularly priests. The belief could be described as a 'premonitory snuffle of post-reformation puritanism', to use McFarlane's phrase.[167] But it is worth noting that, contrary to what Foxe suggested, the defendants differed from the later reformers on several points about the sacraments. For example, they do not seem to have wanted to retain Baptism and the Eucharist as sacraments at all, while they appear to have considered Matrimony one, even though they wished to dispense with the role of the priest in the ceremony.[168]

The belief that man can reach God directly, without the need of intermediaries, recurred constantly in the other charges: in a way the defendants were accusing the Church of using magic, thus reversing the roles played in the trials of witches. Though the belief foreshadows Puritanism, it is not clear how far the defendants were

---

[164] Contrast this with, for example, the trial of Thomas Northorn before the bishop of Bath and Wells in 1454, in which the accused had to give 'yes' or 'no' answers to very slanted questions (*The Register of Thomas Bekynton, bishop of Bath and Wells, 1443–1465*, ed. H. C. Maxwell Lyte and M. C. B. Dawes (Somerset Record Society, xlix–l, 1934–5), number 898).

[165] See pp. 43–51, 72–6, 89–92 and 98–102.

[166] D. Knowles and D. Obolensky, *The Middle Ages* (The Christian Centuries, ii, London, 1972), p. 451; O. Chadwick, *The Reformation* (The Pelican History of the Church, iii, Harmondsworth, 1973), pp. 14–15.

[167] McFarlane, *Wycliffe*, p. 185.

[168] Thomson, 'John Foxe', 253–4.

appealing to the Bible. On the one hand explicit references to it were very few. But this could be because the prosecutors were not willing to include them in the charges, despite their generosity in other respects in giving reasons for the defendants' beliefs. Appeals to the authority of the Bible might well be implied in the defendants' approval or disapproval of various practices: to take but one example, those who were opposed to the taking of oaths may well have had Matthew 5.33–7 in mind.

There is a similar problem about how far the defendants looked to Wycliffe. On the one hand he is never mentioned: the defendants appear to have regarded William White, Hugh Pye and a few others as their teachers. On the other hand the large majority of their views, in common with those of Lollards generally,[169] are clearly traceable to Wycliffe; even though they were often expressed in more extreme and more popularized forms than Wycliffe's were.[170]

What may be called anti-sacerdotalism was a feature which the defendants shared with Lollards generally.[171] It ranged from anti-clericalism in the sense of criticism of the behaviour of priests and nuns, especially of the financial greed of priests, to opposition in principle to various powers, such as administering the sacraments and making and enforcing laws, which were claimed by various members of the ecclesiastical hierarchy. Clearly the defendants wanted a reform of the clergy; how far they wanted its abolition is not so obvious. The attacks on the temporalities of the Church, which were one aspect of anticlericalism, had social as well as religious implications. There were social implications, too, in the defendants' views on fighting, killing and various legal processes such as taking oaths and pleading in court.[172] Yet, while the social order would have been greatly affected if the temporalities of the Church had been confiscated and if various others of the defendants' views had been implemented, there was only one, vague mention of the complete overthrow of lay society.[173] In this respect it is noticeable that both defendants who wanted the temporal possessions of ecclesiastics to be confiscated, hoped that the lay lords would do it. In not seeking the overthrow of lay society the accused seem to have been in agreement with most Lollards after Oldcastle's revolt.[174] Indeed, the defendants were clearly in the mainstream of the later Lollard movement; though on the whole, according to Dr Thomson,

---

[169] Thomson, *Later Lollards*, p. 240; Hudson, 'A Lollard Compilation', 66.
[170] See footnotes to Table 2 (p. 11).
[171] Thomson, *Later Lollards*, pp. 244–50.
[172] For what Lollardy implied in the social order, especially in the minds of its opponents, see M. E. Aston, 'Lollardy and Sedition, 1381–1431', *Past & Present*, xvii (1960), 1–44.
[173] See p. 47.   [174] Thomson, *Later Lollards*, p. 249.

they adhered to the more extreme beliefs.[175] The most important difference was the unusual emphasis on the sacraments. As Dr Hudson has suggested, many of the other differences, such as the absence of views about unlicensed preaching and the principle of private religion, and the unusual emphasis on church bells and holy water and blessed bread, were probably largely the result of the particular questionnaire on which the charges were based.[176] A local flavour appeared in only two topics: Our Lady of Walsingham and the denunciation of the bishop of Norwich and his ministers.

iv. *The Sentences*

Probably fourteen defendants denied all the charges brought against them and successfully purged themselves.[177] As for the others, occasionally their pleas or their sentences were not mentioned. But Master Robert Berte was the only one of them for whom there is positive evidence that no punishment was imposed. And his case seems to have been special inasmuch as he was allowed to purge himself apparently because it was not clear that what he admitted— having possessed a copy of *Dives and Pauper*—amounted to heresy.[178]

The penances imposed varied considerably, and usually the guilty person was sentenced to a combination of several kinds of punishment. However, none of the defendants is known to have followed William White, John (or William) Waddon and Hugh Pye in being sentenced to death.[179] With the possible exceptions of John Fynche and Margery Baxter this is not surprising since the death penalty was normally reserved for relapsed heretics,[180] and none of the defendants is known to have been convicted of heresy a second time. John Fynche might have been considered a relapsed heretic since he admitted he had only escaped an earlier conviction by perjuring himself;[181] while Margery Baxter was accused of engaging in heretical activities[182] after she had been convicted of heresy,[183] but there is no record of her being convicted a second time.

Flogging was the most common punishment. It featured in over half the sentences. The number of floggings imposed on an individual varied from one[184] to twelve or more,[185] but normally between three and six were ordered. Usually they were to be received in the

---

[175] Ibid., p. 125.
[176] Hudson, 'Examination of Lollards', 151.
[177] See pp. 39–40, 192–3, 201 and 210–16.   [178] See pp. 99–102.
[179] See p. 8.
[180] McFarlane, *Wycliffe*, p. 150; *Reg Chichele*, ed. Jacob, i, pp. cxxxiv–cxxxv.
[181] See pp. 183–6.   [182] See pp. 43–51.
[183] See p. 42.   [184] See p. 208.
[185] See pp. 35–8, 80, 83 and 168.

penitent's parish church, or its cemetery, during the solemn procession of the parish on one or more Sundays, or in the market-place
of his home town on one or more market-days.[186] Occasionally they
were to be received elsewhere—usually in Norwich, in the market-
place or in the Cathedral church or its cloisters.[187] Clearly, therefore,
the ecclesiastical authorities were eager to make the penances, and
thereby the penitents' recantations, known to the public. Frequently a penitent was given precise instructions that he was to
appear bare-footed, bare-headed and clad only in a shirt and a pair
of breeches, or similar attire, carrying a candle which he was to offer
at the high altar of his parish church as soon as he had finished his
penance.[188]

The most common punishments after flogging were 'solemn
penance' and fasting. The former was to be undergone in Norwich
Cathedral before the bishop or his representative on each Ash
Wednesday and Maundy Thursday for several years.[189] Precisely
what it comprised was never explained. The latter usually entailed
fasting on bread and water every Friday for a year.[190] Sometimes,
however, longer periods or other days, or other food and drink, were
specified.[191] Fasting and 'solemn penance' were the only punishments that were explicitly linked to particular heresies. Both were
frequently imposed as punishments for denying that Christians were
bound to abstain from meat on Fridays and various other days.[192]

Three other punishments were occasionally imposed. The first
was for the convicted person to appear as a penitent, bare-footed,
bare-headed and wearing only a shirt and a pair of breeches, in the
solemn procession of his parish on a given number of Sundays, or in
the market-place of his home town on a given number of market-
days, carrying a candle which he was to offer afterwards at the high
altar of his parish church.[193] The punishment used the trappings of a
flogging but spared the penitent the beating. The second was for the
penitent to hold a torch at the elevation of the host during mass in
his parish church on a number of Sundays. Neither of the two cases
of this punishment was explicitly linked to a denial of transubstantiation, but one of the defendants confessed to having attacked it in
a particularly virulent way, and denying it was one of only two
charges brought against the other.[194] The third punishment was
imprisonment: one defendant was sentenced to 'carceres septen-

---

[186] e.g., pp. 197 and 204.   [187] See pp. 35–8, 78, 188 and 206.
[188] e.g., pp. 197–8 and 200.   [189] e.g., p. 124.
[190] e.g., p. 162.
[191] See pp. 40, 56, 66, 68, 105, 107, 110, 150–1, and 192.
[192] e.g., pp. 56 and 119.
[193] e.g., pp. 151 and 156.
[194] See pp. 90–2 and 106–7.

nales'[195] in a monastery; another to the same term in a place which the bishop said he would specify later.[196]

Flogging, 'solemn penance' and fasting seem to have been imposed much more frequently in these trials than in other trials of Lollards. On the other hand branding and the obligation to wear an embroidered faggot on an outer garment, which were ordered in some other trials, were not mentioned. And the only restrictions on the penitents' movements, apart from their obligations to appear for their penances, were the two prison sentences; restricting a person's movements to his parish or diocese for a number of years, or even for life, was a punishment imposed in some later trials. However, too much significance should not be attached to the differences since the punishments imposed on Lollards generally seem to have followed no uniform pattern.[197]

The severity of the penances bore some relationship to the seriousness of the offences. It was not, however, a very consistent one. Thus John Fynche, the man who had perjured himself, was perhaps fortunate to avoid the death penalty or a specially severe punishment:[198] while John Skylly, with a prison sentence and a seven-year fast on bread and water, John Godesell, John Fyllys, Thomas Love and Henry Lachecold may have considered their sentences unusually severe for their offences.[199] Rather, the severity of the penances seems to have fluctuated with time. Thus, the only two prison sentences were imposed in trials which immediately followed each other:[200] and five of the six sentences imposed on 18 April 1430 were almost identical.[201] The women were sentenced to the same kinds of punishment as the men, but on the whole they seem to have been treated rather more leniently. For example, the sixth person to be sentenced on 18 April 1430 was a woman, and she was ordered two floggings less than each of the five men.[202] Two defendants were treated leniently on other grounds. Thomas Mone had his penance suspended because he was old and weak.[203] This, at least, was the official reason, but it would be interesting to know whether his social position was taken into consideration: for it is unlikely he was a very weak man since he had recently travelled a dozen miles from Loddon to Horning,[204] and he was the only defendant who appears

[195] Probably imprisonment for seven years, but possibly imprisonment for a period of time each year for seven years.
[196] See pp. 56 and 63.
[197] Thomson, *Later Lollards*, pp. 231–5.
[198] See p. 188.
[199] See pp. 56, 63–4, 104–5 and 209.
[200] See pp. 56 and 63.
[201] See pp. 110, 118–19, 124, 129–30 and 138.
[202] See p. 132.   [203] See p. 181.
[204] See p. 76.

clearly as a fairly wealthy man.[205] The second person was Isabel Chapleyn: she had her penance reduced on account of old age, misery and impotence.[206]

The manuscript provides only fragmentary information about whether and how the sentences were enforced. The bishop himself seems to have assumed responsibility for the solemn penances in the Cathedral since he ordered them to be performed before him or his representative.[207] Two notes give some idea of the extent to which they were performed. In itself one note is ambiguous as to whether it is naming those who appeared in the Cathedral to do their solemn penances on Ash Wednesday 1431, or whether it is naming those who were due to appear.[208] But the former is more likely since of the ten people who are recorded elsewhere in the manuscript as due to appear, the names of three are missing from the note, and one of the three was John Fynche,[209] who, the second note states,[210] did not appear on that day. What happened to John Fynche, who was already in trouble for perjuring himself, or to the other two persons,[211] is not recorded. As for the other punishments, the only evidence comes from the records concerning John Kynget, Thomas Chatrys and Thomas Wade and from two notes. Regarding the three men, the bishop laid the responsibility of seeing their floggings were carried out, and indeed of administering many of them, on their parish priests.[212] So possibly the parish priests of the other penitents were held responsible for seeing they performed their penances. The only evidence of responsibility being assumed by a layman is contained in a note concerning Nicholas Drye of Lynn. It states that a fellow citizen of his was bound to the sum of £20 (to whom is not specified) to guarantee that Nicholas performed his penance and kept himself free of heresy.[213] The second note simply states that John Burell performed his penance.[214]

v. *The Defendants and the Practice of Lollardy*

The sixty defendants comprised fifty-one men and nine women. Four were priests: John Midelton, vicar of Halvergate; John Cupper, vicar of Tunstall; Robert Cavell, parish chaplain of Bungay; and Master Robert Berte of Bury St Edmunds, who was described as a chaplain. All the other men whose occupations are known were artisans or servants. Thomas Mone was probably a shoemaker,[215]

---

[205] See pp. 25–6 and 28. For similar cases of leniency being exercised out of regard for social position, see M. Bowker, *The Secular Clergy in the Diocese of Lincoln, 1495–1520* (Cambridge, 1968), pp. 35–6.   [206] See p. 200.
[207] e.g., p. 110.   [208] See pp. 194–5.   [209] See p. 188.
[210] See pp. 188–9.   [211] Edmund Archer and John Pert.
[212] See pp. 35–8 and 83–4.   [213] See p. 174.
[214] See p. 78.   [215] See pp. 76 and 165.

as were three others,[216] one of whom was also a servant of Thomas
Mone,[217] and another of whom had formerly been one.[218] Three
were tailors, and three were skinners. There were also two glovers,
two carpenters, another servant of Thomas Mone, a miller, a parch-
ment-maker, a wright, a shipman, a waterman, a tiler and a butcher.
As mentioned, Thomas Mone was the only defendant who appears
clearly as a fairly wealthy man. As for the women, three were married to defendants: Sybil Godsell, Matilda Fleccher and Hawisia
Mone; while Margery Baxter's husband seems to have been a well-
known heretic,[219] even though he did not appear as a defendant. At
least Margery Baxter and Hawisia Mone appear to have been active
Lollards,[220] and no mere followers of their husbands!

The home towns and villages of all but one of the defendants were
mentioned.[221] With one exception all came from the diocese of
Norwich: John Fynche came from Colchester, which was in the
diocese of London, but he was in Ipswich, which lay within the
diocese of Norwich, when he was arrested.[222] The most striking
feature is that the large majority came from a group of small towns
and villages in the south and east of Norfolk and north-east Suffolk.
The scarcity of those who came from the cities and larger towns is
also noticeable. This is specially so in the case of Norwich, the largest
and most important city in the diocese, and one which lay near the
area from which most of the defendants came. It seems never to have
been a centre of Lollardy[223] in the way that London,[224] Bristol,[225]
Coventry[226] and some other cities were.

Almost half the defendants were accused of associating with people
suspected or convicted of heresy.[227] The associations revealed by the
accusations throw much light on the spread of heresy. Many of them
were centred on a family or a household. Thomas Mone's household
at Loddon is the best example, and its role paralleled that played
by the Grevill (or Grebill) family in the spread of Lollardy in the
Tenterden area of Kent in the early sixteenth century.[228] Mone, his

---

[216] Edmund Archer, described as a cordwainer (see pp. 164–5); and John
Pert and John Wroxham, described as souters (see pp. 172 and 189).

[217] John Pert (see p. 75).

[218] Edmund Archer (see pp. 76 and 164–5).

[219] William Baxter (see pp. 39, 47–8, 50 and 179).

[220] See pp. 41–51, 75 and 138–44.

[221] See map (p. 27).   [222] See pp. 182 and 185.

[223] N. P. Tanner, 'Popular Religion in Norwich with special Reference to the
Evidence of Wills, 1370–1532' (unpublished Oxford D.Phil. thesis, 1973), pp.
305–11.

[224] Thomson, *Later Lollards*, pp. 139–71.

[225] Ibid., pp. 20–47.   [226] Ibid., pp. 100–16.

[227] See Table 2 (p. 11).

[228] Lambeth Palace Library, Register of Archbishop Warham (1503–12),
fos. 159r–v and 169v–171v.

Map: the Home Towns and Villages of the Defendants*

- South Creake 1
- Thurning 1

Lynn 1

- Martham 4

Framingham Earl

NORWICH 2

- Tunstall 2
- Halvergate 1
- Rockland St Mary 1

1 Mundham

2 Seething

- Bergh Apton 1

Shotesham

- Loddon 7

1 Wymondham •

- Toft Monks 1

1 Bedingham

2 Ditchingham

- Beccles 7

2 Bungay •

- Shipmeadow 1

10 Earsham •

1 Flixton •

2 Harleston •

- Bury St Edmunds 1

- Sizewell 1

- Nayland 2

- Colchester 1

* The numbers indicate how many defendants came from each place. In a few cases the place cannot be identified with certainty. These cases are noted in the footnotes to the text.

B

wife and three men who were, or had been, his servants appeared as
defendants at the trials; a daughter and, perhaps, a godson may have
engaged in heretical activities.[229] Links spread out beyond the Mone
household in several directions. Thus John Burell, one of Mone's
servants, admitted he had been taught heresies by, and taken part
in heretical activities with, a variety of people outside as well as
inside his master's household.[230] And the Mones admitted that
'scoles of heresie' had often been held in 'prive chambres and places'
of theirs—presumably in their 'mansio' at Loddon[231]—which not
only they and two servants of theirs, but also a number of priests
and other people, many of whom came from outside the town, had
attended.[232] Several other families seem to have played similar roles:
William Baxter and his wife, who knew Hawisia Mone[233] and tried
to influence Johanna Clyfland and her two servants;[234] Batild (or
Baty) Burell and her husband, who was John Burell's brother;[235]
the Godsells; the Flecchers; the Loves; John Wardon and his son;
Walter Webbe and his daughter; and the Belwards.

Schools of heresy were held in several places besides the Mones'
house. Those mentioned were Earsham,[236] the Godsells' house at
Ditchingham,[237] Bergh (probably Bergh Apton),[238] the house of a
cordwainer called John Abraham in Colchester[239] and London.[240]
Many defendants said that they had learnt their heresies in these
schools, which helps to explain the comparative uniformity of the
defendants' beliefs. They may also help to explain the development
of what might be called a Lollard vocabulary.[241] Words and phrases
such as 'trufle',[242] 'mawmentries',[243] 'singemesse',[244] 'shakelment',[245] 'the popis peny dawnser',[246] 'every Friday is a free day',[247]
and 'alle trewe Cristis puple' and 'the trewe lawe of Crist'[248] are a
few of the many probable examples of it. Much of the vocabulary
gives the impression that it was used in the context of worship as
well as in that of imparting information. And presumably both
worship and teaching were conducted in English.

Also to be seen in the context of both worship and imparting
knowledge is the reading of books, which, as Dr Hudson has pointed
out,[249] continued in Lollard schools down to the eve of the Reforma-

229 See p. 75.   230 See pp. 73–6.   231 See p. 75.
232 See pp. 140, 176 and 179.   233 See p. 47.   234 See pp. 43–51.
235 See p. 74.   236 See pp. 208–9 and 217.
237 See pp. 60 and 66.   238 See pp. 33, 146 and 218.
239 See pp. 146 and 152–3.   240 See p. 146.
241 I am indebted to Dr Hudson for this point and for most of the examples.
242 e.g., pp. 140 and 153.   243 See pp. 45–6.
244 See pp. 141–2.   245 See pp. 81 and 147.   246 See p. 146.
247 e.g., pp. 74 and 78.   248 See p. 147.
249 Hudson, 'A Lollard Compilation', 80; 'Some Aspects of Lollard Book
Production', *Studies in Church History*, ix (ed. D. Baker, Cambridge, 1972),
148 and 156–7.

tion. There are several references to books, including at least one written in English, being read at schools and other meetings, and being passed around among the defendants and other suspects.[250] The ecclesiastical authorities thought that others lay hidden.[251] According to Foxe, moreover, a deposition, which is not known to survive, named several defendants who were literate and owners of works of Scripture.[252] So perhaps some of those who claimed to be illiterate and unable to read their abjurations[253] were not telling the whole truth, and Dr Thomson's conclusion that the level of literacy among the defendants was low may be unduly pessimistic.[254]

Other practices, which have already been mentioned,[255] were breaking fasts and abstinences prescribed by the Church, giving money to the poor instead of paying tithes, not confessing and not communicating. The first sometimes seems to have been done by a group of people in a kind of ritual meal at which meat was eaten.[256] In many other cases heretical beliefs could be put into practice in various ways: it is noticeable that such beliefs were described by one defendant as commandments.[257]

The manuscript gives the impression that Lollardy was well established in at least parts of East Anglia immediately before the trials. The families which acted as its centres seem to have given it a certain stability, and a few references suggest it had existed in some form for a number of years.[258] There were links, too, with other parts of the country, at least to the south. The frequenting of heretical schools in Colchester and London, and John Fynche's connections with the former place, have been referred to.[259] William Caleys, a priest who seems to have been a leader of the Lollard movement in the diocese of Norwich,[260] was later degraded and burnt outside it—at Chelmsford.[261] Six other leaders of the movement in the diocese had earlier been suspected of heresy in Kent; William White, the priest who had been a leading Lollard in Kent and who was tried and burnt in Norwich towards the end of 1428; John (or William) Waddon; John Fowlyn; Thomas and William Everden; and Bartholomew Cornmonger. Archbishop Chichele had tried, but failed,

[250] See pp. 39, 41, 47–8, 60, 69, 75, 99 and 102.
[251] See p. 100.
[252] Foxe, *Acts*, Book 6 (ed. Pratt, iii, p. 597). It is difficult to know whether Foxe distorted the evidence through wishful thinking, as he did in several other cases (see above, p. 8, n. 47, and p. 20).
[253] See p. 7.
[254] Thomson, *Later Lollards*, p. 130.
[255] See pp. 12, and 15–16.
[256] See pp. 64, 72, 75–6, 104–5 and 165.   [257] See p. 73.
[258] See pp. 73, 89–90 and 217–18.
[259] See pp. 26 and 28.
[260] See under his name in the Index.
[261] See p. 140, n. 164.

to catch them during his persecution from May to July 1428, and they had escaped to East Anglia.[262] That they were leaders of the movement in East Anglia very soon after their escape from Kent suggests that some or all of them had paid previous visits to the region; though it is not clear how far they founded the Lollard society there, rather than inserted themselves into an existing tradition. At all events, it seems likely that their arrival in 1428 gave a strong boost to Lollardy, and was one reason why Bishop Alnwick launched his persecution. The links beyond East Anglia suggest that Lollardy was less isolated there than it is thought to have been in other regions of the country.[263] However, the only evidence of links with the Continent were John Fynche's confession that he had been familiar with a 'Ducheman' suspected of heresy,[264] and a reference to a book which had recently arrived 'de partibus ultramarinis'.[265]

In conclusion, the manuscript suggests that in organization—as well as in doctrine[266]—fifteenth-century Lollardy was considerably more developed than is generally thought. Indeed, it seems possible to speak of a Lollard organization in a strict sense; that the evidence for it is fragmentary is to be expected since it was not the purpose of the manuscript to describe it. Clearly schools existed in which heresies were taught systematically. Other heretical activities, some of the nature of worship, took place in these schools and at other, apparently less formal, meetings. Moreover, there was a group of people, a number of whom came from outside East Anglia, who conducted the schools and played a leading role in the movement generally. Several of them were priests, and others may have held official positions.[267] However, despite its geographically wide links, Lollardy in East Anglia, as in other parts of the country after Oldcastle's revolt,[268] does not appear to have penetrated higher than the middle ranks of lay and ecclesiastical society.[269]

vi. *Editorial Procedure*

In the transcription, punctuation and the use of capital letters have been modernized and paragraphs have been introduced. The division of words has also been modernized (e.g., 'before' not 'be fore'). The forms i and j, and u and v, have been rationalized, and the form ff

---

[262] Thomson, *Later Lollards*, pp. 173–6; *Reg. Chichele*, ed. Jacob, iii, pp. 85 and 199, and iv, pp. 297–301; see above, pp. 7–8, and under their names in the Index.

[263] Thomson, *Later Lollards*, p. 2.

[264] See p. 185.   [265] See p. 75.   [266] See p. 20.

[267] See p. 1, n. 14, and p. 75, n. 100.

[268] McFarlane, *Wycliffe*, p. 187.

[269] For the only possible evidence in the manuscript to the contrary, see p. 90, n. 121, and p. 99, n. 132.

has been reduced to F or f as appropriate. Abbreviations have been expanded, except where the contrary is noted by an abbreviation mark ('). Mistakes, such as obvious mis-spellings and the unnecessary repetition of words, have been corrected but the original, incorrect forms are given in footnotes. The original spelling of proper names has been preserved. However, the modern spelling of a place name is normally given in a footnote after the first time it appears in each trial. In most cases it is impossible to say with any degree of certainty whether or not cancellations of words, and words inserted between lines, are later additions. When it is clear that they are later additions they have been noted as such; otherwise they have been noted simply as deleted or interlined words. Matter that appears in square brackets has been supplied.

If information about a person beyond what is mentioned in the manuscript is known to exist, it is referred to in a footnote after the person's first appearance in the text.

TEXT

[1]

(p. 205)[a] **Johannes Wardon de Lodne**[1]

Anno Domini Millesimo CCCC[mo] XXVIII, indiccione septima,[2] pontificatus domini Martini pape quinti anno undecimo, mensis vero Septembris die secunda, in capella palacii Norwic'[3] coram reverendo in Christo patre ac domino, domino Willelmo[4] Dei gracia Norwicensi episcopo, pro tribunali sedente,[b] in mei, Johannis Excestr,[5] notarii publici, et testium subscriptorum—videlicet magistrorum Johannis Bury,[6] in decretis, et Johannis Sutton,[7] in legibus, bacallariorum, necnon Thome Walsham, clerici—[presencia], assistentibus tunc ibidem magistris Willelmo Worstede,[8] priore[c] ecclesie Cathedralis Norwic', ac Johanne Thorp,[9] ordinis Carmelitarum, sacre pagine doctoribus, necnon Thoma Ryngstede,[10] in decretis, ac Willelmo Ascogh,[11] in sacra theologia, bacallariis, comparuit personaliter Johannes Wardon de Lodne Norwicensis diocesis, notatus de lollardia et heresi.

Qui quidem Johannes Wardon, interrogatus et examinatus per dictum reverendum patrem, iudicialiter fatebatur et recognovit se habuisse sepius familiaritatem et conversacionem cum diversis hereticis, et in specie quod ipse Johannes Wardon habuit sepius

---

[a] *No folio number.*   [b] pro tribunali sedente *interlined.*   [c] *MS.* prioris.

---

[1] Loddon, south-east Norfolk. John (or William?) Wardon is not to be confused with John (or William?) Waddon (see p. 45, n. 45). For his arrest and earlier activities, see pp. 218–19.

[2] Seventh according to the Greek indiction (beginning on 1 September), though sixth according to the more usual Bedan indiction (beginning on 24 September). In the only other cases where the indiction-years differed (see pp. 182 and 189), the Bedan indiction was followed.

[3] The Bishop's Palace, Norwich.

[4] William Alnwick, bishop of Norwich 1426–36 and of Lincoln 1436–49 (see Emden, *BRUC*, p. 11; *DNB*, William Alnwick).

[5] See above, p. 4.

[6] See Emden, *BRUC*, p. 112, John Bury.

[7] See Emden, *BRUC*, p. 567, John Sutton.

[8] Prior of the Benedictine Cathedral Priory, Norwich, 1427–36 (see Emden, *BRUO*, iii, pp. 2089–90, William de Worsted).

[9] See Emden, *BRUC*, p. 586, John Thorpe.

[10] Dean of the secular college of St Mary in the Fields, Norwich, 1426–44 (see Emden, *BRUC*, pp. 499–500, Thomas Ryngstede).

[11] Later bishop of Salisbury, murdered in 1450 (see Emden, *BRUC*, p. 28, William Ayscogh).

accessum ad dominos Willelmum Whyte[12] et Hugonem Pye,[13] hereticos condempnatos, ac cum Thoma Burell, glover, de Lodne,*a* et quod ipse Johannes Wardon habuit multociens*b* accessum ad scolas et sermones ac doctrinas eorundem hereticorum*c* in villa de Bergh'[14] et alibi.

Item idem Johannes Wardon fatebatur et*d* recognovit iudicialiter tunc ibidem se*e* audivisse*f* ex informacionibus et doctrinis hereticorum predictorum*g* confessionem vocalem nulli presbitero fore faciendam nisi soli Deo.

Item nullum presbiterum habere potestatem conficiendi corpus Christi*h* in sacramento altaris, sed quod post verba sacramentalia a sacerdote rite ordinato prolata in sacramento altaris remanet panis purus et materialis.

Item Extremam Unccionem frustra fieri infirmis personis cum oleo materiali.

Item neminem fore astrictum ad observanda ieiunia indicta per Ecclesiam, sed quod licitum est cuilibet*i* comedere carnes et omnia cibaria indifferenter diebus Quatuor Temporum, vigiliis sanctorum, sextis feriis, in Quadragesima et omnibus diebus indictis per Ecclesiam.

Item licitum fore cuilibet viro et mulieri exercere et facere quecumque opera corporalia omnibus diebus Dominicis et aliis festivis indictis per Ecclesiam.

Item decimas et oblaciones*j* posse licite subtrahi*k* ab ecclesiis et viris ecclesiasticis dumtamen hoc prudenter fiat.

---

a ppt' qui *deleted.*   *b* ad *deleted.*
c hereticorum *interlined.*   *d* reg *deleted.*
e tenuisse et credidisse *deleted.*   *f* audivisse *interlined.*
g sacrament' baptis' *deleted.*   *h* sed quod *deleted.*
i cuilibet *interlined*   *j* fore *deleted.*
k An illegible word deleted.

---

[12] See above, pp. 8 and 29–30; Bale, *Scriptorum Catalogus*, i, pp. 564–5; Thomas Netter, *Doctrinale*, 'De Sacramentalibus', lxvi, xcix, cxii, cxiii, cxxviii, cxl, clvi and clxiv (ed. B. Blanciotti, Venice, 1757–9, iii, pp. 412, 630 708–10, 789, 844, 850–1, 940 and 983); *Reg. Chichele*, ed. Jacob, iii, p. 85 and iv, p. 297; Thomson, *Later Lollards*, pp. 173–6.

[13] See above, p. 8; Thomson, *Later Lollards*, p. 120.

[14] Probably Bergh Apton, south-east Norfolk. In addition to one or two other references to the school (see below, pp. 146 and 218), one of the charges brought against William White at his trial in September 1428 (see above, p. 8)—a charge that he denied—was that on Easter Sunday 1428 'in quadam tua camera in parochia de Bergh' nostrae dioecesis Johannem Scutte laicum, tuum discipulum, ut officio presbyteri fungeretur induxisti, ipsumque ut panem frangeret, ac gratias Deo ageret, et panem hujusmodi tibi, tuae concubinae, Willelmo Everdon, Johanni Fowlyn, et Willelmo Caless presbytero, tecum ibidem praesentibus, distribueret, haec verba in sensu proferendo, Accipite et manducate in memoriam passionis Christi, informasti et fecisti, (*Fasciculi Zizaniorum*, ed. W. W. Shirley (Rolls Series, London, 1858), pp. 423–4).

Item continenciam presbiterorum et monialium*a* fore commendabilem, sed magis meritorium eisdem nubere.

Item nullas oraciones deberi fieri alicui sancto in celo nisi soli Deo.

Item nullum honorem exhibendum fore ymaginibus crucifixi, Beate Marie vel alicuius sancti, nec peregrinaciones fieri debere quovis modo.

Quibus*b* si[c peractis, ide]m Johannes Wardon asseruit [......] quod ipse nunquam adhibuit fidem informacionibus et doctrinis dictorum hereticorum in premissis articulis.*c* Subsequenter vero quia prefatus r[everen]dus pater, ut asseruit, reputavit dictum Johannem Wardon vehementer suspectum de heresi occasione [.......] premissorum, ipse [..] Wardon*d* [...
....
....
....
....
....
....]
(p. 206) errores, opiniones, vel doctrinas hereticas ac fidei catholice contrarias tenentes vel docentes publice vel occulte, et quod nunquam decetero ipse Johannes Wardon recipiet vel defendet hereticos vel aliquas personas suspectas de heresi,*e* aut consilium vel favorem eisdem scienter impendet. Quibus sic peractis*f* [et] prestitis per eundem Johannem Wardon, tactis per eum sacrosanctis evangeliis, iuravit de admittendo et adimplendo penitenciam quam dictus reverendus pater pro suis commissis in hac parte sibi duxerit iniungendam. Dictus reverendus pater absolvit eundem Johannem a sentencia excommunicacionis qua premissorum occasione extitit innodatus. Et pro commissis suis in hac parte iniunxit eidem Johanni Wardon ieiunium in pane et aqua singulis sextis feriis usque ad festum Natalis Domini proximum futurum, et duas fustigaciones circa ecclesiam suam parochialem de Lodne duabus diebus Dominicis coram solenni processione eiusdem, pedibus denudatis, portando in manu sua cereum cere ponderis*g* dimidie*h* libre, et quod offerat eundem cereum posteriori die Dominica tempore offertorii magne misse ibidem post dictam penitenciam circa ecclesiam suam parochialem peractam.

---

a The script is too faint to see whether monialium (the last clearly visible word on the line) is followed by non. For similarly worded charges, see pp. 95, 148, 158, 160 and 166.
b The contents of much of the remainder of the page are too faint to be legible.
c de deleted.   *d* Wardon interlined.
e vel aliquas personas suspectas de heresi interlined.
f dictus deleted.   *g* j deleted.   *h* dimidie interlined.

[2]

(p. 215 / fo. 19r)[a] **Penitencia Thome Wade, taillour, propter heresim abiuratam**[b]

Willelmus, permissione divina Norwicensis episcopus, dilecto in Christo filio, capellano parochiali ecclesie parochialis Sancte Marie de Coslane[c] civitatis nostre[d] Norwici,[15] salutem, graciam et benediccionem.

Quia nos, in negocio correccionis anime Thome Wade, taillour, dicte ecclesie parochiani[e]—pro eo quod ipse crimen[f] heresis manifeste[g] determinacioni sacrosancte[h] Romane ac universalis Ecclesie[i] notorie[j] repugnantis et per eandem Ecclesiam dampnate infra nostram civitatem predictam nuper[k] tenuit, credidit, asseruit temere[l] et affirmavit—ex officio nostro legitime procedentes, eidem Thome Wade coram nobis in iudicio personaliter constituto, ac[m] crimen[n] heresis huiusmodi sibi per nos[o] iudicialiter obiectum se tenuisse, asseruisse et temere affirmasse humiliter confitenti iuxta confessionem suam[p] in hac parte[q] coram nobis in iudicio factam, penitenciam infrascriptam pro suis commissis modo et tempore inferius annotatis[r] peragendam iniunximus, iusticia suadente[s]—videlicet, tres fustigaciones circa claustrum ecclesie nostre Cathedralis Norwicensis[t] tribus diversis diebus Dominicis[u] coram solenni processione eiusdem, ac totidem fustigaciones circa forum venale civitatis nostre predicte tribus principalibus diebus mercati, necnon sex fustigaciones circa ecclesiam parochialem suam predictam, collo,

[a] *The contents of the whole page are crossed out, except the words* que in alia parte istius folii (*see next footnote*). *Some words and phrases are also crossed out individually, as noted in the footnotes. The contents of the page are, to a considerable extent, repeated on the two following pages, though different dates are given.*
[b] que in alia parte istius folii *follows as a note.*
[c] in *deleted.*
[d] civitatis nostre *interlined.*
[e] ex officio nostro legitime procentes *deleted.*
[f] crimen *interlined.*
[g] infra nostram civitatem predictam tenuit, credidit et affirmavit *deleted.*
[h] matris Ecclesie *deleted.*
[i] notori *deleted.*
[j] notorie *interlined.*
[k] nuper *interlined.*
[l] temere *interlined.*
[m] manifestam *deleted.*
[n] crimen *interlined.*
[o] per nos *interlined.*
[p] huiusmodi *deleted.*
[q] in hac parte *interlined.*
[r] peragend' iniunximus, iusticia id poscente, vobis committimus et ma *deleted.*
[s] peragendam iniunximus, iusticia suadente *interlined.*
[t] coram *deleted.*
[u] ac toti *deleted.*

[15] St Mary of Coslany, Norwich. The parish chaplain is unidentifiable.

capite, tubiis et pedibus denudatis, corpore camisia et femoralibus
solomodo induto, cum cereo cere ponderis unius libre in manibus suis
deferendo, more penitentis humiliter*a* incedendo*b*—vobis committimus et mandamus, in virtute obedientie firmiter iniungentes,
quatinus dictum Thomam Wade moneatis et efficaciter*c* inducatis
quatinus dictam penitenciam modo predicto*d* subeat et peragat*e* in*f*
ecclesia nostra Cathedrali predicta coram processione eiusdem
duobus*g* Dominicis proximis et immediate*h* futuris post datum
presencium, et sex diebus*i* Dominicis ex tunc proximis et immediate
sequentibus circa ecclesiam suam parochialem Sancte Marie de
Coslan' predictam coram solempni processione eiusdem congruo
tempore facienda, necnon*j* circa mercatum civitatis nostre predicte*k* tribus diebus Sabbati proximis et immediate post datum
presencium sequentibus hora decima cuiuslibet illarum dierum,
faciendo qualibet illarum dierum circa marcatum in quatuor par-
ticulis*l* eiusdem*m* unicam pausacionem, et in qualibet pausacione*n*
huiusmodi*o* idem Thomas a vobis trinam cum virga recipiat fustigacionem humiliter et devote in signum satisfaccionis pro commissis suis in premissis.*p* Et si dictus Thomas monicionibus vestris
quin verius nostris, huiusmodi [.......]*q* legitime cessante, non
paruerit et dictam*r* penitenciam sibi iniunctam peregerit cum
effectu, ipsum citetis*s* peremptorie quod compareat coram nobis vel
commissario nostro in capella palacii nostri Norwic' nono die post
citacionem huiusmodi sibi factam, si dies illa iuridica fuerit, sin
autem proxima die iuridica ex tunc sequente, causas racionabiles,
si quas pro se habeat, quare propter suam manifestam offensam in
hac parte non debeat excommunicari et pro*t* excommunicato*u*
publice denunciari in forma iuris proposituri facturique ulterius et
recepturi quod in hac parte iusticia suadebit. Et quid feceritis in

---

a humiliter *interlined.*
b iniunximus, iusticia id poscente *deleted.*
c induti superpellicio *interlined and deleted.*
d modo predicto *interlined.*
e videlicet *rubbed out:* humiliter et devote *interlined and deleted:* ecclesiam *deleted.*
f in *interlined.*
g duobus *sic, even though floggings in the cathedral on three Sundays had been ordered.*
h et immediate *interlined.*
i diebus *interlined.*
j tribus diebus principia' venalibus *deleted.*
k tribus diebus *deleted.*   *l* ipsius mercati *deleted.*
m pausacionem sobriam et singularem *deleted.*
n ipsum Thomam trinis vicibus ter publice fustigetis *deleted.*
o huiusmodi *interlined.*   *p* ond' *deleted.*
q An illegible word.   *r* p' *deleted.*
s vel *deleted.*   *t* sic *deleted.*
u excommunicato *interlined.*

premissis,*a* et si dictus Thomas monicionibus nostris huiusmodi paruerit et penitenciam predictam peregerit*b* [.....],*c* nos citra festum Omnium Sanctorum proximum futurum distincte certificetis litteris patentibus vestris*d* habentibus hunc tenorem auctentice sigillatis.

Datum in palacio nostro Norwici xiij⁰ die mensis Septembris Anno Domini Millesimo CCCC⁰ XXVIII⁰ et nostre consecracionis anno tercio.

(p. 216 / fo. 19v) Willelmus, permissione divina Norwicensis episcopus, dilecto in Christo filio, capellano parochiali ecclesie parochialis Sancte Marie de Coslan civitatis nostre Norwic', salutem, graciam et benediccionem.

Quia nos, in negocio correccionis anime Thome Wade, taillour, nuper dicte ecclesie parochiani—pro eo quod ipse nonnullas hereses et errors quamplures determinacioni sacrosancte ac universalis Ecclesie Romane notorie repugnantes et per eandem Ecclesiam dampnatas infra dictam parochiam et aliis diversis locis civitatis predicte tenuit, credidit, asseruit pariter et affirmavit, quos et quas idem Thomas coram nobis*e* iudicialiter fatebatur et recognovit—legitime procedentes confessione[m]que eiusdem Thome in hac parte sequentes, eidem Thome penitenciam subscriptam pro suis demeritis in hac parte modo,*f* forma et temporibus inferius annotatis peragendam iniunximus, iusticia id poscente—videlicet, tres fustigaciones coram solenni processione prioris et conventus ecclesie nostre Cathedralis Norwic' tribus diversis Dominicis diebus, ac sex fustigaciones circa ecclesiam parochialem Sancte Marie predictam sex Dominicis diebus coram solenni processione eiusdem, necnon tres fustigaciones circa marcati locum civitatis predicte tribus diversis Sabbati diebus, collo, capite et pedibus ac tibiis denudatis, corpore camisia et femoralibus dumtaxat induto, cereum cere ponderis unius libre manibus deferendo ac humiliter et devote incedendo—vobis tenore presencium committimus et mandamus, in virtute obediencie firmiter iniungendo, quatinus ipsum Thomam Wade moneatis peremptorie et efficaciter inducatis quatinus huiusmodi penitenciam incipiat, subeat et peragat diebus Dominicis coram processionibus predictis in forma predicta ac circa mercati locum predicti die Sabbati proximo post recepcionem presentis nostri mandati, et sic de diebus huiusmodi in dies immediate con-

---

a in premissis *interlined.*
b et penitenciam predictam peregerit *interlined.*
c An illegible word.   *d* patentibus *repeated.*
e nobis *interlined.*   *f* et *deleted.*

tinuando quousque idem Thomas ipsam penitenciam peregerit, ut prefertur. Vobis insuper ut supra mandamus quatinus, superpelicio induti, virgam vestris manibus deferendo, singulis diebus memoratis tempore execucionis presencium dictum Thomam, ut premittitur, incedentem sequamini continue et immediate. Ipsumque Thomam circa mercati locum, ut premittitur, incedentem ad faciendam in quatuor principalibus locis mercati predicti pausacionem sobriam per vos moneri et in qualibet particulari pausacione sic facienda publice fustigari volumus et mandamus. Et si idem Thomas*a* monicionibus vestris quin verius nostris non paruerit cum effectu, ipsum citetis seu citari faciatis peremptorie quod compareat coram nobis vel commissario nostro in capella palacii nostri Norwic' nono die post citacio[nem] huiusmodi sibi (p. 217 / fo. 20r) factam, si iuridicus fuerit, alioquin proximo die iuridico ex tunc sequente, causam, si quam pro se habeat, racionabilem quare propter eiusdem manifestam offensam in hac parte non debeat excommunicari et pro excommunicato publice denunciari in forma iuris proposituri facturique ulterius et recepturi quod in hac parte*b* canonice dictaverint sancciones. De diebus vero recepcionis presencium monicionisque et execucionis eiusdem qualiter et an dictus Thomas nostris monicionibus huiusmodi debite paruerit necne nos vel commissarium nostrum predictum dictis nono die et loco, si idem Thomas premissis monicionibus non paruerit, alias infra triduum post dictam penitenciam peractam, distincte et aperte certificare curetis litteris vestris patentibus habentibus hunc tenorem sigillo auctentico consignatis.

Datum in palacio nostro Norwic' primo die mensis Aprilis Anno Domini Millesimo CCCC^mo Vicesimo Nono et nostre consecracionis anno tercio.

[3]

(p. 207)*c* **Johannes Midelton, vicarius de Halvergate**[16]

Die Martis, videlicet, quinto die mensis Octobris Anno Domini Millesimo CCCC^mo XXVIII, coram reverendo in Christo patre ac domino, domino Willelmo Dei gracia Norwicensi episcopo, in capella

---

a monicit *deleted.*   *b* iusticia suadebit *deleted.*   *c* No folio number.

[16] John Ederych de Midelton was instituted vicar of Halvergate, east Norfolk, on 18 December 1426 (REG/5, Book 9, fo. 22v). On 23 May 1433 he exchanged the vicarage for the rectory of Felthorpe, north Norfolk (REG/5,

palacii Norwicensis episcopalis, comparuit personaliter dominus Johannes Midelton, notatus de crimine heresis. Cui prefatus reverendus pater obiecit[a] iudicialiter et articulabatur quod ipse fuit communis[b] fauctor[c] et receptor hereticorum, et quod ipse recepit in specie in domum suam dominum Willelmum Whyte, hereticum famosum et condempnatum, ac Willelmum Baxter de Martham,[17] wright, de heresi convictum, et quod ipse ministravit eisdem esculenta et poculenta, et quod recepit ab eisdem libros continentes hereses et tenuit conventiculas et doctrinam hereticam cum eisdem. Que omnia et singula per prefatum patrem iudicialiter obiecta prefatus magister Johannes Midelton constanter negavit. Unde prefatus pater prefixit eidem diem Sabbati proximum post festum Sancte Lucie Virginis ex tunc proximum sequens ad purgandum se in eadem capella cum xij manu ordinis sui de vicinato.[d]

Presentibus tunc ibidem magistris Willelmo Bernham[18] et Thoma Ryngstede, in decretis bacallariis, Willelmo Ascogh et Johanne Sutton.

Quo quidem die Sabbati, videlicet xviij die Decembris Anno Domini suprascripto, coram magistro Willelmo Bernham, in decretis bacallario, dicti reverendi patris vicario in spiritualibus generali, in capella palacii predicti iudicialiter sedente, comparuit personaliter dictus magister Johannes Midelton cum suis compurgatoribus: videlicet, dominis Johanne atte Lee, rectore de Redham,[19] magistro Johanne Southoo, rectore de Fornecete,[20] Johanne Aylesham, rectore de Beston iuxta Milham,[21] magistro Petro[e] Nelond, rectore de Heylesdon,[22] magistro Johanne Cok, rectore de Est Bradenham,[23] magistro Johanne Keche, rectore de Cantele,[24] magistro Johanne

---

[a] sibi *deleted.*	[b] communis *interlined.*	
[c] p' *deleted.*	[d] dce *deleted.*	[e] P' *deleted.*

Book 9, fo. 62r). In the entry noting the exchange, as well as a few lines later in the record of his trial, he is styled Master, but he cannot bei dentified with any probability with a university graduate. Probably, too, he was not the same man as the Master John Midelton, M.A., who assisted at many of the later trials.

[17] Martham, east Norfolk.
[18] See Emden, *BRUC,* pp. 57–8, William Bernham.
[19] Reedham, south-east Norfolk.
[20] Forncett, south Norfolk. See Emden, *BRUC,* p. 542, John Southo.
[21] Beeston near Mileham, west Norfolk. See Emden, *BRUC,* pp. 25–6, John Aylesham.
[22] Hellesdon, near Norwich. See Emden, *BRUC,* pp. 461 and 425, Peter Priour de Stokeneylond and Peter Neylond.
[23] East Bradenham, west Norfolk.
[24] Cantley, south-east Norfolk.

Elmham, vicario de Castr' Trinitat',[25] Thoma Arteys, rectore de Wrenyngham,[26] Stephano Drewe, rectore de Braydeston,[27] Willelmo Duffeld, vicario de Lympenhowe,[28] Johanne Rycheman, rectore de Strumpeshawe,[29] Johanne Cupper, vicario de Tunstale,[30] Willelmo Blithe, vicario de Upton,[31] Roberto Walter, rectore de Witton,[32] Willelmo Snell, vicario de Mowton,[33] et Willelmo Cupper, rectore medietatis de Broom iuxta Bungey,[34] cum pluribus aliis circa xxti in numero. Factaque proclamacione publica si qui voluerint obicere contra purgacionem dicti Johannis Midelton, nulloque contradicente, dictus magister Willelmus Bernham admisit purgacionem dicti Johannis Midelton super premissis et restituit eum, quantum in eo fuit, ad pristinam famam et dimisit eum ab officio.

Presentibus tunc ibidem magistr' Johanne Bury, in decretis bacallario, ac Johanne Rykkes, rectore de Swathefeld,[35] Galfrido Joye, clerico, et magistro Petro Werketon, notario publico et, in admissione dicte purgacionis, scriba[a] et notario in absencia magistri Johannis Excestr, registratoris in hac parte existentis, tunc cum dicto reverendo patre celebrante ordines eodem die apud Lavenham.[36]

(Penitencia: quod Die Cinerum proximo futuro et in Cena Domini, ac Die Cinerum et die Cene Domini ex tunc proximis sequentibus,[b] se presentet in ecclesia Cathedrali cum aliis penitentibus; et quod per vij annos ablacta[.............][c] ieiunet in pane et aqua.)[d]

[a] *MS.* scribe.
[b] se' *deleted.*
[c] *The final letters of* ablacta *and the following word are illegible.*
[d] *The bracketed paragraph is at the foot of the page, detached from the other contents of the page. It seems unlikely that it refers to John Midelton since he successfully purged himself. Of those whose trials appear on the preceding page of the manuscript and on the following one, it could refer to John Baker (see pp. 68–70). But this, too, seems unlikely since there is plenty of space after the record of his trial for it to have been written there.*

[25] Caister Trinity, near Yarmouth.
[26] Wreningham, south Norfolk.
[27] Bradeston, east Norfolk.
[28] Limpenhoe, east Norfolk.
[29] Strumpeshaw, east Norfolk.
[30] Tunstall, east Norfolk. See p. 70, n. 85.
[31] Upton, east Norfolk.
[32] Witton, near Blofield, east Norfolk.
[33] Moulton, east Norfolk.
[34] Broome near Bungay, south Norfolk.
[35] Swafield, north Norfolk.
[36] Lavenham, west Suffolk. For the ordinations, see REG/5, Book 9, fos. 124r–v.

[4]

(p. 219 / fo. 20r) **Margeria, uxor Willelmi Baxter, wryght, de Martham**[37]

In Dei nomine, Amen. Per presens publicum instrumentum cunctis appareat evidenter quod Anno Domini Millesimo Quadringentesimo Vicesimo Octavo, indiccione septima, pontificatus sanctissimi in Christo patris et domini nostri, domini Martini divina providencia pape quinti, anno undecimo, mensis Octobris*a* die septima, in capella palacii episcopalis Norwicensis, in mei, Johannis Excestr, clerici, publici auctoritate apostolica notarii, et testium subscriptorum presencia,*b* coram reverendo in Christo patre ac domino, domino Willelmo Dei gracia Norwicensi episcopo, pro tribunali sedente, assistentibus sibi magistris Johanne Thorp, ordinis Carmelitarum, ac Roberto Colman[38] et Johanne Elys, ordinis Minorum, et Johanne Gaysle, ordinis Predicatorum, sacre pagine professoribus, ac Jacobo Walsyngham,[39] in legibus licenciato, necnon Willelmo Bernham, in decretis bacallario, comparuit personaliter Margeria, uxor Willelmi Baxter, wryght, de Martham Norwicensis diocesis, notata de lollardia et heresi. Que quidem Margeria de mandato dicti reverendi patris ad sancta Dei*c* evangelia per ipsam corporaliter tacta*d* prestitit iuramentum veritatem quam sciverit et noverit super interrogandis ab eadem tangentibus materiam fidei dictura et depositura.

Deinde vero dicta Margeria sic iurata,*e* interrogata et examinata per dictum reverendum patrem fatebatur iudicialiter et recognovit: se novisse dominum Willelmum Whyte, hereticum condempnatum; ac ipsum dominum Willelmum,*f* tanquam hereticum et lollardum fuisse et esse*g* a populo*h* nominatum ac diligenter et sepius quesitum, in domum suam pro refugio habendo ibidem recepisse et per v dies continuos*i* custodivisse et concelasse ac abscondisse;*j* et eidem Willelmo consilium, auxilium et favorem, in quantum potuit, dedisse et prebuisse; ac libros ipsius Willelmi Whyte a villa de Jernemuth[40] ad villam de Martham occulte cariavisse et abscondisse ibidem.

---

a anno *deleted.*   *b* con *deleted.*   *c* gr *deleted.*
d p *deleted.*   *e* sic iurata *interlined.*   *f* per ordinarios et viros v *deleted.*
g fuisse et esse *interlined.*   *h* catholico *deleted.*
i per v dies continuos *interlined.*   *j* ac abscondisse *interlined.*

---

[37] Martham, east Norfolk.
[38] See Bale, *Scriptorum Catalogus*, i, p. 563.
[39] See Emden, *BRUC*, p. 613, James de Walsingham.
[40] Yarmouth.

Postmodum vero tunc ibidem prefata Margeria fatebatur et recognovit*a* iudicialiter coram dicto patre quod, ex doctrina et informacione quas ipsa Margeria habuit*b* a dicto Willelmo Whyte, ipsa tenuit, credidit et affirmavit articulos sive opiniones subscriptas, videlicet:

i. Quod non est aliquis Christianus in terra*c* nisi qui custodit precepta Dei.

ii. Item quod confessio vocalis nullo modo facienda est presbiteris, eo quod sub colore Confessionis plurima committuntur*d* inconveniencia*e* et peccata quia quiscumque proponens confiteri ante Confessionem peccat sub spe venie, quod non faceret si non confiteretur.

iii. Item quod peregrinaciones non deberent fieri quovis*f* modo nisi tantum pauperibus,*g* nec ymagines adorari quovis modo eo quod Lucifer post casum quod non potuit obtinere in celo iam habet cotidie in terris in adoracione of stokkes and stones and ded mennes bones.

iiii. Item quod nullo modo licet interficere quemquam, nec per processum legis dampnare reum.

v. Item quod quilibet bonus homo est sacerdos, et quod nullus homo finaliter veniet in celum nisi sacerdos.

vi. Item quod iuramenta sunt solum ordinata ad servandam famam coram iudice.

Quibus quidem articulis prescriptis per dictum patrem tanquam erroneis*h* et*i* hereticis coram dicta Margeria iudicialiter declaratis, placuit eidem Margerie prescriptas hereses et quascumque alias hereses et errores,*j* ut asseruit, abiurare. Et deinde, (p. 220 / fo. 20v)*k* tactis per eandem Margeriam corporaliter sacrosanctis evangeliis tunc ibidem sponte, ut apparuit, publice iuravit ad ea*l* quod ab hac hora in antea ipsa nunquam tenebit vel affirmabit scienter aut docebit errores sive hereses nec opiniones aliquas determinacioni sacrosancte Ecclesie Romane et eius sane doctrine contrarias; nec hereticos vel aliquas personas de*m* heresi suspectas seu opiniones aliquas sane doctrine sancte Romane Ecclesie*n* contrarias tenentes, docentes sive affirmantes sustentabit,*o* manutenebit*p* aut*q* recipiet; nec huiusmodi personis prebebit consilium, auxilium vel favorem

---

a q *deleted.*
b ex *deleted.*
c in terra *interlined.*
d inconvencia *deleted.*
e inconveniencia *interlined.*
f nullo *interlined and deleted.*
g quovis modo nisi tantum pauperibus *interlined.*
h heret *deleted.*
i et *interlined.*
j abiurare *deleted.*
k et *deleted.*
l ad ea *interlined.*
m de *interlined.*
n contras *deleted.*
o vel *deleted.*
p nec omi eisdem *deleted.*
q aut *interlined.*

publice vel occulte sub pena iuris.[a] Quam quidem[b] penam prefatus reverendus pater declaravit eidem Margerie in vulgari[c] fore penam mortis.

Deinde[d] vero, prestito per eandem iuramento corporali de peragendo penitenciam pro suis commissis sibi iniungendam, prefatus pater iniunxit eidem Margerie pro suis commissis in hac parte: quatuor fustigaciones circa ecclesiam parochialem de Martham coram solenni processione eiusdem iiij diebus Dominicis cum cereo cere ponderis unius libre suis manibus deferendo, collo, capite et pedibus denudatis, corpore curtello solomodo induto; et duas fustigaciones circa mercatum sive forum de Ocle[e][41] simili modo ut supra; et insuper quod feria quarta in Capite Ieiunii proxima futura et in Cena Domini ex tunc proxima sequente in ecclesia Cathedrali Norwic' coram dicto reverendo patre aut eius successore cum aliis penitentibus se presentet, actura solempnem penitenciam pro commissis.

Acta sunt hec prout supra scribuntur et recitantur: scilicet Anno Domini, indiccione, pontificatu, mense, die et loco quibus supra. Presentibus tunc ibidem discretis viris magistris Nicholao Derman, in decretis, Willelmo Ascogh, in sacra theologia, bacallariis, Hugone Acton, notario publico, Willelmo Bamburgh et Thoma Rodelond, capellanis, ac Thoma Walsham, clerico, et aliis quampluribus testibus.

(p. 273 / fo. 60r) *Depositiones contra Margeriam, uxorem Willelmi Baxter, wryght*

Die prima mensis Aprilis Anno Domini Millesimo CCCC[mo] XXIX[o] Johanna Clyfland, uxor Willelmi Clifland, commorans in parochia Sancte Marie Parve[42] in Norwico, citata comparuit personaliter coram reverendo in Christo patre et domino, domino Willelmo Dei gracia Norwicensi episcopo, in capella palacii sui iudicialiter sedente. Et[f] de mandato dicti patris iuravit ad sancta Dei evangelia per ipsam corporaliter tacta de veritate dicenda in et super omnibus et singulis interrogandis ab eadem que concernunt materiam fidei.

Quo quidem iuramento sic prestito, ipsa Johanna Clifland dixit[g] quod die Veneris[43] proximo ante festum Purificacionis Beate Marie

[a] sub pena iuris *interlined*.   [b] penitenciam *deleted*.   [c] in vulgari *interlined*.
[d] Deinde dominus extra iudicium dispensavit cum dicta Margeria quod possit habere unum sotularem in altero pede suo, scilicet egroto *written in the margin in a different hand*.
[e] solio *deleted*.   [f] in *deleted*.   [g] dixit *interlined*.

---

[41] Probably Acle, east Norfolk.
[42] St Mary the Less.   [43] 28 January 1429.

ultimum Margeria Baxter, uxor Willelmi Baxter, wright, nuper commorantis in Martham Norwicensis diocesis, sedens et suens cum ista iurata in camera eiusdem iuxta camenum in presencia istius iurate ac Johanne Grymell et Agnetis Bethom, servencium istius iurate, dixit, et informavit istam iuratam et servientes suas predictas quod nullo modo iurarent, dicens in lingua materna: 'dame, bewar of the bee, for every bee wil styngge, and therfor loke that ȝe swer nother be Godd ne be Our Ladi ne be non other seynt, and if ȝe do the contrarie the be will styngge your tunge and*a* veneme your sowle.'

Deinde dicit ista iurata quod prefata Margeria quesivit ab ea quid ipsa fecit sic omni die in ecclesia. Et ista respondebat sibi dicens quod primo post introitum suum in ecclesiam ipsa solebat, genuflectendo ante crucem, dicere in honore crucifixi quinquies Pater Noster et totidem Ave Maria in honore Beate Marie, matris Christi. Et tunc dicta Margeria, increpando, dixit isti iurate, 'vos male facitis sic genuflectendo et orando coram ymaginibus in talibus ecclesiis quia Deus nunquam erat in tali ecclesia nec unquam exivit nec exibit de celo, nec vult magis meritum tibi prebere vel concedere pro*b* talibus genufleccionibus, adoracionibus vel oracionibus factis in talibus ecclesiis quam lumen accensum et sub lata coopertura fontis baptismalis undique absconditum*c* potest tempore nocturno prebere lumen existentibus in ecclesia quia non est maior*d* honor exhibendus ymaginibus in ecclesiis nec ymaginibus crucifixi quam est exhibendus furcis super quas*e* frater vester esset suspensus,' dicens in lingua materna, 'lewed wrightes of stokkes hewe and fourme suche crosses and ymages, and after that lewed peyntors glorye thaym with colours, et si vos affectatis videre veram crucem Christi ego volo monstrare eam tibi hic in domo tua propria.' Et ista iurata asseruit se libenter videre velle veram crucem Christi. Et prefata Margeria dixit, 'vide', et tunc extendebat brachia sua in longum, dicens isti iurate, 'hec est vera crux Christi, et istam crucem tu debes et potes*f* videre et adorare omni die hic in domo tua propria, et adeo tu in vanum laboras quando vadis ad ecclesias ad adorandas sive orandas aliquas ymagines vel cruces mortuas.'

Et deinde dixit ista iurata quod prefata Margeria quesivit ab ea quomodo ipsa credidit de sacramento altaris. Et ista iurata, ut asseruit, sibi respondebat dicens (p. 274 / fo. 60v) quod ipsa credidit quod ill[u]d sacramentum altaris post consecracionem*g* est verum corpus Christi in specie panis. Et tunc dicta Margeria dixit isti iurate,*h* 'tu male credis quia si*i* quodlibet tale sacramentum esset*j*

---

a bryng *deleted.*   *b* tol *deleted.*   *c MS.* abscondita.
d maior *interlined.*   *e* ho *deleted.*   *f* omni die *deleted.*
g ve *deleted.*   *h* tu male credis *deleted.*   *i* quol *deleted.*
j *An illegible word deleted.*

Deus et verum corpus Christi, infiniti sunt dii, quia mille sacerdotes et plures omni die conficiunt mille tales deos et postea tales deos comedunt et commestos emittunt per posteriora in sepibus turpiter fetentibus,[a] ubi potestis tales deos sufficientes[b] invenire si volueritis perscrutari; ideoque sciatis pro firmo quod illud quod vos dicitis sacramentum altaris nunquam erit Deus meus per graciam Dei, quia tale sacramentum fuit falso et deceptorie ordinatum per presbiteros in Ecclesia ad inducendum populum simplicem ad ydolatriam, quia illud sacramentum est tantum panis materialis.'

Deinde dicta Margeria interrogata per istam iuratam dixit isti iurate, ut asseruit, quod ille Thomas Cantuariensis quem populus vocat[c] Sanctum Thomam Cantuar' fuit falsus proditor et est dampnatus in inferno eo quod dotavit ecclesias iniuriose possessionibus et suscitavit ac supportavit plures hereses in Ecclesia que seducunt simplicem populum, et ideo si Deus fuerit benedictus idem Thomas[d] fuit et est maledictus, et si Thomas fuerit et sit benedictus Deus fuit et est maledictus, et isti falsi presbiteri qui dicunt quod idem Thomas paci, ter sustinuit mortem suam coram altari menciuntur quia tanquam falsus vecors proditor, fugiendo, occisus fuit in ostio ecclesie.

Deinde dixit ista iurata quod prefata Margeria, interrogata per istam iuratam, dixit sibi quod isti maledicti papa, cardinales, archiepiscopi, episcopi et in specie episcopus Norwicensis et alii qui supportant et sustentant hereses et ydolatrias regnantes generaliter in populo habebunt infra breve eandem vel peiorem[e] vindictam quam habuit that cursed Thomma of Canterbury, for thay falsly and cursedly desseyve the puple with thair false mawmentryes and lawes ad extorquendas pecunias a simplici populo ad sustentandam ipsorum superbiam, luxuriam et ociositatem; et sciatis indubie quod vindicta Dei cito veniet in eos[f] qui[g] crudelissime occiderunt sanctissimos Dei filios et doctores—videlicet[h] sanctum patrem Abram,[44] Willelmum White,[i] sanctissimum et doctissimum doctorem legis divine, ac[j] Johannem Waddon[45] et alios de secta legis Christi—

[a] MS. fetentes.	[b] sufficientes *interlined*.
[c] MS. vocant.	[d] e *deleted*.
[e] ve *deleted*.	[f] eo q' *deleted*.
[g] qui *interlined*.	[h] p *deleted*.
[i] Willelmum White *interlined*.	[j] et suo *deleted*.

---

[44] *Sanctum patrem Abram* probably refers to William White; though it could refer, as Dr Thomson thought, to the John Abraham who was a leader of the Lollards in Colchester and who may have been executed in 1428 or 1429. The latter may earlier have been the John Abraham of Woodchurch, Kent, who was suspected of heresy and who had disappeared from his home by the summer of 1428 (see below, p. 152; Thomson, *Later Lollards*, pp. 121–2; *Reg. Chichele*, ed. Jacob, iv, p. 298).

[45] See above, pp. 8 and 29–30. Throughout this manuscript, as well as in Archbishop Chichele's register (*Reg. Chichele*, ed. Jacob, iv, p. 297), he is called John. In the treasurer of Norwich's record of his burning he is called

que quidem vindicta venisset in dictum Caypham,[46] Norwicensem
episcopum, et eius ministros, qui sunt membra diaboli, ante istud
tempus nisi papa transmisisset ad istas partes illas falsas indul-
gencias[47] quas illi Cayphe impetrarunt falso ad inducendum populum ad faciendas processiones pro statu ipsorum et Ecclesie, que
indulgencia induxit populum simplicem ad ydolatriam maledictam.

(p. 275 / fo. 61r)[a] Item dixit ista iurata quod prefata Margeria
dixit sibi quod nullus puer sive infans natus habens parentes Christianos[b] debet baptizari in aqua secundum usum communem quia
talis infans sufficienter baptizatur in utero matris, et ideo illa
mamentria et idolatria quas isti falsi et maledicti sacerdotes faciunt
cum intingunt infantes in fontes in ecclesiis, hoc tantum faciunt ad
extorquendas pecunias a populo a[d] manutenendos ipsos[c] sacerdotes
et[d] concubinas eorundem.

Item quod eadem[e] Margeria dixit isti iurate tunc ibidem quod
solus consensus mutui amoris inter virum et mulierem sufficit pro
sacramento matrimonii, absque expressione aliorum verborum[f] et
absque solennizacione in ecclesiis.

Item quod eadem Margeria dixit isti iurate quod nullus fidelis
homo vel mulier tenetur[g] ieiunare in Quadragesima, diebus Quatuor
Temporum, sextis feriis, vigiliis sanctorum et aliis [diebus] indictis
per Ecclesiam; et quod quilibet potest licite[h] dictis[i] diebus et
temporibus comedere carnes et omnimoda alia cibaria; et quod
melius esset cuilibet comedere carnes remanentes[j] die Jovis de
fragmentis[k] in diebus ieiunalibus quam ire in mercatum et[l] indebitare
se emendo pisces; et quod Papa Sylvester constituit xlam'.[48]

---

[a] Contra Margeriam Wryght (*i.e.*, Contra Margeriam, [uxorem Willelmi
Baxter,] wryght (*see lines 24–5 of p. 43*)?) *at top of page.*
   [b] Christianos *interlined.*   [c] ipsos *interlined.*
   [d] con *deleted.*   [e] ur' *deleted.*   [f] so *deleted.*
   [g] ieiur *deleted.*   [h] licite *interlined.*   [i] uxor Mone *in margin.*
   [j] diebus Jovis *deleted.*   [k] die Jovis de fragmentis *interlined.*   [l] e *deleted.*

William (*The Records of the City of Norwich*, ed. W. Hudson and J. Tingey
(Norwich, 1906–10), ii, p. 66). But it is clear that the same person is being
referred to.

John (or William) Waddon is not, however, to be confused with the Wardon
of Loddon who appeared as a defendant at the trials (see: above, pp. 32–4;
and below, p. 176, where the two men are mentioned separately). It is not clear
whether the latter, too, was called John or William. However, two lists (see
pp. 176 and 179), which seem to be listing the same people, suggest that in this
case, too, only one person was involved; though William Wardon may have
been the unnamed son (see p. 76) of John Wardon.

[46] i.e., Caiaphas.   [47] These indulgences are not recorded elsewhere.

[48] i.e., *Quadragesima.* See Canon 5 of the Council of Nicaea, 325 (C. J. Hefele
and H. Leclerq, *Histoire des Conciles* (Paris, 1907–), ii, p. 548). The forty days
mentioned in the canon may not refer to the fast before Easter, but the earliest
unambiguous reference to the forty-day fast before Easter also dates from the
pontificate of Sylvester I, 314–35 (*The Catholic Dictionary of Theology*, ed.
H. F. Davis, J. Crehan and others (London 1961–), 'Lent', iii, pp. 199–200).

Item eadem Margeria dixit isti iurate quod Willelmus Whyte, qui fuit condempnatus[a] falso pro heretico, est[b] magnus sanctus in celo et sanctissimus[c] doctor ordinatus et missus[d] a Deo; quodque omni die ipsa oravit ad eundem sanctum Willelmum Whyte, et omni die vite sue orabit ad eum ut ipse dignetur intercedere pro ipsa ad Deum celi; et quod dictus Willelmus White dixit eidem Margerie, ut ipsa asseruit isti iurate, quod ipsa Margeria sequeretur post eum ad locum supplicii sui quia ipsa tunc videret quod ipse faceret plura mirabilia quia ipse voluit convertere populum per predicacionem suam et facere populum insurgere et[e] occidere omnes proditores qui steterunt contra ipsum[f] et doctrinam suam, que fuit lex Christi.[g] Que quidem Margeria dixit isti iurate quod ipsa Margeria fuit[h] ad locum[i] mortis dicti W. White ut videret quid fieret per ipsum Willelmum White, et[j] ipsa Margeria videbat quod quando dictus W. White, in loco ubi fuit combustus, voluit predicasse populo verbum Dei, tunc unus diabolus, discipulus Cayphe episcopi, percuciebat ipsum W. White super labia et obturabat manu sua[k] os dicti sancti doctoris sic quod nullo modo potuit proponere voluntatem Dei.

Item dixit ista iurata quod prefata Margeria docuit et informavit eandem iuratam quod ipsa nunquam iret peregre ad Mariam de Falsyngham[49] nec ad aliquem sanctum vel alium locum.

Dixit eciam eadem Margeria quod uxor[50] Thome Mone est secretissima[l] et sapientissima mulier in doctrina W. White, et quod filius[51] fratris Ricardi Belward fuit bonus doctor et primo informavit eam in doctrina et opinionibus suis.[m]

(p. 276 / fo. 61v)[n] Dixit eciam ista iurata quod dicta Margeria rogavit istam iuratam quod ipsa et prefata Johanna, famula sua, venirent secrete in cameram dicte Margerie noctanter et ibidem ipsa audiret maritum suum legere legem Christi eisdem, que lex fuit scripta in uno libro[52] quem dictus maritus solebat legere eidem

---

[a] *An illegible word deleted.* [b] valde sanctus *deleted.*
[c] sanctus *deleted.* [d] et missus *interlined.*
[e] memorandum de uxore H'ubler' de Martham *in margin.*
[f] et eciam ipsa Mar' *deleted.*
[g] et doctrinam suam, que fuit lex Christi *interlined.*
[h] *MS.* iuit. [i] Item de *in margin.*
[j] on' *deleted.* [k] *An illegible word.*
[l] Falsyngham *in margin.,*
[m] memorandum de Johanna West, commorante in cimiterio de Marisco *in bottom right-hand corner of page.* [n] Contra Margeriam Baxter *at top of page.*

---

[49] A pun on St Mary of Walsingham.
[50] Hawisia Mone. [51] Possibly John Belward, junior.
[52] The book cannot be identified with certainty. *Lex Christi* is not known to have been the title of a Lollard book, but Wycliffe and others frequently used the phrase to mean the Scriptures (e.g., *Trialogus*, iii. 31 (pp. 238–43)), and Margery Baxter may well have been using it in the same sense.

Margerie noctanter,*a* et dixit quod maritus suus est optimus doctor Christianitatis.

Dixit eciam dicta Margeria quod ipsa*b* communicavit cum Johanna*c* West, muliere commorante in cimiterio Sancte Marie de Marisco,*d* 53 de*e* lege Christi, et ipsa Johanna est in bona via salvacionis.

Dixit insuper dicta Margeria isti iurate sic:*f* 'Johanna, apparet per vultum tuum quod tu intendis et proponis revelare istud consilium quod dixi tibi episcopo.' Et ista iurata iuravit quod ipsa nunquam voluit revelare consilium suum in hac parte nisi ipsa Margeria dederit sibi occasionem hoc faciendi. Et tunc dixit*g* dicta Margeria eidem iurate, 'et si tu accusaveris me dicto episcopo, ego faciam tibi sicut feci cuidam fratri Carmelite de Jernemuth,54 qui fuit doctissimus frater tocius patrie.' Cui dixit ista iurata*h* et respondebat, petens ab ea quid ipsa fecit dicto fratri. Et illa Margeria*i* respondebat quod ipsa communicavit cum dicto fratre, increpans eum quia sic mendicabat et quod non fuit elemosina facere nec dare sibi bonum nisi voluerit dimittere habitum suum et ire ad aratrum, et sic quod ille placeret magis Deo quam sequendo*j* vitam aliquorum aliorum fratrum. Et tunc ipse frater*k* quesivit ab eadem Margeria si aliquid aliud ipsa sciverit dicere vel docere sibi. Et ipsa Margeria, ut asseruit isti iurate, exposuit dicto fratri evangelia in lingua Anglicana. Et tunc dictus frater*l* recessit ab eadem Margeria, ut asseruit isti iurate. Et postea idem frater accusavit eandem Margeriam de heresi. Et prefata Margeria audiens quod dictus frater ipsam accusavit sic, ipsa Margeria accusavit ipsum fratrem quod ipse*m* voluit eam carnaliter cognovisse, et quia ipsa noluit sibi consentire ipse frater accusavit eam de heresi. Et propterea dicta Margeria dixit quod maritus suus voluit ipsum fratrem propterea occidisse, et sic propter metum ille frater tacuit et recessit a partibus cum verecundia.

Dixit eciam dicta Margeria isti iurate quod ipsa fuit sepius ficte confessa decano de Campis*n* 55 ad finem quod ipse decanus reputaret

---

a in prioratu Norwic' *deleted.*   *b* bene informavit Johannam *deleted.*
c communicavit cum Johanna *interlined.*   *d* in *deleted.*
e de *interlined.*   *f* sic *interlined.*   *g* ist *deleted.*
h Margeria *deleted.*   *i* Margeria *interlined.*   *j* sequendo *interlined.*
k pe *deleted.*   *l* frater *interlined.*   *m* ve *deleted.*
n et ista iurata quesivit ad quid ipsa s *deleted.*

---

53 Probably the parish church of St Mary in the Marsh, Norwich.
54 Yarmouth. The friar is unidentifiable.
55 i.e., the dean of the secular college of St Mary in the Fields, Norwich. Thomas Ryngstede, who attended many of the trials, though not Margery Baxter's, had been dean since October 1426 (Emden, *BRUC*, pp. 499–500). His predecessor was John Rickinghall, who was dean from 1405 until his promotion to the bishopric of Chichester in 1426 (Emden, *BRUC*, p. 480; though Dr Emden is not correct in saying that he had had a previous spell as dean, beginning in 1395).

eam esse bone vite. Et propterea ipse sepius dedit eidem Margerie pecuniam. Et tunc ista iurata dixit sibi nunquid est confessa sacerdoti de omnibus peccatis suis.[a] Et ipsa Margeria dixit quod ipsa nunquam egit malum alicui sacerdoti, et ideo ipsa nunquam voluit confiteri sacerdoti nec obedire se[b] alicui sacerdoti, quia[c] nullus sacerdos habet potestatem absolvendi quemquam a peccatis, et presbiteri gravius peccant omni die quam alii homines. Et eciam dixit eadem Margeria quod omnis homo et omnis mulier qui sunt de opinione eiusdem Margerie sunt boni sacerdotes, et quod sancta Ecclesia est tantum[d] in locis habitacionum omnium existencium de secta sua. Et ideo ipsa Margeria dixit quod confitendum est soli Deo, et nulli[e] alii sacerdoti.

Item dixit dicta Margeria isti iurate[f] quod populus honorat diabolos qui ceciderent cum Lucifero de celo,[g] qui quidem diaboli cum cadendo in terram intrarunt in ymagines stantes in ecclesiis, et in eisdem continue habitarunt et adhuc habitant latitantes, ut populus adorans[h] eosdem sic committeret[i] ydolatriam.

Item dixit quod dicta Margeria informavit istam iuratam quod[j] aqua benedicta vel panis benedictus sunt nisi truphe et nullius virtutis, et quod omnes campane sunt depellende et destruende ab ecclesiis, et quod omnes qui ordinarunt campanas in ecclesiis sunt excommunicati.[k]

Dixit eciam eadem Margeria[l] isti iurate quod ipsa Margeria non deberet comburi, licet ipsa fuerit convicta de lollardiis, quia ipsa Margeria, ut asseruit isti iurate, habuit et habet unam cartam salvacionis in utero suo.

Item eadem Margeria dixit quod ipsa vincebat in iudicio dominum Norwicensem episcopum et Henricum Inglese ac dominos abbates existentes cum eisdem.

(p. 277 / fo. 62r)[m] Item dicta iurata dicit quod Agnes[n] Bethom, famula istius iurate, missa ad domum dicte Margerie die Sabbati[o] [56] proximo post Diem Cinerum ultimo elapso, dicta Margeria non existente in domo sua, invenit unam ollam eneam stantem supra ignem, in qua quidem olla bullivit[p] una pecia salse carnis porcine cum farina avene in eadem olla, prout dicta Agnes retulit isti iurate.

[a] MS. vestris. [b] sibi deleted.
[c] su deleted. [d] tantum interlined.
[e] MS. nullo. [f] MS. iurati.
[g] et ca' Deus deleted. [h] MS. adorantes.
[i] MS. committerent. [j] quod interlined.
[k] MS. excommunicate. [l] quod deleted.
[m] Contra Margeriam Baxter at top of page.
[n] de deleted.
[o] ac prima ebdomada deleted.
[p] An illegible word and salse deleted.

[56] 12 February 1429.

Johanna Grymle, serviens*a* Willelmi Clyfland etatis xvj annorum et amplius, iurata de veritate dicenda in hac parte, interrogata et examinata de et super omnibus et singulis singillatim que dicta Johanna Clyfland supra deposuit, dicit ista iurata in virtute iuramenti sui prestiti quod ipsa fuit presens una cum dicta Johanna Clyfland et Agnete Bethom in camera dicte contestis supraexaminate, iuxta camenum ignis, ubi ista iurata audivit prefatam Margeriam Baxter dicere omnia et singula contenta in deposicionibus dicte contestis supraexaminate. Et insuper addidit ista iurata quod prefata Margeria dixit eidem quod maritus suus noctanter*b* exivit sepius septa dicti*c* prioratus per magnas portas, et venit ad domum suam propriam per venellam fratrum Minorum Norwici, et nullus monachus scivit inde.[57] Dixit eciam ista iurata quod ipsa audivit dictam Agnetam Bethom dicere quod ipsa vidit dicto die Sabbati ollam eneam bullientem cum carnibus salsis porcine et farina avene in domo eiusdem Margerie. Et in aliis dicit ista*d* iurata quod ipsa audivit totam communicacionem habitam inter dictam Margeriam et prefatam contestem suam prout continetur in deposicionibus suis, et concordat cum eadem conteste sua.

Agnes Bethom, serviens Willelmi Clyfland de Norwico etatis quatuordecim annorum, iurata de veritate dicenda super interrogandis ab eadem omnibus et singulis*e* que concernunt materiam fidei, interrogata, requisita et*f* examinata*g* super omnibus et singulis que prefata Johanna Clyfland supra deposuit, dicit et concordat in omnibus cum dicta Johanna Clyfland, hoc addito sive mutato: quod dicta Margeria dixit circa festum Purificacionis Beate Marie ultimum elapsum[58] in presencia istius iurate ac Johanne Clyfland et Johanne Grymle in domo dicte Johanne Clyfland quod illud sacramentum quod presbiteri post consecracionem elevant supra capita sua et ostendunt populo*h* non [est] corpus Christi, sicut illi falsi presbiteri affirmant ad decipiendum populum, sed est nisi torta panis pistata per pastorem, quam tortam panis sic consecratam presbiteri comedunt et per posteriora emittunt in sepibus, et ideo illud sacramentum nunquam erit Deus meus, sed magnus antiquus

---

a Johannis C *deleted.*   *b* veniet *deleted.*
c p' *deleted.*   *d* quod *deleted.*
e An illegible word deleted. *f* interrogata *deleted.*
g examinata *interlined.*   *h* One or two illegible letters deleted.

---

[57] It is not clear which priory was being referred to. Possibly it was the Benedictine Cathedra[1] Priory in Norwich, since it was the only house of monks in the city and lay next to the Franciscan friary.
[58] 2 February 1429.

Deus qui nunquam exivit nec exibit*a* de celo erit Deus meus, et non iste Deus quem populus colit hiis diebus;*b* eciam addens ista (p. 278 / fo. 62v) iurata dixit*c* quod die Sabbati⁵⁹ proximo*d* post Diem Cinerum ultimum elapsum ista iurata, missa ad domum dicte Margerie pro uno scabello faciendo per magistram suam, vidit unam ollam eneam stantem supra ignem in domo dicte Margerie bullientem et coopertam et, dicta Margeria non existente in domo illa, ista iurata discooperuit ollam et vidit in eadem unam peciam de bakon bullientem in aqua cum farina avene.

[5]

(p. 220 / fo. 20v) **Johannes Skylly de Flixton***e* ⁶⁰

Anno Domini Millesimo Quadringentesimo Vicesimo Octavo, indiccione septima, pontificatus sanctissimi in Christo patris et domini nostri, domini Martini divina providencia pape quinti huius nominis, anno duodecimo, mensis Marcii die quintadecima, in capella palacii Norwic', in mei, Johannis Excestr, clerici, notarii publici, et testium infrascriptorum presencia, coram reverendo in Christo patre ac domino, domino Willelmo Dei gracia Norwicensi episcopo, pro tribunali sedente, assistentibus sibi tunc ibidem magistris Willelmo Worstede, priore ecclesie Cathedralis Norwic', sacre pagine professore, Ricardo Caudray,⁶¹ [archidiacono] in ecclesia Norwic', ac*f* Johanne Kenynghale,⁶² Johanne Thorpe, Petro de Sancta Fide⁶³ et [. . . . .]*g* Wychyngham,⁶⁴ ordinis Carmelitarum, sacre pagine professoribus, ac Willelmo Bernham, in decretis, [et] Willelmo Ascogh, in sacra theologia, bacallariis, adductus fuit personaliter Johannes Skylly de Flixton, millar; quem Willelmus Westbury, Johannes Fray et Ricardus Weltden, justiciarii domini nostri regis

a nec exibit *interlined.*   *b* dixit *deleted.*   *c* dixit *interlined.*
d proximo *interlined.*   *e* Johannes Skylly de Flixton *repeated in margin.*
f adductus fuit ad iudicium personaliter Johannes Skylly de Flixton Norwicensis d *deleted.*   *g* Blank in MS.

---

⁵⁹ 12 February 1429.
⁶⁰ Flixton, north-east Suffolk. For John Skylly's earlier activities, see pp. 217–19.
⁶¹ Archdeacon of Norwich and later chancellor of Cambridge University (see Emden, *BRUC*, pp. 126–7, Richard Caudray).
⁶² Later prior provincial of the English Carmelites (see Emden, *BRUO*, ii, pp. 1035–6).
⁶³ See Emden, *BRUC*, p. 502, Peter of S. Faith.
⁶⁴ Possibly Henry Wichingham (see Emden, *BRUO*, iii, p. 2045).

ad gaolam domini regis castri Norwic' de prisonibus ibidem existentibus deliberandam assignati apud Thetford die Lune in vigilia
Sancti Petri in Cathedra anno regni regis Henrici sexti septimo per
Henricum Drury, tunc vicecomitem Norff' et Suff', dicto patri*a* per
recordatorem fecerunt liberari ad iudicium*b* (p. 221 / fo. 21r)*c* super
crimine heretice pravitatis responsurum.[65]

Qui quidem Johannes Skylly, coram dicto patre ibidem in iudicio
personaliter constitutus, recognovit et fatebatur se recepisse hereticos in domum suam—videlicet Willelmum Whyte, hereticum
condempnatum, ac Johannem Whaddon, skynner, hereticum
similiter condempnatum—ac eosdem et ipsorum doctrinas erroneas
et hereticas admisisse et manutenuisse et supportasse, ac eisdem in
hac parte prebuisse consilium, auxilium vel favorem, ac ex eorum
hereticorum doctrinis didicisse, tenuisse et affirmasse articulos
subscriptos omnes et singulos.

Videlicet, quod sacramenta Baptismi facti in aqua necnon Confirmacionis facte per episcopos in forma communi usitata in Ecclesia
modice vel nullius*d* sunt*e* virtutis et nichil ponderanda si parentes
pueri*f* non baptizati sunt Christiani.

Item quod confessio vocalis non deberet fieri alicui sacerdoti, sed
tantum soli Deo, quia nullus sacerdos habet potestatem absolvendi
quemquam peccatorem a peccato.

Item quod nullus sacerdos habet potestatem conficiendi corpus
Christi in sacramento altaris; et quod post verba sacramentalia, a
quocumque presbitero quantumcumque rite aut debite sint prolata, remanet purus panis materialis in altari.

Item quod solus consensus mutui amoris inter virum et mulierem
sufficit ad matrimonium, absque aliqua expressione verborum*g* aut
solennizacione in ecclesia.

Item quod quilibet homo existens in vera caritate est sacerdos Dei,
et quod nullus sacerdos habet maiorem potestatem ad ministranda
aliqua sacramenta in Ecclesia quam habet aliquis laicus non
ordinatus.

Item quod nemo tenetur ieiunare diebus Quadragesimalibus nec
in diebus iiij*or* Temporum, sextis feriis nec vigiliis alicuius sancti.
Sed licitum est cuilibet fideli dictis diebus et temporibus edere

---

a lib *deleted.*
b ad iudicium (*both words deleted*)
  per (*deleted*)
  super crimine
  in bottom right-hand corner of page.
c Joh' Skylly, miller *in top right-hand corner of page.*
d est *deleted.*   *e* sunt *interlined.*
f baptizandi *deleted.*   *g* sive *deleted.*

---

[65] For this gaol delivery, see pp. 217–19.

carnes et omnimoda cibaria indifferenter ad eorum libitum*a* tociens quociens sine offensione Dei, quia Deus nunquam ordinavit tali[a] ieiunia*b* observari a populo.

Item quod papa Romanus est Antechristus, ac episcopi et alii prelati Ecclesie sunt*c* discipuli Antecristi, et quod papa non habet potestatem ligandi et solvendi in terra.

Item quod licitum est cuilibet Christiano facere et exercere quecumque opera*d* corporalia,*e* peccato duntaxat excepto, diebus Dominicis et aliis festivis indictis per Ecclesiam.

Item quod licitum est quibuscumque presbiteris capere et habere uxores, et quibuscumque monialibus capere et habere maritos et cohabitare*f* simul ut mariti et uxores, et quod illa vita esset magis commendabilis quam*g* vivere caste.

Item quod excommunicaciones et censure ecclesiastice late per episcopos et prelatos Ecclesie nullo modo sint timende nec ponderande.

Item quod non est licitum iurare in aliquo casu.

Item quod nulla peregrinacio deberet fieri.

Item quod nullus honor est exhibendus ymaginibus crucifixi, Beate Marie vel alicuius sancti.

(p. 222 / fo. 21v)*h* Item quod aqua benedicta a presbiteris in ecclesiis non est sanccior nec maioris virtutis quam est aqua torrentis vel fontis non sanctificata per presbiterum, quia Dominus benedixit aquas in prima creacione earundem.*i*

Item quod licitum est omnibus detinere et subtrahere decimas ab ecclesiis et curatis, et oblaciones similiter,*j* quia decime et oblaciones faciunt presbiteros esse superbos.

Item quod mors Sancti Thome, martyris, nunquam fuit sancta nec*k* meritoria.

Item quod reliquie sanctorum, scilicet carnes et ossa hominis mortui, non debent a populo venerari, nec de monumento fetido extrahi, nec in capsis reponi.

Item quod nullo modo licet pugnare pro patria, pro iure hereditario, nec placitare coram iudice pro aliquo iure.

Item quod omnes ecclesie materiales sunt nisi synagoge et ad modicum deserviunt, quia oraciones vel preces dicte in*l* campo vel nemore*m* sunt*n* ita acceptabiles in conspectu Dei sicut*o* oraciones vel preces facte sive dicte in ecclesiis.

---

a quo *deleted*.
b fier *deleted*.
c dissi *deleted*.
d servilia *deleted*.
e corporalia *interlined*.
f cum *deleted*.
g vita communis presbiterorum et monialium *deleted*.
h Joh' Skylly *at top of page*.
i ubi fu *deleted*.
j for thay make prestes prowde *deleted*.
k oni *deleted*.
l eu *deleted*: in *repeated*.
m est *deleted*
n sunt *interlined*.
o sicut *repeated*.

Item quod non est orandum alicui*a* sancto in celo nisi tantum soli Deo.

Item quod campane in ecclesiis et pulsaciones earundem ad nichil fuerunt ordinate nisi tantum ad colligendas pecunias in bursas presbiterorum.

Item quod non est peccatum contravenire preceptis Ecclesie ex contemptu.

Quibus*b* quidem articulis prescriptis omnibus et singulis per prefatum Johannem Skilly coram dicto patre iudicialiter confessatis, prefatus Johannes Skilly dixit et asseruit quod dictus Willelmus White et Johannes Waddon docuerunt et informaverunt*c* eum dictos articulos, et quod ipse credidit eorum doctrine in hac parte. Et deinde prefatus pater declaravit eidem Johanni Skilly quod dicti articuli continent in se errores et hereses quamplures determinacioni sancte Ecclesie Romane contrarias. Et tunc prefatus Johannes Skilly*d* asseruit se velle ex tunc dictas hereses ac quascumque alias hereses*e* puro corde dimittere et pro perpetuo abiurare. Unde prefatus pater prefixit sibi*f* diem duntaxat Martis, videlicet xv*m* diem dicti mensis Marcii,[66] ad abiurandas dictas et quascumque alias hereses in eodem loco.*g*

Quibus die et loco, coram dicto reverendo patre iudicialiter sedente,*h* assistentibus sibi tunc ibidem magistro Willelmo Worstede, priore ecclesie Cathedralis Norwici, sacre pagine professore, ac magistro Ricardo Caudray, archidiacono Norwic', necnon magistris Johanne Thorp, ordinis Carmelitarum, sacre pagine professore, Thoma Hunter,[67] in artibus magistro, et aliis iurisperitis in multitudine copiosa, adductus fuit personaliter ad iudicium dictus Johannes Skylly; volens, ut asseruit, dictas hereses et quascumque alias avido desiderio pro perpetuo abiurare secundum formam et tenorem*i* cuiusdam scripti cirographi et indentati tunc ibidem in iudicio sibi ostensi, et cuius tenorem per prius, ut asseruit, audivit et

---

a scor *deleted.*
b Jhon Whyte, Jhon Wadden *written in the margin in a different hand.*
c *MS.* docuit et informavit.   *d* ut *deleted.*
e ex tunc *repeated.*   *f* dcm' *deleted.*
g Presentibus in actibus dicte diei magistris J. Sutton, in legibus bacallario, Johanne [W]ylly, capellano, Roberto [Ay]lmer, notariis, et aliis *in margin. For the supplied letters, which have disappeared from the manuscript as the edge of the page has worn away, see pp.* 55 *and* 63.
h adductus fuit ad iudiciu *deleted.*   *i* et tenorem *interlined.*

---

[66] Presumably a mistake for Friday 18 March 1429: that was the day on which John Skylly was later said to have abjured (see p. 59), whereas Tuesday 15 March was the day on which he had just been tried (see p. 51).
[67] See Emden, *BRUO*, ii, p 987, Thomas Hunter.

plenarie*a* intellexit. Et quia asseruit se esse laicum et nescire legere tenorem illius abiuracionis, idem Johannes Skylly commisit organum vocis sue dicto magistro Ricardo Caudray, archidiacono Norwic',*b* et plenariam potestatem ad legendam vice et nomine suis eandem abiuracionem. Qui quidem*c* magister Ricardus*d* Caudray, onus huiusmodi in se suscipiens,*e* tenorem eiusdem scripti indentati de verbo ad verbum plenarie [et] publice in iudicio perlegit; dicto Johanne Skilly interim continue manum suam dexteram [super librum evangeliorum]*f* tenente et ascultante. Et ipso tenore abiuracionis perlecto, prefatus Johannes iuravit ad sancta Dei evangelia, per ipsum tunc tacta, quod omnia contenta in eodem scripto indentato bene et fideliter iuxta effectum eiusdem scripti in omnibus observabit.*g* (p. 223 / fo. 22r)*h* Quibus sic peractis, prestito per eundem Johannem alio iuramento ad sacra evangelia tunc ibidem de peragendo penitenciam sibi pro suis commissis in hac parte iniungendam, dictus pater absolvit eum a sentencia excommunicacionis—qua [extitit innodatus] propter hereses predictas,*i* quas, ut premittitur, tenuit, credidit et affirmavit—tunc ibidem in iudicio*j* secundum formam in quadam papyri cedula, quam in manibus suis tunc tenuit et legit,*k* inscriptam [et] conceptam. Cuius cedule tenor,*l* una cum tenore abiuracionis eiusdem, inferius*m* est insertus.

Presentibus*n* in actibus istius ultimi diei magistris Johanne Bury, in decretis bacallario, Johanne Sutton, in legibus bacallario, Ada Cokelot, Thoma Rodelond, Johanne Willy et aliis pluribus.

In Dei nomine, Amen. Quia nos, Willelmus, permissione divina Norwicensis episcopus, contra te, Johannem Skilly de Flixton nostre diocesis, miller, subditum nostrum, ex officio nostro legitime procedentes, per tuam confessionem coram nobis iudicialiter factam invenimus te infra nostram diocesim hereticos*o* famosos, notorios et condempnatos in domum tuam recepisse, concellasse, supportasse et manutenuisse, ac multas*p* hereses et errores quamplures fidei catholice et determinacioni sacrosancte et universalis Ecclesie repugnantes—de quibus in quodam cirographo super tua abiuracione concepto et indentato, cuius una pars in archivis nostris

---

a et *repeated.*   *b* ad *deleted.*
c q *deleted.*   *d* Car *deleted.*
e te *deleted.*
f For the words supplied, see pp. 62 and 109 and elsewhere.
g quibus sic peractis *in bottom right-hand corner of page.*
h Joh' Skilly *in middle of top of page:* J. Skylly *in top right-hand corner of page.*
i q' *deleted.*   *j* absolvit *repeated:* sub hac que *deleted.*
k conce *deleted.*   *l* et est talis infer *deleted.*
m sequitur et est *deleted.*
n MS. presentes erant.   *o* notorios et *deleted.*   *p* err *deleted.*

noscitur remanere, ad quam nos referimus et pro hic inserta haberi
volumus, plenior fit mencio—tenuisse, credidisse et affirmasse, ac
per hoc in excommunicacionis sentenciam incidisse; nunc autem,
usus consilio saniori, petis misericordiam et sponte redis ad Ecclesie
unitatem; inprimis abiurata per te omni heresi et recepta per nos a
te secundum ritum Ecclesie iuratoria caucione de parendo[a] mandatis Ecclesie, te absolvimus ab omni excommunicacionis vinculo
quo tenebaris astrictus. Et quia per predicta que tenuisti, credidisti
et affirmasti in Deum et sanctam matrem Ecclesiam temere deliquisti, tibi pro pena penitenciali carceres septennales in monasterio
de Langele[68] dicte nostre diocesis iniungimus per presentes; et quia
in sextis feriis quibus sepius temporibus preteritis carnibus vesci
consueveras, per septem annos iam proximos futuros in pane et
aqua ieiunes; et[b] quod[c] per duos[d] annos proximos et immediate post
dictum septennium sequentes omni[e] iiij[a] [f] feria in Capite Ieiunii[g] et
quintis feriis in Cenis[h] Domini in ecclesia nostra Cathedrali Norwic'
coram nobis vel successore nostro aut in hac parte nostrum locum
tenente qui pro tempore fuerit cum aliis penitentibus te presentes,
acturus solennem penitenciam pro commissis.

Abiuracio Johannis Skylly de Flyxton

In the name of God, tofore you, the worshipful fadir in Crist,
William, be the grace of God bisshop of Norwich, Y, John Skylly of
Flixton, miller, of your diocese, your subject, defamed and noted
hugely of heresie, felyng and undirstandyng that afore this tyme Y
afermed opin errours and heresies, holdyng, belevyng, afermyng and
techyng,

That the sacramentes of Baptem doon in watir and of Confirmacion (p. 224 / fo. 22v)[i] doon[j] be a bisshop in fourme customed in
holi Churche be but of litell availe and not to be pondred if the fadir
and the modir of a child hadde Cristendom.

Also that Y held, beleved and afermed that confession shuld be
made unto no prest, but only to God, for no prest hath poar to
asoile a man of synne.

[a] iuri *deleted.*
[b] Penitencia solennis ij annis post septennium elapsum *in margin.*
[c] p' *deleted.*
[d] per duos *interlined:* duos (*not interlined*) *repeated.*
[e] sexta *deleted.*   [f] iiij[a] *interlined.*
[g] et *deleted.*   [h] in Cenis *repeated.*
[i] salvetur spacium *written in the margin in a different hand.*
[j] in watir *deleted.*

---

[68] The Premonstratensian abbey of Langley, Norfolk.

Also that Y held and afermed that no prest hath poar to make Cristis body in forme of bred in the sacrament of the auter, and that aftir the sacramentall wordys said of a prest at messe ther remayneth pure material bred on the auter.

Also that Y held and afermed that oonly consent of love betuxe man and woman is sufficiant for matrimonie, withowte expressyng of wordis and withowte solempnizacion in churche.

Also that Y held and afermed that every trewe man and woman being in charite is a prest, and that no prest hath more[a] poar in[b] mynystryng of the sacramentes than a lewed man hath.

Also that Y held and afermed that no man is bounde to faste in Lenton, in Quater Temps, Fridais, vigilis of seintes ne other days commaunded of the Churche to be fasted, and that it is leful to ete flessh all suche days and tymes withowte offence of God, for God mad never law to binde the puple to suche fastis.

Also that Y held,[c] afermed and taght that the pope of Rome is Antecrist, and bisshopes[d] and other prelates ben disciples of Antecrist, and that the pope hath no poar to bynde ne to lose.[e]

Also that Y held, afermed and taght that it is leful prestes to take vyves and nunnes to take husbondes and dwelle togeder as wyff and husbond, holdyng that lyff more commendable than to lyve chaste.[f]

Also that Y held,[g] afermed and taght that it is leful all men and women to doon all maner bodely werkes on Sonedays and other festival days commaunded of the Churche to be halwed.

Also that Y held, afermed and taght that censures and cursynges of bisshopes and prelates ar not to be dred ne pondred.

Also that Y held, afermed and taght that it is not leful to swere in ony case.

Also that Y held and afermed and taght that no pilgrimage oweth to be do, ne no maner of worship owith to be do unto ony ymages of the crucifix, of Our Lady or of ony other seyntes.

Also that holy watir halwed be a prest is of no mor effect than the watir of the ryver or of a welle is, for as moche as God blessed all thinges that he maked.

Also that Y held, taght and afermed that it is leful all men to withdrawe and take away tithes and offeryngges from churches and prestes, for offeryngges and tithes make prestes proude.

Also that Y held, taght and afermed that if the deth of Crist was precious and profitable, the deth of Seynt Thomas of Cantirbury was unholy and onprofitable.

---

[a] more *interlined*.
[b] myns *deleted*.
[c] and *deleted*.
[d] and bisshopes *repeated*.
[f] a (*interlined*) *follows* chaste.

[e] b (*interlined*) *follows* lose.
[g] and *deleted*.

Also that (p. 225 / fo. 23r)[a] Y held, taght and afermed that relikes of seyntes, that is to say flessh or boon of ony ded man, shuld not be worsheped of the puple ne shryned.

Also that Y held, taght and afermed that it is not leful ony mon to fighte or do bataile for a[b] reawme or a cuntre, or to plete in lawe for ony right or wrong.

Also that Y held, taght and afermed that material churches be but of litel availe and owyn to be but of litell reputacion, for every mannys prayer said in the feld is as good as the prayer said in the churche.

Also that Y held, taght and afermed that prayer shuld be maad unto no seynt in hevene, but oonly to God.

Also that Y held, taght and afermed that[c] ryngyng of belles in churches availyth to nothyng but oonly to gete mony into prestes purses.

Also that Y held, taght and afermed that it is no synne to doon agayn the preceptes and lawes of holy Churche.

Because of whyche and many other errours and heresies whyche Y have holde,[d] afermed and taght to your subjectes in your diocese, Y am called tofore you, worshipful fadir, whyche have cure of my soule. And be you fully enformed that the said myn holdyng, belevyng, techyng and afermyng ben opin errours and heresies and contrarious to the determinacion of the Churche of Roome, wherfore Y wyllyng folwe and sewe the doctrine of holy Churche, and departe from all maner of errour and heresie, and turne with good will and herte to the oonhed of the Churche. Considerand that holy Churche spereth not hyr bosom to hym that will turne agayn, ne God will not the deth of a synner but rather that he be turned and lyve, with a pure herte Y confesse, deteste and despise my said errours and heresies, and the said opinions Y confesse heretikous and erroneous and to the faith of the Church of Rome and all universall holy Churche repugnant. And for as moche as be the said thinges that Y wikkedly so afermed, said,[e] beleved and taght Y shewed meself corrupt and unfaithful, that from hensforth Y shewe me uncorrupt and faithful the faith and doctrine of holy Churche trewly to kepe Y promitte. And all maner of errour and heresie,[f] doctrine and opinion agayn the faith of the Churche and determinacion of the Churche of Roome—and namely the opinions before rehersed—Y abjure and forswere, and swere be theese holy gospels be me bodely touched that from hensforth Y shal never holde errour ne errours,

---

[a] salvetur spacium *written in the top right-hand corner of the page in a different hand.*

[b] rew *deleted.*
[d] taght and *deleted.*
[f] doctir *deleted.*

[c] ryngg *deleted.*
[e] and *deleted.*

heresie ne heresies ne fals doctrine agayn the [....]ᵃ faith of holy Churche and determinacion of the Churche of Roome. Ne no suche thinges Y shal obstinatly defende, ne ony man holdyng or techyng suche maner of thinges be me or ony other persone opinly or prively Y shal defende. [Y] shal never aftir this time be no recettour, fautour, confortour, concellour or defensour of heretikes or of ony men or women suspect of heresie. Ne Y shal trowe to thaym. Ner wittingly Y shal felaship with thaym, ne be hoomly with thaym. Y shal never yeve consell, favour, yeftes ne confort to thaym. If Y knowe ony heretik or of heresie ony man or woman suspect or of thaym fautours, confortours, consellours or defensours, or of ony men or women making prive conventicules or assembles, or holdyng ony diverse or singuler opinions from the commune doctrine of the Churche, Y shal late you, worshipful fadir, or your vicar generall in your absence or the diocesanes of suche men have soone and redy knowyng. So help me God atte holy doom and theese holy gospels.

In wittenesse of whiche thinges Y subscribe here with myn owyn hand a cross +.ᵇ And to this partie endented to remayne in your registre Y sette my signet. And that other partie endented Y receyve undir your seal to abide with me unto my lyves ende. Yoven at Norwich in your chapell of your palaice the xviij day of the moneth of March the yer of our Lord a thousand four hundred and xxviij.

[6]

(p. 226 / fo. 23v) **John Godesell,**⁶⁹ **parchemyn-maker**

Anno Domini Millesimo CCCCᵐᵒ XXVIII, indiccione septima, pontificatus sanctissimi in Christo patris et domini nostri, domini Martini divina providencia pape quinti, anno duodecimo, mensis Marcii die xviij, in capella palacii Norwic', in mei, Johannis Excestr, clerici, notarii publici, et testium subscriptorumᶜ [presencia], coram reverendo in Christo patre ac domino, domino Willelmo Dei gracia Norwicensi episcopo, iudicialiter sedente, assistentibus sibi magistro Willelmo Worstede, priore ecclesie Cathedralis Norwic', sacre

---

ᵃ *A short word has been almost totally obscured by a drop of ink.*

ᵇ *As elsewhere in the manuscript, the + is in the same hand as the rest of the text.*

ᶜ videlicet magistri Johannis Sutton, in legibus bacallarii, Johannis Wylly, notarii publici, Roberti Aylmer notarii publici, Thome Rudlond et Johannis Shuldham, capellanorum, presencia *deleted.*

---

⁶⁹ For his arrest and earlier activities, see pp. 217–19.

c

pagine professore, necnon magistris Ricardo Caudray, archidiacono
Norwici, ac Thoma Hunter, in artibus magistro, et aliis nonnullis
viris ecclesiasticis, adductus fuit ad iudicium Johannes Godesell,
parchemen-maker de Dychyngham[70] Norwicensis diocesis.

Cui prefatus reverendus pater dixit [et] proposuit quod ipse[a] fuit
vehementer suspectus de heresi et pro heretico notorio[b] in civitate
et diocese Norwicensi habitus, tentus et reputatus, et quod in
specie[c] idem J. Godesell recepit in domum suam sepius hereticos
notorios et famosos, et eosdem sustentavit,[d] supportavit, concelavit
et manutenuit, ac eisdem prebuit consilium, auxilium et favorem,
et quod idem J.G. eosdem hereticos permisit scienter tenere scolas
et legere libros in domibus suis, et quod ipse fuit discipulus eorundem. Qui quidem Johannes Godesell[e] respondens[f] iudicialiter
publice et expresse fatebatur, dicens se scienter recepisse in domos
suas vicibus iteratis hereticos et lollardos—videlicet dominos Willelmum White, presbiterum, Hugonem Pye, presbiterum, ac Bartholomeum Cornemonger,[71] Johannem Waddon, Johannem Fowlyn[72]
et Thomam Everdon[73] ac alios—ac quod ipse Johannes Godesell,
sciens dictos Willelmum White, Hugonem, Bartholomeum, Johannem, Johannem et Thomam esse hereticos notorios, ipsos supportavit, concelavit et manutenuit iuxta posse suum, et quod ipse permisit scienter[g] eosdem hereticos legere et docere hereses et errores,[h]
et quod ipse Johannes Godesell didicit ab eisdem hereticis et doctrinis eorundem omnes hereses et errores subscriptos, quas et quos
idem Johannes, ut asseruit, tenuit et affirmavit.

Inprimis, videlicet, idem Johannes dixit iudicialiter et fatebatur se
tenuisse, credidisse et affirmasse quod sacramentum Baptismi,
factum in aqua in forma consueta usitata in ecclesiis, modicum vel
nichil est ponderandum si parentes infantis sint fideles.

Item fatebatur se tenuisse,[i] credidisse et asseruisse quod sacramentum Confirmacionis, factum per episcopum in forma communi
usitata in Ecclesia, non requiritur nec est meritarium fieri pro eo
quod quamcito infans pervenerit ad discrecionem ad recipiendum et
intelligendum verbum Dei, est sufficienter confirmatus.

Item quod confessio vocalis non deberet fieri alicui sacerdoti nisi
tantum soli Deo, eo quod nullus presbiter habet potestatem ad
absolvendum aliquem de peccato.

[a] ipse *interlined*.   [b] pu in diocese et c *deleted*.
[c] *MS.* specia.   [d] et *deleted*.
[e] respondebat iudicialiter s dicens *deleted*.
[f] et dicens *deleted*.   [g] scienter *interlined*.
[h] subscriptos quas et quos *deleted*.   [i] et *deleted*.

[70] Ditchingham, south-east Norfolk.
[71] See above, pp. 29–30; *Reg. Chichele*, ed. Jacob, iii, p. 199 and iv, p. 297.
[72] See above, pp. 29–30 and p. 33, n. 14; *Reg. Chichele*, ed. Jacob, iv, p. 298.
[73] See above, pp. 29–30; *Reg. Chichele*, ed. Jacob, iv, p. 297.

Item fatebatur se tenuisse et affirmasse quod nullus sacerdos habet potestatem conficiendi corpus Christi in sacramento altaris, et quod post verba sacramentalia rite prolata a presbitero remanet in altari purus panis materialis.

Item quod solus consensus mutui amoris inter virum et mulierem sufficit pro sacramento matrimonii, absque aliqua expressione verborum aut solennizacione in ecclesia.

Item fatebatur se tenuisse et affirmasse quod papa est Antecristus et caput draconis de quo fit mencio in sacra Scriptura,*a* [74] et quod episcopi et ecclesiarum prelati sunt*b* corpus draconis, et quod fratres mendicantes sunt cauda draconis.

Item fatebatur se tenuisse et credidisse quod quilibet fidelis homo et quelibet fidelis mulier est sacerdos, et habet plenam potestatem conficiendi corpus Christi adeo bene sicut aliqui sacerdotes.

(p. 227 / fo. 24r)*c* Item fatebatur idem Johannes Godesell*d* se tenuisse et affirmasse quod est licitum cuilibet fideli exercere et facere quecumque opera servilia, peccato dumtaxat excepto, diebus Dominicis et aliis festivis inductis per Ecclesiam, dummodo fit occulte ad evitandum scandalum.

Item quod*e* Ecclesia catholica est congregacio solum salvandorum.

Item quod omnes ecclesie materiales sunt nisi synagoge, ac modicum vel nichil deberent haberi*f* in reverencia, quia Deus exaudit preces orantis in campo tam bene sicut preces orantis in tali synagoga.

Item quod nemo tenetur ieiunare diebus ieiunalibus indictis per Ecclesiam, sed licitum est omni populo comedere carnes indifferenter in Quadragesima, sextis feriis, diebus Quatuor Temporum et vigiliis sanctorum.

Item quod nullus honor exhibendus est aliquibus ymaginibus.

Item quod peregrinaciones nullo modo deberent fieri.

Item quod licitum est quibuscumque presbiteris capere uxores, et monialibus capere maritos, et sic simul vivere quasi sub coniugio.

Item quod licitum est subtrahere et auferre decimas et oblaciones ab ecclesiis et curatis, et dare eas pauperibus.

Item quod censure et excommunicaciones late per episcopos sive ordinarios nullo modo sunt timende.

Item quod nullo modo licitum est pugnare pro regno vel pro iure hereditario, nec placitare pro aliqua causa.

Item quod pulsaciones campanarum ad nichil penitus deserviunt nisi tantum ad colligendas pecunias in bursas hominum.

---

a MS. Sciriptura.
c Joh' Godesell *at top of page.*
e congregacio *deleted.*

b sunt *repeated.*
d quod e *deleted.*
f in reverencia *deleted.*

---

[74] Revelation 12–14.

Quibus quidem articulis prescriptis omnibus et singulis per prefatum Johannem Godesell coram dicto patre iudicialiter confessatis, prefatus pater declaravit eidem Johanni dictos articulos continere in se errores et hereses quamplures*a* fidei catholice et determinacioni Ecclesie Romane contrarios. Et prefatus Johannes Godesell voluit, ut asseruit iudicialiter*b* et puro corde affectavit, dictas ac quascumque alias hereses pro perpetuo dimittere et abiurare re et verbo, ac simpliciter abiurare, et redire ad Ecclesie unitatem. Unde prefatus pater prefixit sibi diem Lune, videlicet xxi^imum^ die[m] mensis Marcii predicti, ad abiurandos huiusmodi errores et hereses inscriptos in eodem loco.

Presentibus tunc ibidem magistris Johanne Bury, in decretis, Johanne Sutton et Ada Cokelot, in legibus bacallariis, Johanne Wylly, notario, et Thoma Rodeland, capellano, et aliis quampluribus.

Quo die Lune, videlicet xxj⁰ die dicti mensis Marcii, coram dicto reverendo patre in capella palacii predicti iudicialiter sedente, assistentibus sibi tunc ibidem magistro Willelmo*c* Worstede, priore ecclesie Cathedralis Norwic', sacre pagine professore, necnon magistris Willelmo Bernham et Johanne Bury, in decritis bacallariis, et aliis iurisperitis, in mei, Johannis Excestr, notarii prescripti, et testium subscriptorum presencia, adductus fuit ad iudicium personaliter dictus Johannes Godesell, asserens se audivisse plenarie et intellexisse tenorem abiuracionis sue in quodam cirographo*d* scripto et indentato concepte, sub qua quidem forma voluit libenter, ut asseruit, abiurare. Et quia asseruit se fore laicum et nescire legere*e* tenorem dicte abiuracionis, ipse Johannes commisit organum vocis sue magistro (p. 228 / fo. 24v) Roberto Aylmer, notario publico, Consistorii Norwicensis procuratori, tunc ibidem presenti, ad legendum pro ipso et nomine suo ac vice persone sue tenorem abiuracionis predicte. Qui quidem magister Robertus Aylmer, onus legendi dictam abiuracionem vice et nomine dicti Johannis Godesell in se*f* suscipiens, tenorem huiusmodi abiuracionis de verbo ad verbum publice ac alta et intelligibili voce perlegit; dicto Johanne Godesell manum suam dexteram super librum evangeliorum interim continue tenente, et iurante ad ea se velle firmiter et inviolabiliter observare iuramentum in dicto*g* cirographo*h* indentato scriptum iuxta ipsius cirographi exigenciam et tenorem. Et in testimonium huius rei idem Johannes Godesell in utraque parte dicti cirographi

---

a determi *deleted.*
c Bernham *deleted.*
e legere *interlined.*
g scripto *deleted.*

b iudicialiter *interlined.*
d An illegible word *deleted.*
f s sic req *deleted.*
h scrip *deleted.*

indentati signum crucis[a] subscripsit manu sua propria. Et deinde, prestito per eundem iuramento iterato[b] ad sancta evangelia per ipsum corporaliter tacta de parendo mandatis Ecclesie et de peragendo penitenciam sibi pro suis commissis iniungendam, prefatus reverendus pater absolvebat eundem a sentencia excommunicacionis qua propter premissa extitit innodatus iuxta formam in quadam papiri cedula conceptam, quam prefatus pater tunc ibidem iudicialiter tenuit et perlegit. Cuius quidem cedule tenor,[c] una cum tenore dicti cirographi indentati, inferius continetur.

Presentibus tunc ibidem[d] Johanne Sutton, in legibus, Ada Cokelot, in decretis, Johanne Benet, Johanne Blitheburgh, Thoma Rodelond, capellanis, ac Roberto Aylmer, notario publico, et aliis quampluribus testibus ad premissa vocatis specialiter et rogatis.

In Dei nomine, Amen. Quia nos, Willelmus, permissione divina Norwicensis episcopus, contra te, Johannem Godesell, parchemener de Dychyngham nostre diocesis, subditum nostrum, ex officio nostro legitime procedentes, per tuam confessionem coram nobis iudicialiter factam invenimus te infra nostram diocesim plures hereticos notorios et famosos in domum tuam sepius recepisse,[e] ac eisdem favisse consilium et auxilium prebuisse, ac eosdem supportasse et concelasse, teque multas hereses et errores quamplures fidei orthodoxe et determinacioni sacrosancte ac universalis Ecclesie repugnantes—de quibus in quodam cirographo super tua abiuracione concepto et indentato, cuius una pars in archivis nostris noscitur remanere, ad quam nos referimus et pro hic inserta[f] haberi volumus, plenior fit mencio—tenuisse, credidisse et affirmasse, et per hoc in excommunicacionis sentenciam incidisse; nunc autem, usus consilio saniori, petis misericordiam et sponte redis ad Ecclesie unitatem; idcirco, inprimis abiurata per te omni heresi et recepta per nos secundum ritum Ecclesie iuratoria caucione de parendo mandatis Ecclesie, te absolvimus ab omni excommunicacionis vinculo quo tenebaris astrictus. Et quoniam per predicta que perpetrasti, tenuisti, credidisti et asseruisti in Deum et sanctam matrem Ecclesiam temere deliquisti, tibi pro pena penitenciali carceres septennales per nos postmodum assignandos[g] iniungimus per presentes. Et quia tenuisti, credidisti et affirmasti fore licitum cuicumque fideli edere

[a] manu *follows* crucis.
[b] de *deleted.*
[c] sequitur sub hac forma verborum inferius de *deleted.*
[d] presentibus tunc ibidem *repeated.*
[e] *MS.* recipisse.
[f] hari *deleted.*
[g] tibi *repeated.*

carnes ac omnimoda cibaria indifferenter sextis feriis, diebus Quadragesimalibus.*

[7]

(p. 265 / fo. 56r) **Isabella Davy**

Isabella Davy, filia Ricardi Davy de Toft',[75] fatetur coram domino
xxij ¦die Marcii Anno Domini CCCC° XXVIII° in parlario de
Thorp'[76] sedente*b* quod Thomas Pert, capellanus, docuit ipsam:

Quod non deberet credere in sacramentis Ecclesie, nec quod
accederet ad ecclesiam diebus festivalibus.

Item docuit ipsam quod presbiteri non habent potestatem conficiendi corpus Christi in sacramento altaris, sed quod remanet
purus panis materialis post consecracionem.

Item quod ymagines nullo modo sunt adorande.

Item quod peregrinaciones nullo modo deberent fieri.

Item quod*c* nemo tenetur ieiunare sextis feriis, vigiliis sanctorum,
iiij*or* Temporum et in Quadragesima.

Dicit eciam quod ipsamet comedit pullos columbarum in Quadragesima in domo*d* Walteri Webbe apud Dawne Hill'.[77]

Item quod non licet iurare quovis modo.

Item quod licitum est operari diebus festivalibus ac aliis indictis
per Ecclesiam.

Item dicit quod docuit ipsam quod sacramentum Baptismi et
sacramentum Confirmacionis sunt nichil*e* [vel] parum ponderanda.

Item quod licitum fuit sacerdotibus capere uxores, et monialibus
capere maritos.

Item quod est licitum auferre oblaciones et decimas ab ecclesiis et
curatis.

Dicit eciam quod ipsa credidit doctrinis dicti Thome Pert et
Johanne, filie Walteri Webbe predicti.

---

*a The text ends here, at the end of a line in the manuscript and towards the foot
of the page. It may have continued on the following folio (fo. 25), which no longer
survives.*
b Contra Thomam Pert in margin.
c licitum est cuilibet deleted.
d MS. domio.　　　　　　　　　　　　　　　*e An illegible word probably deleted.*

[75] Probably Toft Monks, south-east Norfolk; possibly West Tofts, south-
west Norfolk.
[76] i.e., in a parlour of the bishop's manor-house at (Bishop's) Thorpe, near
Norwich (see p. 66).
[77] The place is unidentifiable.

Deinde eadem Isabella voluit, ut asseruit, dictas hereses et quascumque*a* alias hereses dimittere et abiurare.*b* Et tunc iuravit ad sancta evangelia coram eodem patre quod ab hac hora in antea nunquam tenebit errores sive hereses nec doctrinas sive opiniones contra fidem Ecclesie catholice et determinacionem sacrosancte Ecclesie Romane. Et in specie opiniones suprascriptas eadem Isabella tunc ibidem iudicialiter abiuravit. Et iuravit ad sancta Dei evangelia per ipsam corporaliter tacta quod amodo in futurum nullas errores sive hereses pertinaciter defendet; nec aliquam personam tenentem vel docentem errores sive hereses, aut aliam opinionem fidei catholice et determinacioni sacrosancte*c* Ecclesie Romane contrariam, per ipsam vel mediam personam publice vel occulte defendet; et quod nunquam recipiet vel defendet hereticos, aut eisdem prebebit consilium, auxilium vel favorem; et quod nunquam credet hereticis, nec scienter cum hereticis se associabit, nec erit familiaris scienter cum eisdem. Et si noverit aliquos hereticos sive aliquam personam suspectam de heresi, vel talium personarum suspectarum fautores, confortatores, consiliatores vel defensores, aut aliquas personas facientes privatas conventiculas vel congregaciones aut tenentes diversas sive singulares opiniones a communi doctrina Ecclesie et fide catholica, quod ipsa faciet dictum reverendum patrem aut eius vicarium in spiritualibus generalem, sive ipsius*d* (p. 266 / fo. 56v) successorem qui pro tempore fuerit, habere de talibus personis celarem et certam noticiam.

Presentibus tunc ibidem magistris Johanne Sutton, in legibus bacallario, ac Roberto Aylmer et Hugone Acton, notariis publicis, necnon Caldebek', armigero, Thoma Walsham, clerico, et aliis.

Quibus sic ut premittitur expeditis, dicta Isabella iuravit ad sancta Dei evangelia per eam tunc ibidem iudicialiter tacta de parendo mandatis Ecclesie et peragendo*e* penitenciam sibi pro suis commissis iniungendam. Et deinde dictus pater*f* absolvit eam a sentencia excommunicacionis qua, propter hereses predictas [quas] prius tenuit, credidit et affirmavit, [extitit innodata]. Et eciam idem

---

a he *deleted.*
b dimittere et abiurare *interlined.*
c et determinacioni *repeated.*
d Isabella Davy   Ricardus Clerk
  Sibilla Godsell   Thomas White
                   Katerina Wryght
  Et pro commissis per vij Quadragesimas in sextis feriis in pane et aqua, et quod iij annis presentet se (*i.e., Isabel Davy*) in ecclesia Cathedrali *written at foot of page.*
e s *deleted.*
f excommunicavit *deleted.*

pater iniunxit sibi iudicialiter pro commissis quod singulis sextis feriis per septem Quadragesimas proximas et immediate sequentes in pane et aqua ieiunet; et*a* quod per tres annos proximos et immediate post dictum xxij diem Marcii sequentes singulis quartis feriis in Capite Ieiunii et singulis quintis feriis in Cena Domini per tempus consimile se coram dicto patre, sive eius vices in hac parte gerente,*b* personaliter presentet, actura solennem penitenciam pro commissis.

Presentibus tunc ibidem testibus proxime prescriptis.

[8]

Sibilla, uxor Johannis Godsell de Dychingham[78]

Comparuit personaliter coram reverendo in Christo patre et domino, domino Willelmo Dei gracia Norwicensi episcopo, in parlario suo infra manerium de Thorp Episcopi[79] situato iudicialiter sedente xxij die Marcii Anno Domini M° CCCC° XXVIII*c* in mei, Johannis Excestr, clerici, notarii publici, et testium subscriptorum presencia.

Que quidem Sibilla fatebatur et recognovit iudicialiter ipsam sepius recepisse in domos suas hereticos notorios et famosos—videlicet Willelmum Whyte et Hugonem Pye, presbiteros, ac Bartholomeum Cornmonger, Johannem Waddon, Johannem Fowlyn et Thomam Everden ac alios—et eisdem prebuisse in eorum doctrinis et opinionibus auxilium, concilium et favorem. Dixit eciam et fatebatur dicta Sibilla iudicialiter tunc ibidem se concepisse, audivisse et tenuisse ex doctrinis*d* dictorum hereticorum, quibus firmiter credidit, ut asseruit, illa vice, omnes et singulas opiniones subscriptas.

Inprimis videlicet quod sacramentum Baptismi, factum in aqua in forma communiter usitata in Ecclesia, nichil vel modicum est ponderandum si parentes infantis sint fideles.*e*

Item quod sacramentum Confirmacionis factum per episcopum in forma communi non requiritur nec est necessarium ad salutem.

Item quod confessio vocalis facta sacerdoti inutilis est et invalida

---

a Penitens (*MS.* penitentes) iij annis Anno Domini M° CCCC° (*MS.* CCC°) XXIX° egit (*MS.* eg*t*) penitenciam solennem *in margin*.
b se *repeated*.
c xxij die Marcii Anno Domini M° CCCC° XXVIII *interlined*.
d do *deleted*.   *e* It *follows* fideles.

---

78 Ditchingham, south-east Norfolk.
79 (Bishop's) Thorpe, near Norwich.

quia nullus sacerdos habet potestatem absolvere quemquam a peccatis; et ideo soli Deo, qui solus peccata dimittit, facienda est confessio.

Item quod nullus sacerdos habet potestatem conficiendi corpus Christi in sacramento altaris, et quod post verba sacramentalia a presbitero rite prolata remanet in altari purus panis materialis.

Item quod solus consensus mutui amoris inter virum et mulierum sufficit ad matrimonium, absque verborum prolacione*a* et absque solempnizacione in ecclesia.*b*

(p. 267 / fo. 57r)*c* Item quod papa est Antechristus et capud draconis de quo fit mencio in sacra Scriptura,[80] episcopus vero et alii prelati Ecclesie sunt corpus draconis, fratres autem mendicantes sunt cauda draconis.

Item quod quilibet fidelis homo et quelibet fidelis mulier est bonus sacerdos et habet adeo bonam potestatem conficiendi corpus Christi sicut aliquis sacerdos ordinatus.

Item quod licitum est cuilibet fideli exercere et facere quecumque opera servilia, peccato duntaxat excepto, diebus Dominicis et aliis festivis indictis per Ecclesiam, dummodo fiat occulte ad evitandum scandalum.

Item quod omnes ecclesie materiales sunt nisi synagoge, ac modicum vel nichil sunt habende in reverencia, quia Deus exaudit orantem in campis adeo bene sicut in talibus ecclesiis.

Item quod nemo tenetur ieiunare diebus ieiunalibus indictis per Ecclesiam, sed licitum est cuilibet esus carnium et*d* omnimodorum cibariorum omni hora dierum Quadragesimalium, sextarum feriarum et vigiliarum*e* sanctorum*f* indifferenter.

Item quod nullus honor exhibendus est aliquibus ymaginibus.

Item quod peregrinaciones nullo modo sunt fiende.

Item quod licitum est fidelibus subtrahere decimas et oblaciones ab ecclesiis et curatis.

Item quod pulsaciones campanarum ad*g* nichil penitus deserviunt nisi solum ut colligant in bursas sacerdotum.

Quibus quidem articulis et opinionibus prescriptis per prefatam Sibillam*h* coram dicto patre iudicialiter confessatis et abiuratis,*i* dicta Sibilla,*j* volens, ut asseruit,*k* ad Ecclesie redire unitatem, iuravit ad sancta Dei evangelia per ipsam corporaliter tacta quod ab hac hora in antea nunquam tenebit errorem vel errores, heresim vel

---

a sive *deleted.*   *b* item quod papa est *in bottom right-hand corner of page.*
c Sibilla *at top of page.*   *d* omnimod *deleted.*   *e* indi' *deleted.*
f indict' per *deleted.*   *g* ad *interlined.*   *h* MS. Isabellam.
i et abiuratis *interlined.*   *j* MS. Isabella.
k oa omnes errores et hereses ac alios quoscumque *deleted.*

[80] Revelation 12-14.

hereses, nec*a* falsam doctrinam aut opinionem contra fidem sancte Ecclesie et determinacionem sancte Romane Ecclesie; nec aliquam personam tenentem vel docentem errores sive hereses aut falsam doctrinam huiusmodi per se vel aliquam aliam personam publice vel occulte defendet; et quod decetero non recipiet, supportabit vel concelabit aliquam personam in hac parte suspectam, nec eidem prebebit consilium, auxilium vel favorem, nec scienter cum*b* talibus*c* erit familiaris nec se*d* associabit cum eisdem. Et si noverit aliquos hereticos vel de heresi aliquas personas suspectas, sive talium personarum fautores, confortatores, conciliatores vel defensores, aut facientes privatas conventiculas aut tenentes singulares opiniones a communi doctrina Ecclesie, ipsa faciet dictum patrem sive (p. 268 / fo. 57v) eius vicarium in spiritualibus generalem aut diocesanos talium personarum*e* de nominibus et personis earundem*f* sertam et scelerem habere noticiam. Quibus sic peractis et prestito per eandem iuramento iterum corporali de parendo mandatis Ecclesie, dictus*g* pater ipsam absolvit a sentencia excommunicacionis qua, occasione premissarum heres[i]um, extitit innodata canonice.*h* Et pro commissis penitenciam sibi iniunxit subsequentem: videlicet, quod per septennium proximum et immediate futurum sextis feriis singulis Quadragesimis dicti septennii in pane et servicia ieiunet, et interim durante eodem septennio singulis vigiliis Beate Marie Virginis in pane et aqua duntaxat ieiunet; et*i* quod in*j* iiij*k* feria Capite Ieiunii proxima futura et in Cena Domini ex tunc proxima sequente coram dicto reverendo patre, sive eius in hac parte locumtenente, in ecclesia sua Cathedrali Norwic' se personaliter cum aliis penitentibus presentet, actura solempnem penitenciam pro commissis.

Presentibus tunc ibidem magistro Johanne Sutton, in legibus bacallario, ac Roberto Aylmer et Hugone Acton, notariis publicis, necnon Henrico Caldebek, armigero, et Thoma Walsham, clerico, et aliis.

[9]

(p. 208)*l* **Johannes Baker alias Ussher de Tunstale**[81]

Anno Domini Millesimo CCCC*mo* Vicesimo Nono, indiccione septima, pontificatus sanctissimi in Christo patris et domini nostri,

a fass *deleted.*	*b* eisdem *deleted.*	*c* talibus *interlined.*
d se *interlined.*	*e* nd *deleted.*	*f* earundem *interlined.*
g pates *deleted.*	*h* absolvit *repeated.*	*i* Penitencia solennis *in margin.*
j sexta *deleted.*	*k* iiij *interlined.*	*l No folio number.*

domini Martini divina providencia pape quinti, anno duodecimo, mensis Marcii die ultima, coram reverendo in Christo patre ac domino, domino Willelmo Dei gracia Norwicensi episcopo, in capella manerii sui de Thorp Episcopi[82] iudicialiter sedente, assistentibus sibi tunc magistris Willelmo Bernham,[a] in decretis, ac Willelmo Ascogh, in sacra theologia, bacallariis, in mei, Johannis Excestr, clerici, notarii publici, [presencia], comparuit in iudicio Johannes Baker alias Ussher, carpenter de Tunstale Norwicensis diocesis, notatus[b] de crimine heretice pravitatis et lollardie.

Et impetitus iudicialiter per dictum patrem, fatebatur et recognovit iudicialiter se habuisse unum librum de Johanne Bunge de Beghton[83] dicte diocesis, qui quidem liber continebat in se Pater Noster et Ave Maria et Credo in[c] lingua Anglicana script'.[d]

Item idem Johannes Baker alias Ussher fatebatur tunc ibidem se didicisse ex informacione et doctrina dicti Johannis Bunge quod nullus honor exhibendus est ymaginibus[e] crucifixi, Beate Marie aut alterius cuiuscumque sancti in ecclesiis.

Item[f] fate[ba]tur et recognovit idem Johannes Baker se didicisse, tenuisse et credidisse ex informacione et doctrina dicti Johannis Bunge quod nemo tenetur ieiunare in Quadragesima, sextis feriis, diebus Quatuor Temporum nec aliis[g] vigiliis vel diebus indictis per Ecclesiam, et quod dictis diebus et temporibus licitus est cuilibet esus carnium et omnium aliorum cibariorum indifferenter.

Item[h] dictus Johannes Baker alias Ussher fatebatur et recognovit iudicialiter coram dicto patre quod ipse didicit eciam ex informacione et doctrina Johannis Pyry de Martham,[84] wright, quod nemo tenetur ieiunare dictis diebus et temporibus, nec abstinere ab esu carnium, sed ieiunare tantum a peccatis.

Item[i] idem Johannes Baker alias Ussher asseruit, fatebatur et recognovit iudicialiter coram dicto reverendo patre se didicisse, tenuisse et credidisse ex doctrina et informacione dicti Johannis Pyry omnes et singulos articulos sive opiniones subscriptas: videlicet, quod confessio vocalis non deberet fieri alicui sacerdoti, sed tantum soli Deo facienda est confessio; item quod omnis oracio facienda est soli Deo et nulli alii sancto in celo; item quod nulla oracio dicenda est nisi tantum Pater Noster.

Quibus quidem heresibus et erroribus suprascriptis per prefatum

---

[a] R' deleted.   [b] dec deleted.
[c] lat deleted.   [d] J. Bunge de Beghton in margin.
[e] et deleted.   [f] quod deleted.
[g] dieb deleted.   [h] Johannes Pyry in margin.
[i] Pyry in margin three times opposite this paragraph.

---

[82] (Bishop's) Thorpe, near Norwich.
[83] Beighton, east Norfolk.
[84] Martham, east Norfolk.

Johannem Baker alias Ussher coram dicto patre iudicialiter confessatis, placuit eidem Johanni Baker, ut asseruit, tunc ibidem abiurare*a* suprascriptas hereses et errores necnon omnes alias hereses et errores quoscumque fidei catholice et determinacioni sacrosancte et universalis Ecclesie Romane contrarios. Et sic personaliter idem Johannes Baker iuravit ad sancta Dei evangelia per ipsum tacta*b* coram dicto reverendo patre iudicialiter tunc ibidem quod ab hac hora in antea ipse nunquam tenebit errores vel hereses nec falsam doctrinam seu opinionem contra fidem catholicam et determinacionem sacrosancte Ecclesie Romane, nec talem falsam doctrinam sive opinionem aut aliquam personam huiusmodi doctrinam sive opinionem tenentem vel docentem*c* recipiet vel defendet, nec tali persone prebebit consilium, auxilium vel favorem scienter, publice vel occulte, sub pena iuris.*d*

[10]

(p. 282 / fo. 64v)*e* **Johannes Cupper, vicarius de Tunstale**[85]

Die ultima mensis Marcii Anno Domini Millesimo CCCC*mo* Vicesimo Nono, indiccione septima, pontificatus sanctissimi in Christo patris et domini nostri, domini Martini divina providencia pape quinti, anno duodecimo, in capella manerii episcopalis in villa de Thorp Episcopi[86] situati, in mei, Johannis Excestr, notarii publici, ac magistri Johannis Sutton, in legibus bacallarii,*f* Johannis*g* Willy, capellani, notarii publici, Willelmi Bamburgh, capellani, et aliorum [presencia], coram reverendo in Christo patre ac domino, domino Willelmo Dei gracia Norwicensi episcopo, iudicialiter sedente, assistentibus sibi magistris Willelmo Bernham, in decretis bacallario, ac Thoma Hunter, in artibus magistro, comparuit personaliter dominus Johannes Cupper,*h* vicarius perpetuus ecclesie parochialis de Tunstale Norwicensis diocesis, conventus ad iudicium responsurus super crimine lollardie et heretice pravitatis.

---

a et quascumque hereses et errores *deleted.*
b iuravit *repeated.*   *c* def rece *deleted.*   *d See p. 40, n. d.*
e The contents of the page are upside down, at the foot of the page.
f Johe *deleted.*   *g* S *deleted.*   *h* rector *deleted.*

---

85 Tunstall, east Norfolk (Tunstall, east Suffolk, was a rectory). John Cupperre, priest, was instituted vicar on 7 April 1422 (REG/4, Book 8, fo. 72v), and on 11 June 1434 he exchanged the benefice for the vicarage of Wighton, north Norfolk (REG/5, Book 9, fo. 69v).
86 (Bishop's) Thorpe, near Norwich.

[11]

(p. 269 / fo. 58r) **Johannes Pyrye de Martham,**[87] **wryght**

Die x⁰ mensis Aprilis Anno Domini Millesimo CCCC^mo Vicesimo Nono, indiccione septima, pontificatus sanctissimi in Christo patris et domini nostri, domini Martini divina providencia pape quinti, anno duodecimo, in quodam claustro infra palacium Norwic'[88] situato, in mei, Johannis Excestr, clerici, notarii publici, ac Johannis Poleyn, civis Norwici, et Thome Walsham, clerici, testium ad hoc specialiter vocatorum, [presencia], constitutus personaliter Johannes Pyrye, wright, commorans, ut asseruit, in villa de Martham Norwicensis diocesis, notatus de crimine heretice pravitatis et lollardie, dixit expresse tunc ibidem se tenuisse^a et audivisse ex informacione Willelmi White, heretici condempnati, opiniones subscriptas.^b

Inprimis videlicet quod nulle oraciones deberent^c fieri alicui sancto in celo nisi tantum soli Deo.

Item quod peregrinaciones nullo modo deberent fieri ad Thomam Cantuariensem nec ad aliqua alia loca sive ymagines, sed ad ymagines Christi que sunt pauperes, quibus erogande sunt pecunie quas populus expendit et consumit in aliis inani[bu]s peregrinacionibus.

Item quod licitum est cuilibet facere et exercere quecumque opera corporalia omnibus Dominicis et aliis festivis diebus indictis per Ecclesiam, peccato duntaxat excepto.

Item quod solus mutuus consensus inter virum et mulierem sufficit ad sacramentum matrimonii sui.^d

Item quod nullo modo licet iurare nec pro aliqua causa pugnare.

Item quod nullo modo licet occidere quemquam, nec per processum legis dampnare reum furti vel homicidii.

Item quod eque meritorium est cuilibet occupato sive laboranti diebus Dominicis absentare se ab ecclesia, dummodo cogitet bene de Deo, sicut est aliis personis interesse^e divinis officiis diebus Dominicis et festivis.

Item^f dictus Johannes Pyrye tunc ibidem dixit quod Johannes Bunge de Beyghton[89] docuit ipsum J. Pyrie quod nullus honor est exhibendus aliquibus ymaginibus sculptis in ecclesiis.

---

^a et credidisse ex infor *deleted.*   ^b Contra W. White *in margin.*
^c fii *deleted.*   ^d pluri' *follows* sui.
^e ntibus *at the end of* interesse *has been almost totally erased.*
^f Contra Johannem Bunge de Beghton *in margin.*

---

[87] Martham, east Norfolk.
[88] The Bishop's Palace, Norwich.   [89] Beighton, east Norfolk.

Quos quidem articulos omnes et singulos prefatus Johannes Pyry credidit, ut asseruit, esse veros.

Deposicio Johannis Baker alias Ussher de Tunstale[90] *contra Johannem Pyry*[a]

Johannes[b] Baker,[c] testis iuratus, coram domino dicit quod Johannes Pyry docuit et informavit istum iuratum quod nemo tenetur ieiunare in Quadragesima, sextis feriis, diebus iiij[or] Temporum, vigiliis sanctorum nec aliis temporibus indictis per Ecclesiam,[d] sed dictis diebus et temporibus licitus est esus carnium cuilibet dummodo se abstineat ab aliis peccatis.

Item quod confessio vocalis non deberet fieri alicui sacerdoti nisi tantum soli Deo.

Item quod omnis oracio facienda est soli Deo, et nullis aliis sanctis.

Item quod nulla oracio[e] dicenda est nisi tantum Pater Noster.

Deposicio Margerie, uxoris Willelmi Wryght,[f] *contra dictum J. Pyry*

Dicta Margeria dicit quod Johannes Pyrye et eadem Margeria bis vel ter comederunt carnes in sextis feriis, scilicet primo in domo dicte Margerie et postmodum in domo dicti Johannis Pyry: idem Johannes Pyrye et eadem Margeria comedebant unam avem assatam vocatam[g] a bernak,[91] quem idem Johannes cepit in marisco.

[12]

(p. 285 / fo. 66[h]r) **Johannes Burell, famulus Thome Mone**

Johannes Burell, filius Ricardi Burell, glover, examinatus de materia heresis, fatebatur die xviij Aprilis Anno Domini Millesimo

---

[a] *For this deposition, see also p. 69.*
[b] Memorandum de obligacione C librarum facta domino quod dictus Johannes Pyrye comparebit coram domino infra 8 dies [........] aliquis fideiussorum suorum [....................] *written in the margin in a different hand; several words are too faint to be legible.*
[c] *MS.* Baxter.   [d] nec *deleted.*   [e] fa *deleted.*
[f] *Possibly* uxoris Willelmi [Baxter], wryght (*see p. 46, n. a*).
[g] *MS.* unum avem assatum vocatum.   [h] 68 *deleted.*

---

[90] Probably Tunstall, east Norfolk; possibly Tunstall, east Suffolk.
[91] i.e., a barnacle (goose).

CCCC^{mo} XXIX° in domo officii registri in palacio Norwic',[92] iuratus*
dixit quod Thomas Burell, frater istius iurati, tribus annis elapsis
docuit istum iuratum Pater, Ave et Credo in lingua Anglicana.

Item dicit quod idem frater suus docuit istum iuratum precepta
Dei in lingua Anglicana, et quod in primo mandato continetur quod
nullus honor est exhibendus aliquibus ymaginibus sculptis in
ecclesiis per manus hominum, ne likened^b after hem in hevene above
ne after hem that be in water benethe erthe, to lowte thaym ne
worsshipe^c thaym.

Item fatebatur et dixit iste iuratus quod Thomas Burell, frater
istius iurati, docuit istum iuratum quod confessio vocalis facienda
est soli Deo^d in loco secreto, et illa confessio duntaxat sufficit pro
remissione peccatorum. Istum articulum Thomas Mone sepius dixit
in presencia istius iurati et semel in presencia Johannis Josse de
Lodne[93] et aliorum vicinorum suorum.

Item^e iste iuratus dicit quod Thomas Mone dixit sepius diversis
vicinis suis quod^f melius^g esset pluribus presbiteris capere sibi
uxores et eis uti carnaliter,^h sicut plures presbiteri faciunt in diversis
partibus remotis, quam vivere secundum vitam communem pres-
biterorum.

Itemⁱ iste iuratus dixit quod Ricardus Belward ac Willelmus
White et dictus Thomas Burell docuerunt istum iuratum quod
nullus sacerdos habet potestatem conficiendi^j corpus Christi in
sacramento altaris; et quod Deus creavit^k omnes sacerdotes, et in^l
quolibet sacerdote capud et^m oculos ad videndum, aures ad audiendum, linguam ad loquendum et omnia membra cuiuslibet hominis;
et illud sacramentum quod tales sacerdotes asserunt esse verum
corpus Christi nec habet oculos ad videndum, aures ad audiendum,
os ad loquendum, manus ad palpandum nec pedes ad ambulandum
sed est torta panis facta deⁿ farina frumenti.

Item^o dixit iste iuratus quod Ricardus Belward et Thomas
Burell, frater suus, et Thomas Mone docuerunt ipsum sepius diversis vicibus quod Ecclesia catholica est anima cuiuslibet boni Christiani, et quod oraciones dicte devote in campis vel nemoribus sunt
adeo acceptabiles in conspectu Dei sicut oraciones facte cum tanta
devocione in ecclesiis.

---

^a iuratus *interlined:* Contra Thomam *in margin.*   ^b af *deleted.*
^c hem *deleted.*   ^d et nulli sacerdoti *deleted.*
^e Contra Thomam Mone *in margin.*   ^f bonum *deleted.*
^g melius *interlined.*   ^h et hoc esset *deleted.*
ⁱ Contra Ricardum Belward *in margin.*   ^j sacramentum *deleted.*
^k in omni sa *deleted.*   ^l omnes sacerdotes et in *interlined.*
^m et *interlined.*   ⁿ far *deleted.*
^o q' *deleted:* Contra Ricardum Belward *in margin.*

---

⁹² The Bishop's Palace, Norwich.   ⁹³ Loddon, south-east Norfolk.

Item*a* dicit iste iuratus quod quidam sutor,[94] famulus Thome
Mone, docuit istum iuratum quod nullus homo tenetur*b* ieiunare
diebus Quadragesimalibus nec sextis feriis nec vigiliis apostolorum,
quia talia ieiunia nunquam erant instituta ex precepto divino sed
tantum ex ordinacione presbiterorum, for every Fryday is fre day et*c*
ideo omni*d* die Veneris quilibet potest indifferenter edere pisses vel
carnes secundum sui appetitus desiderium.

Item dicit este iuratus quod*e* nemo tenetur observare aliqua festa
indicta per Ecclesiam nisi tantum diem Dominicam, quam tantum*f*
Deus precepit ab operibus observari, et quidem quilibet potest
omnibus diebus indictis per Ecclesiam licite exercere et facere
quecumque opera corporalia ad eorum libitum, diebus Dominicis
duntaxat exceptis.*g*

Item*h* peregrinaciones nullo modo sunt faciende ad Mariam de
Falsyngham[95] nec ad Thomam Cantuar' nec ad aliqua alia loca
nisi tantum ad*i* vicinos indigentes.*j*

Item quod*k* non est licitum in aliquo casu iurare nisi cum
homo fuerit in periculoso casu concernente vitam suam.

Item*l* dicit iste iuratus quod Ricardus Belward et Thomas Burell
docuerunt istum iuratum quod nemo tenetur solvere decimas vel
oblaciones presbiteris, quia Deus non habet aliquam partem de
aliquibus decimis vel oblacionibus solutis presbiteris, et quod
quilibet tenetur decimare animam suam tantum Deo quia oblaciones
et decime faciunt presbiteros superbos esse.

Item*m* quod Ricardus Belward docuit istum quod*n* iste mundus
est locus purgatorii, et omnis anima quamcito egressa fuerit de
corpore statim sine medio transit ad celum sive ad infernum, et
adeo frustra fiunt oraciones vel misse dicte vel facte pro defunctis.

(p. 286 / fo. 66v)*o* Item*p* dixit iste iuratus quod Batild, uxor Thome
Burell, fratris istius iurati, que moratur in parochia Sancti Martini,[96]

---

a famulus Thome Mone *in margin.*
b ieiur *deleted.*
d ideo omni *interlined.*
f tantum *interlined.*
h nem *deleted.*
j Hoc docuit uxor fratris sui *in margin.*
k nemo *deleted.*
l quod *deleted:* Contra R. Belward et Thomam Burell *in margin.*
m Contra R. Belward *in margin.*
n non est *deleted.*
o Joh' Burell *at top of page.*
p Contra uxorem T. Burell *in margin.*

c illa *deleted.*
e quod *interlined.*
g MS. excepto.
i proximos *deleted.*

[94] Probably John Pert (see pp. 75 and 172).
[95] A pun on St Mary of Walsingham.
[96] It is not clear which parish was being referred to. Thomas Burell, his wife
and his brother seem to have come from the parish of Loddon (see pp. 77,
146 and 175), which was dedicated to the Holy Trinity.

dixit isti iurato in crofto Thome Mone*a* quod nulle*b* misse erunt amplius celebrate per capellanos usque ad finem mundi, prout continetur in quodam libro[97] qui iam*c* nuper venit de partibus ultramarinis ad istas partes.

Item eadem Batild dixit*d* isti iurato*e* quod fratres destruent istum mundum.

Item*f* die v*ta* Julii anno suprascripto, in claustro ducente ad celarium vini,*g* Johannes Burell dixit*h* Johanni Excestr quod die Pasche[98] mane Anno Domini Millesimo CCCC*mo* XX*mo* Octavo vidit in le botery retro altum scannum aule mansionis Thome Mone de Lodne unum quarterium porcelli*i* coctum*j* farcitum frigidum. Et*k* iste Johannes suspicatur quod dictus porcellus*l* fuit occisus et*m* paratus*n* ac coctus de consilio uxoris[99] Thome Mone;*o* et eciam quod residuum eiusdem porcelli fuit comestum per*p* Thomam*q* Burell, fratrem istius Johannis Burell, ac uxorem Thome Mone et*r* per*s* Johannem Pert, famulum dicti Thome Mone, ac per alium hominem toga de russeto[100] indutum,*t* cuius nomen iste Johannes dixit se*u* nescire, in vigilia Pasche predicta. Et dicto die Pasche uxor Thome Mone misit per filiam suam dictum residuum porcelli ad domum Thome Burell. Dicit eciam iste Johannes,*v* interrogatus per quid scitur se scire dictum porcellum sic fuisse per dictos T. Burell, uxorem Thome Mone, Johannem Pert et alium hominem sibi ignotum fore*w* comestum in vigilia Pasche,*x* quod hoc fuit presumendum eo quod

a dixit *deleted.*
b *Just possibly* mille.
c vi *deleted.*
d eid *deleted.*
e MS. iurate.
f *Contra uxorem* T. Mone *in margin.*
g *Possibly* vnu' (*i.e.,* unum): dixit michi *deleted.*
h Johannes Burell dixit *interlined.*
i assa assatu' *deleted.*
j coctum *interlined.*
k Contra T. Burell *in margin.*
l fuit *deleted.*
m eo *deleted.*
n ait *deleted.*
o de consilio (*possibly* confilio) uxoris Thome Mone et *interlined.*
p Johannem *deleted.*
q Thomam *interlined.*
r uxorem Thome Mone et *interlined.*
s Contra Johannem Pert *in margin.*
t q *deleted.*
u Edmundus Archer scit informare de commestione dicti porcelli eo quod ipse fuit invitatus ad eundem *in margin.*
v q' *deleted.*
w MS. fire.
x dicit *repeated.*

[97] Unidentifiabie.
[98] 4 April 1428.
[99] Hawisia Mone.
[100] According to Knighton 'principales pseudo-Lollardi prima introductione hujus sectae nefandae vestibus de russeto utebantur pro majore parte, illorum quasi simplicitatem cordis ostendentes' (Henry Knighton, *Chronicon* (ed. J. R. Lumby, Rolls Series, 1889–95), ii, p. 184). Walsingham gave a similar description (Thomas Walsingham, *Historia Anglicana* (ed. H. T. Riley, Rolls Series, 1863–4), i, p. 324). William Ramsbury was clad in a tunic and mantle of russet when he was 'ordained' a Lollard priest in 1385 (A. Hudson, 'A Lollard Mass', *Journal of Theological Studies*, xxiii (1972), 411).

omnes ille persone fuerunt recluse in quadam camera, vocata le chesehous chambr, secrete dum Thomas Mone fuit apud mercatum de Hornyng*a* [101] in vigilia dicti festi Pasche ante nonam,*b* isto Johanne nesciente, et tandem eodem die Sabbati iste Johannes videbat omnes illas personas exeuntes de dicta camera.

Item*c* iste Johannes Burell*d* dixit die Sabbati[102] proximo post festum Translacionis Sancti Thome Martyris anno prescripto quod iste Johannes Burell, tenens in manu sua unum fagothook,*e* una cum*f* Edmundo Archer, cordewaner commorante in Lodne olim cum Thoma Mone sed modo cum Johanne Josse commorante in Stubbes Grene[103] prope mansum Bakones,[104] et dum iste Johannes et prefatus*g* Edmundus Archer pergebant per viam usque Lodne erga vesperam, videbant quandam veterem crucem iacentem prope portam aule vocate Lodne Hall.[105] Quam crucem iste Johannes Burell*h* percuciebat cum dicto fagothook. Et tunc*i* filius Johannis Wardon, existens cum eisdem, interrogavit ab isto Johanne quare ipse sic percuciebat illam crucem. Et iste Johannes asserit se respondere sibi dicendo, 'quamvis gravius et acucius percuterem istam crucem cum acuciori instrumento, nunquam cruentaret illa crux.'

Item*j* idem Johannes Burell dicit quod dictus Edmundus Archer et Johannes, clericus de Lodne,*k* [106] sunt lollardi eo quod iste Johannes et prefatus Edmundus comederunt carnes die Sabbati in quadam cymba, navigantes versus Jernemuth.[107]

Item quod clericus*l* de Lodne cremelat ymagines in Lodne.

(p. 234 / fo. 37v)*m* In Dei nomine, Amen. Per presens publicum instrumentum cunctis appareat evidenter quod Anno ab Incarna-

a et *deleted.*   *b* et postmodum in exit *deleted.*
c Contra Johannem Burell *in margin.*
d quod *deleted.*   *e* venit *deleted.*
f Contra Edmundum Archer *in margin.*
g Johannes *deleted.*   *h* percuscie *deleted.*   *i* iste Johannes *deleted.*
j Contra clericum de Lodne *in margin* (*the initial* c *of* clericus *is a small letter in the MS.*).
k *Possibly* Johannes Clericus de Lodne (*the initial* c *of* clericus *is a capital letter in the MS.*).
l *The initial* c *is a small letter in the MS.*
m Johannes Burell, famulus Thome Mone *at top of page.*

[101] Horning, north-east Norfolk.   [102] 10 July 1428.
[103] Stubbs Green is an area on the edge of Loddon.
[104] Probably the manor-house of the Bacon family (see Blomefield, *Norfolk*, x, pp. 156–7).
[105] Loddon Hall (see Blomefield, *Norfolk*, x, p. 160).
[106] The man is unidentifiable.   [107] Yarmouth.

cione Domini secundum cursum et computacionem Ecclesie Anglicane Millesimo CCCC^{mo} Tricesimo, indiccione nona, pontificatus
sanctissimi in Christo patris et domini nostri, domini Martini
divina providencia pape quinti, anno quartodecimo, mense Decembris die nona, in capella palacii reverendi in Christo patris et domini,
domini Willelmi Dei gracia Norwicensis episcopi, in civitate Norwic'
situati, in mei, Johannis Excestr, clerici, notarii publici, ac Roberti
Aylmer, notarii publici, Thome Walsham et Willelmi Fraunceys,
clericorum, testium ad infrascripta vocatorum et requisitorum,
[prescencia], coram discreto viro, magistro Willelmo Bernham, in
decretis bacallario, dicti reverendi patris, domini Norwicensis
episcopi, vicario in spiritualibus generali, pro tribunali sedente,
comparuit personaliter Johannes Burell, famulus Thome Moone,
nuper commorantis^a in Lodne Norwicensis diocesis, de heresi et
heretica pravitate notatus multipliciter et diffamatus, et ea occasione ad iudicium evocatus personaliter responsurus. Qui quidem
Johannes Burell, super crimine heretice pravitatis per dictum
vicarium in spiritualibus generalem, iudicem in hac parte, allocutus^b
personaliter^c et impetitus, fatebatur et recognovit iudicialiter tunc
ibidem se infra diocesim Norwicensem tenuisse, credidisse et affirmasse omnes hereses et errores in subscriptis articulis conscriptos.

Inprimis quod omnis confessio facienda est soli Deo in loco secreto,
et illa confessio duntaxat sufficit pro remissione omnium peccatorum.

Item quod nullus sacerdos habet potestatem conficiendi corpus
Christi sub specie panis et vini in sacramento altaris ad missam, sed
Deus creavit omnes sacerdotes, et illud sacramentum quod sacerdotes asserunt esse verum corpus Christi est nisi torta panis facta de
farina frumenti.

Item quod nemo tenetur solvere decimas nec oblaciones ecclesiis
nec curatis, quia Deus non habet aliquam partem de eisdem, sed
tales decime et oblaciones faciunt presbiteros esse superbos.

Item quod nemo tenetur sanctificare aliquod festum indictum per
Ecclesiam nisi tantum diem Dominicum, quem solum ipse Deus ab
omnibus operibus abstineri et sanctificari [precepit], et omnibus aliis
diebus indictis per Ecclesiam licitum est cuilibet facere et exercere
quecumque opera corporalia.

Item quod melius esset presbiteris capere sibi uxores, et eis
carnaliter uti, quam vivere secundum vitam communem presbiterorum.

Item quod Ecclesia catholica est anima cuiuslibet boni Christiani.
Et quod omnes oraciones devote dicte in campis vel nemoribus

---

^a MS. commorant'. ^b in iudicio *deleted*.
^c personaliter *interlined*.

sunt adeo acceptabiles in conspectu Dei sicut consimiles oraciones dicte in ecclesiis cum tanta vel consimili devocione.

Item quod nemo tenetur ieiunare diebus Quadragesimalibus, diebus Quatuor Temporum, vigiliis apostolorum nec sextis feriis quia talia ieiunia nunquam erant instituta ex precepto divino sed ex ordinacione presbiterorum, sed omnibus talibus diebus quilibet potest tociens quociens sibi placuerit edere pisces vel carnes indifferenter secundum proprium desiderium appetitus. And every Friday is a fre day to al manere metys, bothe flessh and fissh indifferently. Et iste comedit carnes quodam Sabbato.

Item quod peregrinaciones nullo modo sunt faciende nisi tantum pauperibus.

Item quod nullus honor est exhibendus aliquibus imaginibus sculptis vel depictis in ecclesiis nec extra.

Item quod nullo modo licet iurare nisi in casu periculoso concernente vitam alicuius.

Item quod frustra fiunt oraciones et celebrantur misse pro defunctis, quia anime omnium defunctorum aut sunt in celo aut in inferno, quia non est alius locus purgatorii quam iste mundus.

Quibus omnibus et singulis per dictum Johannem iudicialiter confessatis, iudex intimavit eidem quod dicti articuli continent in se nonnullas hereses et errores. Ideoque idem Johannes asseruit se velle eosdem hereses et errores ac quoscumque alios re et verbo dimittere et abiurare, ac puro corde redire ad Ecclesie unitatem. Et tunc idem Johannes, tenens manum suam dexteram ad librum evangeliorum, iuravit iudicialiter ad ea quod ab hac hora in antea ipse nunquam tenebit, credet nec affirmabit errorem nec heresim nec aliquam opinionem vel doctrinam fidei catholice et determinacioni Ecclesie Romane[a] repugnantem; nec hereticos vel personas de heresi suspectas recipiet vel supportabit; nec eis prebebit consilium, auxilium vel favorem. Et tunc iudex denunciavit sibi periculum relapsus. Et deinde, prestito per eum iuramento de agendo penitenciam pro commissis, absolutus est. Et pro commissis iudex iniunxit sibi iiij fustigaciones circa ecclesiam parochialem Sancti Georgii ad Portas[108] et totidem circa mercatum Norwici, capite et pedibus denudatis, corpore camisia et bracciis tantum induto, cum cereo cere ponderis dimidie libre offerendo dicte ecclesie post penitenciam peractam.

Quam penitenciam peregit in forma sibi limitata.

[a] contra' *deleted.*

---

[108] St George at the Monastery Gates, more commonly called St George at Tombland, Norwich.

[13]

(p. 209 / fo. 16r) **Johannes Kynget**^{a}

Die vicesima mensis Augusti Anno Domini Millesimo CCCC^{mo} Vicesimo Nono, coram reverendo in Christo patre ac domino, domino Willelmo Dei gracia Norwicensi episcopo, in capella^b manerii sui de Thorp^c ^{109} iudicialiter sedente, comparuit personaliter Johannes Kynget de Nelond.^{d} ^{110} Per dictum patrem iudicialiter impetitus super crimine heretice pravitatis, fatebatur iudicialiter se^e fuisse notatum et defamatum quod ipse recepisset, supportasset et manutenuisset hereticos—scilicet Willelmum White, Hugonem Pye,^{f} presbiteros, Bartholomeum^g Thaccher, Thomam James et alios hereticos famosos. Quorum doctrinis et informacionibus ipse Johannes Kynget instructus, ut asseruit, et informatus, ipse Johannes tenuit, credidit [et] asseruit hereses et errores in indenturis super abiuracione eiusdem Johannis inscriptos, conceptos, contentos plenius et specificatos. Quos quidem errores et hereses omnes et singulos prefatus Johannes voluit, ut asseruit, puro corde re et verbo totaliter dimittere pariter et abiurare pro perpetuo iuxta formam in huiusmodi indenturis^h conscriptam in ydeomate Anglicano. Quarum tenorem prefatus reverendus pater per magistrum Willelmum Ascogh, sacre pagine bacallarium, prefato Johanni Kynget publice perlegi [precepit] in iudicio tunc ibidem. Quarum indenturarum tenore per ipsum magistrum Willelmum Ascogh eidem Johanni Kynget sic perlecto et per ipsum Johannem, ut asseruit,^{i} plenarie intellecto, ipse Johannes Kynget fatebatur et recognovit se in et de premissis erroribus et heresibus in dictis indenturis conscriptis fuisse et esse reum et culpabilem, et eosdem errores et hereses iuxta formam huiusmodi sibi, ut premittitur, prius lectam^j [velle] abiurare. Sed quia ipse tunc, ut asseruit, fuit oculorum visu debilitatus, ipse non potuit huiusmodi abiuracionem legere. Ideo^k ipse Johannes Kynget constituit dictum magistrum Willelmum Ascogh organum vocis sue ad legendam huiusmodi abiuracionem nomine suo et pro eo. Qui quidem magister Willelmus Ascogh, onus lecture huiusmodi in se

^{a} re' in iiij^{to} folio precedente *follows as a note.*
^{b} palacii Norwic' *deleted.*
^{d} alias *follows* Nelond.
^{f} habito *deleted.*
^{h} conce *deleted.*
^{j} *One or two illegible letters deleted.*

^{c} manerii sui de Thorp *interlined.*
^{e} recepiss *deleted.*
^{g} Cornemonger alias *deleted.*
^{i} publice perlecto *deleted.*
^{k} pe' *deleted.*

^{109} (Bishop's) Thorpe, near Norwich.
^{110} Nayland, south Suffolk (see p. 80, n. 112).

assumens, tenorem dictarum indenturarum abiuracionem dicti
Johannis Kynget in se continentem de verbo ad verbum plenarie
perlegit publice in iudicio tunc ibidem; dicto Johanne K. interim
ascultante et manum suam dexteram super librum evangeliorum
continue tenente. Et sic idem Johannes omnes errores et hereses
huiusmodi abiuravit. Et in testimonio huiusmodi abiuracionis ipse
Johannes K. manu sua propria in utraque parte dictarum indenturarum signum + subscripsit. Et uni parti earundem indenturarum penes registrum dicti patris remanenti sigillum suum
apposuit. Et postea, prestito per eundem Johannem Kynget tunc
ibidem iuramento corporali ad librum evangeliorum per ipsum
tactum de stando mandatis Ecclesie et de peragendo penitenciam
sibi pro suis commissis iniungendam a dicto patre in hac parte, prefatus pater ipsum Johannem Kynget a sentencia excommunicacionis, quam occasione premissorum incurrebat, absolvebat. Et pro
commissis suis in hac parte idem pater iniunxit eidem Johanni
Kynget tres fustigaciones circa cimiterium capelle de Nelond coram
solenni processione eius tribus diebus Dominicis proximis et immediate sequentibus post festum Sancti Bartholomei ex tunc
proximum sequens, collo, capite et pedibus denudatis, corpore
camisia et femoralibus duntaxat induto, unum cereum cere ponderis
unius libre*a* in manibus deferendo, et alium cereum ultima Dominica
post*b* penitenciam huiusmodi peractam tempore offertorii magne
misse summo altari offerendo; et quod incedat eodem modo*c* circa
mercatum de Nedham,[111] dictum vel consimilem cereum deferendo,
(p. 210 / fo. 16v)*d* tribus diebus mercati tempus messivum, quod
tunc instabat, proximis et immedia[te] sequentibus; et quod in
quatuor partibus tam dicte processionis quam mercati predicti
magis patentibus singulis diebus Dominicis et diebus mercati idem
Johannes Kynget genuflectat et a vicario de Stoke Nelond,[112] qui
ipsum sequetur superpelliceo indutus, unam fustigacionem recipiat*e* cum virga humiliter et devote.

Presentibus in actis huiusmodi diei et assistentibus dicto reverendo
patri in premissis*f* magistris Thoma Ryngstede, Thoma Ludham,[113]

---

a ponderis unius libre *interlined.*   *b* post *interlined.*   *c* circa *deleted.*
d J. Kynget *at top of page.*   *e* h *deleted.*
f magistris Willelmo Worstede, priore ecclesie Cathedralis Norwicensis, ac
Johanne Elys, ordinis Minorum, sacre pagine professoribus, necnon Willelmo
Bernham, Thoma Ryngstede et Nicholao Derman, in decretis, Willelmo
Ascogh, in sacra pagina, Johanne Sutton et Johanne Pynkeneye,[114] in legibus,
bacallariis, necnon Johanne Cok, notario *deleted.*

---

[111] Probably Needham Market, east Suffolk; possibly Needham, south
Norfolk.
[112] Stoke by Nayland, south Suffolk (Neylond, south Norfolk, was a rectory).
[113] See Emden, *BRUC*, p. 376, Thomas Ludham.
[114] See Emden, *BRUC*, p. 466, John Pynkney.

in decretis, ac Willelmo Ascogh, in sacra pagina, et Johanne Sutton,
in legibus, bacallariis, necnon fratribus*a* Ricardo Barton et Ricardo
Norton, ordinis Minorum, et Johanne Wylly, notario publico, et me,
J. Excestr, actorum scriba, notario publico.

In the name of God, tofore you, the worshipfull fadir in Crist,
William, be the grace of God bisshop of Norwich, I, John Kyngent
of Nelond of your diocese, your subject defamed and noted hugely
of that I have receyved, supported and mayntened heretikes—that
is to say Syr William Whyte, Syr Huwe Pye, Bartholomewe Thaccher,
Thomas James and other famous heretikes—felyng and under-
standyng that be thayr doctrine Y was enformed of these errours
and heresies whyche Y helde and beleved.

That is to say that the sacrament of Baptem, whyche the heretikes
calle the shakelment of Baptem, doon in water in the fourme cus-
timed in the Churche is of none availe ne to be pondred.

Also that confession of mowth made unto a prest is of noon availe
ne plesyng to God, for confession oweth to be made oonly to God and
to non other prest.

Also that no prest hath powar to make Goddys body in the sacrament of the awter, but God made alle prestes, and no prest hath
powar to make God, for God was made longe tyme or the prestes
were made.

Also that no matrimoyn shuld be solennized in the churche, but
oonly consent in hert betuxe man and woman suffiseth for matrimoyn.

Also that no man is bownde to faste on Fridays, vigiles of seyntes
ne other days and tymes bodey be the Churche to be fasted.

Also that prayer shuld be made oonly to God, and to noon other
seynt.

Also that no*b* prayer shuld be said but oonly the Pater Noster.

Also that no pilgrimage oweth to be mad but only to poure
puple.

Also that ryngyng of belles (p. 211 / fo. 17r) be but Antecristis
hornes.

Because of whyche errours and heresies Y am called tofore you,
worshipful fadir, whiche have cure of my soule. And be you fully
enformed that the said articules that Y have confessed before you
ben opyn errours and heresies and contrarious to the*c* determinacion
of the Churche of*d* Roome, wherfor Y wyllyng folwe and suwe the

a fratribus *interlined.*   *b* no *interlined.*
c doctrine *deleted.*
d tho oh *deleted.*

doctrine of holy Churche, and departe from all maner of errour and heresie, and turne with good will and hert to the oonhed of the Churche. Considerant[a] that holy Churche spereth not hir bosom to hym that will turne agayn, ne God will not the deth of a synner but rather that he be turned and lyve, with a pure herte Y confesse, deteste and despise my said errours and heresies, and the said opinions Y confess heretikous and erroneous and to the faith of the Churche of Roome and all universall holy Churche repugnant. And for as muche as be the said thinges that Y wykkedly so held and beleved Y shewed meself corrupt and unfaithful, that from hensforth Y shewe me uncorrupt and faithful, the faith and doctrine of holy Churche truly to kepe Y promitte. And all maner of errour and heresie, doctrine and opinion agayn the faith of holy Churche and the determinacion of the Churche of Roome—and namely the opinions before rehersed—Y abjure and forswere, and swere be these holy Gospels be me bodely touched that from hensforth Y shal never holde errour ne errours, heresie ne heresies ne fals doctrine agayn the faith of the Churche and determinacion of the Churche. Ner no suche thynges Y shal obstinatly defende, ne ony man or woman holdyng or techyng suche maner of thynges be me or ony other persone opynly or prively Y shal defende. Y shall never aftir this tyme be no recettour, fautour, counsellour or defensour of heretikes or ony men or women suspect of heresie. Ner Y shal trowe to thaym.[b] Ne wittyngly Y shall felaship with thaym, ne be hoomly with thaym. Y shal never yeve consell, favour, yeftes ne confort to thaym. Yf Y knowe ony heretik or of heresie ony man or woman suspect or of thaym fautours, confortours, consellours or defensours, or ony men or women makyng prive conventicules[c] or assembles, or holding divers or singuler opinions from the comune doctrine of the Churche, Y shal late you, worshipfull fadir, or your vicar generall in your absens or the diocesans of suche (p. 212 / fo. 17v) men have soone and redy knowyng. So help me God atte holy doom and these holy Gospels.

In witnesse of whiche thing Y subscribe here with myn owyn hand a crosse +. And to this partie endented to remayne in your registre Y[d] sette to my signet. And that other partie endented Y receyve undir your seal to abide with me unto my lyves ende. Yoven in the chapell of your maner of Thorp the xxti day of the moneth of August the yer of oure Lord a thousand four hundred and xxixti.

---

[a] q' deleted.
[b] yf Y knowe ony heretik or of heresie ony man or woman suspect deleted.
[c] ons deleted.
[d] se deleted.

(p. 213 / fo. 18r) *Penitencia Johannis Kynget et Thome Chatrys de Nedham propter crimen heresis*

Willelmus, et cetera, dilecto in Christo filio, vicario ecclesie parochialis de Stoke Neylond nostre diocesis, salutem, graciam et benediccionem.

Quia nos, in negocio correccionis animarum Johannis Kynget de Nelond dicte diocesis et Thome Chatris de eadem, subditorum nostrorum de et super crimine heretice pravitatis multipliciter diffamatorum, ex officio nostro legitime procedentes, eisdem pro eorum commissis in hac parte coram nobis iudicialiter confessatis penitenciam iniunximus infrascriptam—videlicet, utrique eorundem tres fustigaciones circa cimiterium capelle de Nedham coram solenni processione eiusdem tribus diebus Dominicis proximis et immediate sequentibus proxime post festum Sancti Bartholomei proximum facienda, collo, capite et pedibus denudatis, corpore camisia et femoralibus duntaxat induto, portando manibus utriusque eorundem unum cereum cere ponderis unius libre, quos cereos ultima die Dominica huiusmodi*a* post penitenciam ipsam peractam*b* post evangelium magne misse summo altari dicte capelle offerri per eosdem humiliter et devote volumus et mandamus, quodque tribus diebus mercati, instans tempus messivum, proximis et immediate sequentibus incedant, et ipsorum uterque incedat, modo predicto circa mercatum de Nedham predictum, dictos vel consimiles cereos in manibus suis deferentes, et quod in quatuor partibus dicte processionis et dicti mercati magis patentibus singulis diebus Dominicis et diebus mercati predictis dicti incedentes genuflectant et a vobis, quem superpelicio indutum singulis diebus predictis sequi [volumus], unam fustigacionem recipere humiliter et devote volumus et mandamus—iusticia id poscente, vobis committimus et mandamus, in virtute obedientie firmiter iniungendo itemque, [quatinus] moneatis et inducatis moneri*c* et induci faciatis sic*d* peremptorie prefatos J.K. et T.C., quos nos eciam tenore presencium peremptorie monemus, quod dictam penitenciam per nos eisdem, ut prefertur, iniunctam subeant et peragant humiliter et devote, sicque subeat et peragat uterque eorundem. Et si monicionibus nostris huiusmodi non paruerint et ipsorum uterque non paruerit cum effectu, ipsos vel ipsum huiusmodi monicionibus non parentes vel parentem citetis seu citari faciatis peremptorie quod compareant seu compareat coram nobis vel commissario nostro in capella palacii nostri Norwic' die xij post citacionem*e* huiusmodi, si dies illa iuridica fuerit, sin autem

a peremptorie peract' *deleted.*
b post penitenciam ipsam peractam *interlined.*
c ve *follows* moneri.   *d* faciatis *repeated.*   *e* huius *deleted.*

proxima die iuridica ex tunc sequente, causas racionabiles, si quas pro se habeant vel eorum alter habeat pro se, quare pro manifesta offensa eorum vel alterius eorundem non debeant, seu alter eorundem dictis monicionibus non parens [non] debeat, excommunicari in forma iuris proposituri facturique ulterius et recepturi quod in ea parte canonice dictaverint sancciones. De diebus vero recepcionis presencium monicionumque et induccionum per vos in hac parte faciendarum, et quid feceritis qualiterque, et an dicti Johannes et Thomas ac uterque eorundem monicionibus nostris huiusmodi[a] paruerint et ipsorum uterque paruerit in premissis, nos vel commissarios nostros huiusmodi dictis die et loco distincte certificetis per litteras vestras patentes harum seriem continentes sigillo auctentico consignatas.

Datum fuit in manerio de Thorp Episcopi xx die Augusti Anno Domini M⁰ CCCC^mo XXIX et nostre consecracionis anno quarto.

[14]

(p. 329 / fo. 90r) **Ricardus Fleccher de Beccles**[115]

In Dei nomine, Amen. Per presens publicum instrumentum cunctis appareat evidenter quod Anno Domini ab Incarnacione eiusdem Millesimo Quadringentesimo Vicesimo Nono, indiccione septima, pontificatus sanctissimi in Christo patris et domini nostri, domini Martini divina providencia pape quinti, anno duodecimo, mense vero Augusti die vicesima septima, in capella palacii reverendi in Christo patris et domini, domini Willelmi Dei gracia Norwicensis episcopi, in civitate Norwic' situati, in me[i], Johannis Excestr, clerici, notarii publici, et testium subscriptorum presencia, coram dicto reverendo patre, domino Willelmo Norwicensi episcopo, pro tribunali ad reddenda iura—prout michi, notario prescripto, pro tunc apparebat—iudicialiter sedente, assistentibus tunc eidem reverendo patri venerabilibus et discretis viris, magistris Willelmo Worstede, priore ecclesie Cathedralis Norwicensis, ac Johanne Derham, priore[b] celle ecclesie Sancte Margarete de Lenn Episcopi,[116] sacre pagine professoribus, ac Willelmo Bernham et Willelmo Sekyngton, in decretis bacallariis, Ricardus Fleccher de Beccles

---

[a] parui' *deleted.*   [b] ecci *deleted.*

[115] Beccles, north-east Suffolk.
[116] John Derham, prior of Norwich Cathedral Priory's cell at Lynn from 1422, or earlier, until 1436 (see Emden, *BRUO*, i, p. 572, John Dereham).

Norwicensis diocesis, de et super crimine heretice pravitatis, ut dicebatur, multipliciter diffamatus et super eodem crimine personaliter responsurus, in vinculis[a] ad iudicium fuit adductus. Cui quidem Ricardo Fleccher prefatus reverendus pater, iudicialiter sedens,[b] omnes et singulos articulos in quodam scripto cirographo super abiuracione dicti Ricardi concepto et indentato, cuius tenor inferius continetur,[c] scriptos et[d] contentos ac hereses et errores in eisdem articulis habitos et contentos, dixit, proposuit et obiecit. Quos quidem articulos omnes et singulos, ac universas hereses et omnimodos errores in eisdem articulis habitos et contentos, idem Ricardus Fleccher fatebatur et recognovit se infra diocesim Norwicensem diu tenuisse, credidisse,[e] docuisse et affirmasse prout[f] in dicto scripto indentato plenarie continetur. Idcirco idem Ricardus volens, ut asseruit, et affectans puro corde redire ad Ecclesie unitatem, ac omnes hereses et quoscumque errores re et verbo dimittere pro perpetuo et abiurare secundum tenorem dicti cirographi indentati,[g] cuius tenorem, ut asseruit, prius cum matura deliberacione audivit et plenarie intellexit, et quia idem Ricardus asseruit se fore oculorum lumine aliqualiter caligatum et ipsam abiuracionem legere non valentem propria in persona, ipse Ricardus constituit iudicialiter magistrum Johannem Willy, notarium publicum, organum vocis sue. Cui quidem magistro Johanni Wylly ipse Ricardus commisit plenariam et liberam potestatem nomine suo et pro se dictam abiuracionem suam coram prefato reverendo patre legendi et interponendi. Qui quidem Johannes Wylly, organum vocis dicti Ricardi in se assumens, omnes et singulas hereses et errores universos per ipsum Ricardum coram dicto reverendo patre prius iudicialiter confessatos ac alios hereses et errores quoscumque in personam dicti Ricardi Fleccher pro perpetuo abiuravit, ceteraque fecit prout plenius continetur[h] in dicto scripto[i] cirographo in hac parte concepto et indentato, cuius tenor de verbo ad verbum sequitur et est talis.

In the name of God, tofore you, the worshipful fadir in Crist, William, be [the] grace of God bisshop of Norwich, Y, Richard Fleccher of Beccles of your diocese, your subject, knoweleche and confesse that Y have be conversaunt with heretikes and thaym receyved into myn hous wittyngly and thaym supported, faverd and conselod—that is to say with Syr William Whyte, Syr Huwe

---

[a] adductus fuit *deleted.*
[c] cuius tenor inferius continetur *interlined.*
[d] indentatos *deleted.*
[f] in eodem *deleted.*
[h] plenius continetur *interlined.*

[b] proposuit et obiecit *deleted.*
[e] et aff *deleted.*
[g] qi *deleted.*
[i] indentato *deleted.*

Pye, William Everden,[117] Richard Belward, Bartholomew Monk, John[a] (p. 330 / fo. 90v)[b] Skylly, millere, and William Wright[c] of Martham—and of thaym Y have receyved the errours and heresies, the whiche be contened in these indentures, whiche Y have beleved, affermed and taught, that is to say,

That the sacrament of Baptem doon in water in forme custumed in the Churche is nother necessarie ne vailable to mannys salvacion.

Also that confession shuld oonly be made to God, and to noon other[d] prest.

Also that no prest hath poar to make Cristis body in [the] sacrament of the auter.

Also that only consent betuxe man and woman, with consent of the frendys of bothe parties, suffiseth for matrimony, withoute expressyng of wordis or solennizacion in churche.

Also that every Cristen man is a prest.

Also that the pope of Roome is Antecrist, and other prelates[e] and persones of the Churche ben disciples of Antecrist.

Also that no man is bounde to kepe the holydays, but that it is leful everybody to do all bodyly werkes on Sundays and other festival days boden be the Churche.

Also that no man is bounde to offre in churches.

Also no man is bounde to paye mortuaries to churches, for suche payng of mortuaries and other thinges to the Churche makyn prestes proude.

Also that no worship shuld be do to ony ymages, but that all ymages owyn to be destroied and do away.

Also that holy water and holy bred ben of noon vertu, and that it were better prestes to halwe wellis and flodis ordeyned for mannys mete and drynk than to blesse water in churche whiche men springe on here clokes.

Also that every[f] prayer shuld oonly be made unto God, and to noon other seynt.

Also that commune blessyng that men use and make with here right hand, it availeth to nothing elles but to skere away flies.

Also that in no maner it is lefull to sle a man, nether be processe of lawe to dampne a man that is gulty of thefte or of manslawght.

---

[a] Ricardus Fleccher	Nicholaus Drye
Matilda Fleccher	Willelmus Hardy
Johannes Eldon	Hawysia Mone
Robertus Cawell	Johannes Pert

written in bottom left-hand corner of page.
[b] Ric' Fleccher *in top left-hand corner of page.*
[c] *Possibly* William [Baxter], wright (*see p. 46, n. a*).
[d] seyntes *deleted.* [e] *MS.* prefates. par *deleted.*

---

[117] See above, pp. 29–30, 33, n. 14; *Reg. Chichele*, ed. Jacob, iv, pp. 297–8.

Also that it is not leful in ony case to swere ne to lye.

Also that no pilgrimage shuld be do but oonly to pore puple.

Because of whiche errours and heresies Y am called tofore you, worshipful fadir, whiche have cure of my soule. And be you fully enformed that the said myn affermyng, holdyng, belevyng and techyng ben opin errours and heresies and contrarious to the determinacion of the Churche of Roome, wherfor Y wyllyng folwe a[nd] sue the doctrine of holy Churche and departe from all maner of errour and heresie, and turne with good will and hert to the oonhed of the Churche. Considerand that holy Churche spereth not hir bosum to hym that will turne agayn, ne God will not the deth of a synner but rather that^a (p. 331 / fo. 91r)^b he be turned and lyve, with a pure hert Y confesse, deteste and despise my said errours and heresies, and the said opinions Y confesse heretikous and erroneous and to the faith of the Churche of Roome and all universal holy Churche repugnant. And for as moche as be the said thinges that Y wikkedly so affermed, seid, beloved and taught Y shewed meself corrupt and unfaithful, that from hensforth Y shewe me uncorrupt and faithful the faith and doctrine of holy Churche truly to kepe Y promitte. And all maner of errour and heresie, doctrine and opinion agayn the faith of the Churche and determinacion of the Churche of Roome—and namely the opinions before rehersed—Y abjure and forswere, and swere be these holy Gospels be me bodely touched that from hensforth Y shal never holde errour ne errours, heresie ne heresies ne fals doctrine agayn the faith of holy Churche and determinacion of the Churche of Rome. Ne no suche thinges Y shal obstinatly defende, ne ony^c man^d holdyng or techyng suche maner of thinges be me or ony other persone opinly or prively Y shal defende. Y shal never aftir this tyme be no recettour, fautour, consellour or defensour of heretikes or of ony men or women suspect of heresie. Ne Y shal trowe to thaym. Ne wittingly Y shal felaship with thaym, ne be hoomly with thaym. Y shal never yeve consell, favour, yeftes ne confort to thaym. Yf Y knowe ony heretik or of heresie ony man or woman suspect or of thaym fautours, confortours, consellours or defensours, or of ony men or women makyng prive conventicules or assembles, or holdyng ony divers or singuler opinions from the commune doctrine of the Churche, Y shal late you, worshipful fadir, or your vicar generall in your absence or the diocesanes of suche men have soone and redy knowyng. So help me God atte holy doom and these holy Gospels.

In wittenesse of whiche thing Y subscribe here with myn owyn

---

^a he be turned *in bottom right-hand corner of page.*
^b Ricardus Fleccher *in top right-hand corner of page.*
^c person *deleted.*   ^d man *interlined.*

hand a crosse ╋. And to this partie endented to remayne in your registre Y sette my signet. And that other partie endented Y receyve undir your seal to abide with me unto my lyves ende. Yoven at Norwich in the chapell of your palaice*ᵃ* the xxvij day of moneth of August the yer of our Lord a thousand four hundred and xxix*ti*.

Qui quidem Ricardus Fleccher iuravit ad sacra evangelia per ipsum tacta corporaliter tunc ibidem quod ab hac hora in antea ipse omnia et singula in dicto*ᵇ* cirographo indentato super abiuracione sua concepto ac coram dicto reverendo patre per prefatum magistrum Johannem Wylly, organum vocis dicti Ricardi Fleccher, ut (p. 332 / fo. 91v) [premittitur], gerentem, publice perlecto et per ipsum Ricardum, ut asseruit, plenarie intellecto contenta iuxta ipsius cirographi exigenciam et tenorem inviolabiliter observabit. Et in huius rei testimonium in utraque parte dicti scripti indentati cum penna signum crucis ╋ fecit manu sua propria et subscripsit, ac uni parti eiusdem scripti indentati penes registrum dicti reverendi patris remansure sigillum suum apposuit, et aliam partem eiusdem scripti indentati,*ᶜ* sub sigillo dicti reverendi patris sigillatam, idem Ricardus recepit in iudicio tunc ibidem penes ipsum Ricardum, ut asseruit, toto vite sue tempore permansuram. Prestitoque per eundem iuramento ut supra de parendo mandatis Ecclesie et de agendo penitenciam sibi pro suis commissis suprascriptis iniungendam, dictus reverendus pater absolvit ipsum Ricardum Fleccher ab omni excommunicacionis sentencia qua premissorum occasione extitit innodatus, et penitenciam iniunxit eidem pro commissis sub eo qui sequitur verborum tenore.

In Dei nomine, Amen. Quia nos, Willelmus, permissione divina Norwicensis episcopus, contra te, Ricardum Fleccher de Beccles nostre diocesis, subditum nostrum et subiectum, ex officio nostro legitime procedentes, per tuam confessionem coram nobis iudicialiter factam invenimus te hereticos notorios et famosos in domum tuam recepisse, supportasse, concelasse et defendisse, ac multas hereses et errores quamplures fidei orthodoxe ac determinacioni sacrosancte ac universalis Ecclesie repugnantes—de quibus in quodam cirographo super abiuracione tua scripto et indentato, cuius una pars in archivis nostris noscitur remanere, ad quam nos referimus et pro hic inserta haberi volumus, plenior fit mencio—tenuisse, credidisse et affirmasse; nunc autem, usus concilio saniori,

---

ᵃ th *deleted*.   ᵇ scripto *deleted*.
ᶜ idem Ricardus Fleccher *deleted*.

petis misericordiam et sponte redis ad Ecclesie unitatem; idcirco, inprimis abiurata per te omni heresi et recepta per nos a te secundum ritum Ecclesie iuratoria caucione de parendo mandatis Ecclesie, te absolvimus ab omni excommunicacionis vinculo quo tenebaris astrictus. Et quia per predicta que tenuisti, credidisti et affirmasti in Deum et sanctam matrem Ecclesiam temere deliquisti, tibi [iniungimus] pro pena penitenciali [.....]*a* fustigaciones circa cimiterium ecclesie parochialis de Beccles predict' coram solenni processione eiusdem horis consuetis facienda, capite et pedibus denudatis, corpore femoralibus duntaxat induto, more penitentis incedendo ac unum cereum cere ponderis unius libre in manibus suis deferendo; et totidem circa mercatum de Beccles predict' iiij*or* diebus mercati ibidem, capite et pedibus denudatis, corpore camisia et femoralibus duntaxat induto, dictum cereum portando. Et quia tenuisti, credidisti et affirmasti fore licitum cuicumque fideli edere carnes diebus Quadragesimalibus, diebus Quatuor Temporum, sextis feriis et sanctorum vigiliis indictis per Ecclesiam, tibi iniungimus quod omni sexta feria per annum iam proximum futurum in pane et aqua ieiunes.*b*

[15]

(p. 293 / fo. 70r) **Willelmus Colyn, skynner, de Creyk**118

Die xxiij Octobris Anno Domini Millesimo CCCCmo XXIXo in domo habitacionis mei, Johannis Excestr, in Norwico in meique, notarii subscripti, ac Thome Hard de South Creyk, husbondman, ac Roberti Merlowle de Waterdon,119 hosbondeman, et Jacobi Crake-shild de South Creyk, husbondman, [presencia], constitutus Willelmus Colyn,*c* in*d* South Creyk trahens moram et natus in Snetesham,120 skynner, alias per reverendum in Christo patrem et dominum, dominum Willelmum Dei gracia Norwicensem episcopum, propter suspicionem heresis arrestatus, dixit, asseruit et fatebatur*e* quod:

Circiter xiiij annis elapsis quidam dominus Thomas Baxter, tunc capellanus paroch' de South Creyk, iniunxit isti Willelmo Colyn

a Blank in MS.
b Matildis Fleccher *and (all three words deleted)* Joh' Eldon, glover *in bottom right-hand corner of page.*
c di *deleted.*   *d* in *interlined.*
e se hactenus dixisse et asseruisse erro *deleted.*

---

118 South Creake, north-west Norfolk.
119 Waterden, north-west Norfolk.
120 Snettisham, north-west Norfolk.

pro suis commissis eidem Thome in foro[a] penitenciali revelatis penitenciam subscriptam: videlicet, ad dicendum v Pater Noster et totidem Ave coram ymagine pietatis Beate Marie dicte ecclesie[b] flexis[c] genibus. Et quia iste Willelmus asseruit et dixit eidem capellano quod magis esset sibi meritorium dicere dict' v Pater Noster et Ave coram Deo in sacramento altaris, et sic coram sacramento altaris ipse dixit et fecit dictam penitenciam et non coram ymagine pietatis, et eo pretextu reputabatur iste lollardus.

Item dicit quod ipse dixit domine Le Straunge,[121] que fuit mater Edi' Oldhall, quod ipse affectavit osculare pedes[d] dicte domine Le Straunge quam pedes Domine Nostre de Walsyngham, et quod ipse mallet pedem dicte Domine de Walsyngham fore extra mucturam quam pedem dicte domine Le Straunge pati minimam lesuram.

Item dicit quod iste Willelmus[e] dixit domino Johanni, vicario de South Creyk,[122] publice in taberna hec verba: 'domine vicarie, ego dicam vobis unum: quod genus humanum magis tenetur[f] secunde persone in Trinitate, scilicet Filio, quam tenetur Patri quia Pater creavit primum hominem, qui fuit causa dampnacionis humani generis, et Christus, Filius Dei, per passionem suam et mortem redemit humanum genus et vite pristine restauravit.'

Item iste dicit quod ipse dixit in presencia Thome Hardy de Creyk et aliorum predictorum quod ipse mallet capere membrum secretum mulieris quam sacramentum altaris.

Die Lune, videlicet xx Marcii Anno Domini prescripto, coram dicto[g] reverendo in Christo patre ac domino, domino Willelmo Dei gracia Norwicensi episcopo, in aula manerii[h] sui de Thorneg'[123] iudicialiter sedente, prefatus Willelmus Colyn, skynner, prius arestatus de heresi eo quod ipse tenuit, credidit et affirmavit errores et hereses subscriptos, comparuit. Cui dominus fecit obici articulos subscriptos, quibus ipse respondebat prout post eosdem articulos plenius continetur. Presentibus tunc ibidem magistris Willelmo Ascogh, in sacra theologia bacallario, Johanne Sutton, in legibus bacallario, et Johanne Wylly, notario publico.

[a] consciencie deleted.
[b] dicte ecclesie interlined.
[c] ge' deleted.
[d] domine nostre deleted.
[e] quod repeated.
[f] filio deleted.
[g] patre deleted.
[h] de and (deleted) p follow manerii.

---

121 Probably Emma Oldhall, mother of Sir Edmund Oldhall, who seems to have been married at one time to Sir Peter L'Estrange (Blomefield, Norfolk, vi, p. 16; viii, p. 353 and x, p. 265).

122 John Goleth of Little Walsingham, vicar of South Creake from 28 February 1405 until sometime before 27 June 1444 (REG/3, Book 6, fo. 315v and REG/5, Book 10, fo. 53v).

123 Thornage, north Norfolk.

Inprimis quod nullus honor est exhibendus ymaginibus in ecclesiis, nec truncus ymaginis Beate Marie de Walsyngham nullo modo est adorandus. Istum articulum dictus Willelmus Colyn negavit.

Item*a* quod ipse Willelmus Colyn dixit yconimis ecclesie de South Creyk, instantibus penes parochianos dicte ecclesie ad contribuendum pro pictura ymaginum ipsius ecclesie, quod ipse mallet dare xij*d* ad comburendam aliquam imaginem quam unum obolum pro pictura alicuius ymaginis. Istum articulum dicto Willelmo obiectum idem Willelmus fatebatur iudicialiter et recognovit.

(p. 294 / fo. 70v)*b* Item*c* tibi proponimus, dicimus et articulamur quod infra nostram diocesim tu tenuisti, credidisti et asseruisti quod malles ire ad Walsyngham ad videndum regem Anglie quam ire ad ostium domus in qua fuisti ad videndum sacramentum altaris. Istum articulum dicto Willelmo obiectum idem Willelmus expresse fatebatur iudicialiter et recognovit.

Item*d* quod*e* tu asseruisti te malle videre secretum membrum mulieris quam sacramentum altaris. Ad istum articulum idem Willelmus dixit et fatebatur iudicialiter quod ipse dixit*f* se*g* velle libencius tangere secretum membrum mulieris quam sacramentum altaris.

Item quod tu tenuisti et asseruisti quod omnes mulieres deberent esse communes. Fatetur se dixisse quod vellet matrimonium fuisse annulatum per*h* aliquod tempus notabile.

Item quod tu tenuisti et asseruisti quod confessio facienda est soli Deo, et nulli sacerdoti. Negat articulum istum sibi obiectum.

Item quod tu tenuisti et affirmasti publice quod a tempore Incarnacionis Christi nulla anima intravit celum. Negat istum articulum sibi obiectum.

Item quod tu tenuisti, asseruisti et affirmasti quod omnes homines plus tenentur Filio, Christo, quam Patri quia Pater creavit primum hominem, Adam, qui fuit causa dampnacionis generis humani, et Christus, Filius Dei, per passionem suam et mortem genus humanum redemit et vite pristine restauravit. Fatetur quod humanum genus magis tenetur Filio quam Patri quia Filius redemit nos omnes.*i*

Qui quidem reverendus pater recepit ab eodem Willelmo Colyn iuramentum ad sacra evangelia per ipsum tacta de peragendo penitenciam sibi pro suis commissis suprascriptis coram eodem patre iudicialiter, ut premittitur, confessatis. Que penitencia est ista:

---

a Fatetur *in margin.*
b Contra Willelmum Colyn, skynner, de Creyk *at top of page.*
c Fatetur *in margin.*
d Negat, ut fatetur quod dixit tangere *in margin.*
e malles vid *deleted.*　　　　　　　*f* et *deleted.*
g mall *deleted.*　　　　　　　　　　*h* septennium vel *deleted.*
i nos omnes *interlined:* quod pater per creacionem (*not interlined*) *deleted.*

D

videlicet, quod offerat magno altari dicte ecclesie de South Creyk unum torticum precii xl denariorum; et quod omni Dominica, durante dicto tortico, tenebit ipsum torticum tempore elevacionis sacramenti altaris coram magno altari; et quod, capite, tubiis et pedibus [denudatis], corpore curtello sive cota*a* vel camisia induto, iiij diebus coram solenni processione dicte ecclesie facienda more penitentis incedat, dictum torticum in manibus suis deferendo. Quibus sic peractis, dictus Willelmus ad evangelia sacra per ipsum tacta*b* iuravit quod de cetero ab hac hora in ante nunquam tenebit hereses nec errores nec opiniones aliquas contra determinacionem sancte Romane Ecclesie, nec hereticos sustentabit vel supportabit, nec prebebit eis consilium, auxilium vel favorem; et si poterit cognoscere aliquos hereticos vel de heresi aliquas personas suspectas, quod de*c* eisdem dictum patrem vel eius vicarium generalem quamcito poterit debet reddere cerciorem. Et deinde idem pater declaravit eidem quod si in futurum in premissis vel aliis heresibus fuerit convictus criminaliter, igne*d*

[16]

(p. 341 / fo. 96r) **Robertus Cavell, capellanus**

In Dei nomine, Amen. Per presens publicum instrumentum cunctis appareat evidenter quod Anno [Domini] ab Incarnacione eiusdem secundum cursum et computacionem Ecclesie Anglicane Millesimo CCCC° XXIX°, indiccione octava, pontificatus sancti in Christo patris et domini nostri, domini Martini divina providencia pape quinti, anno terciodecimo,*e* mensis Marcii die*f* secunda,*g* in mei, Johannis Excestr, clerici, notarii publici et in negocio subscripto actorum scribe, necnon Roberti Aylmer, Johannis Wylly et Johannis Walpooll, notariorum publicorum, ac Thome Walsham et Willelmi*h* Steynwar, clericorum Norwicensis diocesis, presencia,*i* in capella palacii episcopalis infra civitatem*j* Norwici situati*k* pariter

---

a MS. cote.
b ad evangelia sacra per ipsum tacta *interlined.*
c nominibus *deleted.*
d The text ends here, at the end of a line in the manuscript and towards the foot of the page: Ricardus Kyng de Wymu *in bottom right-hand corner of page.*
e MS. terciodecima.
f An illegible word and tercia *deleted.*
g secunda *interlined.*
h MS. Willelmo.
j Norwicen' *deleted.*
i cora *deleted.*
k onr ex *deleted.*

existencium, coram reverendo in Christo patre ac domino, domino
Willelmo Dei gracia Norwicensi episcopo, in dicta capella iudicialiter
sedente, ad iura reddenda—prout michi, Johanni Excestr, notario
prescripto, tunc apparebat—pro tribunali sedente,[a] assistentibus[b]
dicto reverendo patri[c] tunc ibidem venerabilibus et discretis viris,
Willelmo Worstede, priore ecclesie Cathedralis Sancte Trinitatis
Norwici,[d] ordinis Sancti Benedicti, ac Johanne Thorp, ordinis Carmelitarum, sacre pagine professoribus, necnon magistris Johanne
Ingham,[124] in sacra theologia, et Willelmo Bernham ac Thoma
Ryngstede, in decretis, et Johanne Sutton, in legibus, bacallariis, ac
Thoma Hunter, in artibus magistro, Robertus Cavel, capellanus parochialis de Bungey[125] Norwicensis diocesis, notatus de heresi et ea
occasione arestatus, adductus fuit ad iudicium in vinculis coram dicto
reverendo patre super crimine heretice pravitatis responsurus. Qui
quidem Robertus, coram dicto reverendo patre tunc ibidem iudicialiter constitutus,[e] ad sancta evangelia per ipsum corporaliter tacta
iuravit de veritate dicenda in et super interrogandis et examinandis
ab eodem materiam fidei tangentibus. Quo quidem iuramento sic
per ipsum Robertum prestito, idem Robertus coram prefato reverendo patre interrogatus et examinatus fatebatur iudicialiter et
recognovit quod ipse antea habuit communicacionem frequentem
cum nonnullis hereticis famosis—videlicet cum Willelmo[f] Whyte,
Hugone Pye et aliis notoriis hereticis[g]—in scolis privatis[h] eorundem.
De quorum hereticorum informacionibus et doctrinis erroneis[i] idem
Robertus instructus, ut asseruit, et informatus,[j] fatebatur iudicialiter
se didicisse,[k] tenuisse, credidisse et affirmasse errores et hereses in
articulis subscriptis contentos,[l] qui in quodam scripto[m] cirographo
super ipsius Roberti abiuracione concepto et indentato, cuius[n] tenor
subscribitur,[o] plenarie continentur. Quos quidem articulos omnes et
singulos ac hereses et errores in eis contentos idem Robertus voluit,
ut asseruit, pro perpetuo dimittere et abiurare. Unde prefatus pater
prefixit eidem Roberto diem[p] crastinum, videlicet tercium diem dicti
mensis Marcii, ad abiurandos dictos errores et hereses tunc coram
dicto patre iudicialiter confessatos secundum formam quam prefatus
pater sibi duxerit assignandam.[q]

[a] adductus fuit ad *deleted.*	[b] tu *deleted.*
[c] patri *interlined.*	[d] et *deleted.*
[e] v *deleted.* [f] Will *deleted.*	[g] exia *deleted.*

[h] MS. scol' privat'; *but see p. 94, where the two words are in the plural.*

[i] erroneis *interlined.*	[j] informatus *interlined.*
[k] didicisse *interlined.*	[l] que *deleted.*
[m] scripto *interlined.*	[n] t' t' *deleted.*
[o] seriatim conscribuntur *deleted.*	
[p] lune *deleted.*	[q] quo quidem *deleted.*

---

124 See Emden, *BRUC*, p. 326 (John de Ingham).
125 Bungay, north-east Suffolk.

Die vero Veneris, videlicet (p. 342 / fo. 96v)[a] tercio die Marcii Anno Domini suprascripto, adveniente, coram dicto reverendo patre in ecclesia collegiata Beate Marie de Campis in Norwico[126] iudicialiter sedente, assistentibus sibi tunc ibidem fratre Johanne Thorp, ordinis Carmelitarum, sacre pagine professore, ac magistris Willelmo Bernham et Thoma Ryngstede,[b] Nicholao Derman, in decretis bacallario, ac Johanne Aylesham[127] et Thoma Hunter, in artibus magistris,[c] presentibus tunc ibidem Johanne Wylly, Hugone Acton et Nicholao Stanhowe ac Johanne Excestr, scribente, notariis publicis, ac aliis quampluribus fidedignis, comparuit personaliter prefatus dominus Robertus[d] Cavell, volens, ut asseruit, et affectans puro corde omnimodos[e] errores et hereses in dicto scripto indentato specificatos, cuius tenorem prius solus per se[f] perlegit, ut tunc asseruit, et intellexit, iuxta formam in eodem scripto conscriptam dimittere re et verbo ac pro perpetuo abiurare. Cuius scripti indentati unam partem idem Robertus Cavell in manibus suis tenens coram dicto patre legit publice. Et tenens manum suam dexteram super librum evangeliorum, ad ea iuravit se contenta in eodem scripto iuxta omnem vim, formam et effectum eorundem in quantum poterit impleturum. Et in huius rei testimonium signum sancte crucis in utraque parte dicti scripti indentati idem Robertus Cavell coram dicto patre tunc ibidem in iudicio subscripsit. Cuius scripti indentati tenor de verbo ad verbum sequitur et est talis.

In Dei nomine, Amen. Coram vobis, reverendo in Christo patre ac domino, domino Willelmo Dei gracia Norwicensi episcopo, ego, Robertus Cavel, capellanus parochialis[g] ecclesie parochialis de Bungeye vestre[h] Norwicensis diocesis, subditus vester et subiectus, considerans et perpendens quod ante istud tempus infra vestram diocesim cum hereticis famosis frequentem habui communicacionem —videlicet cum Willelmo Whyte, Hugone Pye, hereticis postmodum condempnatis, ac cum aliis hereticis notoriis—in eorum scolis privatis, ex quorum doctrinis erroniis et perversis concepi, credidi et tenui omnes articulos qui[i] sequuntur, quibus pro tunc adhibui plenam fidem.

Inprimis videlicet quod sacramentum Baptismi, factum in aqua secundum formam in Ecclesia usitatam, modicum vel parum est

---

[a] Rob' Cavell *in top left-hand corner of page.*
[b] in decretis bacallariis *deleted.*
[c] necnon *deleted.*
[d] Ca *deleted.*
[e] omnimodos *interlined.*
[f] intellexit *deleted.*
[g] de *deleted.*
[h] dioc' *deleted.*
[i] MS. que.

---

[126] The secular college of St Mary in the Fields, Norwich.
[127] Possibly John Aylesham, rector of Beeston (see p. 39).

ponderandum pro eo quod, quamcito anima infantis in utero matris est corpori unita, infunditur gracia Spiritus Sancti, per quam parvulus est sufficienter baptizatus. Et cum idem infans parvulus ad annos pervenerit maturiores ita quod sciat intelligere verbum Dei, est sufficienter confirmatus.

Item quod confessio vocalis non est facienda alicui sacerdoti, sed soli Deo, qui solus peccata dimittit.

Item quod omnis*a* remissio peccatorum solum a Deo est, et ideo penitencia non est a sacerdote vel ab homine peccatore*b* iniungenda.

Item quod nullus sacerdos secundum ritum Ecclesie ordinatus habet potestatem conficiendi corpus Christi in sacramento altaris, sed post verba*c* (p. 343 / fo. 97r)*d* sacramentalia a tali presbitero prolata in altari purus panis remanet materialis.

Item quod in Quadragesima, diebus Quatuor Temporum, sextis feriis et vigiliis sanctorum prohibitis per Ecclesiam nullus fidelis obligatur ad ieiunium, sed licitum est cuilibet fideli dictis diebus et temporibus comedere carnes et omnia cibaria indifferenter.

Item quod omnibus diebus Dominicis et aliis festivis indictis per Ecclesiam licitum est cuilibet fideli operari et quecumque opera facere et exercere, preterquam opera servilia, que dicti heretici in eorum doctrinis fore peccata sive vicia declararunt.

Item quod decime et oblaciones sunt a clericis et ecclesiis subtrahende, dumtamen hoc prudenter fiat.

Item quod reliquie sanctorum, scilicet carnes et ossa hominis mortui, nullo modo deberent a populo venerari, nec de monumento fetido extrahi, nec in capsa aurea vel argentea recludi, quia sic facientes committunt ydolatriam.

Item quod continencia presbiterorum et monialium non est commendabilis, sed melius esset eis nubere.

Item quod solus mutuus consensus amoris in Jhu' Christo sufficit pro matrimonio inter virum et mulierem, absque verborum expressione seu aliqua solennizacione in ecclesia.

Item quod non est peccatum contravenire preceptis Ecclesie.

Item quod censure ecclesiastice nec excommunicaciones prelatorum sunt timende.

Item quod non est orandum alicui sancto, sed tantum soli Deo est orandum.

Item quod nullus honor est exhibendus ymaginibus crucifixi, Beate Marie nec alicuius sancti, eo quod arbores crescentes in silvis sunt maioris viriditatis et virtutis et eo cicius adorande quam lapis vel lignum mortuum sculptum ad similitudinem hominis.

a R deleted. *b* MS. peccatori.
c R. Cavell *in bottom right-hand corner of page.*
d R. Cavell *in top left-hand corner of page:* Rob' Cavell *in top right-hand corner of page.*

Item quod si passio Christi fuerit utilis et preciosa, mors Sancti Thome, martiris, fuit maledicta, vilis pariter et vituperanda.

Item quod peregrinaciones nullo modo faciende sunt, nisi tantum pauperibus.

Item quod nullo modo licet interficere quemquam nec per processum legis dampnare reum furti vel homicidii.

Item quod nulli licet pro iure suo hereditario vel pro patria pugnare nec placitare, quia sic facientes amittunt caritatem.

Quorum errorum et heresum occasione ego, Robertus Cavel suprascriptus, coram vobis, reverendo patre supradicto, iudicialiter evocatus et per vestram paternitatem instructus plenarie et informatus quod premissi articuli per me coram vobis, ut premittitur, iudicialiter confessati, quos credidi, tenui et affirmavi, continent in se errores notorios et hereses manifestas ac determinacioni sacrosancte Romane Ecclesie contrarias et repugnantes, quocirca ego, volens sequi doctrinam sancte matris Ecclesie, consideransque quod sancta mater Ecclesia nulli claudit gremium rediri volenti, (p. 344 / fo. 97v) nec misericors Deus vult mortem peccatoris sed ut maius convertatur et vivat, cum puro corde detestor, despicio pariter et renuncio errores meos et hereses suprascriptos ac alios quoscumque, premissasque opiniones coram vobis fateor fore hereticas et erroneas, ac fidei sancte matris ac universalis Ecclesie Romane contrarias et repugnantes. Et quia per errores et hereses huiusmodi, quos et quas sic nequiter tenui, credidi et affirmavi, meipsum probavi publice corruptum pariter et incredulem, quod ab hac hora in antea me reddam incorruptum pariter et fidelem, fidem et doctrinam sancte matris Ecclesie promitto me amodo fideliter servaturum. Ac omnimodos errores et hereses, doctrinas et opiniones fidei et determinacioni sacrosancte Ecclesie Romane contrarias, et precipue articulos sive opiniones suprascriptas per me coram vobis iudicialiter confessatas, renuncio pariter et abiuro. Et ad hec sancta Dei evangelia per me coram vobis corporaliter tacta iuro quod ab hac hora in antea ego nunquam tenebo, credam vel affirmabo errorem nec errores, heresim ve[l] hereses nec falsam doctrinam contra fidem sancte matris Ecclesie et determinacionem Ecclesie Romane. Nec talia obstinaciter defendam. Nec aliquam personam errores sive hereses tenentem, credentem sive affirmantem per me vel per aliquam mediam personam obstinaciter defendam. Nec hereticis vel aliquibus personis de heresi suspectis prebebo consilium, auxilium vel favorem. Nec eis credam, nec familiaris ero cum eisdem. Et si hereticos sive aliquas personas de herese suspectas aut hereticorum fautores, confortatores, consiliatores sive defensores aut aliquas personas [facientes] privatas conventiculas vel [tenentes] diversas aut singulares opiniones a communi doctrina Ecclesie discrepantes in futurum cognoscere potero seu reperire, vos, reverendum patrem, sive in vestra absencia vestrum in spiritualibus vicarium generalem, si sint infra vestram diocesim, et alias diocesanos locorum huiusmodi personarum, faciam de eisdem habere certam et celerem noticiam. Sicut me Deus adiuvet et hec evangelia sacrosancta.

In cuius rei testimonium ego, Robertus Cavel suprascriptus, manu mea propria signum sancte crucis + hic subscribo. Ac isti parti huius scripti indentati penes vos in registro vestro remansure sigillum meum appono. Alteram vero partem eiusdem scripti indentati sigillo vestro sigillatam penes me recipio, mecum[a] quoad vixero permansuram. Datum in ecclesia collegiata de Campis in Norwico sub sigillo vestro tercio die mensis Marcii Anno Domini Millesimo CCCC[mo] XXIX[o].

Qua quidem abiuracione,[b] prout superius continetur, per ipsum Robertum Cavell coram dicto reverendo patre, ut premittitur, facta publice et perlecta, [et] prestito per eundem dominum Robertum iuramento[c] (p. 345 / fo. 98r)[d] ad sacra evangelia per ipsum corporaliter tacta de parendo mandatis Ecclesie et de peragendo penitenciam sibi a dicto patre pro suis commissis suprascriptis iniungendam, prefatus pater ipsum dominum Robertum a sentencia excommunicacionis, qua premissorum occasione tenebatur astrictus, absolvit sub eo[e] qui sequitur tenore verborum.

In Dei nomine, Amen. Quia nos, Willelmus, permissione divina Norwicensis episcopus, contra te, Robertum Cavell, capellanum parochialem de Bungeye nostre diocesis, subditum nostrum et subiectum, ex officio nostro legitime procedentes, per tuam confessionem coram nobis iudicialiter factam invenimus te cum hereticis notoriis et famosis et postmodum condempnatis communicacionem frequentem et familiarem sepius habuisse, ac eisdem et eorum opinionibus et doctrinis erroneis favisse, eisdemque prebuisse concilium, auxilium et favorem, ac nonnullos hereticos supportasse ac concelasse, teque multas hereses et errores quamplures fidei orthodoxe et determinacioni sacrosancte ac universalis Ecclesie contrarias et repugnantes—de quibus in quodam cirographo super tua abiuracione concepto et indentato, cuius una pars in archivis nostris noscitur remanere, ad quam nos referimus et pro hic inserta haberi

---

[a] quod deleted.   [b] prescri deleted.
[c] ad sacra evangelia, Cavell in bottom right-hand corner of page.
[d] Cavell in top left-hand corner of page.
[e] quit deleted.

volumus, plenior fit mencio—tenuisse, credidisse et affirmasse, et per
hoc in excommunicacionis sentenciam incidisse; nunc autem, usus
concilio saniori, petis misericordiam et sponte redis ad Ecclesie
unitatem; idcirco inprimis abiurata per te omni heresi et recepta per
nos a te secundum ritum Ecclesie iuratoria caucione de parendo iuri
et mandatis Ecclesie, te absolvimus ab omni excommunicacionis
vinculo quo tenebaris astrictus, penitenciam pro tuis commissis
suprascriptis respectantes tibi postmodum iniungendam.

Acta sunt hec prout suprascribuntur et superius recitantur sub
Anno Domini, indiccione, pontificatu, mense, diebus et locis superius
recitatis; presentibus tunc ibidem testibus proxime prescriptis.
J. Excestr.

[17]

(p. 289 / fo. 68r) **Magister Robertus Bert de Bury**[128]

In Dei nomine, Amen. Per presens publicum instrumentum
cunctis appareat evidenter quod Anno Domini ab Incarnacione
eiusdem secundum cursum et computacionem Ecclesie Anglicane
Millesimo Quadringentesimo Vicesimo Nono, indiccione octava,
pontificatus sanctissimi in Christo patris et domini[a] nostri, domini
Martini divina providencia pape quinti, anno terciodecimo, mensis
Marcii die secunda, in capella[b] palacii episcopalis in civitate Norwici situati, in mei, Johannis Excestr, clerici, notarii publici, dicti
reverendi patris actorum scribe, necnon Roberti Aylmer, Johannis
Wylly et Johannis Walpooll, publicorum auctoritate apostolica
notariorum, ac Thome Walsham et Willelmi Steynwar,[c] clericorum
Norwicensis diocesis, ad infrascripta testium vocatorum, [presencia],
coram reverendo in Christo patre[d] ac domino, domino Willelmo Dei
gracia Norwicensi episcopo, constitutus [est] personaliter[e] magister
Robertus Berte, capellanus, de heretica pravitate notatus, ut
dicebatur, multipliciter et diffamatus ac ea occasione coram dicto
patre[f] responsurus ad dictos diem et locum ad iudicium evocatus.

[a] dm *deleted.*	[b] episcopal' eo *deleted.*
[c] test *deleted.*	[d] patre *repeated.*
[e] discretus vir *deleted.*	[f] per *deleted.*

[128] Bury St Edmunds. Apart from his being styled Master here and elsewhere in the manuscript, there seems to be no evidence that he was a university graduate.

Qui,*a* per prefatum reverendum patrem tunc ibidem iudicialiter impetitus, dixit iudicialiter et recognovit quod ipse olim habuit quendam librum vocatum *Dives et Pauper*.[129] Cui quidem Roberto dictus pater dixit quod ille liber continet in se plures errores et hereses quamplures. Et prefatus Robertus respondit dicens,*b* si in dicto libro iam co[n]tineantur hereses sive errores, huiusmodi hereses sive errores sunt de novo scripti et in dicto libro collocati post tempus quando ipse vendidit eundem librum*c* cuidam homini commoranti iuxta Hychene,[130] cuius nomen et cognomen dixit se ignorare. Dixit eciam idem Robertus iudicialiter tunc ibidem quod ipse*d* concessit et tradidit dictum librum cuidam fratri ordinis Predicatorum conventus Sudbur'*e* [131] nominato Nicholao, cuius cognomen dixit se ignorare, ad usum domini Andree Boteler, militis,[132] copiandum. Qui quidem frater Nicholaus ipsum librum incepit scribere. Et Robertus Dykkes de Bury*f* [133] residuum eiusdem libri scripsit et plenarie consummavit. Dixit insuper et asseruit dictus Robertus quod*g* tempore quo ipse habuit dictum librum in custodia sua ipse nunquam scivit*h* fuisse nec esse errores vel hereses in eodem.

Deinde vero prefatus reverendus pater dicto Roberto proposuit, obiecit et articulabatur, eidem dicens quod ipse Robertus infra diocesim Norwicensem habuit secretam et frequentem familiaritatem cum hereticis famosis, et precipue cum domino Johanne Poleyn,*i* qui*j* fuit pro heretico reputatus, et quod hereticos supportavit et sustinuit*k* eisdem et eorum opinionibus concilium, favorem et auxilium impendendo. Ad istum articulum dictus Robertus respondit, dicens quod ipse nunquam habuit secretam

---

a liber Dives et Pauper *written in the margin in a different hand.*
b domino *deleted.*
d tra *deleted.*
f tenor *deleted.*
h fore *deleted.*
c cu' fratri *deleted.*
e copian *deleted.*
g nunquam *deleted.*
i D. Jon' Poloyn *written in the margin in a different hand.*
j p *deleted.*
k *MS.* sustunuit.

---

[129] *Dives and Pauper*, an anonymous work written in English between 1405 and about 1410 (*Dives and Pauper*, ed. P. H. Barnum (Early English Text Society, Original Series, vols. 275–, 1976–), i, p. ix). As Dr Hudson has pointed out, its orthodoxy would seem to be assured by the fact that Abbot Whethamstede paid for a copy of it to be made for St Albans (Hudson, 'Examination of Lollards', 145).
[130] Hitchin, Hertfordshire.
[131] Sudbury, south-west Suffolk. The friar is unidentifiable.
[132] Sir Andrew Butler (or Boteler), knight.
[133] Robert Dykkes of Bury St Edmunds, scrivener, had been described as vehemently suspect of heresy during the bishop of Norwich's investigations into heresy in Bury St Edmunds on 14 December 1428 (REG/5, Book 9, fo. 109v).

communicacionem[a] (p. 290 / fo. 68v) nisi[b] semel, et hoc in camera[c] ipsius.[d] Et ulterius idem Robertus negavit quod unquam fuit fautor, supportator vel manutentor[e] hereticorum aut ipsorum opinionibus vel doctrinis aliqualiter adherens, nec habuit cum eis communicacionem nisi ad ipsorum confusionem.

Deinde vero idem reverendus pater dicto Roberto Berte ulterius articulabatur, proposuit et obiecit quod ipse Robertus infra diocesim Norwicensem tenuit, asseruit et populo predicavit quod decime nullo modo sunt solvende alicui viro ecclesiastico qui est in peccato mortali, item quod nullus honor est exhibendus[f] ymaginibus crucifixi, Beate Marie nec alicuius sancti, item quod nulle peregrinaciones sunt faciende. Quos quidem [articulos] dictus Robertus Berte constanter negavit.

Unde prefatus reverendus pater prefixit dicto Roberto,[g] de speciali gracia et favore ad parcendum ipsius Roberti laboribus et expensis in hac parte, ad purgandum se cum[h] vij manu presbiterorum sue conversacionis noticiam obtinencium apud Lavenham[134] vel apud Novum Mercatum,[135] in progressu ipsius patris versus London' post festum Pasche proximum futurum faciendo, secundo die post premunicionem ex parte dicti patris sibi in hac parte faciendam. Quibus die et loco per premunicionem huiusmodi sibi faciendam limitandis eidem, dictus Robertus ad sacra evangelia iuravit iudicialiter tunc ibidem se coram eodem patre personaliter compariturum. Quos diem et locum eidem sic limitandos prefatus reverendus pater eidem Roberto tunc ibidem prefixit[i] iudicialiter et recognovit. Quibus die et loco idem Robertus consenciit tunc ibidem. Quibus sic peractis, prefatus reverendus pater monuit dictum magistrum Robertum Berte primo, secundo et tercio quod dicto die vel citra ipse Robertus tradat et exhibeat prefato patri omnes et singulos libros in Anglicano idiomate scriptos et in custodia sua existentes, reddat et exhibeat sub pena excommunicacionis maioris.

Deinde vero die vicesima mensis Aprilis Anno Domini Millesimo Quadringentesimo Tricesimo, coram reverendo in Christo patre ac

[a] Magister Robertus Bert
Willelmus Colyn
Ricardus Kyng
Thomas Ploman
Johannes Fyllys
written at foot of page.
Thomas Love
Johannes Reve
Ricardus Knobbyng
Ricardus Grace
Baldwynus Couper
Johannes Skylan
Edmundus Archer

[b] ad p' cu' *deleted.*
[d] Roberti *deleted.*
[f] aliquibus *deleted.*
[h] vj *deleted.*
[c] istius *deleted.*
[e] herecut *deleted.*
[g] diem ad p' *deleted.*
[i] prefixit *interlined.*

---

[134] Lavenham, west Suffolk.   [135] Newmarket.

domino, domino Willelmo Dei gracia Norwicensi episcopo, in can-
cello ecclesie parochialis Sancti Jacobi infra procinctum monasterii
Sancti Edmundi de Bury Norwicensis diocesis situate,[136] in mei,
Johannis Excestr, clerici, notarii publici et in negocio infrascripto
dicti reverendi patris actorum scribe, ac testium subscriptorum
presencia, pro tribunali ad reddenda iura—prout michi, notario
prescripto, pro tunc apparebat—iudicialiter sedente, comparuit
personaliter prefatus magister Robertus Berte, supplicans dicto
reverendo patri quatinus purgacionem eiusdem magistri Roberti de
et super premissis articulis per ipsum alias coram ipso reverendo
patre, ut premittitur,[a] iudicialiter denegatis [admittat]. Quam
purgacionem idem magister Robertus gratus obtulit faciendam
iudicialiter tunc ibidem. Et produxit compurgatores, quorum
nomina sunt hec: Robertus Westyngton, rector de Berwe,[137]
Ricardus Norwold, rector de Rougham,[138] Johannes de Lyr', rector
de Chevyngton,[139] Gilbertus, rector de Halfstede,[140] Nicholaus,
rector de[b] Thorp,[141] et Robertus Cope, rector de Russhbrook.[c] [142]

(p. 291 / fo. 69r)[d] Et subsequenter postmodum coram dicto patre
tunc ibidem dictus magister Robertus Berte, tactis per ipsum
evangeliis sacrosanctis, ad ea iuramentum iudicialiter prestitit
corporale quod ipse nunquam tenuit,[e] credidit nec affirmavit quod
decime non sunt solvende alicui viro ecclesiastico existenti in
peccato mortali, item[f] quod ipse nunquam tenuit nec affirmavit
quod nullus honor est exhibendus ymaginibus crucifixi, Beate Marie
aut alicuius sancti, item quod nunquam tenuit nec affirmavit quod
nulle peregrinaciones sunt faciende. Et ulterius idem Robertus
iuravit ad eadem evangelia quod ipse nunquam fuit fautor, supportator vel manutentor aliquorum hereticorum, nec fuit aliqualiter
adherens ipsorum opinionibus vel doctrinis, et quod ipse nunquam
habuit communicacionem cum hereticis nisi ad ipsorum confusionem.
Quo iuramento sic prestito, omnes et singuli compurgatores sui
suprascripti, tactis eisdem evangeliis, iurarunt se credere prefatum

---

[a] d deleted.   [b] R follows de.
[c] et subsequenter in bottom right-hand corner of page.
[d] Robertus Berte de Bury in top right-hand corner of page.
[e] tenuit (repeated) deleted.   [f] idem deleted.

---

[136] The parish church of St James within the precincts of the Benedictine
abbey of Bury St Edmunds.
[137] Barrow, west Suffolk.
[138] Rougham, west Suffolk.
[139] Chevington, west Suffolk.
[140] Gilbert Mylde of Stradishall, rector of Hawstead, west Suffolk (REG/4
Book 8, fo. 74r).
[141] Probably Nicholas Huxteve, rector of Thorpe Morieux, west Suffolk
(REG/4, Book 7, fo. 77v).
[142] Rushbrooke, west Suffolk.

magistrum Robertum in hac parte verum prestitisse iuramentum. Quibus sic peractis, quia prefatus reverendus pater asseruit se habere prefatum Robertum Berte de heresi vehementer suspectum, nonobstante purgacione sua huiusmodi, pro eo quod ipse Robertus Berte tamdiu habuit secum dictum librum vocatum *Dives et Pauper*, in quo continentur multi errores et hereses quamplures, super quibus quidem erroribus et heresibus idem magister Robertus est multipliciter diffamatus in diocese Norwicensi, idem Robertus Berte iuravit iterum ad sacra evangelia*ᵃ* predicta per ipsum tunc ibidem in iudicio corporaliter tacta quod ab hac hora in antea ipse nunquam tenebit*ᵇ* nec affirmabit errorem nec errores, heresim nec hereses nec falsam doctrinam aut aliquam opinionem contra fidem Ecclesie et determinacionem sancte Romane Ecclesie. Nec aliquam personam tenentem, docentem vel affirmantem errores vel hereses aut falsam doctrinam per se nec per aliam personam defendet publice vel occulte. Et quod nunquam recipiet, supportabit, concelabit seu defendet aliquam personam de heresi suspectam. Nec eidem scienter prebebit concilium, auxilium vel favorem. Nec cum talibus erit familiaris, nec se associabit aliqualiter cum eisdem. Et si noverit aliquos hereticos vel aliquas personas de heresi suspectas sive talium personarum fautores, confortatores, consiliatores, manutentores vel supportatores, aut aliquas personas facientes privatas conventiculas aut tenentes singulares opiniones a communi doctrina Ecclesie discrepantes, ipse magister Robertus Berte faciet dictum reverendum patrem sive eius vicarium generalem aut diocesanos talium personarum de nominibus et personis earundem certam et celerem habere noticiam.

Presentibus tunc ibidem magistris Willelmo Ascogh, in sacra theologia, ac Johanne Sadde, rectore ecclesie parochialis de Lavenham,[143] in decretis, Johanne Sutton, in legibus, bacallariis, necnon Thoma Hunter, in artibus magistro, ac me, Johanne Excestr, scribente, et aliis quampluribus in multitudine copiosa.

[18]

(p. 296 / fo. 71v) **Thomas Ploman**

Die octava mensis Marcii Anno Domini Millesimo CCCC*ᵐᵒ* XXIX°, coram reverendo in Christo patre ac domino, domino Willelmo Dei

---

ᵃ pretact *deleted.*   *ᵇ* ei *deleted.*

[143] Lavenham, west Suffolk.

gracia Norwicensi episcopo, in capella palacii sui[144] iudicialiter sedente, adductus fuit personaliter in vinculis Thomas Ploman, ship-man,[a] natus, ut asseruit, in villa sive hameletto de Cyswell infra parochiam de Leyston situata,[145] notatus et vehementer suspectus de heresi. Cui quidem Thome Ploman prefatus pater proposuit iudicialiter et obiecit, dicens[b] quod ipse Thomas tenuit et affirmavit errores et hereses subscriptos.

Videlicet inprimis quod sacramenta ecclesiastica modicum vel nichil sunt ponderanda.

Et propterea idem Thomas non fuit confessus et communicatus nec solvit aliquas decimas[c] sive oblaciones aliquibus ecclesiie sive curatis per septennium ultimo elapsum et amplius.

Quos quidem articulos eidem Thome obiectos per ipsum patrem idem Thomas negavit, isto articulo duntaxat excepto: videlicet quod ipse non solvit decimas ecclesiis nec curatis, sed dedit huius-modi decimas pauperibus, quod facere[d] asseruit se credere fore licitum. Et propterea submisit se correccioni domini. Et iuravit ad sacra evangelia per ipsum corporaliter tacta in iudicio tunc ibidem quod ipse nunquam ab hac hora in antea tenebit nec affirmabit errores nec hereses nec falsam doctrinam seu singularem opinionem contra fidem sancte matris Ecclesie et determinacionem Ecclesie Romane, nec cum hereticis erit familiaris, nec eisdem hereticis aut ipsorum doctrinis prebebit consilium, auxilium, auditum vel favorem publice vel occulte sub pena iuris.

Presentibus tunc ibidem religiosis viris, fratribus Willelmo Worstede, priore ecclesie Cathedralis Norwicensis, ac Clemente Felmyngham,[146] ordinis Heremitarum Sancti Augustini, sacre pagine professoribus, ac discretis viris, magistris Willelmo Bernham et Thoma Ludham, in decretis bacallariis, et me, Johanne Excestr, scribente.

[19]

Johannes Fyllys

Eisdem die et loco, coram prefato reverendo patre iudicialiter sedente, adductus fuit ad iudicium in vinculis Johannes Fyllys de

[a] shipman *interlined*.   [b] dicens *interlined*.   [c] alicui ecclesie *deleted*.
[d] facere *interlined*.

---

[144] Presumably the Bishop's Palace in Norwich—Richard Kyng's trial, which immediately precedes Thomas Ploman's in the manuscript, took place there (see p. 105).   [145] Sizewell, within the parish of Leiston, east Suffolk. [146] See Emden, *BRUO*, ii, p. 675, Clement Felmyngham.

Framyngham Comitis,[147] suspectus de heresi pro eo quod in domo Thome Love de Rokelond iuxta Surlyngham,[148] contra prohibicionem Ecclesie, comedit carnes in vigilia Sancti Thome Apostoli ultimo elapsa.[149] Cui quidem Johanni Fyllys dictus pater prefatum articulum proposuit iudicialiter et obiecit. Et idem Johannes Fyllys dictum crimen sibi obiectum fatebatur iudicialiter et recognovit. Et capta inquisicione per dictum patrem inter vicinos eiusdem Johannis habentes noticiam vite et conversacionionis sue si idem Johannes fuerit super crimine heretice pravitatis quovis alio modo maculatus sive eciam respersus, nichil sinistrum detectum[a] sive delatum extitit contra eundem. Quia ipse pater habuit prefatum Johannem de heresi vehementer suspectum, idem reverendus pater fecit ipsum Johannem iurare ad sacra evangelia per ipsum corporaliter tacta in iudicio tunc ibidem quod ab hac hora in antea ipse numquam tenebit nec affirmabit errores nec hereses[b] neque falsam doctrinam nec singularem opinionem contra fidem Ecclesie et determinacionem Ecclesie Romane, et quod nunquam cum hereticis erit familiaris, nec hereticis aut ipsorum doctrinis prebebit consilium, auxilium vel favorem publice vel occulte sub pena iuris.

Presentibus testibus in actu proximo prescripto recitatis et me, J. Excestr.

Et prestito per eundem Johannem Fyllys iuramento de stando mandatis Ecclesie et de agendo penitenciam pro suis commissis in hac parte sibi iniungendam, dominus iniuxit sibi iij fustigaciones circa ecclesiam suam parochialem coram solenni processione iij diebus Dominicis, cum cereo cere precii ij[d], induto curtello, pedibus denudatis et cetera.[c]

[20]

(p. 297 / fo. 72r) **Thomas Love**

Thomas Love de Rokelond iuxta Surlyngham,[150] watirman, notatus quod fuit et est fautor hereticorum et heresis, et quod ipse Thomas precepit filie sue etatis sex annorum dare Johanni Fyllys de Framyngham[151] carnes ad manducandum in vigilia Sancti Thome

---

[a] extitit *deleted.*   [b] nq *deleted.*
[c] Thomas Love *in bottom right-hand corner of page.*

---

[147] Framingham Earl, east Norfolk.
[148] Rockland St Mary, near Surlingham, east Norfolk.
[149] 20 December 1429.
[150] Rockland St Mary, near Surlingham, east Norfolk.
[151] Framingham Earl, east Norfolk.

Apostoli ultimo elapsa*a* 152—quas quidem carnes idem Johannes Fyllys in domo et in presencia istius Thome Love in dicta vigilia Sancti Thome contra prohibicionem Ecclesie manducavit, isto Thoma presente, sciente et tolerante—comparuit coram dicto reverendo patre, in capella palacii sui153 iudicialiter sedente, die octava mensis Marcii Anno Domini Millesimo CCCCmo XXIXº. Ac dictum articulum sibi per prefatum iudicialiter obiectum fatebatur iudicialiter et recognovit. Ideo iuravit ad sacra evangelia per ipsum corporaliter tunc tacta quod ab hac hora in antea ipse nunquam tenebit nec affirmabit errores nec*b* hereses neque falsam doctrinam seu opinionem singularem contra fidem Ecclesie et determinacionem Ecclesie Romane; et quod nunquam recipiet hereticos, nec eis prebebit consilium, auxilium vel favorem publice vel occulte sub pena iuris. Et iuravit de agendo penitenciam pro commissis. Deindeque dictus pater iniunxit sibi vj fustigaciones circa ecclesiam suam parochialem vj diebus Dominicis more penitentis cum cereo cere ponderis dimidie libre offerendo per eum summo altari dicte ecclesie tempore offertorii ultimo Dominico penitencia huiusmodi peracta, et quod omni vigilia Sancti Thome per septennium in pane et aqua ieiunet.

Presentibus tunc ibidem Willelmo Worstede, priore ecclesie Cathedralis Norwic', Clemente Felmyngham, pagine sacre professoribus, magistris Willelmo Bernham et Thoma Ludham, in decretis bacallariis, ac J. Excestr.

[21]

(p. 295 / fo. 71r) **Richardus Kyng de Wymundham**154

Die x mensis Marcii Anno Domini Millesimo CCCCmo Vicesimo Nono, coram reverendo in Christo patre ac domino, domino Willelmo Dei gracia Norwicensi episcopo, in capella palacii sui Norwici iudicialiter sedente, assistentibus eidem patri magistro Clemente Felmyngham, ordinis Heremitarum Sancti Augustini, sacre pagine professore, ac magistro Willelmo Bernham, in decretis bacallario, adductus fuit in vinculis Ricardus Kyng de Wymondham, prius de heresi suspectus et diucius incarceratus. Cui quidem Ricardo idem reverendus pater,

---

a MS. elapso.   *b* re *deleted.*

152 20 December 1429.
153 Presumably the Bishop's Palace in Norwich (see p. 103, n. 144).
154 Wymondham, south Norfolk.

ex officio suo ad correccionem anime dicti Ricardi procedens, hereses subscriptos proposuit et obiecit.

Inprimis videlicet quod idem Ricardus Kyng infra diocesim Norwicensem tenuit, credidit et affirmavit quod in sacramento altaris post prolacionem verborum sacramentalium, a quocumque presbitero quantumcumque rite prolatorum,[a] remanet tantum purus panis materialis, et non corpus Christi.

Item quod idem Ricardus tenuit et affirmavit quod nullus honor est exhibendus aliquibus ymaginibus in ecclesiis nec alibi.

Quas quidem hereses idem Ricardus Kyng fatebatur et recognovit se tenuisse, credidisse et affirmasse. Volens tamen, ut asseruit, ad Ecclesie unitatem redire, ac dictas hereses per ipsum sic iudicialiter confessatas necnon quascumque alias hereses et omnes errores re et verbo puro corde dimittere pro perpetuo et abiurare, coram dicto reverendo patre tunc in iudicio ad sacra evangelia per ipsum corporaliter tacta iuravit quod ab hac hora in antea ipse Ricardus nunquam tenebit nec affirmabit errorem nec errores,[b] heresim nec hereses nec falsam doctrinam seu opinionem contra fidem Ecclesie et determinacionem sancte Romane Ecclesie. Nec aliquam personam tenentem, docentem sive affirmantem errorem vel heresim aut falsam doctrinam huiusmodi per se nec per aliam personam defendet publice vel occulte. Et quod nunquam recipiet, supportabit [vel] concelabit aliquam personam de heresi suspectam. Nec talibus personis scienter prebebit concilium, auxilium vel favorem. Nec cum talibus erit familiaris, nec se associabit cum eisdem. Et quod[c] si noverit aliquos hereticos vel aliquas personas de heresi suspectas aut talium personarum fautores, confortatores, conciliatores, manutentores vel supportatores, aut aliquas personas facientes privatas conventiculas aut tenentes singulares opiniones a communi doctrina Ecclesie discrepantes, ipse Ricardus Kyng de nominibus et personis talium personarum faciet dictum reverendum patrem sive ipsius vicarium in spiritualibus generalem aut diocesanos earundem personarum habere certam et celerem agnicionem. Quibus sic peractis, idem Ricardus Kyng ad evangelia sacra per ipsum tunc ibidem corporaliter tacta iuravit de stando mandatis Ecclesie et de agendo penitenciam pro suis commissis sibi a dicto patre iniungendam. Quo iuramento sic prestito, dictus pater absolvit eundem Ricardum a sentencia excommunicacionis, qua premissorum occasione tenebatur astrictus. Et pro suis commissis in hac parte dominus iniunxit eidem Ricardo Kyng tres fustigaciones circa ecclesiam suam parochialem de Wymundham coram solenni processione eiusdem tribus diebus Dominicis more solito facienda, portans unum cereum cere in manu sua ponderis unius libre; quodque illum cereum ultimo die Dominico

---

[a] *MS.* prolata. [b] *MS.* hereses. [c] quod *interlined.*

huiusmodi penitencia sic peracta offerat summo altari dicte ecclesie; et quod omni Dominica per unum annum continuum tempore elevacionis corporis Christi ad magnam missam unam torcheam precii duorum solidorum, per ipsum Ricardum Kyng sumptibus suis propriis providendam, ob reverenciam sacramenti predicti teneat; quodque singulis vigiliis festi Corporis Christi per triennium in pane et aqua ieiunet.

Presentibus tunc ibidem magistro Johanne Sutton, in legibus bacallario, ac domino Johanne Blytheburgh, capellano, Thoma Rodelond et Thoma Walsham ac me, J. Excestr, notario scribente.

[22]

(p. 297 / fo. 72r) **Johannes Reve de Becles,**[155] **glover**

Die xviij*ᵃ* mensis Aprilis Anno Domini Millesimo Quadringe[nte]simo Tricesimo, coram reverendo in Christo patre ac domino, domino Willelmo Dei gracia Norwicensi episcopo, in capella palacii sui Norwici iudicialiter sedente, adductus fuit Johannes Reve de Becles Norwicensis diocesis, glover, ad iudicium in vinculis, pro heretico notorio multipliciter diffamatus. Qui quidem Johannes Reve, coram dicto reverendo patre in iudicio personaliter constitutus, fatebatur et recognovit iudicialiter se tenuisse, credidisse et affirmasse errores et hereses in articulis subscriptis contentos, et per prefatum reverendum patrem sibi iudicialiter obiectos.

Inprimis videlicet quod sacramentum Baptismi, factum in aqua in forma*ᵇ* in Ecclesia communiter usitata, parum vel modicum est ponderandum si parentes infantis nati sint Christiani.

Item quod sacramentum Confirmacionis*ᶜ* factum per episcopum nullo modo proficit, nec est necessarium ad salutem animarum.

Item quod soli Deo facienda est confessio, et non alicui alteri presbitero, quia nullus presbiter habet potestatem absolvendi quemquam a peccato.

Item quod nullus presbiter habet potestatem conficiendi corpus Christi in sacramento altaris ad missam, sed quod post verba sacramentalia, a presbitero in missa quantumcumque rite prolata, nichil remanet in altari nisi tantum torta panis materialis.

Item quod solus consensus mutui amoris in Jhu' Christo inter

ᵃ videlicet *deleted.*   *ᵇ* in forma *repeated*
ᶜ MS. Baptismi, *but see pp. 111, 115 and elsewhere.*

---

[155] Beccles, north-east Suffolk.

E

virum et mulierem Christiane fidei sufficit ad sacramentum matrimonii, absque aliquo contractu per verba et sine solennizacione in
ecclesia.

(p. 298 / fo. 72v)[a] Item quod solus Deus habet potestatem conficiendi et ministrandi sacramenta, et nulla alia creatura.

Item quod nulla creatura fidei Cristiane tenetur ieiunare diebus
Quadragesimalibus, diebus iiij[or] Temporum, sextis feriis, vigiliis
sanctorum neque aliis temporibus indictis per Ecclesiam, sed quod
licitum est omni populo Christiane fidei omnibus diebus et temporibus predictis edere carnes et omnimoda cibaria indifferenter.
Et eciam idem Johannes Reve fatebatur quod ipsemet comedit
carnes sextis feriis et aliis diebus prohibitis.

Item quod licitum est omni populo Christiano facere et exercere
quecumque opera corporalia singulis diebus Dominicis et aliis
festivis indictis per Ecclesiam, peccatis duntaxat exceptis.

Item quod quilibet homo potest licite subtrahere et retinere
decimas et oblaciones ab ecclesiis et curatis, dumtamen hoc fiat
prudenter.

Item quod licitum est contravenire preceptis Ecclesie.

Item quod censure ecclesiastice nec excommunicacionum sentencie late per episcopos, prelatos vel ordinarios nullo modo sunt
ponderande nec timende, quia cum episcopus vel ordinarius aliquem
hominem excommunicat, Christus ipsum absolvit et benedicit.

Item quod soli Deo faciende sunt oraciones, et nullis aliis sanctis
in celo.

Item quod nullus honor est exhibendus aliquibus ymaginibus
crucifixi, Beate Marie vel alicuius alterius sancti.

Item quod nullo modo faciende sunt peregrinaciones, nisi tantum
pauperibus.

Item quod nullo modo licet iurare.

Item quod papa Romanus est Antechristus, et non habet aliquam
potestatem in Ecclesia, prout Jhus' commisit Petro, nisi sequatur
vestigia Petri in conversacione vite.

Item quod omnes episcopi,[b] prelati et presbiteri et viri ecclesiastici
sunt discipuli Antechristi.

Item quod eque bonum et eque meritorium est cuilibet homini
post mortem sepiliri in prato, campo,[c] nemore vel sterquilinio sicut
in ecclesia et cimiterio.

Quibus quidem articulis suprascriptis omnibus et singulis per
prefatum Johannem Reve prout suprascribuntur coram dicto
reverendo patre iudicialiter confessatis, prefatus reverendus pater[d]
declaravit et asseruit dicto Johanni Reve quod dicti articuli con-

---

[a] Joh' Reve *in top left-hand corner of page.*
[b] sunt *deleted.*   [c] stercore v *deleted.*   [d] decre *deleted.*

tinent in se nonnullos errores et hereses quamplures fidei orthodoxe et determinacioni Ecclesie Romane contrarios et repugnantes. Ideoque idem Johannes Reve, [volens] ad Ecclesie unitatem redire ac omnes errores et hereses in suprascriptis articulis notatos[a] ac omnes[b] alios errores et hereses quascumque cum puro corde re et verbo dimittere pro perpetuo et abiurare in forma in quodam scripto cirographo super ipsius abiuracione inscripta concepto et indentato per ipsum Johannem, ut asseruit, post audita plenarie et intellecta, et quia idem Johannes Reve asseruit se fore laicum et nescire legere dictam abiuracionem, ipse constituit magistrum Johannem Sutton, in legibus bacallarium, notarium publicum, tunc ibidem presentem, organum vocis sue in hac parte. Cui commisit potestatem abiuracionem huiusmodi pro se et nomine suo[c] tunc ibidem coram dicto patre iudicialiter legendi. Qui quidem magister Johannes Sutton, onus negocii huiusmodi in se assumens,[d] (p. 299 / fo. 73r)[e] tenorem et formam dicte abiuracionis vice et nomine dicti Johannis Reve perlegit publice tunc ibidem; prefato Johanne Reve manum suam dexteram super librum evangeliorum interim tenente, et tenorem dicte abiuracionis diligenter ascultante, ut asseruit, et plenarie intelligente. Quibus sic peractis, prefatus Johannes Reve ad evangelia predicta per ipsum sic tacta corporaliter iuravit in iudicio tunc ibidem quod omnia et singula in dicto abiuracionis sue scripto contenta, quatenus ad ipsum attinuit et attinet, faciet et[f] iuxta exigenciam et effectum eiusdem abiuracionis in omnibus inviolabiliter observabit. Et in[g] huius rei evidenciam manu sua propria signum crucis[h] in utroque scripto indentato super huiusmodi abiuracione sua concepto cum penna coram dicto patre[i] fecit pariter et subscripsit. Ac uni parti eiusdem scripti penes registrum dicti patris remanenti sigillum suum apposuit. Alteram vero partem eiusdem scripti idem Johannes Reve recepit ibidem sub sigillo dicti patris consignatam quoad vixerit, ut asseruit, remansuram.[j] Quibus sic peractis, recepto ab eodem Johanne Reve iuramento corporali ad evangelia pretacta de parendo iuri et mandatis Ecclesie ac de peragendo penitenciam sibi pro suis commissis ab ipso patre iniungendam, prefatus ipsum Johannem Reve a sentencia excommunicacionis, qua premissorum occasione extitit innodatus, absolvit et penitenciam iniunxit subscriptam sub eo qui sequitur tenore verborum.

---

[a] re *deleted.*   [b] er *deleted.*   [c] *MS.* sue.
[d] tenorem dicte abiuracionis *in bottom right-hand corner of page, the last two words being deleted.*
[e] Joh' Reve *in top right-hand corner of page.*
[f] inviolabiliter *deleted.*   [g] in *interlined.*
[h] signum crucis *interlined.*
[i] signum crucis (*interlined*) *repeated.*   [j] acta sunt hec *deleted.*

In Dei nomine, Amen. Quia nos, Willelmus, permissione divina Norwicensis episcopus, contra te, Johannem Reve de Beccles nostre diocesis, glover, subditum nostrum et subiectum, ex officio nostro procedentes, per tuam confessionem coram nobis iudicialiter factam invenimus te infra nostram diocesim[a] communicacionem familiarem cum hereticis notoriis et famosis sepius habuisse, ac hereticis huiusmodi favisse ac prebuisse consilium, auxilium[b] et[c] favorem, eosque pro posse tuo supportasse et concelasse, teque multas hereses et errores quamplures fidei orthodoxe et determinacioni sacrosancte ac universalis Ecclesie repugnantes—de quibus in quodam cirographo super tua abiuracione concepto et indentato, cuius una pars in archivis nostris noscitur remanere, ad quam nos referimus et pro hic inserta haberi volumus, plenior fit mencio—tenuisse, credidisse et affirmasse, et per hoc in excommunicacionis sentenciam incidisse; nunc autem, usus concilio saniori, petis misericordiam et sponte redis ad Ecclesie unitatem; idcirco inprimis abuirata per te omni heresi et recepta per nos secundum ritum Ecclesie iuratoria caucione de parendo mandatis Ecclesie, te absolvimus ab omni excommunicacionis vinculo quo tenebaris astrictus. Et quoniam per predicta que perpetrasti, tenuisti, credidisti et affirmasti in Deum et sanctam matrem Ecclesiam temere deliquisti, tibi pro pena penitenciali [iniungimus] iiij[or] fustigaciones circa ecclesiam parochialem de Becles iiij Dominicis diebus[d] coram solenni processione eiusdem cum cereo cere ponderis unius libre in manibus tuis,[e] capite et pedibus denudatis, corpore camisia et femoralibus duntaxat induto, more penitentis incedendo, et totidem fustigaciones circa mercatum de Beccles predict'. Et quia[f] tenuisti, credidisti et affirmasti[g] fore licitum cuicumque fideli edere carnes et omnimoda cibaria indifferenter sextis feriis, diebus Quadragesimalibus et diebus Quatuor Temporum ac vigiliis sanctorum indictis per Ecclesiam, tibi iniungimus quod (p. 300 / fo. 73v)[h] omni sexta feria per triennium proximum sequens in pane et aqua ieiunes, et[i] quod per tres annos proximos futuros singulis quartis feriis in Capite Ieiunii et singulis quintis feriis in Cena Domini in ecclesia nostra Cathedrali Norwic' coram nobis, vel nostras vices in hac parte gerente, cum aliis penitentibus personaliter te presentes, acturus solennem penitenciam pro commissis.

[a] m deleted.
[b] vel deleted.
[c] et interlined.
[d] iiij Dominicis diebus interlined.
[e] MS. suis.
[f] tenuisti, credidisti et affirmasti deleetd.
[g] tenuisti, credidisti et affirmasti interlined.
[h] Johannes Reve in top left-hand corner of page: quod repeated.
[i] Solennis penitencia iij annis in margin.

Tenor vero dicti scripti cirographi super abiuracione dicti Johannis Reve concepti et indentati de verbo ad verbum sequitur et est talis.*a*

In the name of God, tofore you, the worshipfull fadir in Crist, William, be the grace of God bisshop of Norwich, I, John Reve, glover of Becles in your diocese, your subject, felyng and undirstandyng that Y have holde, beleevyd and affermed errours and heresies whyche be contened in this indentur, that is to say,

That Y have holde, beleved and affermed that the sacrament of Baptem done in water in fourme customed in the Churche is of non avail and not to be pondret if the fadir and modir of the childe be cristened and of Cristene beleve.

Also that the sacrament of Confirmacion doon be a bisshop ys not profitable ne necessarie to mannys salvacion.

Also that confession oweth to be made to no prest, but only to God, for no prest hath poar to assoile a man of synne.

Also that Y have holde, beleved and affermed that no prest hath poar to make Goddis body in the sacrament of the auter, and that aftir the sacramentall wordis said of a prest at messe ther remaneth nothyng but only a cake of material bred.

Also that only consent of love in Jhu' Crist betuxe man and woman of Cristene beleve ys sufficiant for the sacrament of matrimony, withoute contract of wordes or solempnisacion yn churche.

Also that Y have holde, beleved and affermed that oonly God hath poar to make the sacramentes, and non other creatur.

Also that Y have holde, beleved and affermed that no creature of Cristene beleve is bounde to faste in Lenton, Ymbren Days, Frydays, vigiles of seyntes ne other tymes whyche be commaunded of the Churche to be fasted, but it is leful all puple of Crystene beleve all suche days and tymes to ete*b* flessh. And in affermyng of this opinion Y have ete flessh on Frydays and other days before rehersed.

Also*c* Y have hold, beleved*d* (p. 301 / fo. 74r)*e* and affermed that it is leeful to all Crystis puple to do all bodely werk as on Sondays and all other days whyche be commaunded of the Churche to be*f* had holy, if the peple kepe hem from other synnes soche days and tymes.

Also Y*g* have holde, beleved and affermed that every man may

---

a in Dei nomine, Amen *deleted.*
b ssh *deleted.*
c that *deleted.*
d and affermed *in bottom right-hand corner of page.*
e Joh' Reve *in top right-hand corner of page.*
f fasted *deleted.*   *g* hal *deleted.*

lefully and withoute synne[a] withholde and withdrawe his tithes and offrynges from churches and curates, so it be do prudently.

Also that Y have holde, beleved and affermed that it is lefull to Goddis peple to do the contrarie of the preceptes of the Churche.

Also that censures of holy Churche and sentences of cursyng yoven be[b] bisshops, prelates or other ordinaries be not to be pondred ne to be dred, for as sone as soche bisshops or ordinaries acurse ony man, Crist hymself asoileth hym.

Also that Y have beleved, hold and affermed that no maner of worship owith to be doo to ony ymages of the crucifix, of Our Lady ne of non other seyntes.

Also that no maner of pilgrimage oweth to be doo to ony places of seyntes, but only to pore peple.

Also that Y have hold and beleved that it is not leful to swere in ony caas.

Also that Y have holde, beleved and affermed that the pope of Rome is Antecrist and hath no poar in holy Churche as Seint Petir hadde but if he folwe the steppis of Peter in conversacion of lyvyng.

Also that all bisshops, prelates and prestes of the Churche be Antecristis disciples.

Also that Y have holde, beleved and affermed that it is as meritorie and as medful and as profitable to all Cristis peple to be byryed in myddynges, medues or in the wilde feldes as it is to be byryed in churches or churcheyerdes.

Because of whiche and many other errours and heresies whiche Y have hold, beleved and affermed[c] withynne your diocese, Y am called tofore you, worshipfull fadir, whiche have cure of my sowle. And be you fully enfourmed that the saide myn holdyng, belevyng and affermyng be opin errours and heresies and contrarious to the Churche of Rome, wherfor Y willyng folwe and sue the doctrine of holy Churche and departe from all maner of errour and heresie and turne with good will and herte to the oonhed of the Churche. Considerant that holy Churche spereth not hir bosom to hym that will turne ageyn, ne God will not the deth of a synner but rather that he be turned and lyve, with a pure (p. 302 / fo. 74v)[d] herte Y confesse, deteste and despise my sayd errours and heresies, and the said opinions Y confesse hereticous and erroneous and to the faith of the Churche of Rome and all universal holy Churche repugnant. And for as moche as be the said thinges that Y so held, beleved and affermed Y shewed meself corrupt and[e] unfaithful, that from hensforth Y shewe me uncorrupt and faithful, the faith and doctrine of

---

[a] wih *deleted*.   [b] a *deleted*.
[c] whit *deleted*.   [d] Joh' Reve *in top left-hand corner of page*.
[e] a *deleted*.

holi Churche truly to kepe Y promytte. And al maner of errour and heresie, doctrine and opinion agein the faith of holy Churche and determinacion of the Churche of Rome—and namely the opinions before rehersed—Y abjure and forswere, and swere be these holy gospels be me bodely touched that from hensforth Y shal never holde errour ne heresie ne fals doctrine ageyn the faith of holy Churche and the determinacion of the Churche of Rome. Ne no suche thinges Y shal obstinatly defende. Ne ony persone holdyng or techyng soche maner of thinges Y shal obstinatly defende be me or ony other persone opinly or prively. Y shal never aftir this time be no recettour, fautour, consellour or defensour of heretikes or of ony persone suspect of heresie. Ne Y shal never trowe to thaym. Ne wittyngly Y shal felaship with thaym, ne^a gyve thaym consell, yeftes, socour, favour ne confort. Yf Y knowe ony heretikes or of heresie ony persones suspect, or of thaym fautours, confortours, consellours or defensours, or of ony persones makyng prive conventicules or assembles, or holdyng ony senguler opinions from the comune doctrine of the Churche, Y shal late you, worshipful fadir, or your vicar general in your absence or the diocesans of suche persone[s] have soone and redy knowyng. So help me God atte holy doom and these holy gospels.

In wittenesse of whiche thinges Y subscribe here with myn owyn hand a crosse +. And to this partie endented to remayne in your registre Y sette my signet. And that other partie endented Y receyve undir your seal to abide with^b me unto my lyves ende. Yoven at Norwich in your chapell of your palais, xviij day of the moneth of Aprill the yer of oure Lord a thousand four hundred and thretty.

[23]

(p. 303 / fo. 75r) **Ricardus Knobbyng de Beccles**[156]

In Dei nomine, Amen.^{c} Per presens publicum instrumentum cunctis appareat evidenter quod Anno Domini ab Incarnacione eiusdem secundum cursum et computacionem Ecclesie Anglicane Millesimo Quadringentesimo Tricesimo, indiccione octava, pontificatus sanctissimi in Christo patris et domini nostri, domini Martini divina providencia pape quinti, anno terciodecimo, mensis Aprilis

---

^{a} y *deleted.* ^{b} v *deleted.*
^{c} Ricardus Knobbyng *in margin.*

---

156 Beccles, north-east Suffolk.

die decimaoctava, in mei, Johannis Excestr, clerici, publici auctoritate apostolica notarii, ac testium subscriptorum presencia, coram reverendo in Christo patre ac domino, domino Willelmo Dei gracia Norwicensi episcopo, in capella palacii sui infra civitatem Norwicensem situati pro tribunali ad iura reddenda—prout michi, notario prescripto, tunc apparebat—iudicialiter sedente, assistentibus eidem reverendo patri tunc ibidem venerabilibus et discretis viris, magistris Willelmo Worstede, priore ecclesie Cathedralis Norwic', ac Johanne Elys, ordinis Minorum, sacre pagine professoribus, necnon fratre Edmundo Snetisham, priore ecclesie sive prioratus de Cokesford,[157] ac magistris Willelmo Bernham et Thoma Ryngstede ac Johanne Bury, in decretis, et Willelmo Ascogh, in sacra theologia, bacallariis,[a] Ricardus Knobbyng de Beccles, multipliciter, ut dicebatur, diffamatus de crimine heretice pravitatis et ea occasione responsurus,[b] in vinculis ad iudicium[c] personaliter fuit adductus, ac de et super omnibus et singulis heresibus et erroribus in quodam scripto cirographo super abiuracione eiusdem Ricardi Knobbyng concepto et indentato contentis plenarie et conscriptis per prefatum[d] reverendum patrem iudicialiter impetitus. Qui quidem Ricardus Knobbyng omnes et singulas hereses et errores omnimodos[e] in dicto scripto indentato,[f] cuius tenor inferius describitur, contentos et per prefatum reverendum patrem eidem Ricardo Knobbyng tunc ibidem obiectos iudicialiter et articulatos fatebatur et recognovit[g] iudicialiter se infra diocesim Norwicensem tenuisse, credidisse et affirmasse. Et subsequenter tunc ibidem idem Ricardus, volens et affectans, ut asseruit, puro corde ad Ecclesie unitatem redire, ac omnes hereses et errores in dicto scripto indentato contentos et specificatos ac per ipsum tunc ibidem coram prefato patre iudicialiter confessatos ac alios errores et hereses quascumque re et verbo dimittere pro[h] perpetuo et abiurare secundum formam et tenorem in dicto scripto cirographo indentato specificatos, quos, ut asseruit, prius audivit et plenarie intellexit, et quia idem Ricardus Knobbyng asseruit se esse mere laicum et legere nescientem, ipse constituit magistrum Johannem Sutton, in legibus bacallarium, tunc ibidem presentem, organum vocis sue. Cui ipse Ricardus commisit plenariam potestatem nomine suo et pro se dictam abiuracionem in prefato scripto indentato[i] conceptam et contentam coram ipso

---

[a] iudicialiter sedente . . . bacallariis *partly interlined and partly in the margin.*
[b] ad iudicium adductus fuit *deleted.* [c] it *deleted.*
[d] patrem *deleted.* [e] MS. omnimodas.
[f] cuius unam partem sub sigillo dicti reverendi patris sigillatam idem Ricardus *deleted.*
[g] fo *deleted.* [h] MS. per.
[i] oc *deleted.*

---

[157] The priory of Augustinian canons, Coxford, Norfolk.

reverendo patre*ᵃ* legendi et interponendi iudicialiter tunc ibidem. Et deinde idem magister Johannes Sutton,*ᵇ* organum vocis ipsius Ricardi in hac parte*ᶜ* in se assumens,*ᵈ* abiuracionem*ᵉ* eiusdem*ᶠ* Ricardi Knobbyng fecit, legit et interposuit secundum formam in dicto scripto indentato contentam, cuius tenor de verbo ad verbum sequitur et est talis.

In the name of God, tofore you, the worshipful fadir in Crist, William, be the grace of God bisshop of Norwich, Y, Richard Knobbyng, duellyng in Becles of your diocese, your subject, felyng and undirstandyng that Y have be familier with heretekes and many tymes conversant with thaym, of whos doctrine and informacion Y have lerned, conceyved and reported the errours and heresies wiche be conteyned in this indenture, which errours and heresies Y have holde, beleved and afermed in your said diocese, that it to say,

That the sacrament of Baptem doon in watir in forme custumed*ᵍ* of the Church*ʰ* is of noon availe ne not to be pondred if the fadir and modir of the child borne have Cristendom.

Also that the sacrament of Confirmacion doon of a bisshop, as the commune*ⁱ* us is hadde, is nother profitable ne (p. 304 / fo. 75v)*ʲ* necessarie to the salvacion of mennys sowlis.

Also that confession oweth to be made unto God oonly, and to non other prest, for non other prest hath poar of assoile a man of ony synne.

Also that no prest hath poer to make Cristis varay body in the sacrament of the auter at messe, and that aftir the sacramental wordes said of ony prest at messe ther remayneth nothyng but oonly a cake of material bred.

Also that oonly consent of love in Jhu' Crist be*ᵏ* tuex man and woman of Cristes beleve is sufficient for the sacrament of matrimonye, withoute contract made be wordis or solennizacion in Chirche.

Also that no prest in erthe hath poer to make the sacramentes, but God oonly hath that poar and noon other prest.

Also that no Cristen peple is bounde to faste in Lenton time,*ˡ* Ymbrin Days, Fridays, vigiles of seyntes ne other tymes which ben commaunded of the Churche to be fasted, but all suche days and

---

ᵃ f *deleted.*   *ᵇ* onus negocii huiusmodi *deleted.*
ᶜ organum vocis ipsius Ricardi in hac parte *interlined.*
ᵈ d *deleted.*   *ᵉ* dicti *deleted.*
ᶠ eiusdem *interlined.*   *ᵍ* in *deleted.*
ʰ if *deleted.*   *ⁱ* do *deleted.*
ʲ Ric' Knobbyng *in top left-hand corner of page*: ne *repeated.*
ᵏ tux *deleted.*   *ˡ* yb *deleted.*

tymes it is leful to alle Cristen peple to ete flesshe and all maner of metes indifferently as ofte as lust and appetit cometh.

Also that it is leful to al Cristis peple to do al maner bodyly werkes on Sondayes and all other festival days whiche be commaunded be holy Churche to be had in reverence and holy, so that the peple kepe hem from other synnes suche days and tymes.

Also that every man may lefully withoute synne withdrawe and withholde his tithes and his offerynges from churches and curates, so it be do prudently.

Also that it is leful and no synne to do the contrarie of the preceptes of holy Churche.

Also that censures and cursynges yoven be*a* bisshops and other ordinaries of holy Churche bynde not in conscience, ne be not to be pondred ne dredde, for whann suche bisshops and ordinaries acursen ony persone, Crist blisseth and assoileth the same persone.

Also that al maner of prayer shuld be made to God oonly, and to noon other seyntes.

Also that no maner worship owith to be doo to any ymages of the crucifix, of Oure Lady ne of noon other seyntes.

Also that noon pilgrimage owith to be doo to ony places or seyntes, be oonly to the pore peple.

Also that it is not leful to swere in ony caas.

Also that the pope of Rome is veray Antecrist and hath no poar of God to bynde ne to lose as Petir hadde, for he sueth not the steppes of Petir in conversacion of holy levyng.

Also that all other bisshops and prelates and prestes of the Churche be Antecristis disciples.

Because of whiche and many other errours and heresies which Y have holde, beleved and affermed withynne your said diocese, Y am called tofore you, worshipful fader, whiche have cure of my sowle. And be you fully informed that the said my belevyng, holdyng and affermyng be*b* (p. 305 / fo. 76r)*c* opin errours and heresies and contrarious to the Churche of Rome, wherfor Y wyllyng folwe and sue the doctrine of holy Churche, and departe from all maner of errour and heresie, and turne with good wille and herte to the oonhed of the Churche. Considerant that holy Churche spereth not hir bosom to hym that wil turne ageyne, ne God will not the deth of a synner but rather that he be turned and lyve, with a pure herte Y confesse, detest and despise my said errours and heresies, and these sayd opinions Y confesse hereticous and erroneous and to the faith of the Churche of Rome and all universall holy Churche repugnant. And

---

a a *deleted.*
b be opin errours *in bottom right-hand corner of page.*
c Ric' Knobbyng *in top right-hand corner of page:* be *repeated.*

for as moche as be the saide thinges that Y so held, beleved and affermed Y shewed meself corrupt and unfaithful, that from hensforth Y shewe me uncorrupt and faithful, the faith and doctrine of holy Churche truly to kepe Y promitte. And all maner of errour and heresie, doctrine and opinion agayn the faith of holy Church and determinacion of the Churche of Rome—and namely these opinions before rehersed—Y abjure and forswere, and swere be these holy gospels be me bodyly touched that from hensforth Y shal never holde errour ne heresie ne fals doctrine agayn the faith of holy Churche and determinacion of the Churche of Rome. Ne no suche thinges Y shal obstinatly defende. Ne no persone holdyng or techyng suche thinges Y shal obstinatly defende be me or ony other persone opinly or prively. Y shal never aftir this tyme be no recettour, fautour, consellour or defensour of heretikes or of ony persones suspect of heresie. Ne Y shal never trowe to thaym. Ne wittyngly Y shal felaship with thaym, ne be homly with thaym, ne geve thaym consell, yeftes, sokour, favour or confort. Yf Y knowe ony heretikes or of heresie ony persones suspect, or of thaym fautours, confortours, consellours or defendours, or of ony persones makyng prive conventicules or assembles, or holdyng ony singuler opinions from the comune doctrine of the Churche, Y shal late you, worshipful fadir, or your vicar general in your absence or the diocesanes of suche[a] persones have sone and redy knowyng of thaym. So help me God atte holy dome and these holy gospels.

In wittenesse of whiche thing Y subscribe here with myn hand [a] crosse +. And to this partie endented to remayne in youre registre Y sette my sygnet. And the other partie endented Y receyve undir your seal to abide with me into my lyves ende. Yoven at Norwich in your chapell of your palays the xviij day of the moneth of Aprill the yer of oure Lord a thousand foure hundred and thretty.

Qui quidem Ricardus Knobbyng continue, dum prefatus magister Johannes Sutton tenorem dicte abiuracionis [legit], (p. 306 / fo. 76v)[b] manum suam dexteram tenuit super librum evangeliorum[c] et tenorem dicte abiuracionis assidue ascultavit. Et iuravit ad evangelia predicta quod ab hac hora in antea ipse inviolabiliter observabit omnia et singula contenta in abiuracione sua predicta iuxta ipsius exigenciam et tenorem. Et in maiorem huius rei evidenciam idem Ricardus Knobbyng manu sua propria in utroque scripto cirographo indentato super huiusmodi abiuracione sua concepto coram

---

[a] pic *deleted*.
[b] Ricardus Knobbyng *in top left-hand corner of page*.
[c] tenuit *repeated*.

dicto reverendo patre in iudicio tunc ibidem cum penna signum sancte crucis fecit pariter et subscripsit. Ac uni parti eiusdem scripti indentati, penes registrum dicti reverendi patris residenti, sigillum suum apposuit. Et alteram partem eiusdem scripti indentati idem Ricardus Knobbyng receipt in iudicio tunc ibidem, sigillo dicti reverendi patris consignatam, penes eundem Ricardum durante vite sue tempore, ut asseruit, remansuram. Quibus sic peractis, idem Ricardus, de novo tactis per eum evangeliis sacrosanctis, iuravit ad ea^a iudicialiter tunc ibidem de stando et parendo^b mandatis Ecclesie ac de peragendo penitenciam sibi pro commissis suis predictis a prefato reverendo patre iniungendam. Et deinde idem reverendus pater ipsum Ricardum^c ab omni excommunicacionis vinculo quo premissorum occasione tenebatur astrictus rite et canonice absolvebat sub eo qui sequitur tenore verborum.

In Dei nomine, Amen. Quia nos, Willelmus, permissione divina Norwicensis episcopus, contra te, Ricardum Knobbyng de Beccles nostre diocesis, subditum nostrum et subiectum, ex officio nostro legitime procedentes,^{d} per tuam confessionem coram nobis iudicialiter factam invenimus te infra nostram diocesim privatam communicacionem familiariter cum hereticis notoriis et famosis sepius^e fecisse et habuisse, ac hereticis huiusmodi favisse ac prebuisse concilium, auxilium et favorem, eosdemque pro posse tuo supportasse et concelasse, teque multas hereses et errores quamplures fidei orthodoxe et determinacioni^f sacrosancte ac universalis Ecclesie repugnantes—de quibus in quodam cirographo super tua abiuracione concepto et indentato, cuius una pars in archivis nostris noscitur remanere, ad quam nos referimus et pro hic inserta haberi volumus, plenior fit^g mencio—tenuisse, credidisse et affirmasse, et per hoc in excommunicacionis sentenciam incidisse; nunc autem, usus concilio saniori, petis misericordiam et sponte redis ad Ecclesie unitatem; idcirco, inprimis abiurata per te omni heresi et recepta per nos secundum ritum Ecclesie iuratoria caucione de parendo mandatis Ecclesie, te absolvimus ab omni excommunicacionis vinculo quo tenebaris astrictus. Et quoniam per predicta que tenuisti, credidisti et affirmasti in Deum et sanctam matrem Ecclesiam temere deliquisti, tibi pro pena penitenciali [iniungimus] quatuor fustigaciones circa cimiterium ecclesie parochialis de Beccles nostre diocesis quatuor diebus Dominicis coram solenni processione eiusdem,

---

^{a} t *deleted.* ^{b} et parendo *interlined.*
^{c} a sentencia *deleted.*
^{d} ex officio nostro legitime procedentes *interlined.*
^{e} familiariter *repeated.* ^{f} ecclesie *deleted.*
^{g} mens *deleted.*

capite et pedibus denudatis, corpore camisia et femoralibus induto, cum cereo cere ponderis unius libre tuis*a* manibus deferendo, et more penitentis incedendo; et totidem fustigaciones circa mercatum de Beccles quatuor diebus mercati principal' eiusdem ville eodem modo supradicto. Et quia tenuisti, credidisti et affirmasti fore licitum cuicumque fideli edere carnes et omnimoda cibaria indifferenter sextis feriis, diebus Quadragesimalibus, diebus Quatuor Temporum et vigiliis sanctorum indictis per Ecclesiam, tibi iniungimus quod omni sexta feria per unum annum iam proximum futurum in pane et aqua ieiunes, et*b* quod per duos annos iam proximos futuros omni quarta feria in Capite Ieiunii et omni quinta feria in Cena Domini coram nobis vel nostrum locum tenente in hac parte in ecclesia nostra Cathedrali Norwic' cum aliis penitentibus te personaliter presentes, acturus*c* solennem penitenciam pro commissis.

Acta sunt hec prout suprascribuntur sub Anno Domini, indiccione, pontificatu, mense, die et loco predictis. Presentibus tunc ibidem magistris Thoma Hunter, in artibus magistro, Willelmo Bamburgh, presbiteris, Henrico Sharyngton et Roberto Aylmer, notariis publicis, ac aliis quampluribus in multitudine numerosa, et me, J. Excestr.

[24]

(p. 307 / fo. 79r) **Ricardus Grace, skynner, de Beccles**[158]

In Dei nomine, Amen. Per presens publicum instrumentum cunctis appareat evidenter quod Anno Domini ab Incarnacione eiusdem Millesimo CCCC*mo* Tricesimo, pontificatus sanctissimi in Christo patris et domini nostri, domini Martini divina providencia pape quinti, anno terciodecimo, mensis Aprilis die decimaoctava, in mei, Johannis Excestre, clerici, publici auctoritate apostolica notarii, ac testium subscriptorum presencia, coram reverendo in Christo patre ac domino, domino Willelmo Dei gracia Norwicensi episcopo, in capella palacii sui infra civitatem Norwic' situati pro tribunali ad iura reddenda—prout michi, notario prescripto, pro tunc apparebat—iudicialiter sedente, assistentibus eidem reverendo

---

a MS. suis.
b Solennis penitencia ij annis *in margin.*
c p *deleted.*

---

158 Beccles, north-east Suffolk.

patri tunc ibidem venerabilibus et discretis viris, magistris Willelmo Worstede, priore ecclesie Cathedralis Norwic', ac Johanne Elys, ordinis Minorum, sacre pagine professoribus, necnon fratre Edmundo Snetesham, priore ecclesie sive prioratus de Cokesford, ac magistris Willelmo Bernham et Thoma Ryngsted ac Johanne Bury, in decretis, et Willelmo Ascogh, in sacra theologia, bacallariis, Ricardus Grace, [s]kynner de Beccles Norwicensis diocesis, de et super crimine heretice pravitatis, ut dicebatur, multipliciter diffamatus et super eodem crimine personaliter responsurus, in vinculis ad iudicium fuit adductus. Cui quidem Ricardo Grace prefatus reverendus pater iudicialiter sedens omnes et singulos articulos in quodam scripto cirographo super abiuracione dicti Ricardi concepto et indentato, cuius tenor inferius continetur, scriptos [et] contentos ac hereses et errores in eisdem articulis specificatos dixit, proposuit et obiecit. Quos quidem articulos omnes et singulos, ac universas hereses et omnimodos^a errores in eisdem articulis habitos et contentos, idem Ricardus Grace fatebatur et recognovit se infra diocesim Norwicensem diu tenuisse, credidisse, docuisse et affirmasse, prout in eodem^b dicto scripto indentato plenarie continetur. Idcirco idem Ricardus, volens, ut asseruit, et affectans puro corde redire ad Ecclesie unitatem, ac omnes hereses et quoscumque errores re et verbo dimittere pro perpetuo et abiurare secundum tenorem dicti cirographi indentati, cuius tenorem, ut asseruit, prius cum matura deliberacione audivit et plenarie intellexit, et quia idem Ricardus asseruit se^c esse mere laicum et legere nescientem, ipse Ricardus constituit magistrum Johannem Sutton, in legibus bacallarium, tunc ibidem presentem, organum vocis sue. Cui ipse Ricardus commisit plenariam potestatem nomine suo et pro se dictam abiuracionem in prefato scripto indentato conceptam et contentam coram ipso reverendo patre legendi et interponendi iudicialiter tunc ibidem. Et deinde idem magister Johannes Sutton, organum vocis ipsius Ricardi in hac parte in se assumens, abiuracionem eiusdem Ricardi Grace fecit, legit et interposuit secundum formam in dicto scripto indentato contentam, cuius tenor de verbo ad verbum sequitur et est talis.

In the name of God, tofore you, (p. 308 / fo. 79v) the worshipfull fadir in Crist, William, be the grace of God bysshop of Norwych, Y, Richard Grace, skynner, dullyng in^d Beccles of your diocese, your subject, felyng and undirstandy[ng] that afore this time Y affermed

---

^a MS. omnimodas. ^b in *repeated*.
^c fore oculorum lumine aliqualiter *crossed out*.
^d p *crossed out*.

errours and heresies, sayng, affermyng and belevyng withynne your said diocese,

That the sacrament of Baptem doon in water in fourme custumed of the Churche ys litell to be pondred for as muche as whan a child cometh to yeres of discrecion and receyvyth Cristis lawe and hys commaundments he ys sufficiently baptized and so he may be saved withowtyn ony other baptem.

Also that the sacrament of Confirmacion doon be a bysshop is unvaillable and not profitable to mannys sowle ne to hys lyve.

Also that confession oweth to be made unto no prest, but oonly to God, for no prest hath poar to assoile a man of ony synne.

Also that Y held, beleved and affermed that no prest hat poar to make Goddys body in the sacrament of the auter, and that after the sacramentall wordis said of a prest at messe ther remayneth but oonly a cake of material bred.

Also that only consent of love in Jhu' Crist betuxe man and woman suffiseth for the sacrament of matrymon', withowtyn contract of ony wordis or solempnizacion in churche.

Also that Y have holde, beleved and affermed that oonly God hath poar to make the sacramentes, and noon other erthely man.

Also that no man ne woman is bounde to faste in Lenton, Ymbre Days, Fridays, vigiles of seyntes ne other tymes whyche ar commaunded of the Churche to be fasted, but it is leful to every persone all suche days and tymes to ete flessh and all maner of metis indifferently at hys owyn lust.

Also Y have holde, beleved and affermed that it is leful to every Cristene persone to do alle bodely werkys on Sonedays and alle other days whiche ar commaunded of the Churche to be had holy, if a man kepe hym from other synnes suche days.

Also that Y have holde, beleved and affermed that every man may lefully withdrawe and withholde tythes and offrynges from churches and curates, so it be do prudently.

Also Y have holde, beleved and affermed that it is no synne to the Cristene peple to do the contrarie of the preceptes of holy Churche.

Also that censures of the Churche be not to be dredde ne fered, for as soone as the bisshops and ordinaries acurse ony man, God assoileth hym.

Also Y have[a] (p. 309 / fo. 80r)[b] holde, beleved and affermed that all prayers shuld be made oonly to God, and to none other seyntes.

Also Y have holde, beleved and affermed that no maner of worship owith to be do to ony ymages of the crucifix, of Our Lady Seynt Marie ne of none other seyntes.

[a] holde, beleved *in bottom right-hand corner of page.*
[b] Ric' Grace *in top right-hand corner of page.*

Also that Y have holde, beleved and affermed that no maner of*a* pylgrymages*b* owith to be do to ony seyntes, but the expenses whiche shuld be do and made in suche pilgrimages shuld be yoven to pore puple.

Also that Y held and have beleved that it is not lefull a man to swere in ony caas.

Also Y have holde and affermed that the pope is Antecrist, and hath no poar in holy Churche as Seynt Peter hadde but if he folwe the steppis of Petir in levyng, and all bisshops, prelates and prestes of the Churche ar*c* Antecristes disciples.

Because of whiche and many other errours and heresies Y am called tofore you, worshipful fadir, whiche have cure of my sowle. And be you fully enfourmed that the sayd myn affermyng, belevyng and holdyng be opin errours and heresies and contrarious to the determinacion of the Churche of Rome, wherfor Y wyllyng folwe and sue the doctrine of holy Churche, and departe from all maner of errour and heresie, and turne with good will and herte to the oonhed of the Churche. Considerand that holy Churche spereth not hir bosom to hym that will turne ageyn, ne God will not the deth of a synner but rather that he be turned and lyve, with a pure herte Y confesse, deteste and despise my sayd errours and heresies, and these said opinions Y confesse hereticous and erroneous and to the faith of the Churche of Rome and all universal holy Churche repugna[n]t. And for as muche as be the said thinges that Y so*d* held, beleved and affermed Y shewed meself corrupt and unfaithful, that from hensforth Y shewe me uncorrupt and faithful, the faith and doctrine of holy Churche truly to kepe Y promitte. And all maner of errour and heresie, doctrine and opinion ageyn the feyth of holy Churche and determinacion of the Churche of Rome—and namely the opinions before rehersed—Y abjure and forswere, and swere be these holy gospels be me bodyly touched that from hensforth Y shal never (p. 310 / fo. 8ov) holde errour ne heresie ne fals doctrine ageyn the feith of holy Churche and determinacion of the Churche of Rome. Ne no suche thinges Y shal obstinatly defende. Ne no persone holdyng or techyng suche maner of thinges Y shal obstinatly defende be me or ony other persone opinly or prively. Y shal never after this time be no recettour, fautour, consellour or defensour of heretikes or of ony persone suspect of heresie. Ne Y shal never trowe to thaym. Ne wittyngly Y shal felaship with thaym, ne be hoomly with thaym, ne geve thaym consell, yeftes, sokour, favour ne confort. Yf Y knowe ony heretikes or of heresie ony persones suspecte or of

---

a worship owith to be *deleted, followed by* do (*not deleted*).
b *The* s *of* pylgrymages *has been almost completely rubbed out.*
c ante cr *deleted.*   *d* w *deleted.*

thaym fautours, confortours, concellours or defensours, or of persones makyng prive conventicules or assembles, or holdyng ony
divers or singuler opinions from the comune doctrine of the Churche,
Y shal late you, worshipful fadir, or your vicar general in your
absence or the diocesanes of suche persones have soone and redy
knowyng. So help me God atte holy doom and these holy gospels.

In wittenesse of whiche thyng Y subscribe here with myn owyn
hand a crosse +. And to this partie endented to remayne in your
registre Y sette my signet. And that other partie endented Y receyve under your seel to abide with me unto my lyves ende. Yoven
at Norwich in your chapell of your palaice, xviij day of the moneth
of Aprilli the yer of oure Lord a thousand foure hundred and thretty.

Qui quidem Ricardus Grace—dum magister Johannes Sutton,
organum vocis ipsius Ricardi gerens, ut prefertur, fuit in legendo[a]
abiuracionem prescriptam[b]—tangens manu sua dextera librum
evangeliorum, iuravit ad ea[c] quod ab hac hora in antea ipse omnia
et singula in dicto scripto cirographo contenta, in quantum personam suam concernunt, iuxta ipsius scripti indentati exigenciam et
tenorem inviolabiliter observabit. Et in huius rei testimonium in
utraque parte dicti scripti[d] super abiuracione sua concepti et indentati signum crucis[e] cum penna manu sua propria fecit pariter et
subscripsit coram dicto reverendo patre iudicialiter tunc ibidem. Ac
uni parti eiusdem scripti indentati, penes registrum dicti reverendi
patris remansure, sigillum suum apposuit. Et alteram partem
eiusdem scripti indentati idem Ricardus Grace recepit in iudicio
tunc ibidem, sub sigillo ipsius reverendi patris sigillatam, penes
ipsum Ricardum durante tocius vite sue tempore, ut asseruit,
permansuram. Et deinde idem Ricardus iuravit ad sacra evangelia
pretacta iudicialiter de parendo mandatis Ecclesie et de peragendo
bene et fideliter penitenciam sibi per dictum reverendum patrem in
hac parte iniungendam pro suis commissis superius recitatis. Et
subsequenter idem reverendus pater ipsum Ricardum a sentencia
excommunicacionis, qua premissorum occasione tenebatur[f] (p. 311 /
fo. 81r)[g] astrictus, rite et canonice absolvebat sub eo qui sequitur
tenore verborum.

In Dei nomine, Amen. Quia nos, Willelmus, permissione divina
Norwicensis episcopus, contra te, Ricardum Grace de Beccles nostre
diocesis, subditum nostrum et subiectum, per tuam, ex officio nostro

---

[a] tenor *deleted.*   [b] idem Ru *deleted.*   [c] iuravit ad ea (*repeated*) *deleted.*
[d] indentat *deleted.*   [e] in utroque et *deleted.*
[f] astrictus *in bottom right-hand corner of page.*
[g] Ricardus Grace *in top right-hand corner of page.*

legitime procedentes,[a] confessionem coram nobis iudicialiter factam invenimus te infra nostram diocesim multas hereses et errores quamplures fidei orthodoxe et determinacioni sacrosancte ac universalis Ecclesie repugnantes—de quibus in quodam cirographo super tua abiuracione concepto et indenta[to], cuius una pars in archivis nostris noscitur remanere, ad quam nos referimus et pro hic inserta haberi volumus,[b] plenior fit mencio—tenuisse, credidisse et affirmasse, et per hoc in excommunicacionis sentenciam incidisse; nunc autem, usus consilio saniori, petis misericordiam et sponte redis ad Ecclesie unitatem; idcirco, inprimis abiurata per te omni heresi et recepta per nos a te secundum ritum Ecclesie iuratoria caucione de parendo mandatis Ecclesie, te absolvimus ab omni excommunicacionis vinculo quo tenebaris astrictus. Et quoniam per predicta que tenuisti, credidisti et affirmasti in Deum et sanctam matrem Ecclesiam temere deliquisti, tibi pro pena penitenciali [iniungimus] quatuor fustigaciones circa cimiterium ecclesie parochialis de Beccles[c] coram solenni processione eiusdem quatuor diebus Dominicis horis consuetis facienda, capite et pedibus denudatis, corpore camisia et femoralibus duntaxat induto, more penitentis incedendo, et unum cereum cere ponderis unius libre manu sua publice deferendo; et quatuor fustigaciones circa mercatum de Beccles predict' quatuor diebus mercati ibidem, nudis capite et pedibus, dictum cereum, ut premittitur, deferendo, corpore camisia et femoralibus duntaxat induto. Et quia tenuisti, credidisti et affirmasti fore licitum cuicumque fideli edere carnes et omnimoda cibaria indifferenter sextis feriis, diebus Quadragesimalibus, diebus Quatuor Temporum et vigiliis sanctorum indictis per Ecclesiam, tibi iniungimus quod omni sexta feria per annum iam proximum futurum in pane et aque ieiunes, et[d] quod per duos annos continuos iam proximos et immediate sequentes omni quarta feria in Capite Ieiunii et omni quinta feria in Cena Domini coram nobis vel nostrum locum tenente in hac parte in ecclesia nostra Cathedrali Norwic' cum aliis penitentibus te presentes personaliter, acturus solennem penitenciam pro commissis.

Acta sunt hec prout suprascribuntur et recitantur sub Anno Domini, indiccione, pontificatu, mense die et loco predictis. Presentibus discretis viris, magistro Thoma Hunter, in artibus magistro, et Willelmo Bamburgh, presbiteris, necnon magistris Henrico Sharyngton et Roberto Aylmer, notariis publicis, Thoma Rodelond, Johanne Blytheburgh et aliis quampluribus tunc ibidem presentibus in multitudine numerosa; me, Johanne Excestr, scribente.

---

[a] ex officio nostro legitime procedentes *interlined*.
[b] et mandamus *deleted*.   [c] et t quatuor diebus Dominicis *deleted*.
[d] Penitencia solennis ij annis *in margin*.

[25]

(p. 312 / fo. 81v) **Baldewinus Cowper de Beccles**[159]

In Dei nomine, Amen. Per presens publicum instrumentum cunctis appareat evidenter quod Anno Domini ab Incarnacione eiusdem Millesimo CCCC^mo Tricesimo, pontificatus sanctissimi in Christo patris et domini^a nostri, domini Martini divina providencia pape quinti, anno terciodecimo, mensis Aprilis die decimaoctava, in mei, Johannis Excestre, clerici, publici auctoritate apostolica notarii, ac testium subscriptorum presencia, coram reverendo in Christo patre ac domino, domino Willelmo, Dei gracia Norwicensi episcopo, in capella palacii sui infra civitatem Norwic' situati pro tribunali ad iura reddenda—prout michi, notario prescripto, pro tunc apparebat—iudicialiter sedente, assistentibus eidem reverendo patri tunc ibidem venerabilibus et discretis viris, magistris Willelmo Worstede, priore ecclesie Cathedralis Norwic', ac Johanne Elys, ordinis Minorum, sacre pagine professoribus, necnon fratre Edmundo Snetesham, priore ecclesie sive prioratus de Cokesford, ac magistris Willelmo Bernham et Thoma Ryngstede ac Johanne Bury, in decretis, et Willelmo Ascogh, in sacra theologia, bacallariis, Baldewinus Cowper de Beccles Norwicensis diocesis, de et super crimine heretice pravitatis, ut dicebatur, multipliciter diffamatus et super eodem crimine personaliter responsurus, in vinculis ad iudicium adductus [fuit]. Cui quidem Baldewino Cowper prefatus reverendus pater iudicialiter sedens omnes et singulos articulos in quodam scripto cirographo super abiuracione dicti Baldewini concepto et indentato, cuius tenor inferius continetur, scriptos [et] contentos ac hereses et errores in eisdem articulis specificatos dixit, proposuit et obiecit. Quos quidem articulos omnes et singulos, ac universas hereses et omnimodos^b errores in eisdem articulis habitos et contentos, idem Baldewinus fatebatur et recognovit se infra diocesim Norwicensem diu tenuisse, cred[id]isse, docuisse et affirmasse, prout in eodem dicto scripto indentato plenarie continetur. Idcirco idem Baldewinus, volens, ut asseruit, et affectans puro corde redire ad Ecclesie unitatem, ac omnes hereses et quoscumque errores re et verbo dimittere pro perpetuo et abiurare secundum tenorem dicti cirographi indentati, cuius tenorem, ut asseruit, prius cum matura deliberacione audivit et plenarie intellexit, et quia idem Baldewinus

---

^a dm' *deleted.*   ^b *MS.* omnimodas.

---

159 Beccles, north-east Suffolk.

asseruit se esse mere laicum et legere nescientem, ipse Baldewinus constituit magistrum Johannem Sutton, in legibus bacallarium, tunc ibidem presentem, organum vocis sue. Cui ipse Baldewinus commisit plenariam potestatem nomine suo et pro se dictam abiuracionem in prefato scripto indentato conceptam et contentam coram ipso reverendo patre legendi et interponendi iudicialiter tunc ibidem. Et deinde idem magister Johannes Sutton, organum vocis ipsius Baldewini in hac parte se assumens, abiuracionem eiusdem Balde-wini fecit, legit et*a* interposuit secundum formam in dicto scripto indentato contentam, cuius tenor de verbo ad verbum sequitur et est talis.

(p. 313 / fo. 82r) In the name of God, tofore you, the worshipful fadir in Crist, William, be [the] grace of God bysshop of Norwich, Y, Baldewyn Cowper of Beccles of your [diocese], felyng and undir-standyng that Y have be familier with heretikes, that is to say with Sir Huwe Pye and many others, be whos untrewe doctrine Y was enformed of these errours and heresies, whiche Y have holde, beleved and affermed withynne your diocese, that is to say,

That the sacrament of Baptem doon in watir in forme customed in the Churche is of noon availe and not to be pondred if the fadir and modir of the [child] be cristned and of Cristen beleve.

Also that the sacrament of Confirmacion doon be a bisshop is unvaillable and not profitable to mannys sowle nei to hys lyve.

Also that confession oweth to be made unto [no] prest, but oonly to God, for no prest hath poar to assoile a man of ony synne.

Also Y have holde, beleved and affermed that no prest hath poar to make Goddis body in the sacrament of the auter, and that aftir the sacramental wordis said of the prest at messe ther remayneth nothyng but oonly a cake of material bred.

Also that oonly consent of love in Jhu' Crist betuxe man and woman suffiseth for the sacrament of matrimon, withoute contracte of ony wordis or solempnizacion in churche.

Y have holde, beleved and affermed that oonly God hath poar to make the sacramentes, and non other erthely man.

Also that no man ne woman is bounde to*b* do ony penance whiche i[s] enjoyned to hym of ony prest in Confession, because that no prest hath poar to assoile a man of synne.

Also that Y held, beleved and afermed that no man ne woman is

---

a t' *follows* et.
b faste in Lenton, Ymbre Days, Fridays, vigiles of seyntes ne none other tymes whiche ar commaunded of the Churche to be fasted, but it is leful *deleted.*

bownde to faste in Lenton, Ymbr' Days, Fridays, vigiles of seyntes ne other tymes whiche ar commaunded of the Churche to be fasted, but it is leful to every persone alle suche days and tymes to ete flessh indifferently at is own lust.

Also Y have holde, beleved and affermed that it is leful to every Cristene persone to do alle bodely werkes on Sondays and alle other days whiche ar commaunded of the Churche to*a* be had holy, if a man kepe hym from other synnes suche days.

Also Y have holde, beleved and affermed that every man may leefully withdrawe and withholde tithes and offrynges from churches and curates, so it be do prudently.

Also that Y have holde, beleved and affermed that it is no synne to the peple to do the contrarie of the preceptes of holy Churche.

Also tha[t] censures of the Churche be not to be dred ne fered, for*b* as sone as the bysshops acurse*c* ony*d* man, (p. 314 / fo. 82v)*e* God*f* assoileth and blesseth hym.

Also Y have holde, beleved and affermed that all prayers shuld be made only to God, and to noon other seyntes.

Also Y have holde, beleved and affermed that no maner of worship oweth to be do to ony ymages of the crucifix, of Our Lady Seynt Marie ne of noo other seyntes.

Also that no maner of pilgrimage oweth to be doo to ony seyntes, but the expenses whiche shuld be doo*g* or made in suche pilgrimages shuld be yoven to pore men.

Also Y held and have beleved that it is not leful a man to swere in ony caas.

Also Y have holde, beleved and affermed that the pope is Antecrist, and hath no poar in holy Churche as Seynt Petir hadde but if he folwe the*h* steppis of*i* Petr' in lyvyng, and all bisshops, prelates and prestes of the Churche ar Antecristes disciples.

Because of whiche and many other errours and heresies Y am called tofore you, worshipful fadir, whiche have cure of my soule. And be you fully informed that the said myn affermyng, belevyng and holdyng be opin errours and heresies and contrarious to the determinacion of the Churche of Rome, wherfor Y wyllyng folwe and sue the doctrine of holy Churche, and departe from alle maner of errour and heresie, and turne with good will and herte to the oonhed of the Churche. Considerant that holy Churche spereth not hir bosom to hym that will turne ageyn, ne God will not the deth of a synner but rather that he be turned and lyve, with a pure herte Y

---

a h *deleted.*
b af *deleted.*
c a *deleted.*
d ony *interlined.*
e Baldewinus Cowper *in top left-hand corner of page.*
f assoitle *deleted.*
g to ony ymages *deleted.*
h sp deleted.
i Per *deleted.*

confesse, deteste and despise my said errours and heresies, and the said opinions Y confesse hereticous and erroneous and to the faith of the Churche of Rome and al universal holy Churche repugnant. And for as moche as be the said thinges that Y so held, beleved and affermed Y shewed meself corrupt and unfaithful, that from hensforth Y shewe me uncorrupt and faithful, the faith and doctrine of holy Churche truly to kepe Y promitte. And all maner of errour and heresie, doctrine and opinion agayn the faith of holy Churche and determinacion of the Churche of Rome—and namely the opinions before rehersed—Y abjure and forswere, and swere be these holy gospels be me bodely touched that from hensforth Y shal never holde errour ne heresie ne fals doctrine ageyn the feith of holy Churche and determinacion of the Churche of Rome. Ne no suche thinges Y shal obstinatly defende. Ne no persone holdyng or teching suche maner of (p. 315 / fo. 83r)[a] thinges Y shal obstinatly defende be me or ony other persone opinly or prively. Y shal[b] never aftir this tyme be no recettour, fautour, consellour or defensour of heretikes or of ony persone suspect of heresie. Ne Y shal never trowe to thaym. Ne wittyngly Y shal felaship with, ne be hoomly with, thaym; ne gyve thaym consell, yeftes, sokour, favour ne confort. Yf Y knowe ony heretikes or of heresie ony persones suspect or of thaym fautours, confortours, consellours or defensours, or of ony persones makyng prive conventicules or assembles, or holdyng ony singuler opinions from the comune doctrine of the Churche, Y shal lete you, worshipful fadir, or your vicar general in your absence or the diocesanes of suche persones have sone and redy knowyng. So help me God atte holy doom and these holy gospels.

In wittenesse of whiche thynges Y subscribe here with myn hand a crosse +. And to this partie indented to remayne in your registre Y sette my signet. And that other partie indented Y receyve undir your seel to abyde with m[e] to my lyves ende. Yoven at Norwich in your chapell of your palaice the xviij day of the moneth of Aprill the yer of our Lord a thousand four hundred and thretty.

Qui quidem[c] Baldewinus Cowpere—dum magister Johannes Sutton, organum vocis ipsius Baldewini gerens, ut prefertur, fuit in legendo abiuracionem prescriptam—tangens manu sua dextera librum evangeliorum, iuravit ad ea quod ab hac hora in antea ipse omnia et singula in dicto scripto cirographo contenta, in quantum personam suam concernunt, iuxta ipsius scripti indentati exigenciam et tenorem inviolabiliter observabit. Et in huius rei testimonium in

---

[a] Baldewinus Cowper *in top right-hand corner of page.*
[b] late you *deleted.*   [c] Joh *deleted.*

utraque parte dicti scripti, super abiuracione sua concepti et indentati, signum crucis cum penna manu sua propria fecit pariter et
subscripsit coram dicto reverendo patre iudicialiter tunc ibidem.
Ac uni parti eiusdem scripti indentati, penes registrum dicti reverendi
patris [remansure, sigillum suum apposuit. Et alteram partem
eiusdem scripti indentati idem Baldewinus Cowper recepit in iudicio
tunc ibidem, sub sigillo ipsius reverendi patris]ᵃ sigillatam, penes
ipsum Baldewinum durante tocius vite sue tempore, ut asseruit,
permansuram. Et deinde idem Baldewinus iuravit ad sacra evangelia pretacta iudicialiter de parendo mandatis Ecclesie et de
per[ag]endo bene et fideliter penitenciam sibi per dictumᵇ rever-
endumᶜ patrem in hac parte iniungendam pro suis commissis
superius recitatis. Et subsequenter idem reverendus pater ipsum
Baldewinum a sentencia excommunicacionis, qua premissorum
occasione tenebatur astrictus, rite et canonice absolvebat sub eo
qui sequitur tenore verborum.

In Dei nomine, Amen. Quia nos, Willelmus, permissione divina
Norwicensis episcopus, contra te, Baldewinum Couper de Beccles
nostre diocesis, subditum nostrum et subiectum, per tuam, ex
officio (p. 316 / fo. 83v)ᵈ nostro legitime procedentes, confessionem
coram nobis iudicialiter factam invenimus te infra nostram diocesim
multas hereses et errores quamplures fidei orthodoxe et determinacioni sacrosancte ac universalis Ecclesie repugnantes—de quibus in
quodam cirographo super tua abiuracione concepto et indentato,
cuius una pars in archivis nostris noscitur remanere, ad quam nos
referimus et pro hic inserta haberi volumus, plenior fit mencio—
tenuisse, credidisse et affirmasse, et per hoc in excommunicacionis
sentenciam incidisse; nunc autem, usus consilio saniori, petis
misericordiam et sponte redis ad Ecclesie unitatem; idcirco, inprimis abiurata per te omni heresi et recepta per nos a te secundum
ritum Ecclesie iuratoria caucione de parendo mandatis Ecclesie, te
absolvimus ab omni excommunicacionis vinculo quo tenebaris
astrictus. Et quoniam per predicta que tenuisti, credidisti et affirmasti in Deum et sanctam matrem Ecclesiam temere deliquisti, tibi
pro pena penitenciali [iniungimus] quatuor fustigaciones circa cimiterium ecclesie parochialis de Beccles coram solenni processione
eiusdem quatuor diebus Dominicis horis consuetis facienda, capite
et pedibus denudatis, corpore camisia et femoralibus duntaxat
induto, more penitentis incedendo, et unum cereum cere ponderis

---

ᵃ *For the words supplied, see pp.* 118 *and* 123 *and elsewhere.*
ᵇ Baldewinum *deleted.*　　　　　　　　　ᶜ reverendum *interlined.*
ᵈ Baldewynus Cowper *in top left-hand corner of page.*

unius libre manu sua publice deferendo; et quatuor fustigaciones circa mercatum de Beccles predict' quatuor diebus mercati ibidem, nudis capite et pedibus, dictum cereum, ut premittitur, deferendo, corpore camisia et femoralibus duntaxat induto. Et quia tenuisti, credidisti et affirmasti fore licitum cuicumque fideli edere carnes et omnimoda cibaria indifferenter sextis feriis, diebus Quadragesimalibus, diebus Quatuor Temporum et vigiliis sanctorum indictis per Ecclesiam, tibi iniungimus quod omni sexta feria per annum iam proximum futurum in pane et aqua ieiunes, et*a* quod per duos annos*b* iam proximos et immediate sequentes omni quarta feria in Capite Ieiunii et omni quinta feria in Cena Domini coram nobis vel nostrum locum tenente in hac parte in ecclesia nostra Cathedrali Norwic' cum aliis penitentibus te presentes personaliter, acturus solennem penitenciam pro commissis.

Acta sunt hec prout suprascribuntur et recitantur sub Anno Domini, indiccione, pontificatu, mense, die et loco predictis. Presentibus discretis viris, magistris Thoma Hunter, in artibus magistro, et Willelmo Blytheburgh, presbiteris, necnon magistris Henrico Sharyngton et Roberto Aylmere, notariis publicis, Thoma Rudlond, Johanne Blytheburgh et aliis quampluribus tunc ibidem presentibus in multitudine numerosa; me, Johanne Excestre, scribente.

[26]

(p. 333 / fo. 92r) **Matildis, uxor Ricardi Fleccher de Beccles**[160]

In Dei nomine, Amen. Per presens publicum instrumentum cunctis appareat evidenter quod Anno ab Incarnacione Domini secundum cursum et computacionem Ecclesie Anglicane Millesimo Quadringentesimo Tricesimo, indiccione octava, pontificatus sanctissimi in Christo patris et domini nostri, domini Martini divina providencia pape quinti, anno terciodecimo, mense Aprilis die decimaoctava, in capella palacii reverendi in Christo patris et domini, domini Willelmi Dei gracia Norwicensis episcopi, in civitate Norwic' situati, in mei, Johannis Excestr, clerici, notarii publici, et testium subscriptorum presencia,*c* coram dicto reverendo patre pro tribunali ad iura reddenda—prout michi, notario prescripto, tunc apparebat—sedente, assistentibus tunc eidem reverendo patri

---

a [Pe]nitencia solennis *in margin.*
b continuos *deleted.*   *c* com *deleted.*

---

160 Beccles, north-east Suffolk.

venerabilibus et discretis viris, magistris Willelmo Worstede, priore ecclesie Cathedralis Norwicensis, ac[a] Johanne Elys, ordinis Fratrum Minorum, sacre pagine professoribus, necnon venerabili et religioso viro, fratre Edmundo Snetesham, priore ecclesie regularis de Cokefford, necnon discretis viris, magistris Willelmo Bernham, Thoma Ryngstede et Johanne Bury, in decretis bacallariis, Matildis Fleccher, uxor Ricardi Fleccher de Beccles Norwicensis diocesis, notata et multipliciter diffamata de heresi, [ad iudicium fuit adducta]. Cui quidem Matildi prefatus reverendus pater, ex officio suo procedens,[b] proposuit et obiecit, dicens eidem quod ipsa infra diocesim Norwicensem nonnullas hereses et errores quamplures tenuit, credidit et affirmavit.

Inprimis videlicet quod sacramentum Baptismi, factum in aqua in forma Ecclesie communiter usitata, parum vel modicum est ponderandum.

Item quod sacramentum Confirmacionis, per episcopos Ecclesie communiter ministratum, nichil proficit ad animarum salutem.

Item quod omnis confessio soli Deo est facienda, et non alteri sacerdoti.

Item quod nullus presbiter habet potestatem conficiendi verum corpus Christi in sacramento altaris, sed quod post omnia verba sacramentalia, a quocumque presbitero quantumcumque rite prolata, remanet in altari purus panis materialis.

Item quod solus consensus mutui amoris inter virum et mulierem sufficit pro sacramento matrimonii, absque[c] verborum expressione vel solennizacione in ecclesia.

Item quod nemo tenetur sanctificare aliquos dies indictos ab Ecclesia, diebus Dominicis dumtaxat exceptis, et licitum est cuilibet fideli[d] omnibus diebus indictis per Ecclesiam facere et exercere quecumque opera corporalia omnibus diebus huiusmodi, Dominicis diebus dumtaxat exceptis.

Item quod nullus honor est exhibendus aliquibus ymaginibus crucifixi vel alterius sancti.

Item quod peregrinaciones nullo modo sunt faciende, nisi tantum pauperibus.

Item quod omnis oracio facienda est soli Deo, et nullis aliis sanctis.

Item quod panis benedictus[e] et[f] aqua benedicta sunt nullius virtutis, nec sunt sancciores nec maioris virtutis propter aliquas benedicciones sive coniuraciones factas per[g] presbiteros super easdem.

---

[a] f *deleted.*
[c] p'la *deleted.*
[e] nec alq' *deleted.*
[g] l *deleted.*

[b] dixit *deleted.*
[d] d *deleted.*
[f] et *interlined.*

Quos quidem articulos omnes et singulos, ac*a* hereses et errores contentos in eisdem, prefata Matildis fatebatur et recognovit*b* iudicialiter se tenuisse, credidisse et affirmasse. Tamen eadem Matildis, super premissis per ipsam iudicialiter confessatis per prefatum reverendum patrem informata, concepit*c* dictos articulos nonnullas hereses et errores quamplures in se continere. Ideoque voluit, asseruit, ad Ecclesie redire unitatem, ac omnes hereses et errores per ipsam coram dicto patre, ut prefertur, iudicialiter confessatos ac omnes alias hereses et errores quoscumque re et verbo dimittere pro perpetuo et abiurare. Et iuravit eadem Matildis ad (p. 334 / fo. 92v)*d* sancta Dei evangelia per ipsam corporaliter tacta quod ab hac hora in antea ipsa nunquam tenebit nec affirmabit hereses nec errores nec falsam doctrinam seu opinionem contra*e* fidem sancte matris Ecclesie et determinacionem Ecclesie Romane; quodque de cetero non recipiet, supportabit nec celabit aliquam personam de heresi suspectam, nec eidem prebebit consilium, auxilium vel favorem; et si noverit aliquos hereticos vel de heresi aliquas personas suspectas sive ipsarum fautores, confortatores, conciliatores vel defensores, vel facientes privatas conventiculas aut [tenentes] singulares opiniones a communi doctrina Ecclesie discrepantes, ipsa faciet dictum patrem sive eius vicarium in spiritualibus generalem*f* aut diocesanos talium personarum de nominibus et personis earundem habere*g* certam et celerem expedicionem. Quibus sic peractis, et prestito per eandem Matildem alio iuramento ad sancta evangelia per ipsam tunc iudicialiter tacta propria in persona de parendo mandatis Ecclesie et de agendo penitenciam pro suis commissis prescriptis eidem a dicto patre iniungendam, prefatus reverendus pater eam absolvit a sentencia excommunicacionis qua premissorum occasione extitit innodata. Et iniunxit eidem Matildi penitenciam que sequitur pro commissis: videlicet, iij fustigaciones circa ecclesiam suam parochialem, corpore camisia solomodo induto,*h* capite et pedibus denudatis, cum cereo cere ponderis dimidie libre manibus suis deferendo, et more penitentis incedendo, coram solenni processione dicte ecclesie de Beccles facienda tribus diebus Dominicis more*i* et tempore solitis;*j* et totidem fustigaciones circa mercatum de Beccles, cum cereo predicto conformiter incedendo.

Acta sunt hec prout suprascribuntur et recitantur sub Anno Domini, indiccione, pontificatu, mense, die et loco suprascriptis. Presentibus tunc ibidem magistris Willelmo Ascogh, sacre pagine,

a er *deleted.*
b t *deleted.*
c One or two illegible letters deleted.
d Matildis, uxor Ricardi Fleccher *in top left-hand corner of page:* ad *repeated.*
e ecclesiam *deleted.*
f de nominibus ipsarum per *deleted.*
g certi' *deleted.*
h MS. induta.
i solit *deleted.*
j faciend' *repeated.*

Johanne Sutton, legum, bacallariis, ac Thoma Hunter, in artibus
magistro, et me, Johanne Excestr, notario publico.

[27]

(p. 335 / fo. 93r) **Johannes Eldon, glover, de Beccles**[161]

In Dei nomine, Amen. Per presens publicum instrument[um]
cunctis appareat evidenter quod Anno Domini ab Incarnacione
eiusdem secundum cursum et computacionem Ecclesie Anglicane
Millesimo CCCC^{mo} Tricesimo, indiccione octava, pontificatus
sanctissimi in Christo patris et domini nostri, domini Martini
divina providencia pape quinti, anno terciodecimo, mensis Aprilis
die decimaoctava, in mei, Johannis Excestre, clerici, publici auctoritate apostolica notarii, ac testium subscriptorum presencia, coram
reverendo in Christo patre ac domino, domino Willelmo Dei gracia
Norwicensi episcopo, in capella palacii sui Norwic' situati pro
tribunali^a ad iura reddenda—prout michi, notario prescripto, tunc
apparebat—iudicialiter sedente, assistentibus eidem reverendo
patri tunc ibidem venerabilibus et discretis viris, magistris Johanne
Elys, ordinis Minorum, sacre pagine professore, necnon fratre
Edmundo Snetesham, priore ecclesie sive prioratus de Cokesford, ac
magistris Willelmo Bernham et Thoma Ryngstede ac Johanne Bury,
in decretis, Johanne Sutton, in legibus, et Willelmo Ascogh, in sacra
theologia, bacallariis, Johannes Eldon, glover de Becles, multipliciter, ut dicebatur, diffamatus de crimine heretice pravitatis et
ea occasione responsurus, in vinculis ad iudicium personaliter fuit
adductus, ac de et super omnibus et singulis heresibus et erroribus,
in quodam scripto cirographo super abiuracione eiusdem Johannis
Eldon concepto et indentato contentis plenarie et conscriptis, per
prefatum reverendum patrem iudicialiter impetitus. Qui quidem
Johannes Eldon omnes et singulas hereses et errores omnimodos in
dicto scripto indentato, cuius tenor inferius describitur, contentos
et per prefatum reverendum patrem eidem Johanni Eldon^b tunc
ibidem obiectos iudicialiter et articulatos fatebatur et recognovit
iudicialiter se infra diocesim Norwicensem tenuisse, credidisse et
affirmasse. Et subsequenter tunc ibidem idem Johannes, volens et
affectans, ut asseruit, puro corde ad Ecclesie unitatem redire, ac

---

^{a} sedent *deleted.* ^{b} tuic *deleted.*

---

[161] Beccles, north-east Suffolk.

omnes hereses et errores in dicto scripto indentato contentos et specificatos ac per ipsum tunc ibidem coram prefato patre iudicialiter confessatos ac alios errores et hereses quascumque*a* re et verbo dimittere pro perpetuo et abiurare secundum formam et tenorem in dicto scripto cirographo indentato specificatos, quos, ut asseruit, prius audivit et plenarie intellexit, et quia idem Johannes Eldon asseruit se esse mere laicum et legere nescientem, ipse constituit*b* discretum virum, magistrum Willelmum*c* Worstede, priorem ecclesie Cathedralis (p. 336 / fo. 93v) Sancte Trinitatis Norwic', sacre pagine professorem, tunc ibidem presentem, organum vocis sue. Cui ipse Johannes commisit plenariam potestatem nomine suo et pro se dictam abiuracionem in prefato scripto indentato conceptam et contentam coram ipso reverendo patre legendi et interponendi iudicialiter tunc ibidem. Et deinde idem magister Willelmus Worstede, organum vocis ipsius Johannis in hac parte in se assumens, abiuracionem eiusdem Johannis Eldon fecit, legit et interposuit secundum formam in dicto scripto indentato contentam, cuius tenor de verbo ad verbum sequitur et est talis.*d*

(p. 337 / fo. 94r)*e* In the name of God, tofore you, the worshipful fadir in Crist, William, be the grace of God bysshop of Norwich, Y, John Eldon, glover of Beccles of your diocese, felyng and undirstandyng that Y have be familier with heretikes, that is to say with Sir Huwe Pye and many other, be whos untrewe doctrine Y was enformed of these errours and heresies, whiche Y have holde, beleved and affermed withynne your diocese,

That is to say that the sacrament of Baptem doon in water in fourme customed in the Churche is of noon availe and not to be pondred if the fadir and modir of the childe be cristened and of Cristen beleve.

Also that the sacrament of Confirmacion doon be a bisshop is unvaillable and not profitable to mannys sowle ne to his lyve.

Also that confession oweth to be made unto no prest, but oonly to God, for no prest hath poar to assoile a man of ony synne.

Also Y have hold, beleved and afermed that no prest hath poar to make Goddys body in the sacrament of the auter, and that aftir the sacramental wordis said of the prest at messe ther remayneth nothing but oonly a cake of material bred.

a et *deleted.*
b v *deleted.*
c Willelmum *repeated.*
d In the (*a deleted* n *ends* the) name of God, prout sequitur in folio proximo sequente *follows* talis.
e John Eldon, glover de Becles *at top of page.*

Also that oonly consent of love in Jhu' Crist to make the sacramentes, and non other erthly man.[a]

Also that man ne woman is bounde to do ony penance whiche is enjoyned to hym of ony prest in Confession because that no prest hath poar of the Churche to be fasted, but it is leful to every persone alle suche days and tymes to ete flessh and all maner of metis indifferently at is own lust.

Also Y have holde, beleved and affermed that it is leful to every Cristene persone[b] to do alle bodyly werkes on Sondays and alle other days whiche ar commaunded of[c] the Churche to be had holy, if a man kepe hym from synnes suche days.

Also that Y have hold, beleved and affermed that every man and woman may leefully withdrawe and withholde tythes and offrynges from churches and curates, so it be do prudently.

Also that [Y] have holde, beleved and affermed that it is no synne to the peple to do the contrarie of the preceptis of holy Churche.

Also that the censures of the Churche be not to be dred ne fered, for as sone as the bisshops acurse ony man, God asoileth and blesseth hym.

Also Y have holde, beleved and affermed that alle prayers shuld be made only to God, and to noon other seyntes.

Also Y have holde, beleved and afermed that no maner of worship owith to be doo to ony ymages of the crucifix, of Our Lady Seynt Marie ne of noon other seyntes.

Also that no maner of pilgrimage oweth to be do to ony seyntes, but the expenses whiche shuld be doo or made in suche pilgrimages shuld be yoven to pore men.

Also Y held and have beleved that it is not lefull a man to swere in ony caas.

Also Y holde, beleved (p. 338 / fo. 94v)[d] and affermed that the pope is Antecrist, and hath no poar in holy Churche as Seint Petir hadde but if he folwe the steppis of Petre in lyvyng, and all bisshops, prelates and prestis of the Churche ar Antecristis disciples.

Because of whiche and many other errours and heresies Y am called tofore you, worshipful fadir, whiche have cure of my sowle. And be you fully informed that the said myn affermyng, belevyng and holdyng be opin errours and heresies and contrarious to the determinacion of the Churche of Rome, wherfor Y willyng folwe and sue the doctrine of holy Churche, and departe from all maner of errour and heresie, and turne with good will and herte to the oonhed

---

[a] *This, and the next, paragraph each consists of two articles conflated into one by mistake.*

[b] alle suche days and tymes *deleted.*

[c] th' *deleted.*

[d] John Eldon *in top left-hand corner of page*

of the Churche. Considerant that holy Churche spereth not hir bosom to hym that will turne*a* ageyn, ne God wil not the deth of a synner but rather that he be turned and lyve, with a pure herte Y confesse, deteste and despise my saide errours and heresies, and these said opinions Y confesse hereticous and erroneous and to the faith of the Churche of Rome and all universall holy Churche repugnant. And for as moche as be the said thinges that Y so held, beleved and afermed Y shewed me*b* self corrupt and unfaithful, that from hensforth Y shewe me uncorrupt and faithful, the faith and doctrine of holy Churche truly to kepe Y promitte. And all maner of errour and heresie, doctrine and opinion ageyn the faith of holy Churche and determinacion of the Churche of Rome—and namely the opinions before rehersed—Y abjure and forswere, and swere be these holy gospels be me bodely touched that from hensforth Y shal never holde errour ne*c* heresie*d* ne fals doctrine ageyn the faith of holy Churche and determinacion of the Churche of Rome. Ne no suche thynges Y shal obstinatly defende. Ne no persone holdyng or techynge*e* suche maner of thinges Y shal obstinatly defende be me or ony other persone opynly or pryvely. Y shal never aftir this time be no recettour, fautour, consellour or defensour of heretikes or of ony persone suspect of heresie. Ne Y shal trowe to thaym. Ne wittyngly Y shal felaship with thaym, ne be hoomly with thaym, ne gyve thaym consel, yeftes, sokour, favour ne confort. Yf Y knowe ony heretikes or of heresie ony persones suspect or of thaym fautours, confortours, consellours or defensours, or of ony persones makyng prive conventicules or assembles, or holdyng ony singuler opinions from the comune doctrine of the Churche, Y shal lete you, worshipful fadir, or your vicar general in your absence or the diocesanes of suche persones, have sone and redy knowyng. So help me God atte holy doom and these holy gospels.

In wittenesse of whiche thinges Y subscribe her with myn owyn hand a crosse +. And to this partie indented to remayne in your registre Y sette my signet. And that other partie indented Y receyve undir your seel to abyde with me into my lyves ende. Yoven at Norwich in your chapell of your palays the xviij day of the moneth [of] Aprill the yer of oure Lord a thousand four hundred and*f* thretty.*g*

(p. 339 / fo. 95r)*h* Qui quidem Johannes Eldon—dum magister Willelmus Worstede, organum vocis ipsius Johannis gerens, ut

a g *deleted.*   *b* ses *deleted.*
c errours *deleted.*   *d* heresie *interlined.*
e MS. tochyng.   *f* tretty *deleted.*
g qui quidem Johannes Eldon *in bottom right-hand corner of page.*
h Johannes Eldon *in top right-hand corner of page.*

prefertur, fuit in legendo abiuracionem prescriptam—ta[n]gens manu sua dextera librum evangeliorum, iuravit ad ea quod ab hac hora in antea ipse omnia et singula in dicto scripto cirographo contenta, in quantum personam suam concernunt, iuxta ipsius scripti indentati exigenciam et tenorem inviolabiliter observabit. Et in huius rei testimonium in utraque parte dicti scripti, super abiuracione sua concepti et indentati, signum crucis cum penna manu sua propria fecit pariter et subscripsit coram dicto reverendo patre iudicialiter tunc ibidem. Ac uni parti eiusdem scripti indentati, penes registrum dicti reverendi patris remansure, sigillum suum apposuit. Et alteram partem eiusdem scripti indentati idem Johannes Eldon [recepit] in[a] iudicio tunc ibidem, sub sigillo ipsius reverendi patris sigillatam, penes ipsum Johannem durante tocius vite sue tempore, ut asseruit, permansuram. Et deinde idem Johannes iuravit ad sacra evangelia pretacta iudicialiter de parendo mandatis Ecclesie et de peragendo bene et fideliter penitenciam sibi per dictum[b] reverendum[c] patrem in hac parte iniungendam pro suis commissis superius recitatis. Et subsequenter idem reverendus pater ipsum Johannem a sentencia excommunicacionis, qua premissorum occasione tenebatur astrictus, rite et canonice absolvebat sub eo qui sequitur tenore verborum.

In Dei nomine, Amen. Quia nos, Willelmus, permissione divina Norwicensis episcopus, contra te, Johannem Eldon de Beccles nostre diocesis, subditum nostrum et subiectum,[d] ex officio nostro legitime procedentes, per tuam[e] confessionem coram nobis iudicialiter factam invenimus te infra nostram diocesim multas hereses et errores quamplures fidei orthodoxe et determinacioni sacrosancte ac universalis Ecclesie repugnantes—de quibus in quodam cirographo super tua abiuracione concepto et indentato, cuius una pars in archivis nostris noscitur remanere, ad quam nos referimus et pro hic inserta haberi volumus, plenior fit mencio—tenuisse, credidisse et affirmasse, et per hoc in excommunicacionis sentenciam incidisse; nunc autem, usus consilio saniori, petis misericordiam et sponte redis ad Ecclesie unitatem; idcirco, inprimis abiurata per te omni heresi et recepta per nos a te secundum ritum Ecclesie iuratoria caucione de parendo mandatis Ecclesie, te absolvimus ab omni excommunicacionis vinculo quo tenebaris astrictus. Et quoniam per predicta que tenuisti, credidisti et affirmasti in Deum et sanctam matrem Ecclesiam temere deliquisti, tibi pro pena penitenciali[f]

---

[a] d deleted.
[b] Johannem deleted.
[c] reverendum interlined.
[d] per tuam deleted.
[e] per tuam interlined.
[f] affirmasti deleted.

[iniungimus] quatuor fustigaciones circa cimiterium ecclesie parochialis de Beccles coram solenni processione eiusdem quatuor diebus Dominicis horis consuetis facienda, capite et pedibus denudatis, corpore camisia et femoralibus dumtaxat induto, more penitentis incendendo, et unum cereum cere ponderis unius libre manu sua publice deferendo; et quatuor (p. 340 / fo. 95v) fustigaciones circa mercatum de Beccles predict' quatuor diebus mercati ibidem, nudis capite et*a* pedibus, dictum cereum, ut premittitur, deferendo, corpore camisia et femoralibus dumtaxat induto. Et quia tenuisti, credidisti et affirmasti fore licitum cuicumque fideli edere carnes et omnimoda cibaria indifferenter sextis feriis, diebus Quadragesimalibus, diebus Quatuor Temporum et vigiliis sanctorum indictis per Ecclesiam, tibi iniungimus quod omni sexta feria per annum iam proximum futurum in pane et aqua ieiunes, et*b* quod per duos annos continuos iam proximos et immediate sequentes omni quarta feria in Capite Ieiunii et omni quinta feria in Cena Domini coram nobis vel nostrum locum tenente in hac parte in ecclesia nostra Cathedrali Norwic' cum aliis penitentibus te presentes personaliter, acturus solennem penitenciam pro commissis.

Acta sunt hec prout suprascribuntur et recitantur sub Anno Domini, indiccione, pontificatu, mense, die et loco predictis. Presentibus discretis viris magistro Thoma Hunter, in artibus magistro, et Willelmo Bamburgh, presbiteris, necnon magistris Henrico Sharyngton et Roberto Aylmere, notariis publicis, Thoma Rodelond, Johanne Blytheburgh et aliis quampluribus tunc ibidem presentibus in multitudine numerosa; Johanne Excestre, scribente.

[28]

(p. 352 / fo. 101v) **Hawisia Moone, uxor Thome Moone de Lodne**[162]

In Dei nomine, Amen. Per presens publicum instrumentum cunctis appareat evidenter quod Anno ab Incarnacione Domini secundum cursum et computacionem Ecclesie Anglicane Millesimo Quadringestesimo Tricesimo, indiccione octava, pontificatus sanctissimi in Christo patris et domini*c* nostri, domini Martini divina providencia pape quinti, anno terciodecimo, mensis Augusti die quarta,*d*

a capite et *interlined*.   *b* Penitencia solennis per duos annos *in margin*.
c d *deleted*.   *d* mensis Augusti die quarta *interlined*.

162 Loddon, south-east Norfolk.

coram reverendo in Christo patre ac domino, domino Willelmo Dei gracia Norwicensi episcopo, in capella palacii sui Norwic' pro tribunali ad reddenda iura—ut michi, Johanni Excestr, clerico, notario publico prescripto, tunc apparebat—in mei, Johannis Excestr, notarii, et testium subscriptorum presencia[a] sedente, assidentibus eidem reverendo patri tunc ibidem magistris Willelmo[b] Worstede, priore ecclesie Cathedralis Norwic', ac Johanne Paas, ordinis Fratrum Minorum, sacre pagine professoribus, ac Willelmo Ascogh et Roberto Woler,[163] sacre theologie bacallariis, necnon Thoma Ryngstede, in decretis bacallario, adducta fuit ad iudicium Hawisia Moone, uxor Thome Moone de Lodne Norwicensis diocesis, diffamata et vehementer suspecta de heresi et ea occasione arestata et sub carcerali custodia servata,[c] personaliter responsura. Cui quidem Hawisie prefatus reverendus pater, contra eam ex officio legitime procedens, dixit, proposuit et obiecit omnes articulos in quodam scripto cirographo, super abiuracione eiusdem Hawisie[d] in lingua Anglicana concepto et indentato, conscriptos ac omnes hereses et errores in eisdem articulis contentos. Quos quidem articulos ac[e] omnes errores et hereses in eis contentos eadem Hawisia fatebatur et recognovit iudicialiter se tenuisse, credidisse, asseruisse et affirmasse.[f] Et deinde ipsa Hawisia, informata per dictum reverendum patrem quod dicti articuli continent in se nonnullas hereses et errores quamplures, asseruit coram dicto patre se velle ipsos articulos ac omnes hereses et errores in eis contentos, necnon omnem heresim in genere, puro corde dimittere pro perpetuo et abiurare sub forma et tenore in dicto scripto indentato contentis. Quos formam et tenorem magister Johannes Wylly, notarius publicus, de mandato domini eidem Hawisie publice perlegit in ydeomate Anglicano. Et[g] quos quidem formam et tenorem ipsa Hawisia, ut asseruit, audivit et plenarie intellexit. Et deinde ipsa Hawisia, asserens se nescire legere tenorem dicte abiuracionis sue, constituit dictum magistrum Johannem Wylly organum vocis sue ad legendam huiusmodi abiuracionem suam vice et nomine ipsius Hawisie. Et ad hoc faciendum eadem Hawisia ipsum magistrum Johannem Wylly requisivit cum instancia et[h] rogavit. Qui quidem magister Johannes Wylly, per ipsam Hawisiam sic rogatus, ut premittitur, et requisitus, tenorem abiuracionis ipsius Hawysee publice in iudicio perlegit. Et interim eadem Hawisia,[i] genuflectens et manum suam dexteram

---

[a] iudicialiter *deleted.*
[b] J *deleted.*
[c] adducta fuit ad iudicium *repeated.*
[d] c *deleted.*
[e] erro *deleted.*
[f] que q *deleted.*
[g] Et *interlined.*
[h] *An illegible word deleted.*
[i] te *deleted.*

---

[163] See Emden, *BRUO*, iii, p. 2076, Robert Woller.

F

super librum evangeliorum [tenens], iuravit ad ea se amodo imperpetuum observaturam omnia et singula contenta in dicto scripto
indentato super ipsius abiuracione[a] sic concepto ac nomine et vice[b]
eiusdem Hawisie perlecto, in quantum concernunt personam ipsius
Hawisie, (p. 353 / fo. 102r) iuxta omnem vim, formam et effectum
dicti scripti indentati, cuius tenor sequitur [et] est talis.

In the name of God, tofore you, the worshipful fadir in Crist,
William, be the grace of God bisshop of Norwich, Y, Hawise Moone,
the wyfe of Thomas Moone of Lodne of your diocese, your subject,
knowyng, felyng and undirstandyng that before this tyme Y have
be right hoomly and prive with many heretikes, knowyng [thaym]
for heretikes, and thaym Y have receyved and herberwed in our
hous, and thaym Y have conceled, conforted, supported, maytened
and favored with al my poar—whiche heretikes names be these, Sir
William Whyte, Sir William Caleys,[164] Sir Huwe Pye, Sir Thomas
Pert, prestes, John Waddon, John Fowlyn, John Gray, William
Everden, William Bate of Sethyng,[165] Bartholomeu Cornmonger,
Thomas Borell and Baty, hys wyf, William Wardon,[166] John Pert,
Edmond Archer of Lodne, Richard Belward, Nicholas Belward,
Bertholomeu Monk, William Wright and many others—whiche have
ofte tymes kept, holde and continued scoles of heresie yn prive
chambres and prive places of oures, yn the whyche scoles Y have
herd, conceyved, lerned and reported the errours and heresies
which be writen and contened in these indentures, that is to say,

Fyrst that the sacrament of Baptem doon in watir in forme cus-
tomed in the Churche is but a trufle and not to be pondred, for alle
Cristis puple is sufficiently baptized in the blood of Crist, and so
Cristis puple nedeth noon other baptem.

Also that the sacrament of Confirmacion doon be a bisshop is of
noon availe ne necessarie to be had for as muche as whan a child hath
discrecion and can and wile undirstande the word of God it is sufficiently confermed be the Holy Gost and nedeth noon other confirmacion.

Also that confession shuld be maad oonly to God, and to noon
other[c] prest, for no prest hath poar to remitte synne ne to assoile a
man of ony synne.

---

[a] con *deleted.*   [b] sup *deleted.*   [c] seynt *deleted.*

---

[164] He was degraded and burnt as a Lollard at Chelmsford on 7 June 1430
(*Annales Monasterii Sancti Albani a Johanne Amundesham conscripti*, ed.
H. T. Riley (Rolls Series, London, 1870–1), i, p. 51). Also, see above, p. 33,
n. 14.
[165] Seething, south-east Norfolk.   [166] See p. 45, n. 45.

Also that no man is bounde to do no penance whiche ony prest enjoyneth [hym]*a* to do for here synnes whyche thei have confessed unto the pr[est], for sufficient penance for all maner of synne is every persone to abstyne hym fro lyyng, bakbytyng and yvel doyng, and no man is bounde to do noon other penance.

Also that no prest hath poar to make Cristis veri body at messe in forme of (p. 354 / fo. 102v)*b* bred, but that aftir the sacramental wordis said at messe of the prest ther remayneth oonly material bred.

Also that the pope of Roome is fadir Antecrist, and fals in all hys werkyng, and hath no poar of God more than ony other lewed man but if he be more holy in lyvyng, ne the pope hath no poar to make bisshops, prestes ne non other ordres, and he that the puple callen the pope of Roome is no pope but a fals extersioner and a deseyver of the puple.

Also that he oonly that is moost holy and moost perfit in lyvyng in erthe is verry pope, and these singemesses that be cleped prestes ben no prestes, but thay be lecherous and covetouse men and fals deceyvours of the puple, and with thar sotel techyng and prechyng, syngyng and redyng piteously thay pile the puple of thar good, and tharwith thay susteyne here pride, here lechery, here slowthe and alle other vices, and alway thay makyn newe lawes and newe ordinances to curse and kille cruelly all other persones that holden ageyn thar vicious levyng.

Also that oonly consent of love betuxe man and woman, withoute contract of wordis and withoute solennizacion in Churche and withoute symbred askyng, is sufficient for the sacrament of matrymoyn.

Also it is but a trufle to enoynt a seke man with material oyle consecrat be a bisshop, for it sufficeth every man at hys last ende oonly to have mende of God.

Also that every man may lefully withdrawe and withholde tythes and offringes from prestes and curates and yeve hem to the pore puple, and that is moore plesyng to God.

Also that the temporal lordis and temporel men may lefully take alle possessions and temporel godys from alle men of holy Churche, and from alle bysshops and prelates bothe hors and harneys, and*c* gyve thar good to pore puple, and therto the temporel men be bounde in payne of dedly synne.

[Als]o that it is no synne ony persone to do the contrarie of the preceptes [of] holy Churche.

---

a The wearing away of the edge of this and the next two folios explains why many letters have been supplied.
b Hawisia Moone *in top left-hand corner of page.*   *c* y *deleted.*

Also that every man and every woman beyng in good lyf oute of synne is as good prest and hath [as] muche poar of God in al thynges as ony prest ordred,*a* be he pope or bisshop.

Also that censures of holy Churche, sentences*b* and cursynges ne of suspendyng yeven be prelates or ordinaries be not to be dred ne to be fered, for God blesseth the cursynges (p. 355 / fo. 103r)*c* [of] the bisshops and ordinaries.

Also that it is not leful to swere in ony caas, ne it is not leful to pletyn for onythyng.

Also that it is not leful to slee a man for ony cause, ne be processe of lawe to dampne ony traytour or ony man for ony treson or felonie to deth, ne to putte ony man to deth for ony cause, but every man shuld remitte*d* all vengeance oonly to the sentence of God.

Also that no man is bounde to faste in Lenton, Ymbren Days, Fridays ne vigiles of seyntes, but all suche days and tymes it is leful to alle Cristis puple to ete flessh and [all] maner metis indifferently at here owne lust as ofte as thay have appetite as wel as ony other days whiche be not commanded to be fasted.

Also that no pilgrimage oweth to be do ne be made, for all pilgrimage goyng servyth of nothyng but oonly to yeve prestes good that be to riche and to make gay tap[s]ters and proude ostelers.

Also that no worship ne reverence oweth be do to ony ymages of the crucifix, of Our Lady ne of noon other seyntes, for all suche ymages be but ydols and maade be werkyng of mannys hand, but worship and reverence shuld be do to the ymage of God, whiche oonly is man.

Also that al prayer oweth be maad oonly to God, and to noon other seyntes, for it is doute if thar be ony suche seyntes in hevene as these singemesse aproven and commaunden to be worsheped and prayed to here in erthe.

Because of whiche and many other errours and heresies Y am called tofore you, worshipful fadir, whiche have cure of my soule. And be you fully informed that the said myn affermyng, belevyng and holdyng be opin errours and heresies and contrarious to the determinacion of the Churche of Roome, wherefor Y willyng folwe and sue the doctrine of holy Churche and departe from al maner of errour and heresie, and turne with good will and herte to the oonhed of the Churche. Considerand that holy Churche spereth not hyr bosom to hym that wil turne agayn, ne God wil not the deth of a synner but rather that he be turned and lyve, (p. 356 / fo. 103v) with a pure herte Y confesse, deteste and despise my sayd errours and heresies, and these

---

a h *deleted.*   *b* of *deleted.*
c Hawis' Mone *in top right-hand corner of page:* the cursynges *repeated.*
d synne *deleted.*

said opinions Y confesse hereticous and erroneous and to the feith
of the Churche of Rome and all universall holy Churche repugnant.
And for as muche as be the said thinges that Y so held, beleved and
affermed Y shewed meself corrupt and unfaithful, that from hensforth Y shewe me uncorrupt and faithful, the feith and doctrine of
holy Churche truly to kepe Y promitte. And all maner of errour and
heresie, doctrine and opinion ageyn the feith of holy Churche and
determinacion of the Churche of Roome—and namely the opinions
before rehersed—Y abjure and forswere, and swere be these holy
gospels be me bodely touched that from hensforth Y shal never
holde errour ne heresie ne fals doctrine ageyn the feith of holy
Churche and determinacion of the Churche of Roome. Ne no suche
thinges Y shal obstinatly defende, ne ony persone holdyng or
techyng suche maner of thynges Y shal obstinatly defende be me or
ony other persone opinly or prively. Y shal never aftir this time be
no recettour, fautour, consellour or defensour of heretikes or of ony
persone suspect of heresie. Ne Y shal never trowe to thaym. Ner
wittyngly Y shal felaship with thaym, ne be hoomly with tham, ne
gyve thaym consell, sokour, favour ne confort. Yf Y knowe ony
heretikes or of heresie ony persones suspect or of thaym fautours,
confortours, consellours or defensours, or of ony persone makyng
prive conventicules or assembles, or holdyng ony divers or singuler
opinions from the commune doctrine of the Churche, Y shal late
you, worshipful fadir, or your vicar general in your absence or the
diocesans of suche persones have sone and redy knowyng. So help me
God atte holy doom and these holy gospels.

In wittenesse of which thinges Y subscribe here with myn owen
hand a cross +. And to this partie indented to remayne in your
registre Y sette^a my signet.^b And that other partie^c indented Y
receyve undir your seel to abide with me unto my lyves ende.
Yoven at Norwich in the chapell of your palays the iiij day of the
moneth of August the yer of our Lord a thousand four hundred and
thretty.

(p. 357 / fo. 104r)^d With a pure herte Y confesse, deteste and
despise my said errours and heresies, and these said opinions Y
confesse hereticous and erroneous and to the faith of the Churche of
Roome and all universal holy Churche repugnant. And for as muche
as be the said thinges that Y so held, beleved and affermed Y shewed
me^e self corrupt and unfaithful, that from hensforth Y shewe me

---

^a y *deleted.*   ^b th *deleted.*   ^c nd *deleted.*
^d H. Mone *in top right-hand corner of page. The contents of this page repeat,
or no apparent reason, those of the previous page.*   ^e ses *deleted.*

uncorrupt and faith[ful], the feith and doctrine of holy Churche truly to kepe Y promitte. And all maner of errour and heresie, doctrine and opinion ageyn the feith of holy Churche and deter-minacion of the Churche of Roome—and namely the opinions before rehersed—Y abjure and forswere, and swere be these holy gospels[a] be me bodely touched that from hensforth Y shal never holde errour ne heresie ne fals doctrine ageyn the feith of holy Churche and determinacion of the Churche of Roome. Ne no suche thinges Y shal obstinatly defende. Ne ony persone holdyng or techyng suche maner of thinges Y shal obstinatly defende be me or ony other persone opinly or prively. Y shal never aftir this tyme be no recettour, fautour, consel[lour] or defensour of heretikes or of ony persone suspect of heresie. N[e] Y shal never trowe to thaym. Ner[b] wyttyngly Y sh[al] felashyip with thaym, ne be hoomly with thaym, ne gyve thay[m] consell, yeftes, sokour, favour ne confort. Yf Y knowe ony heretikes or of heresie ony persones suspect or of thaym fautours, confortours or defensours, or of ony persones makyng prive con-venticules or assembles, or holdyng ony divers or singuler opinions from the commune doctrine of the Churche, Y shal late you, wor-shipful fadir, or your vicar general in your absence or the diocesans of suche persones have soone and redy knowyng. So help me God atte holy doom and these holy gospels.

In wittenesse of which thinges Y subscribe here with myn owen hand a crosse +. And to this partie indented to remayne in your registre Y sett[e] my signet. And that other partie indented Y reseyve undir your seel to abide with me unto my lyves ende. Yoven at Norwich in the chapell of your palaice the iiij day of the moneth [of] August the yer of our Lord a thousand four hundred an[d] thretty.

[29]

(p. 317 / fo. 84r) **Johannes Skylan de Bergh**[167]

In Dei nomine, Amen. Per presens publicum instrumentum cunctis appareat evidenter quod[c] Anno ab Incarnacione Domini secundum cursum et computacionem Ecclesie Anglicane Millesimo Quadringentesimo Tricesimo, indiccione octava, pontificatus sanc-

---

[a] *MS.* golpels. [b] wittyyn *deleted.* [c] qi *deleted.*

[167] Probably Bergh Apton, south-east Norfolk. He may have been the same person as John Skilly of Bergh, for whose arrest and earlier activities see pp. 218–19.

tissimi in Christo patris et domini nostri, domini Martini divina providencia pape quinti, anno terciodecimo,[a] coram reverendo in Christo patre ac domino, domino Willelmo Dei gracia Norwicensi episcopo, in capella palacii sui[b] Norwic'—in mei, Johannis Excestr, clerici, notarii publici, et testium subscriptorum presencia[c]—iudicialiter sedente, assistentibus[d] eidem tunc ibidem venerabilibus et religiosis viris, magistris Willelmo Worstede, priore ecclesie Cathedralis Sancte Trinitatis Norwic', ac Johanne Paas, ordinis Fratrum Minorum, sacre theologie professoribus, ac magistris Willelmo Ascogh et Roberto Woler, in sacra[e] theologia,[f] et Thoma Ryngstede, in decretis, bacallariis, adductus fuit in vinculis Johannes Skylan, filius Walteri Skylan de[g] Bergh Norwicensis diocesis, dicti reverendi patris subditus et subiectus. Propter suspicionem heresis pridium arestatus ac diucius incarceratus,[h] adductus fuit ad iudicium in vinculis super crimine heretice pravitatis personaliter responsurus. Cui quidem Johanni Skylan prefatus reverendus in Christo pater iudicialiter sedens omnes articulos in quodam scripto cirographo super abiuracione dicti Johannis Skylan in hac parte concepto et indentato, cuius tenor inferius continetur, in vulgari Anglicano scriptos et contentos[i] ac omnes hereses et errores in eisdem articulis specificatos dixit, obiecit et proposuit articulando. Quos quidem articulos omnes et singulos, ac universas hereses et errores in eis contentos, eidem Johanni iudicialiter tunc ibidem obiectos idem Johannes fatebatur et recognovit iudicialiter se tenuisse, credidisse et asseruisse. Quos quidem articulos prefatus reverendus pater asseruit dicto Johanni nonnullas hereses et errores quamplures in se[j] notorie continere. Ideoque[k] placuit dicto Johanni Skylan, ut asseruit, dictos hereses ac errores ac generaliter omnem heresim re et verbo dimittere pro perpetuo et abiurare secundum formam et tenorem in dicto cirographo scripto et indentato contentos[l] et coram dicto Johanne de mandato dicti reverendi patris perlectos et per ipsum, ut asseruit, plenarie intellectos. Et quia idem Johannes Skylan asseruit se fore laicum et legere suam abiuracionem nescientem, ipse constituit magistrum Johannem Wylly organum vocis sue, et rogavit ipsum ad legendam abiuracionem suam vice sua. Qui quidem Johannes Wylly, organum vocis dicti Johannis Skylan in se suscipiens, totam abiuracionem[m] ipsius Johannis Skylan vice sua iudicialiter perlegit ceteraque perfecit prout in eodem scripto

---

[a] coram reverendo *deleted*. [b] d *deleted*.
[c] in mei, Johannis Excestr . . . presencia *interlined*.
[d] t *deleted*. [e] *MS.* sacrai.
[f] ba *deleted*. [g] no *deleted*.
[h] super crimine heretice pravitatis *deleted*. [i] *MS.* contentes.
[j] a *deleted*. [k] idem Johannes Skylan voluit *deleted*.
[l] quos quidem tenorem et formam idem Jo *deleted*. [m] suam *deleted*.

cirographo super ipsius*a* Johannis abiuracione huiusmodi, ut prefertur, concepto et indentato continetur, cuius tenor sequitur et est talis.

In the name of God, tofore you, the worshipful fadir in Crist, William, be the grace of God bisshop of Norwich, Y, John Skylan, the sone of Watte Skylan of Bergh of your diocese, your subject, felyng and undirstandyng that be[fore] this tyme Y have [be] muche conversant and hoomly with many sundry heretikes, knowyng thaym for heretikes—that is to say, Sir (p. 318 / fo. 84v) William White, Sir Huwe Pye, Sir Thomas Peert and Sir William Caleys, prestes, John Waddon, John Fowlyn, John Grey, William Everden, Thomas Everden, Bartholomeu Cornmonger, Richard Belward, Nicholas Belward, Thomas Borell of Lodne,[168] Batild, hys wyf, William Bate of Sethyng[169] and many others—whos scoles Y have longe continued and kept, first with Sir William White at Bergh[170] and sythen at Colcestre[171] with John Werkewode and many others and aftir that at London with divers persones, yn whiche scoles Y have herd, conceyved, lerned and reported all the errours and heresies whiche be contened in these articules that folwen, whiche Y have holde, beleved and affermed, that is to say,

First that the sacrament of Baptem doon in watir in forme customed in the Churche is but void and not necessarie to be doon ne had, for all Cristis puple*b* is sufficiently baptized in the blood of Crist and nedeth noo other baptem.

Also that the sacrament of Confirmacion doon be a bisshop is of noon availe, for as muche as whan a child hath discrecion and can and will undirstand the worde of God, it is sufficiently confermed be the Holy Gost and nedeth non other confirmacion.

Also that confession shuld be maad oonly to God and to noon erthely prest, for no prest hath poar to assoile hymself ne noon other persone of synne confessed to hym, thogh he be the popis peny dawnser.

Also that no man ne woman is bounde to do no penance whiche the prest enjoyneth hym to do for synnes whiche he hath confessed to the prest, but sufficeant penance for all maner of synnes is absteynyng from*c* leyng, bakbytyng and*d* evll doyng.

Also that no prest hath poar to make Cristis verray body at messe

a ab ipso *deleted.*   *b* if *deleted.*   *c* ly *deleted.*   *d* ou' *deleted.*

---

[168] Loddon, south-east Norfolk.   [169] Seething, south-east Norfolk.
[170] Probably Bergh Apton, south-east Norfolk. For the school, see p. 33, n. 14.
[171] For the Lollard circle at Colchester, see above, p. 45, n. 44; below, pp. 152–3; Thomson, *Later Lollards*, pp. 119 and 121–2.

in forme of bred, but that aftir the sacramental wordis said at messe of ony prest ther remayneth oonly pure material bred.

Also that ther was never pope aftir the decesse of Petir. And he that is called pope of Rome is fadir Antecrist, fals and cursed in al his werkyng, falsly and sotelly undir colour of holynesse disseyvyng the puple to gete hym goode. And he hath no more poar of God than ony*a* other lewed man (p. 319 / fo. 85r)*b* but if he be more holy in lyvyng. And he hath no*c* poar to make bisshops. And bisshops have no poar to make Ordres, ne to do noon other sacramentes, ne to make prestes. But all persones of the Churche from the hyest to the lowest and all here techyng and prechyng and alle thair shakelment' be fals and cursed and untrewe and oonly ordeyned be these prestes to begyle and deceyve the puple, to gete thaym good, to mayntene thair pride, thair slowthe and thar lecherie withall.

Also that the cursed Cayfaces,[172] bisshopes, and here proude prestes every yer make newe lawes and newe ordinances to kille and brenne alle trewe Cristis puple whiche wolde teche or preche the trewe lawe of Crist, whiche they hede and kepe cloos from knowyng of Goddis puple.

Also that verray pope is that persone that is most holy in erthe.

Also that every good man and good woman is a prest.

Also that oonly consent of love betux man and woman is sufficeant for the sacrament of matrimon, thogh the man and the woman never speke ne never be solennized at churche.

Also that it is but a trufle to enoynte a seke man with material oyle consecrat be a bisshop, for it sufficeth every man at hys last ende oonly to have mende on God.

Also that it is leeful every man to withdrawe and withholde offrynges and tithes from prestes and churches.

Also that all temporel lordis and every temporell man is bounde a peyne of dedly synne to take alle possessions and all temporell godis, hors, harneys and juwell from the covetouse bisshops and proude prelates of the Churche, and yeve thair good*d* to the pore puple, and compelle thaym to sustene thaymself with labour of here owyn handes.

Also that it is no synne to do the contrarie of the preceptes of holy Churche.

Also that censures of holy Churche, cursynges ne suspendynges doon be bisshops or ordinaries be not to be dredde, for whan bisshops or ordinaries cursen ony man, God blesseth the same man.

---

a ony *interlined.*
c more *deleted.*

b J. Skylan *at top of page.*
d MS. puple, *but see p.* 141.

[172] i.e., Caiaphases.

Also that it is not leful to[a] swere in ony caas, ne to plete for no right ne for wrong.

Also that it is not leful to sle a man in ony caas, ne be processe of lawe to dampne ony persone to deth for felonie, treson or ony other cause, but every (p. 320 / fo. 85v) man shuld remitte al vengeance oonly to the sentence of God.

Also that no man is bounde to faste in Lenton, Ymbren Days, Fridays ne vigiles of seyntes whyche be commaunded of the Churche to be fasted, but suche days and tymes it is leeful the puple to ete flessh and all[b] other metes indifferently at alle oures and tymes whan thay have lust and appetite to ete, for all suche days and tymes Y have ete[c] flessh as ofte tymes as Y had lust therto whan Y myght have it.

Also that no pilgrimage shuld be do to the Lefdy of Falsyngham, the Lefdy of Foulpette and to Thomme of Cankerbury,[173] ne to noon other seyntes ne ymages.

Also that no worship ne reverence oweth be doon to ony ymages of Oure Lady ne of noon other seyntes, ne no more reverence oweth be do unto the ymages of the crosse than oweth be doon to the galwes whiche men be hanged on, for al suche ymages be but ydols and the makers of hem be acursed.

Also that the foure doctours, Augustyn, Ambrose, Gregory[d] and Jerom, whiche the Churche of Roome hath aproved for seyntes, were heretikes and here doctrine, which Cristis puple calleth doctours draght, bey opin heresies.

Also that anon as ony man is dede his soule goth straght to hevene or elles to helle, for ther is noon other place of purgatorie but oonly this world.

Also that chastite of prestes seculer and reguler is not commendable ne meritorie, but it is more meritorie, leful and commendable alle prestes to take tham wyves and alle nunnes to take thaym husbondes and bringe forth frute of here bodyes.

Because of whiche and many other errours and heresies Y am called tofore you, worshipful fadir, whiche have cure of my soule. And be you fully informed that the said myn affermyng, belevyng and holdyng be opin errours and heresies and contrarious to the determinacion of the Churche of Roome, wherfor Y willyng folwe and sue the doctrine of holy Churche, and departe from all maner of errour and heresie, and turne with good will and herte to the oonhed of the Churche. Considerand (p. 321 / fo. 86r)[e] that holy Churche

---

[a] sle a man in ony caas ne be processe of lawe *deleted*.   [b] man' *deleted*.
[c] ffh *deleted*.   [d] MS. Gregot'.   [e] J. Skylan *at top of page*.

---

[173] A pun on Our Lady of Walsingham, Our Lady of Woolpit and St Thomas of Canterbury.

spereth [not] hir bosom to hym that will turne agayn,[a] ne God will
not the deth of a synner but rather that he be turned and lyve, with
a pure herte Y confesse, deteste and despise my said errours and
heresies, and these said opinions Y confesse hereticous and erroneous
and to the faith of the Churche of Roome and all universal holy
Churche repugnant. And for as much as be the said thinges that Y
so held, beleved and affermed Y shewed meself corrupt and unfaithful, that from hensforth Y shewe me uncorrupt and faithful,
the feith and doctrine of holy Churche trewely to kepe Y promitte.
And all maner of errour and heresie, doctrine and opinion ageyn the
feith of holy Churche and determinacion of the Churche of Roome—
and namely the opinions before rehersed—Y abjure and forswere,
and swere be the holy gospels be me[b] bodely touched that from
hensforth Y shal never holde errour ne heresie ne fals doctrine
ageyn the feith of holy Churche and determinacion of the Churche of
Roome.[c] Ne no suche thinges Y shal obstinatly defende. Ne no
persone holdyng or techyng suche maner of thinges Y shal obstinatly defende be me or ony other persone opinly or prively. Y shal
never aftir this tyme be no recettour, fautour, consellour, confortour
or defensour of heretikes or of ony persone suspect of heresie. Ne Y
shal never trowe to thaym. Ne wittyngly Y shal felaship with tham,
ne be hoomly with thaym, ne gyve thaym consell, yeftes, sokour,
favour ne confort. Yf Y knowe ony heretikes or of heresie ony
persones suspect or of thaym fautours, consellours, confortours or
defensours, or of ony persones makyng prive conventicules or
assembles, or holdyng ony divers or singular opinions from the
commune doctrine of the Churche, Y shall late [you], worshipful
fadir, or your vicar general in your absence or the diocesans of suche
persones have sone and redy knowyng. So help me God atte holy
doom and these holy gospels.

In wittenesse of whiche thinges Y subscribe her with myn owen
hand a crosse. And to this partie indented to remayne in your
registre Y sette me signet. And that other partie indented Y receyve
undir your seel to abyde with me unto my lyves ende. Yoven at
Norwich in the chapell of your (p. 322 / fo. 86v) palace the fourthe
day of the moneth of August the yer of our Lord a thousand four
hundred and thretty.

Qua quidem abiuracione sic, ut premittitur, facta ac subscripcione
manu propria dicti Johannis[d] Skylan iudicialiter facta, prefatus

---

[a] th *deleted*.　　　　　　　　　　　[b] p *deleted*.
[c] and namely the opinions before rehersed *deleted*.
[d] *MS.* Johannes.

Johannes sigillum suum uni parti dicti scripti indentati, penes dictum patrem remanenti,[a] apposuit. Quibus sic peractis, prestito per eum iuramento de agendo penitenciam sibi pro commissis iniungendam, et tunc dominus ipsum absolvebat a sentencia excommunicacionis, quam premissorum occasione ipso facto incurrebat,[b] sub eo qui sequitur tenore verborum.

In Dei nomine, Amen.[c] Quia nos, Willelmus, permissione divina Norwicensis episcopus, contra te, Johannem Skylan, filium Walteri Skylan de Bergh nostre diocesis, subditum nostrum et subiectum, ad anime tue correccionem ex officio nostro legitime procedere intendentes, per tuam propriam confessionem coram nobis iudicialiter factam invenimus te infra nostram diocesim predictam nonnullas hereses et errores quamplures fidei orthodoxe et determinacioni universalis Ecclesie repugnantes—de quibus in quodam cirographo super tua abiuracione concepto et indentato, cuius una pars in archivis nostris noscitur remanere, ad quam nos referimus et pro hic inserta haberi volumus, plenior fit mencio—tenuisse, credidisse et affirmasse, et per hoc in excommunicacionis sentenciam incidisse; nunc autem, usus consilio saniori, petis misericordiam et sponte redis ad Ecclesie unitatem; idcirco, inprimis abiurata per te omni heresi et recepta per nos a te secundun ritum Ecclesie iuratoria caucione de parendo mandatis Ecclesie, te absolvimus ab omni excommunicacionis vinculo quo tenebaris astrictus. Et quoniam per predicta que tenuisti, credidisti et affirmasti in Deum et sanctam matrem Ecclesiam temere deliquisti, tibi pro pena penitenciali penitenciam[d] iniungere intendimus specialem tibi per nos postmodum assignandam.

Presentibus tunc ibidem magistris Hugone Acton, Roberto Aylmer, Petro Werketon et Johanne Walpool, notariis publicis, ac Thoma Rodelond, capellano, et Thoma Walsham, litterato, testibus.

Postmodum vero die septima dicti mensis Augusti prefatus reverendus pater, in dicta capella palacii sui iudicialiter sedens, iniunxit dicto Johanni Skylan, tunc ibidem coram eo in iudicio personaliter constituto,[e] penitenciam subsequentem: videlicet, quod singulis vigiliis[f] Beate Marie per septennium continuum in pane et aqua ieiunet; et quod singulis sextis feriis per triennium a piscibus et

---

[a] sigillum suum *repeated.*
[b] penitenciam q' reservavit pro commissis sibi postmodum iniungendam *deleted.*
[c] n *deleted.*
[d] tibi *deleted.*
[e] *MS.* constitutu'.
[f] pos *deleted.*

lacticiniis se abstineat; et quod iij Dominicis incedat circa cimiterium ecclesie de Bergh coram solenni processione eiusdem, collo, capite et pedibus denudatis, corpore camisia et braciis solum^a induto,^b more penitentis, cum cereo cere ponderis unius libre, quem ultima^c die Dominica coram summo^d altari post evangelium magne misse ibidem^e offerat; et quod pari forma incedat circa mercatum de Lodne tribus diebus mercati ibidem cum alio cereo dicti ponderis, quem offerat summo altari de Lodne ultimo die mercati huiusmodi post penitenciam suam peractam; et^f quod per tres annos proximos sequentes singulis quartis feriis in Capite Ieiunii ac singulis quintis feriis in Cenis Domini cum aliis penitentibus in ecclesia Cathedrali Norwic' se presentet coram domino vel eius locum tenente, acturus penitenciam solennem pro commissis.

Presentibus in iniunccione^g istius penitiencie magistris Hugone Acton ac Johanne Sutton [et] Thoma Walsham.

[30]

(p. 347 / fo. 99r) **Willelmus Hardy de Mundham,**[174] **tayllour**

In Dei nomine, Amen. Per presens publicum instrumentum cunctis appareat evidenter quod Anno Domini ab Incarnacione eiusdem secundum cursum et computacionem Ecclesie Anglicane Millesimo Quadringentesimo Tricesimo, indiccione octava, pontificatus sanctissimi in Christo patris et domini nostri, domini Martini divina providencia pape quinti, anno terciodecimo, in capella palacii reverendi in Christo patris et domini, domini Willelmi Dei gracia Norwicensi episcopi, in civitate Norwic' situati, in mei, Johannis Excestr, clerici, publici auctoritate apostolica notarii, et testium subscriptorum presencia,^h coram dicto reverendo patre, domino Willelmo Dei gracia Norwicensi episcopo, iudicialiter sedente, assidentibus tunc ibidem magistro Johanne Paas, ordinis Fratrum Minorum, sacre theologie professore, ac Thoma Ryngstede, in decretis, Willelmo Ascogh et Roberto Woler, in sacra theologia, bacallariis,ⁱ Willelmus Hardy de Mundham Norwicensis diocesis, dicti reverendi patris subditus et subiectus, de et super heretica

---

^a d *interlined and deleted.*   ^b corpore camisia . . . induto *interlined.*
^c *MS.* ultimo.   ^d altare *deleted.*
^e dict' *follows* ibidem.   ^f Penitencia solennis *in margin.*
^g ist *deleted.*   ^h constat *deleted.*
ⁱ ac Willelmo Bamburgh, Roberto Synceon et *deleted.*

---

¹⁷⁴ Mundham, south-east Norfolk.

pravitate multipliciter diffamatus ac ea occasione arestatus et incarceratus, adductus fuit ad iudicium super crimine heresis in vinculis personaliter responsurus. Cui quidem Willelmo Hardy prefatus reverendus pater iudicialiter sedens dixit, obiecit et proposuit articulando omnes articulos[a] in quodam cirographo super abiuracione ipsius Willelmi Hardy in vulgari lingua Anglicana concepto et indentato,[b] cuius tenor inferius describitur, conscriptos et specificatos, ac omnes hereses et errores in eisdem articulis contentos. Quos quidem articulos omnes et singulos ac omnes hereses et errores in eis contentos dicto Willelmo obiectos et articulatos[c] prefatus Willelmus Hardy fatebatur et recognovit iudicialiter tunc ibidem se tenuisse, credidisse et affirmasse prout in dicto scripto plenius continetur. Et deinde dictus reverendus pater dixit et intimavit dicto Willelmo Hardy quod prefati articuli in se continent nonnullas hereses et errores quamplures. Ideoque idem Willelmus Hardy voluit, ut asseruit,[d] huiusmodi hereses et errores sibi, ut premittitur, articulatos ac generaliter omnem heresim pro perpetuo dimittere et abiurare secundum tenorem in dicto cirographo super abiuracione sua, ut premittitur, in[e] ydiomate Anglicano concepto et indentato conscriptum. Quem quidem tenorem per magistrum Johannem Wylly, notarium publicum, de mandato dicti patris[f] coram prefato Willelmo Hardy in iudicio publice perlectum idem Willelmus Hardy, ut asseruit, de verbo ad verbum audivit et plenarie intellexit. Et quia idem Willelmus Hardy asseruit se nescire legere dictam abiuracionem suam propria in persona, ipse idem Willelmus in personam dicti magistri Johannis Wylly, notarii publici,[g] organum vocis sue in hac parte commisit publice tunc ibidem. Omnes hereses et errores pro[h] perpetuo abiuravit[i] prout in dicto cirographo indentato plenius continetur, cuius tenor sequitur et est talis.

In the name of God, tofore you, the worshipful fadir in Crist, William, be the grace of God bisshop of Norwich, Y, William Hardy of Mundham of your diocese, tayllor, your subject, felyng and undirstandyng that before this tyme Y have be conversant, familier and hoomly with heretikes, and in especial with on called Sir William Caleys, prest, and be another name cleped Hygon', and with other moo in the hous of John Abraham, cordewaner of Colcestre,[175]

[a] in abiuracione eiusdem Willelmi Hardy *deleted*.
[b] conscriptos et inde *deleted*.
[c] dicto Willelmo obiectos et articulatos *interlined*.
[d] dictos *deleted*.   [e] ling *deleted*.
[f] prefato *follows* patris.   [g] om ipse *follows* publici.
[h] MS. per.   [i] sub eo qui sequitur tenore verborum *deleted*.

kepyng and holdyng scoles of heresie, of whom Y have herd, conceyved and reported the errours and heresies whiche be writen
(p. 348 / fo. 99v)[a] and contened in this indentur, whiche errours and
heresie[s] Y have holde, beleved and affermed withynne your
diocese,

First that the sacrament of Baptem doon in watir in forme customed of the Churche is not necessarie ne profitable to be had, for
every man and child of Crist' beleve is sufficiently baptized in the
passion of Crist and nedeth noon other baptem.

Also that the sacrament of Confirmacion doon be a bisshop in
forme customed of the Churche is but a trufle, for as soon as ai[b]
child hath discrecion and can undirstande the word[c] and the lawe of
God it is sufficiently confermed.

Also that confession oweth to be maade oonly to God, and to noon
other prest, for no prest hath poar to assoile a man of ony synne.

Also that every good Cristen man[d] that hath noon ordre is a good
prest, and hath as moche poar to do and mynystre alle the sacramentes in the Churche as ony other prest ordred.

Also that no prest hath poar to make Cristis verry body in the
sacrament at the auter in forme of bred.

Also that oonly consent of love betuxe man and woman is sufficient for the sacrament of perfit matrimoyn withoute contract of
word or solennizacion in churche, for suche solennizacion is but
vayneglorie induced be covetise of prestes to gete mony of the puple.

Also that it is but a vayne jape to enoynte a seke man in perill of
deth with material oyle consecrat be a bisshop.

Also that it is not leful to swere in ony caas.

Also that it is not leful in ony caas to putte ony man to deth, ne be
processe of lawe to dampne a thef or a traitour.

Also that no man is bounde to halwe[e] the Sonedays ne noon other
festival days, but it is leful to every man all suche Sondays and all
other festival days whiche be commaunded be prestes in the Churche
to be had holy to do all other bodely workes except synne, for
prestes ordined all holy days for covetyse to have offringes and
tithes of the puple.

Also that it is meritorie and charitable all men to withdrawe and
withholde from the prestes and curates alle offringes and tithes, for
offringes and tithes make prestes proude and lecherous and vicious,
and therefor it were more meritorie to spende suche good in (p.
349 / fo. 100r)[f] other use.

[a] Will' Hardy *in top left-hand corner of page.*
[b] *Sic.*   [c] of God *deleted.*
[d] is a prest *deleted.*   [e] s *deleted.*
[f] Willelmus Hardy *in top right-hand corner of page.*

Also that censures and cursynges of bisshops and ordinaries doon to the puple be not to be dredde, for thair cursynges be as good as thar blessynges.

Also that [no] Cristene creitoure is bounde to faste in Lenton, Ymbren Days, Fridays ne vigiles of seyntes whiche the prestes in the Churche commaunden to be fasted, but all men may lefully all suche days and tymes ete flessh and all maner of metes indifferently at here owen lust as ofte as thay will, so a man faste from synnes.

Also that all maner of prayer oweth to be maad oonly to God and to noon other seyntes, for alle seyntes be made be ordinances of popes and other prelates and prestes of the Churche, and therfor it is dowte whedir it be plesyng to God preyers to be maad to ony seyntes or nay.

Also that no pilgrimage oweth to be do to ony seyntes or places, but oonly to pore men.

Also that no worship ne reverence oweth to be do to ony ymages of the crucifix, of Our Lady Seynt Marye ne of noon other seintes, for the signe of the crosse is the signe of Antecrist, and no more worship ne reverence oweth be do to the crosse than oweth be do to the galwes whiche men be hanged on.

Also that ther is no Churche but oonly hevene.

Also that holy bred and holy water is ner the better for all the conjuracions and charmes whiche prestes sayn and syngen therover.

Becaus[e]*a* of whiche and many other errours and heresies Y am called tofore yo[u], worshipful fadir, whiche have cure of my soule. And be you fu[lly] informed that the said myn affermyng, belevyng and holdyng be opin errours and heresies and contrarious to the determinacion of the Churche of Roome, wherfor Y willyng folwe and sue the doctrine of holy Churche, and departe from all maner of errour and heresie, and turne with good will and herte to the oonhed of the Churche. Considerand that holy Churche spereth not hyr bosom to hym that will turne agayn, ne God will not the deth of a synner but rather that he be turned and lyve, with a pure herte Y confesse, deteste and despise my said errours and heresies, and the said opinions Y confesse hereticous and erroneous and to the feith of the Churche of Roome and all universal holy (p. 350 / fo. 100v)*b* Churche repugnant. And for as muche as be the said thinges that Y so held, beleved and affermed Y shewed meself corrupt and unfaithful, that from hensforth Y shewe me uncorrupt and faithful, the faith and doctrine of holy Churche truly to kepe Y promitte. And all

---

a The wearing away of the edge of the page explains why letters have been supplied to Becaus, yo and fu.
b Will' Hardy in top left-hand corner of page.

maner of errour and heresie, doctrine and opinion agayn the feith of holy Churche and determinacion of the Churche of Roome—and namely the opinions before rehersed—Y abjure and forswere, and swere be these holy gospels be me bodely touched that from hensforth Y shal never holde errour ne heresie ne fals doctrine agayn the faith of holy Churche and determinacion of the Churche of Roome. Ne no suche thinges Y shal obstinatly defende. Ne no persone holdyng or techyng suche maner of thinges Y shal obstinatly defende be me or ony other persone opinly or prively. Y shall never aftir this tyme be no recettour, fautour, consellour or defensour of heretikes or of ony persones suspect of heresie. Ne Y shal never trowe to thaym. Ne wittyngly Y shal felaship with thaym, ne be hoomly with thaym, ne gyve thaym consell, yeftes, sokour, favour ne confort. Yf Y knowe ony heretikes or of heresie ony persones suspect or of thaym fautours, confortours or defensours, or of ony persones makyng prive conventicules or assembles, or holdyng ony divers or singuler opinions from the commune doctrine of the Churche, Y shal late you, worshipful fadir, or your vicar general in your absence or the diocesans of suche persones have sone and redy knowyng. So help me God atte holy doom and these holy gospels.

In wittenesse of which thinges Y subscribe here with myn owen hand a crosse +. And to this partie indented to remayne in your registre Y sette*a* my signet. And that other partie indented Y receyve undir your seel to abide with me unto my lyves ende. Yoven at Norwich in the chapell of your palaice the iiij day of the moneth of August the yer of our Lord a thousand four hundred and thretty.

Qua quidem abiuracione per prefatum magistrum Johannem Wylly, organum vocis dicti Willelmi, ut premittitur, gerentem in hac parte, vice prefati Willelmi Hardy solenniter in iudicio facta, dictus Willelmus Hardy, tactis sacris evangeliis, iuravit ad ea quod omnia contenta in dicto scripto cirographo*b* per prefatum magistrum Johannem Wylly vice sua perlecta, in quantum concernunt personam suam, iuxta omnem (p. 351 / 101r)*c* vim, formam et effectum eiusdem scripti*d* cirographi bene et*e* inviolabiliter observabit. Et in huius rei testimonium in utroque scripto cirographo indentato manu sua propria cum penna signum crucis + subscripsit iudicialiter et consignavit, ac uni parti dicti scripti indentati penes registrum dicti patris remansure sigillum suum apposuit iudicialiter tunc ibidem.

---

a y *deleted.*   *b* et *deleted.*
c Willelmus Hardy *in top right-hand corner of page.*
d *Two or three illegible letters deleted.*   *e* *An illegible letter deleted.*

Et deinde, prestito per eundem iuramento ad sacra evangelia predicta de debite agendo penitenciam pro commissis, prefatus pater
ipsum Willelmum Hardy absolvebat a sentencia excommunicacionis,
qua premissorum occasione extitit innodatus, sub hoc*a* qui sequitur
tenore verborum: 'In Dei nomine, Amen', prout continetur in
processu*b* contra Johannem Skylan.*c* Et penitenciam pro commissis dominus reservavit sibi postmodum iniungendam. Et deinde
dictus pater declaravit eidem Willelmo periculum residivacionis si
contravenerit abiuracioni sue suprascripte: videlicet, quod tunc debet
tradi potestati seculari merito comburendus.

Presentibus tunc ibidem magistris Hugone Acton, Roberto
Aylmer, Petro Werketon et Johanne Walpool, notariis publicis, ac
Thoma Rodelond, capellano, et Thoma Walsham, litterato, Norwicensis et Lincolniensis diocesium, testibus ad premissa vocatis
specialiter et rogatis.

Die septima mensis Augusti Anno Domini suprascripto dictus
pater, in capella palacii Norwici iudicialiter sedens, iniunxit dicto
Willelmo Hardy, tunc ibidem coram eodem patre iudicialiter constituto, pro commissis suis suprascriptis penitenciam subsequentem:
videlicet, quod tribus diebus Dominicis incedat circa cimiterium*d* ecclesie Sancti Petri de Mundham*e* coram solenni processione eiusdem,*f*
capite et pedibus denudatis, corpore camisia solomodo induto, cum
cereo cere ponderis unius libre deferendo, quem ultimo die Dominico
offerat summo altari dicte ecclesie de Mundham post penitenciam
suam ibidem peractam; et quod incedat circa mercatum de Lodne,[176]
more predicto indutus, tribus diebus mercati eiusdem ville cum*g* alio
cereo dicti ponderis, quem cereum ultimo die mercati post penitenciam suam circa dictum mercatum peractam offerat summo
altari ecclesie de Lodne humiliter et devote; et quod singulis quartis
feriis in Capite Ieiunii et singulis quintis feriis in Cena Domini per
triennium proximum futurum cum aliis penitentibus coram dicto
patre, sive ipsius locum tenente in hac parte, in ecclesia Cathedrali
Norwic' cum aliis penitentibus se personaliter presentet, acturus
solennem penitenciam pro commissis.

Presentes erant in iniunccione dicte penitencie magist' Hugo
Acton, Johannes Sutton, notarii publici, et Thomas Walsham.

---

a MS. hac.   *b* conta *deleted*.   *c* See p. 150.
d de *deleted*.   *e* tribus dieb *deleted*.
f collo *deleted*.   *g* cereo *deleted*.

---

[176] Loddon, south-east Norfolk.

[31]

(p. 229 / fo. 35r)[a] **Willelmus Bate de Sythyng**[177]

In Dei nomine, Amen. Per presens publicum instrumentum cunctis appareat evidenter quod Anno ab Incarnacione Domini Millesimo Quadringentesimo Tricesimo, indiccione octava, pontificatus sanctissimi in Christo patris et domini nostri, domini Martini divina providencia pape quinti, anno terciodecimo, mensis Augusti die quinta, in capella palacii[b] episcopalis in civitate Norwici situati, in mei, Johannis Excestr, clerici, notarii publici, et testium subscriptorum presencia, coram reverendo in Christo patre ac domino, domino Willelmo Dei gracia Norwicensi episcopo, pro tribunali ad iura reddenda—ut michi, dicto notario, tunc apparebat —[iudicialiter sedente], assistentibus eidem reverendo patri tunc ibidem discretis viris, fratre Willelmo Worstede, priore ecclesie Cathedralis Norwic', ac Johanne Thorp de ordine Fratrum Carmelitarum, sacre pagine professoribus, necnon magistris Willelmo Bernham, in decretis, ac Johanne Sutton, in legibus, bacallariis, et Johanne Midelton,[178] in artibus magistro,[c] Willelmus Bate de Sethyng Norwicensis diocesis, tayllour, de et super heretica pravitate multipliciter diffamatus et ea occasione aliquamdiu incarceratus, adductus fuit in vinculis ad iudicium super crimine heresis et heretice pravitatis personaliter responsurus. Qui quidem Willelmus Bate, per prefatum patrem allocutus ac de crimine heretice pravitatis iudicialiter impetitus, fatebatur et recognovit se infra diocesim Norwicensem subscriptos hereses et errores tenuisse, credidisse et affirmasse.

Inprimis videlicet quod sacramentum Baptismi, factum in aqua in forma in ecclesiis fieri consueta, nichil penitus est ponderandum si parentes infantis sint Christiani.

Item quod sacramentum Confirmacionis, ministratum per aliquem episcopum, nichil proficit nec requiritur ad salvacionem humanam.

Item quod confessio nullo modo est facienda alicui sacerdoti, sed omnis confessio facienda est soli Deo, quia nullus presbiter habet potestatem absolvendi quemquam a peccatis.

[a] i (*i.e., folio 1 of the trial of William Bate*) *in top right-hand corner of page.*
[b] episcopalibus *deleted.*
[c] Edmundus Archer de Lodne Norwicensis diocesis, sewter *deleted.*

---

[177] Seething, south-east Norfolk.
[178] See Emden, *BRUO*, ii, pp. 1276-7 (the third and fourth John Middeltons mentioned). Probably he is not to be identified with John Midelton, vicar of Halvergate (see p. 38, n. 6).

Item quod nullus presbiter habet potestatem conficiendi corpus Christi sub specie panis in sacramento altaris ad missam, sed post verba sacramentalia, quantumcumque a presbitero rite prolata, remanet in altari nisi tantum torta puri panis materialis.

Item quod tantum solus consensus mutui amoris in Jhu' Christo inter virum et mulierem sufficit pro sacramento matrimonii, absque aliquo contractu per verba et absque solennizacione in ecclesia.

Item quod nullus homo[a] tenetur observare aliqua ieiunia Quadragesime, dierum Quatuor Temporum, vigiliarum sanctorum, sextarum feriarum nec aliquorum aliorum temporum indictorum per Ecclesiam, sed quod licitum est cuilibet homini talibus temporibus et diebus edere carnes et omnimoda cibaria indifferenter pro eorum libito appetitus.

Item quod licitum est cuilibet subtrahere decimas et oblaciones ab ecclesiis et curatis, dumtamen hoc prudenter fiat.

Item quod censure ecclesiastice—videlicet sentencie[b] suspensionum, excommunicacionum nec interdictorum—late per prelatos vel ordinarios ecclesiasticos nullo modo sunt timende, quia quamcito aliquis prelatus vel ordinarius aliquem excommunicat, statim eo ipso Jhus' Christus ipsum absolvit et benedicit.

Item quod castitas[c] presbiterorum secularium nec regularium nec monialium est meritoria nec commendabilis quoquomodo, sed omnes presbiteri et moniales possunt sine periculo vel peccato nubere et ducere communem vitam coniugii, et hoc esset maius meritorium quam vivere continenter.

Item quod nulla oracio deberet fieri alicui sancto, sed tantum soli Deo.

Item quod non est licitum iurare in aliquo casu.

Item quod[d] (p. 230 / fo. 35v) nullus honor est exhibendus ligno crucis Christi super quam Jhus' Christus paciebatur, nec alicui ymagini Beate Marie nec alicuius alterius sancti.

Item quod peregrinaciones[e] nullo modo sunt faciende, nisi tantum pauperibus.

Item quod non licet quovis modo pugnare pro iure hereditario, nec pro patria defendenda, eo quod omnes sic pugnantes amittunt caritatem.

Item quod iste artes pictorum et sculpatorum nullo modo deberent exerceri, quia nullo modo sunt necessarie.

---

[a] et *deleted.*   [b] e *deleted.*   [c] monialium *deleted.*

[d] Will' Bate   Joh' Wroxham   Joh' Goodwyn   Joh' Belward, senior
Joh' Burrell   Thomas Mone   Henr' Lacchecold   Joh' Belward, junior
Rob' Grygg'   Isabell Chapleyn   Henr' Goode   Rob' Sherwynd
Joh' Fynch   Will' Masse   Ric' Horn   Will' Sherwynd
                                             Joh' Spyr   Rob' Tolle

written at foot of page.

[e] no *deleted.*

Quibus sic peractis, prefatus reverendus pater asseruit dicto Willelmo quod articuli per ipsum sic iudicialiter confessati continent in se nonnullas hereses et[a] errores fidei catholice et determinacioni Ecclesie Romane repugnantes. Ideoque prefatus Willelmus Bate[b] asseruit se velle redire ad Ecclesie unitatem, ac omnes hereses et errores prescriptos necnon quascumque alias hereses et errores re et verbo puro corde dimittere[c] pro perpetuo et abiurare secundum tenorem in quodam cirographo super ipsius abiuracione in ideomate Anglicano scripto et indentato conceptum.[d] Quem tenorem per magistrum Johannem Wylly, notarium publicum, tunc ibidem presentem,[e] publice perlectum idem Willelmus asseruit se de verbo ad verbum totaliter audivisse et plenarie intellexisse. Et quia idem Willelmus Bate asseruit se fore laicum, ipsam abiuracionem legere nescientem propria in persona, ipse constituit prefatum magistrum Johannem Wylly organum vocis sue. Cui liberam commisit potestatem dictam abiuracionem suam vice et nomine suis prestandi,[f] faciendi et legendi, promittens se ratum, gratum et firmum ac stabile habitum totum et quicquid idem magister Johannes Wylly nomine suo fecerit et legerit in hac parte. Qui quidem magister Johannes Wylly, organum vocis dicti Willelmi Bate in se assumens, totum tenorem[g] abiuracionis ipsius Willelmi publice perlegit. Et prefatus Willelmus Bate, tenens interim manum suam dexteram ad sacra evangelia, iuravit ad ea personaliter se omnia et singula in dicto[h] indentato[i] cirografo deducta, quatenus se et abiuracionem suam concernunt, iuxta omnem vim, formam et effectum eiusdem cirografi pro perpetuo inviolabiliter observaturum. Cuius quidem cirographi super ipsius Willelmi abiuracione in hac parte concepti et indentati tenor sequitur [et] est talis.

In the name of God, tofor you, the worshypful fadir in Crist, William, be the grace of God bisshop of Norwich, Y, William Bate of Sethyng, tayllour, of your diocese, your subject, felyng and undirstandyng that Y have holde, beleved and affermed the errours and heresies whiche be contened in this indenture,

That is to say that Y have holde, beleved and affermed that the sacrament of Baptem doon in watir in forme customed of the Churche is of noon availe and not to be pondred if the fadir and modir of the childe be cristened and of Cristene beleve.

---

[a] here *deleted.*
[b] p' *deleted.*
[c] prop *deleted.*
[d] conceptum *interlined.*
[e] quem prefatus Willelmus Bate constituit organum vocis sue in hac parte tunc ibidem *deleted.*
[f] et *deleted.*
[g] ipsius *deleted.*
[h] scripto *deleted.*
[i] indentato *interlined.*

Also that the sacrament of Confirmacion doon be a bisshop ys not profitable ne necessarie to mannys salvacion.

Also that confession oweth to be made to no prest, but oonly to God, for a prest hath no poar to assoile a man of synne.

Also that no prest hath poar to make Goddys body in the sacrament of the (p. 231 / fo. 36r)[a] auter, and that aftir the sacramental wordis said of a prest at messe ther remayneth nothing but oonly a cake of material bred.

Also that oonly consent of love in Jhu' Crist betuxe man and woman is sufficient for the sacrament of matrimon, withoute contract of wordis or solempnizacion in churche.

Also that no man is bounde to faste in Lenton, Ymbren days, Fridays, vigiles of seyntes ne other tymes whiche be commaunded of the Churche to be fasted, but that it is leful to all maner of puple all suche days and tymes to ete flessh and all maner of metis indifferently at her owyn lust.

Also that it is leful to every persone to withholde and withdrawe tithes and offringes from churches and curates, so it be do prudently.

Also that censures of holy Churche and sentences of cursyng yoven be[b] bisshops, prelatis and other ordinaries be not to be pondred ne to be dred, for as soone as suche bisshops or ordinaries acurse ony man, Crist hymself assoileth hym and blesseth hym.

Also that chastite of prestes seculer ne reguler ne of nunnes is not commendable, but all prestis and all nunnes may lefully be wedded and maried and use the comon lyf of wedlok, and that lyf ys more meritorie than is to lyve continent and chast.

Also that not preyer shuld be maad to ony seint, but oonly to God.

Also that it is not leful to swere in ony caas.

Also that no maner of worship shuld be do to the crosse whiche Crist deyed upon, ne to noon ymages of Our Lady ne of noon other seint.

Also that no maner of pilgrimage shuld be do, but oonly to pore puple.

Also that it is not leful to fighte ne plete for heritage ne for a cuntre, for all thoo that do so thay lese here charite.

And that these craftys of peyntours and gravours in no maner shuld be used, for all suche craftys be nother necessarie ne nedfull to be had.

Because of whiche and many other errours and heresies Y am called tofore you, worshipful fadir, whiche have cure of my soule. And be you fully informed that the said myn affermyng, belevyng and holdyng be opin errours and heresies and contrarious to the

---

[a] Will' Bate, ii *in top right-hand corner of page.*
[b] a *deleted.*

determinacion of the Churche of Roome, wherfor Y wyllyng folwe and sue the doctrine of holy Churche, and departe from all maner of errour (p. 232 / fo. 36v) and heresie, and turne with good will and herte to the oonhed of the Churche. Considerand that holy Churche spereth not hir bosom to hym that will turne agayn, ne God will not the deth of a synner but rather that he be turned and lyve, with a pure herte Y confesse, deteste and despise my said errours and heresies, and these said opinions Y confesse hereticous and erroneous and to the faith of the Churche of Rome and all universal holy Churche repugnant. And for as muche as be the said thinges that Y so held, beleved and affermed Y shewed meself corrupt and unfaithful, that from hensforth Y shewe me uncorrupt and faithful, the faith and doctrine of holy Churche truly to kepe Y promitte. And all maner of errour and heresie, doctrine and opinion agayn the faith of holy Churche and determinacion of the Churche of Roome— and namely the opinions before rehersed—Y abjure and forswere, and swere be these holy gospels be me bodely touched that from hensforth Y shall never holde errour ne heresie ne fals doctrine ageyn the faith of holy Churche and determinacion of the Churche of Rome. Ne no suche thinges Y shal obstinatly defende. Ne no persons holdyng or techyng suche maner of thynges Y shal obstinatly defende be me or ony other persone opinly or prively. Y shal never aftir this time be no recettour, fautour, consellour or defensour of heretikes or of ony persone suspect of heresie. Ne Y shal never trowe to thaym. Ne wittyngly Y shal felaship with thaym, ne be homly with thaym, ne gyve thaym consell, yeftes, sokour, favor ne confort. Yf Y knowe ony heretikes or of heresie ony persones suspect or of thaym fautours, confortours or defensours, or of ony persones makyng prive conventicules or assembles, or holdyng ony divers or singuler opinions from the comune doctrine of the Churche, Y shal late you, worshipful fadir, or your vicar general in your absence or the diocesanes of suche persones have sone and redy knowyng. So help me God atte holy doom and these holy gospels.

In wittenesse of whiche thinges Y subscribe here with my owyn hand a crosse +. And to this partie indented to remayne in your registre Y sette my signet. And that other partie indented Y receyve undir your seel to abide with me unto my lyves ende. Yoven at Norwich in the chapell of your palaice the fifte day of the moneth of August the yer of our Lord a thousand four hundred and thretty.

(p. 233 / fo. 37r)[a] Quo quidem iuramento sic, ut premittitur, prestito, prefatus Willelmus Bate, in signum et testimonium quod

[a] Will' Bate, iii *in top right-hand corner of page.*

huiusmodi iuramentum ratum habuit et gratum, cum penna signum crucis in dicto cirographo indentato manu sua propria coram dicto reverendo patre subscripsit iudicialiter tunc ibidem, et uni parti eiusdem scripti indentati penes registrum dicti patris remansure sigillum suum apposuit. Et deinde prefatus pater declaravit et asseruit dicto Willelmo Bate quod si imposterum contravenerit dictum iuramentum suum vel in heresim fuerit relapsus, tradetur curie seculari, ignis supplicio comburendus. Et deinde prefatus Willelmus Bate iuravit ad sacra evangelia per ipsum corporaliter tacta de agendo debite penitenciam quam prefatus pater pro suis commissis sibi duxerit iniungendam. Quo iuramento sic prestito, prefatus reverendus pater ipsum Willelmum Bate a sentencia excommunicacionis, quam premissorum occasione incurrebat, absolvit sub hac forma.

In Dei nomine, Amen. Quia nos, Willelmus, permissione divina Norwicensis episcopus, contra te, Willelmum Bate de Sethyng nostre diocesis, subditum nostrum et subiectum, ad anime tue correccionem ex officio nostro legitime procedere intendentes, per tuam propriam confessionem coram nobis iudicialiter factam invenimus te infra dictam nostram diocesim nonnullas hereses et errores quamplures fidei orthodoxe et determinacioni universalis Ecclesie repugnantes—de quibus in quodam cirographo super tua abiuracione concepto et indentato, cuius una pars in archivis nostris noscitur*a* remanere, ad quam nos referimus et pro hic inserta haberi volumus, plenior fit mencio—tenuisse, credidisse et affirmasse, et per hoc in excommunicacionis sentenciam incidisse; nunc autem, usus concilio saniori, petis misericordiam et sponte redis ad Ecclesie unitatem; idcirco inprimis abiurata per te omn' heresi et recepta per nos a te secundum ritum Ecclesie iuratoria caucione de parendo mandatis Ecclesie, te absolvimus ab omni excommunicacionis vinculo quo tenebaris astrictus. Et quia per predicta que tenuisti, credidisti et affirmasti in Deum et sanctam matrem Ecclesiam temere deliquisti, tibi pro pena penitenciali iniungimus quod a festo Natalis Domini proximo futuro singulis sextis feriis per unum annum continuum in pane et aqua ieiunes; et quod*b* quatuor diebus Dominicis circa cimiterium ecclesie parochialis de Sethyng predict' coram solenni processione eiusdem et quatuor diebus mercati circa mercatum de Lodne,[179] capite et pedibus denudatis, corpore camisia et femoralibus dumtaxat induto, cum cereo cere ponderis dimidie libre tuis

---

a c *deleted.*   *b* per *follows* quod.

[179] Loddon, south-east Norfolk.

manibus deferendo, more penitentis incedas, quem cereum proxima Dominica*a* post penitenciam huiusmodi peractam summo altari ecclesie de Sethyng per te offerri et ibidem dimitti iniungimus et mandamus; et*b* quod per triennium proximum*c* singulis quartis feriis in Capite Ieiunii et singulis quintis feriis in Cena Domini per triennium coram nobis vel nostro locumtenente in hac parte in ecclesia nostra Cathedrali Norwic' cum aliis penitentibus personaliter te presentes, acturus publicam penitenciam pro commissis.*d*

Presentibus tunc ibidem dominis Willelmo Bamburgh, Johanne Blytheburgh et Thoma Rodelond, capellanis, ac Thoma Walsham et Willelmo Steynewar, clericis.

[32]

(p. 323 / fo. 87r) **Edmundus Archer de Lodne**[180]

In Dei nomine, Amen. Per presens publicum instrumentum cunctis appareat evidenter quod Anno ab Incarnacione Domini secundum cursum et computacionem Ecclesie Anglicane Millesimo CCCC*o* XXX*o*, indiccione octava, pontificatus sanctissimi in Christo patris et domini nostri, domini Martini divina providencia pape quinti, anno terciodecimo, mensis Augusti die quinta,*e* in capella [palacii] reverendi in Christo patris et domini, domini Willelmi, Dei gracia Norwicensis episcopi, in civitate Norwic' situati, in mei, Johannis Excestr, clerici, notarii publici dictique reverendi patris registrarii, et testium subscriptorum presencia, coram reverendo in Christo patre ac domino, domino*f* Willelmo Dei gracia Norwicensi episcopo prescripto, pro tribunali ad reddenda iura—ut michi, notario prescripto, tunc apparebat—sedente, assistentibus eidem reverendo patri tunc ibidem venerabilibus viris, fratre Willelmo Worstede, priore ecclesie Cathedralis Sancte Trinitatis Norwic',Clemente Denston archidiacono Sudbur',[181] Willelmo Bernham, in decretis bacallariis, Johanne Thorp, ordinis Carmelitarum,*g* sacre pagine professore,*h* Johanne Middelton, magistro in artibus, Johanne Sutton, in legibus bacallario,

---

a MS. proxim' Dominicam.   *b* Penitencia solennis iij annis *in margin.*
c per triennium proximum *interlined.*
d tamen ex certis causis ipsum reverendum patrem *deleted.*
e mensis Augusti die quinta *interlined.*   *f* wl *deleted.*
g Joh' de Sancta Fide, ordinis Minorum *deleted.*
h MS. professoribus.

---

[180] Loddon, south-east Norfolk.
[181] Sudbury, south-west Suffolk. See Emden, *BRUC*, p. 182, Clement Denston.

[et] Johanne Holdernesse, notario publico, Edmundus Archer de Lodne Norwicensis diocesis, dicti reverendi patris, domini Norwicensis episcopi, subditus et subiectus, de et super heretica pravitate multipliciter diffamatus, adductus fuit in vinculis ad iudicium, super dicto crimine personaliter responsurus. Cui quidem Edmundo prefatus reverendus pater iudicialiter obiecit et proposuit articulando omnes articulos in quodam cirographo super abiuracione eiusdem Edmundi concepto et indentato, cuius tenor inferius describitur, contentos, conscriptos pariter et specificatos. Quos quidem articulos, ac omnes et singulos hereses et errores in eis contentos, prefatus Edmundus Archer iudicialiter coram ipso patre recognovit se tenuisse,[a] credidisse et affirmasse, prout in dicto scripto super ipsius abiuracione concepto et indentato plenius continetur. Et deinde idem Edmundus, informatus ibidem per dictum reverendum patrem quod dicti articuli continent in se nonnullos hereses et errores, asseruit se velle ad Ecclesie unitatem redire, ac dictos et quoscumque alios hereses et errores re et verbo dimittere et pro perpetuo abiurare secundum tenorem in dicto cirographo super ipsius abiuracione inscripto in ydeomate Anglicano conceptum.[b] Cuius[c] tenorem, per magistrum Johannem Wylly, notarium publicum tunc ibidem presentem, de mandato dicti reverendi patris[d] coram dicto Edmundo publice perlectum, idem Edmundus Archer asseruit se de verbo ad verbum[e] totaliter audivisse et plenarie intellexisse. Et quia idem Edmundus asseruit insuper se fore laicum, nescientem legere dictam abiuracionem propria in persona, ipse Edmundus constituit dictum magistrum Johannem Wylly organum vocis sue in hac parte. Cui liberam commisit[f] potestatem ipsam abiuracionem vice et nomine suis[g] legendi, promittens se ratum, gratum et firmum habiturum totum et quicquid idem magister Johannes[h] vice et nomine suis in eodem scripto abiuracionis sue legerit et fecerit in hac parte. Qui quidem magister Johannes Wylly, organum vocis ipsius Edmundi in se assumens, totum[i] tenorem dicte[j] abiuracionis ipsius Edmundi publice perlegit. Et sic idem[k] Edmundus, tenens manum suam dexteram super evangelia, iuravit ad ea se omnia contenta in ipso scripto indentato suam abiuracionem continente iuxta omnem vim, formam et effectum eiusdem inviolabiliter observaturum. Cuius quidem abiuracionis tenor sequitur et est talis.

In the name of God, tofore you, the worshipful fadir in Crist, William, be the grace of God bisshop of Norwich, Y, Edmund

---

[a] ti *deleted.*   [b] que' quidem *deleted.*   [c] Cuius *interlined.*
[d] publice perlectum *deleted.*   [e] aud *deleted.*   [f] commisit *interlined.*
[g] t *deleted.*   [h] nomine *deleted.*   [i] totum *interlined.*
[j] MS. dicti.   [k] Willelmus *deleted.*

Archer of Lodne of your diocese, cordewaner, sumtyme preyntys and servant with Thomas Moone of the same (p. 324 / fo. 87v) toun, your subject, felyng and undirstandyng that Y have be right familier, conversant and homly with many notorie and famous heretikes—that is to say with Sir William Whyte, Sir Hughe Pye, Sir William Caleys, Sir Thomas Pert, Sir Robert Cavel, prestes, with Bertholomeu Cornmonger, John Fowlyn, Thomas Everden, William Everden and John Bayser and many other heretikes—whos scoles Y have kept and continued longe tyme, and of whom Y have herd, lerned and reported the fals doctrine and untrewe opinions whiche be writen and contened in these articules undirwriten, whiche Y confesse hereticous and erroneous and whiche Y have holde, beleved and affermed, that is to say,

First that the sacrament of Baptem, doon in watir as the comoun forme is used in the Churche, is of litel effecte and litel to be pondred, if the fadir and modir of the persone whiche shuld be baptized be of Crist' beleve.

Also that the sacrament of Confirmacion, doon be a bisshop as the comoun use is had in the Churche, is nother expedient ne necessarie unto the salvacion of mannys soules.

Also that confession oweth to be made oonly to God, and to noon ertly prest, for noon erthly prest hath poar to assoyle a man of synne.

Also that no prest hath poar to make Cristis verry body at messe in the sacrament of the auter, but that aftir the sacramental wordis said of ony prest at messe ther remayneth not ellis but oonly a cake of material bred.

Also that oonly consent of love betuxe man and woman suffiseth for the sacrament of matrimon, withoute contract of wordis or solennizacion in churche.

Also that no persone is bounde to faste in Lenton, Ymbren Days, Fridays, vigiles of seyntes ne other days and tymes whiche be commaunded of the Churche to be fasted, but that it is leful to all Cristis puple suche days and tymes at all ours to ete flessh and all maner of metis at here owyn lust; and in affermyng of this opinion Y, Edmund Archer, with Sir William Whyte, Sir William Caleys, Sir Huwe Pye and with other heretikes have ete flessh and all maner of metis indifferently as ofte as Y had lust to ete alle suche days and tymes.

Also Y have holde, beleved and affermed that Goddis puple is not bounde to kepe the holydays wich be commaunded of the Churche to be had holy, but it is leful al Cristis puple to do all bodely werkes all festival and holy days, except oonly the Sondays.

Also Y have holde, beleved and affermed that all Cristis puple may lefully withholde and withdrawe all maner of tithes and offerynges from churches and curates, so it be do prudently.

Also Y have holde, beleved and affermed that every good Cristen man is a good[a] prest, and hath as muche (p. 325 / fo. 88r)[b] poar as ony prest ordred, be he a bysshop or a pope.

Also Y have holde, beleved and affermed that chastite of monkes, chanons, freres, nonnes, prestes and of ony other persones is not commendable ne meritorie, but it is more commendable and more plesyng unto God al suche persones to be wedded and bringe forth frute of hare bodyes.

Also Y have holde, beleved and affermed that it is no synne to doon the contrierie of the preceptes of holy Churche.

Also that censures of holy Churche doon be a bysshop or ony other ordinarie be but truphes and not to be dredde.

Also Y have holde, beleved and affermed that all preyers oweth to be made oonly to God, and to noon other seint.

Also that Y have holde, beleved and affermed that it is not leful to swere in ony caas.

Also Y have holde, beleved and affermed that no maner of pilgrimage oweth to be made, but only to por men.

Also Y have holde, beleved and affermed that no maner of worship oweth to be do ne maad to ony ymages of the crucifix, of Our Lady Seint Maryne of noon other seintes, and in especial to noon ymage of Cristis crosse, for every suche crosse is the signe and the tokene of Antecrist.

Also Y have holde, beleved and affermed that it is not leful to putte ony man to deth for ony cause.

Because of whiche and many other errours and heresies Y am called tofore you, worshipful fadir, which have cure of my soule. And be you fully informed that the said myn affermyng, belevyng and holdyng be opin errours and heresies an contrarious to the determinacion of the Churche, wherfor Y willyng folwe and sue the doctrine of holy Churche, and departe from all maner of errour and heresie, and turne with good will and herte to the oonhed of the Churche. Considerand that holy Churche spereth not hyr bosom to hym that will turne agayn, ne God will not the deth of a synner but rather that he be turned and lyve, with a pure herte Y confesse, deteste and despise my sayd errours and heresies, and these said opinions Y confesse hereticous and erroneous and to the faith of the Churche of Roome and all universal holy Churche repugnant. And for as muche[c] (p. 326 / fo. 88v)[d] as be the said thinges that Y so held,

---

[a] g deleted.   [b] Ed' Archer in top right-hand corner of page.

[c] Penitencia Edmundi Archer et Johannis Pert: uterque sex fustigaciones circa ecclesiam de Lodne et totidem circa mercatum ibidem, itemque a festo Natalis Domini (abst (deleted) follows Domini) singulis vj[tis] feriis per annum ieiunet in pane et aqua, et quod per triennium agat penitenciam solennem written at the foot of the page in a different hand.

[d] Edmundus Archer in top left-hand corner of page.

beleved and affermed Y shewed meself corrupt and unfaithful, that from hensforth Y shewe me uncorrupt and faithful, the feith and doctrine of holy Churche truly to kepe Y promitte. And all maner of errour and heresie, doctrine and opinion ageyn the feith of holy Churche and determinacion of thei Churche of Roome—and namely the opinions before rehersed—Y abjure and forswere, and swere be these holy gospels be me bodely touched that from hensforth Y shal never holde errour ne heresie ne fals doctrine ageyn the feith of holy Churche and determinacion of the Churche of Roome. Ne no suche thinges Y shal obstinatly defende. Ne no persone holdyng or techyng suche maner of thinges Y shal obstinatly defende be me or ony other persone opinly or prively. Y shal never aftyr this tyme be no re-cettour, fautour, consellour or defensour of heretikes or of[a] ony persones suspect of heresie. Ne Y shal trowe to thaym. Ne wittyngly Y shal felaship with thaym, ne be hoomly with ne gyve thaym consell, yeftes, sokour, favour ne confort. Yf Y knowe ony heretikes or of heresie ony persones suspect or of thaym fautours, confortours or defensours, or of ony persones makyng prive conventicules or assembles, or holdyng ony divers or singuler opinions from the commune doctrine of the Churche, Y shal late you, worshipful fadir, or your vicar general in your absence or the diocesanes of suche persones have soone and redy knowyng. So help me God atte holy doom and these holy gospels.

In wittenesse of whiche thinges Y subscribe here with myn owyn hand a crosse +. And to this partie indented to remayne in your registre Y sette my signet. And that other partie indented Y receyve undir your seel to abyde with me unto my lyves ende. Yoven at Norwich in the chapell of your palaice the fyfte day of the moneth of August the yer of our Lord a thousand four hundred and thretty.

Quo quidem iuramento sic, ut premittitur, prestito, prefatus Edmundus Archer, in signum et testimonium quod dictum iura-mentum ratum habuit et gratum, tale signum crucis + in dicto cirographo indentato coram dicto patre iudicialiter tunc ibidem cum penna manu sua propria subscripsit, ac uni parti eiusdem indenture penes registrum dicti patris remansure sigillum suum apposuit. Et deinde prefatus reverendus pater declaravit dicto Edmundo peri-culum relapsus, dicens sibi quod si ipse postmodum relapsus (p. 327 / fo. 89r) fuerit in heresim et inde convictus,[b] propter ipsius incorrigibilitatem in hac parte Ecclesia ex tunc relinquet eum secularis potestatis iudicio comburendum. Et deinde, prestito per eundem Edmundum iuramento ad sacra evangelia per ipsum

[a] heresie *deleted*.　　　　　　　　[b] ex ti *deleted*.

corporaliter tacta de agendo debite*a* penitenciam quam prefatus reverendus pater sibi pro suis commissis prescriptis duxerit iniungendam,*b* reverendus pater ipsum Edmundum absolvit a sentencia excommunicacionis, qua premissorum occasione extitit aligatus, sub hac forma et cetera ut supra. Et pro suis commissis sibi iniunxit vj fustigaciones circa ecclesiam suam parochialem de Lodne et totidem circa mercatum,*c* quodque a festo Natalis Domini proximo ex tunc futuro singulis sextis feriis per unum annum continuum in pane et aqua ieiunet, et*d* quod per triennium proximum singulis iiij*tis* feriis in Capite Ieiu[n]ii et singulis quintis feriis in Cena Domini coram dicto reverendo patre, sive eius in hac parte vices gerente, in ecclesia Cathedrali cum aliis penitentibus se personaliter presentet, acturus solennem penitenciam pro commissis.

Presentibus tunc ibidem magistro Johanne Holdernesse, notario publico, ac Thoma Walsham, clerico, et aliis testibus et cetera. J. Excestr.

[33]

(p. 359 / fo. 105r) **Johannes Pert de Lodne**[182]

In Dei nomine, Amen. Per presens publicum instrumentum cunctis appareat evidenter quod Anno Domini ab Incarnacione eiusdem secundum cursum et computacionem Ecclesie Anglicane Millesimo CCCCº XXXº, indiccione octava, pontificatus sanctissimi in Christo patris et domini nostri, domini Martini divina providencia pape quinti, anno terciodecimo,*e* mensis Augusti die quinta, in capella palacii Norwici, in mei, Johannis Excestr, notarii, et testium presencia subscriptorum,*f* coram reverendo in Christo patre ac domino, domino Willelmo Dei gracia Norwicensi episcopo, iudicialiter sedente, assistentibus eidem reverendo patri tunc ibidem venerabilibus viris, Willelmo, priore ecclesie Cathedralis Norwicensis, ac Johanne Thorp, ordinis Carmelitarum, sacre pagine professoribus, necnon Clemente Denston, archidiacono Sudbur', et Willelmo Bernham, in decretis bacallariis, et aliis in utroque iure graduatis, Johannes Pert de Lodne, dicti patris subiectus et*g* de et

---

a qui *deleted.*   *b* et deinde *repeated.*
c q *deleted.*   *d* Penitencia solennis iij annis *in margin.*
e in capella palacii Norwic' *deleted.*
f in mei, Johannis Excestr . . . subscriptorum *interlined.*
g subiectus *repeated.*

---

182 Loddon, south-east Norfolk.

super crimine heretice pravitatis notatus et multipliciter diffamatus, adductus fuit ad iudicium in vinculis super dicto crimine heresis personaliter. Cui quidem Johanni Pert prefatus reverendus pater proposuit iudicialiter et obiecit omnes articulos in quo[dam] cirographo super abiuracione ipsius Johannis in ydeomate Anglicano concepto et indentato conscriptos et specificatos. Quos articulos omnes et singulos prefatus Johannes Pert fatebatur et recognovit iudicialiter tunc ibidem se tenuisse, credidisse et affirmasse. Et ideo idem Johannes, per prefatum patrem informatus quod dicti articuli continent in se errores et hereses quamplures, voluit, ut asseruit, omnes[a] hereses re et verbo dimittere pro perpetuo et abiurare ac ad Ecclesie unitatem redire. Et deinde, tenore abiuracionis sue coram ipso publice perlecto et per eum audito, ut asseruit,[b] et plenarie intellecto, placuit eidem, ut dixit, sub eadem forma in dicto cirographo concepta omnem heresim abiurare. Et quia asseruit se fore laicum et abiuracionem suam huiusmodi legere nescientem, ipse constituit magistrum Johannem W[ylly],[c] notarium publicum, organum vocis sue ad legendum tenorem abiuracionis sue. Et in pers[ona] ipsius magistri Johannis Wylly, organum vocis ipsius Johannis Pert in hac parte geren[tis, idem] Johannes omnem heresim—tenens interim manum suam dextram super evangelia[d]— public[e et] solenniter abiuravit sub[e] forma in dicto cirographo[f] indentato concepta. Cuius cirographi tenor sequitur et est talis.

In the name of God,[g] tofor you, the worshipful fadir in Crist, William, be the grace of God bysshop of Norwich, I, John Peert of Lodon of your diocese, your subject, felyng and undirstandyng that afore this tyme Y have holde errours and heresies, sayng, belevyng and affermyng withynne your said diocese,

That the sacrament of Baptem doon in water in forme customed of the Churche ys litel to be pondred for as muche as whan a [child comes] to yeres of discrecion and receyveth Cristis lawe and h[........], he is sufficiently baptized and so he may be saved with[oute ony other] baptem.

Also that the sacrament of Confirmacion doon [be a bisshop is] unvaillable and not profitable to mannys[h] so[wle ne to his] lyve.

Also[i] that[j] the sacrament of Confession oweth not [to be made]

---

[a] huiusmodi *deleted*.   [b] ut asseruit *interlined*.
[c] *The wearing away of the edge of this and the next folio explains why many letters have been supplied. For the supplied letters, see pp. 134-8 and elsewhere.*
[d] al *deleted*.   [e] hoc *deleted*.   [f] MS. crigrapho.
[g] et c' prout continetur in indentur' *deleted*.
[h] salvaci *deleted*.   [i] that *deleted*.   [j] that *interlined*.

(p. 360 / fo. 105v) [a] to prest, but oonly to God, for a prest hath no poar to assoyle a man of ony synne.

Also Y held, beleved and affermed that no prest hath poar to make Goddys body in the sacrament of the auter, and that aftir the sacramental wordis said of a prest at messe ther remayneth but oonly a cake of material bred.

Also that oonly consent of love in Jhu' Crist betuxe man and woman suffiseth for the sacrament of matrimon, withowtyn contract of ony wordis or solennizacion in churche.

Also that Y held, beleved and affermed that no man is bounde to faste in Lenton, Ymbre Days, Fridays, vigiles of seyntes ne other tymes whiche be commaunded of the Churche to be fasted, but it is leful to every persone alle suche days and tymes to ete flessh and alle maner of metis indifferently at her owyn lust; and in affermyng of this opinion Y have ete flessh on Fridays and in Lenton and other days before rehersed.

Also Y have holde, beleved and affermed that it is leful to every Cristen persone to do all bodely werkes on holydays whyche be commaunded of the Churche to be had holy, saf oonly the Soneday, if a man kepe hym from other synnes suche days.

Also that Y held, beleved and affermed that every man may lefully withdrawe and witholde tithes and offringes from churches and curatis, so it be do prudently.

Also that Y held, beleved and affermed that it [is] no synne to the Cristene puple to do the contrarie of the preceptis [of] holy Churche.

Also that censures of the Churche be not to be dred [ne] fered, for as sone as the bisshops or ordinaries acurse a man, [God] assoileth hym.

Also Y have holde, beleved and affermed that all [pray]ers shuld be made oonly to God, and to none other seyntes.

Also Y held, beleved and affermed that no maner of worship oweth to be do to ony ymages of the crucifix, of Our Lady Seint Mary ne of non other seyntes.

Also Y have holde, beleved and affermed that no maner of[b] pylgrimage oweth to be do to ony seyntes, but the expenses whiche shuld be do and made in suche pilgrimages shuld be yoven to the pore puple.

Also Y held, beleved and affermed that [the pope o]f Rome is Antecrist, and hath no poar in holy Churche [as Seint P]etir hadde but if he folwe the steppis of Petir in [lyvyng, and] all bysshops, prelates and prestes of the Churche [ar Antecristis] desciples.

---

[a] Joh' Pert *in top left-hand corner of page.*
[b] worship oweth to be do to ony ymages of the crucifix *per* deleted.

Because of whiche and many other errours [and heresies] Y am
called tofore you, worshipful fadir, whiche [have cure] of my soule.
And be you fully informed that the said (p. 361 / fo. 106r) myn
affermyng, belevyng and holdyng be opin errours and [heresies]
and contrarious to the determinacion of the Churche of Rome,
w[herfor] Y willyng folwe and sue the doctrine of holy Churche, and
departe from all maner of errour and heresie, and turne with good
will and herte to the oonhed of the Churche. Considerand that holy
Churche spereth not hyr bosom to hym that will turne agayn, ne
God will not the deth of a synner but rather that he be turned and
lyve, with a pure herte Y confesse, deteste and despise my said
errours and heresies, and these said opinions Y confesse hereticous
and erroneous and to the faith of the Churche of Rome and all
universal holy Churche repugnant. And for as muche as be the said
thinges that Y so held, beleved and affermed Y shewed meself
corrupt and unfaithful, that fro[m] hensforth Y shewe me uncorrupt
and faithful, the faith a[nd doctrine] of holy Churche truly to
kepe Y promitte. And all maner o[f errour] and heresie, doctrine and
opinion ageyn the faith of holy Church[e and] determinacion of the
Churche of Rome—and namely the opinions bef[ore] rehersed—Y
abjure and forswere, and swere be these holy gospels [be] me bodely
touched that from hensforth Y shal never holde err[our ne] heresie
ne fals doctrine ageyn the feith of holy Churche and [determi]nacion
of the Churche of Roome. Ne no suche thinges Y shal ob[stinatly]
defende. Ne no persone holdyng or techyng [suche maner of thinges]
Y shal ostinatly [defende] be me or ony other persone opinly or
prively. Y shal never aftir thi[s time] be no recettour, fautour, consellour or defensour of heretikes or o[f ony] persone suspect of
heresie. Ne Y shal trowe to thaym. Ne wittyngly [Y shal] felaship
with thaym, ne be homly with thaym, ne gyve thaym consell,
[yeftes,] sokour, favour ne confort. Yf Y knowe ony heretikes or of
her[esie] ony persones suspect or of thaym fautours, confortours or
defen[sours], or of*a* ony persones makyng prive conventicules or
assembles, [or] holdyng ony divers or singuler opinions from the
commune [doctrine] of the Churche, Y shal late you, worshipful
fadir, or yo[ur vicar] general in your absens or the diocesanes of
suche person[es have sone] and redy knowyng. So help me God atte
holy doom a[nd these holy gospels].

In wittenesse of whiche thinges Y subscribe here wit[h myn]
owyn hand a crosse +. And to this partie indented [to remayne in
your] registre Y sette my signet. And that other partie indented
[Y receyve undir] your seal to abide with me unto my lyves ende.
Y[oven at Norwich] in the chapell of your palayce the fifte day of

a of *repeated and deleted.*

G

the monet[h of August] the yer of our Lord a thousand four hundred and t[hretty].*a*

(p. 362 / fo. 106v) [Qua qu]idem abiuracione sic, ut premittitur, facta, in signum et testimonium quod idem Johannes Pertiura[ment]um huiusmodi ratum habuit et gratum, idem Johannes manu sua propria signum crucis in dicto cirografo subscripsit in iudicio tunc ibidem, ac uni parti eiusdem cirografi penes registrum dicti patris remanenti sigillum suum apposuit. Et deinde iuravit ad sacra evangelia per ipsum corporaliter tacta de agendo penitenciam, quam prefatus pater sibi pro suis commissis in hac parte decreverit iniungendam. Et hiis omnibus peractis, prefatus reverendus pater absolvit ipsum Johannem Pert a sentencia excommunicacionis, qua extitit alligatus occasione premissorum. Cuius quidem absolucionis forma sequitur et est talis.

In Dei nomine, Amen. Quia nos, Willelmus, permissione divina Norwicensis episcopus, contra te, Johannem Pert, sowter de Lodne nostre diocesis, subditum nostrum et subiectum, ad anime tue correccionem ex officio nostro legitime procedere intendentes, per tuam propriam confessionem coram nobis [iudicia]liter factam invenimus te infra dictam nostram diocesim nonnullas hereses et errores quam[plures] fidei orthodoxe et determinacioni universalis Ecclesie repugnantes—de quibus in quodam ciro[grapho] super tua abiuracione concepto et indentato, cuius una pars in archivis nostris noscitur [rema]nere, ad quam nos referimus et pro hic inserta haberi volumus, plenior fit mencio—[tenui]sse, credidisse et affirmasse, et per hoc in excommunicacionis sentenciam incidisse; nunc autem, [usus con]cilio saniori, petis misericordiam et sponte redis ad Ecclesie unitatem; idcirca, inprimis [abiurata] per te omni heresi et recepta per nos a te*b* secundum ritum Ecclesie iuratoria [caucione] de parendo mandatis Ecclesie, te absolvimus ab omni excommunicacionis vinculo quo tenebaris astrictus. [Et quoniam] per predicta que tenuisti, credidisti et affirmasti in Deum et sanctam matrem Ecclesiam temere [deliqu]isti, tibi pro pena penitenciali iniungimus quod a festo Natalis Domini proximo futuro singulis sextis [feriis per] unum annum continuum in pane et aqua ieiunes; et quod quatuor diebus Dominicis circa [cimiterium] ecclesie parochialis de Lodne predict' coram solenni processione eiusdem et quatuor diebus

---

a For the supplied words in this sentence, see p. 168.
b iuratoria caucione deleted.

mercati [circa merc]atum de Lodne, capite et pedibus denudatis, corpore camisia et femoralibus duntaxat [induto, cum] cereo cere ponderis dimidie libre*ᵃ* tuis*ᵇ* manibus deferendo,*ᶜ* more penitentis*ᵈ* [incedas], quem cereum proxima Dominica post penitenciam huius-modi peractam summo altari ecclesie de Lodne per te offerri [et dim]itti iniungimus et mandamus; et quod singulis quartis feriis in Capite Ieiunii et singulis [quintis f]eriis in Cena Domini per triennium coram nobis vel nostrum locum tenente in hac parte in [ecclesia] Cathedrali Norwic' cum aliis penitentibus personaliter te presentes, acturus publicam penitenciam pro [commissis. ......] ex certis causis ipsum reverendum patrem monentibus, prefatus pater asseruit se velle [................] dicte penitencie usque alias, penitencia tamen panis et aque sextis feriis predictis [......................].*ᵉ*

Presentibus tunc ibidem*ᶠ* dominis Willelmo Bamburgh, Johanne Blytheburgh, [....................d], capellanis, ac Thoma Walsham et Willelmo Steynwar, clericis. J. Excestr.

[34]

(p. 346 / fo. 98v) **Nicholaus Drye de Lenn**[183]

Nicholas Drye de Lenn Episcopi, notatus et suspectus de heresi, die septima mensis Augusti Anno Domini Millesimo CCCC⁰ Tricesimo adductus fuit in vinculis coram reverendo in Christo patre ac domino, domino Willelmo Dei gracia Norwicensi episcopo, in capella palacii Norwici iudicialiter sedente; assedentibus tunc eidem reverendo patri magistro Johanne Paas, ordinis Fratrum Minorum, sacre pagine professore, ac magistris Nicholao Derman et Johanne Bury,*ᵍ* in decretis bacallariis. Cui quidem Nicholao Drye prefatus reverendus pater dixit, obiecit et proposuit, articulando quod,

Ipse tenuit, credidit, asseruit et affirmavit infra diocesim Nor-wicensem nulli homini vel mulieri fore licitum confiteri peccata sua alicui sacerdoti, nisi tantum in mortis extremo articulo.

Item quod ipse dixit, in villa de Wymondham[184] die Pasche ultimo elapso,[185] se ipsum non fuisse confessum per quatuor annos ultimos elapsos.

ᵃ suis *deleted.*　　　　　　　*ᵇ* tuis *interlined.*
ᶜ p *deleted.*　　　　　　　　 *ᵈ* incedendo *deleted.*
ᵉ For his penance, see also p. 166, n. c.
ᶠ dn *deleted.*　　　　　　　　*ᵍ* or *deleted.*

---

[183] Lynn, Norfolk.　　[184] Wymondham, south Norfolk.　　[185] 16 April 1430.

Item quod in die Pasche ultimo elapso non fuit communicatus sacramento Eucaristie, ut ceteri fideles Christiani.

Quos quidem articulos dicto Nicholao obiectos per ipsum reverendum patrem iudicialiter, ut prefertur, idem Nicholaus Drye fatebatur et recognovit in forma sibi articulata. Et quia ipse reverendus pater habuit ipsum Nicholaum de heresi vehementer suspectum, ut asseruit, idem Nicholaus Drye, tactis sacris evangeliis, iuravit ad ea quod ex tunc ipse nunquam tenebit dictos errores vel hereses nec aliquos alios errores vel hereses nec opinionem vel doctrinam[a] fidei catholice et determinacioni sacrosancte[b] Ecclesie Romane contrariam:[c] nec aliquos hereticos vel aliquas personas de heresi suspectas recipiet, sustentabit vel supportabit; nec hereticis prebebit consilium, auxilium vel favorem publice vel occulte. Quibus sic factis, prefatus reverendus pater declaravit eidem Nicholao quod, si amodo in futurum poterit de heresi vel heretica pravitate legitime convinci, propter ipsius incorrigibilitatem debet committi potestati seculari,[d] pena mortis[e] puniendus. Et deinde, prestito per eundem iuramento de agendo penitenciam pro commissis, dominus ipsum absolvebat a sentencia excommunicacionis, qua premissorum occasione extitit innodatus. Quam penitenciam dominus reservavit sibi postmodum assignandam.

Presentibus tunc ibidem magistris Hugone Acton et Petro Werketon, notariis publicis, Thoma Rodelond, capellano, et Thoma Walsham, litterato,[f] et me, J. Excestr, actorum scriba, scribente.

Willelmus Brystowe, shipwryght de Lenn, obligatur pro dicto Nicholao per suum scriptum obligatorium in xx libras, cum condicione quod[g] Nicholaus[h] Drye prescriptus aget suam penitenciam sibi, ut premittitur, iniunctam et quod de cetero[i] servabit se ab omni heresi incorruptum.

Die xiiij Augusti Anno Domini suprascripto dictus pater[j] commisit Willelmo Bernham, officiali suo[k] principali, potestatem iniungendi dicto Nicholao penitenciam subscriptam.[l]

---

[a] determinacioni *deleted*.   [b] r *deleted*.
[c] MS. contrarium.   [d] mortali *deleted*.
[e] mortis *interlined*.   [f] et *deleted*.
[g] ipse *deleted*.   [h] Dreye *deleted*.   [i] ab *deleted*.
[j] iniunxit prefato Nicholao pro commiss' *deleted*.
[k] commisit Willelmo Bernham, officiali suo *interlined*.
[l] Willelmus Hardy *in bottom right-hand corner of page*.

[35]

(p. 243 / fo. 44r) **Thomas Mone de Lodne**[186]

In Dei nomine, Amen. Per presens publicum instrumentum cunctis appareat evidenter quod Anno ab Incarnacione Domini secundum cursum et computacionem Ecclesie Anglicane Millesimo CCCC^{mo} Tricesimo, indiccione octava, pontificatus sanctissimi in Christo patris et domini[a] nostri, domini Martini divina providencia pape quinti, anno terciodecimo, mensis Augusti die decimanova, in capella palacii reverendi in Christo patris et domini, domini Willelmi Dei gracia Norwicensis episcopi, in civitate Norwic' situati, in mei, Johannis Excestr, clerici, publici auctoritate apostolica notarii, dictique reverendi patris actorum scribe et registrarii, ac testium subscriptorum presencia, coram dicto reverendo patre, domino Willelmo Norwicensi episcopo, ad reddenda iura—prout michi, notario prescripto, tunc apparebat—pro tribunali sedente, assistentibus tunc eidem reverendo patri venerabili in Christo patre,[b] domino Roberto Dei gracia Graden' episcopo,[187] necnon discretis viris magistris Willelmo Bernham, dicti reverendi patris officiali principali, ac Thoma Ryngstede, decano ecclesie collegiate Beate Marie de Campis in Norwico, in decretis bacallariis, necnon Willelmo Ascogh, in sacra pagina licenciato,[c] Thomas Mone de Lodne Norwicensis diocesis, dicti reverendi patris subditus et subiectus, de et super crimine heresie et heretice pravitatis, ut dicebatur, multipliciter notatus et vehementer suspectus, adductus fuit ad iudicium,[d] super dicto crimine heresis personaliter responsurus. Cui quidem Thome prefatus reverendus pater proposuit et obiecit iudicialiter omnes et singulos articulos subscriptos, qui secuntur sub hac forma.

In Dei nomine, Amen. Nos, Willelmus permissione divina Norwicensis episcopus, contra te, Thomam Mone de Lodne nostre diocesis, subditum nostrum et subiectum, ex officio nostro dicimus, proponimus ac tibi obicimus articulos subscriptos[e] coniunctim et divisim, et quamlibet particulam eorundem, ad anime tue

---

[a] dm *deleted.*   [b] ac d *deleted.*   [c] ch' *deleted.*
[d] adductus fuit ad iudicium *repeated.*   [e] co *deleted.*

---

[186] Loddon, south-east Norfolk.
[187] Robert Ryngman, a Franciscan friar; as 'episcopus Gradensis' (Gardar in Greenland) he acted as suffragan to the bishops of Norwich between 1425, or 1426, and 1452 (see B. Burnham, 'The Episcopal Administration of the Diocese of Norwich in the Later Middle Ages' (unpublished Oxford B.Litt. thesis, 1971), pp. 138, 140 and 224–5; *Hierarchia Catholica medii et recentioris aevi*, ed. C. Eubel and others (Regensburg: Padua, 1898–), i, p. 270).

correccionem et omnem alium iuris effectum qui ex infrascriptis, vel eorum aliquo, sequi poterit vel debebit.

Inprimis*ᵃ* tibi proponimus, obicimus et articulamur quod infra nostram diocesim Norwicensem tu sepius habuisti suspiciosam familiaritatem et suspectam communicacionem cum nonnullis hereticis, sciens illos hereticos, quos in domos tuas sepius recepisti, ac eos concelasti, confortasti, supportasti et manutenuisti, ac eisdem iuxta vires prebuisti consilium, auxilium et favorem. Quorum hereticorum nomina sunt hec: dominus Willelmus White, dominus Hugo Pye, dominus Willelmus Caleys, dominus Thomas Pert, capellani, Johannes Waddon, Ricardus Belward, Willelmus Baxter, wright, Thomas Burell, glover, Willelmus Everden, Johannes Greye, Willelmus Bate de Sythyng,[188] Johannes Wardon, Johannes Fowlyn, Johannes Pert, Edmundus Archer. Qui sepius tenuerunt scolas de heresi in domibus tuis. Quibus scolis tu sepius interfuisti. Articulum istum prefatus Thomas fatebatur et recognovit in iudicio tunc ibidem.

Item tibi p[ro]ponimus, obicimus et articulamur quod tu infra nostram diocesim tenuisti, credidisti et affirmasti omnes hereses et errores in subscriptis articulis contentos et specificatos.

Inprimis quod sacramentum Baptismi, factum in aqua in forma fieri consueta in Ecclesia, est nisi trupha et nichil ponderandum, quia plebs Christi est sufficienter baptizatus in sanguine Christi, et sic plebs Christi non indiget alio baptismo.

Item quod sacramentum Confirmacionis ministratum per aliquem episcopum non est validum nec necessarium, quia cum aliquis infans habet discrecionem ac scit et vult intelligere verbum Dei, est sufficienter confirmatus per Spiritum Sanctum et non indiget aliqua alia confirmacione.

Item quod omnis confessio deberet fieri soli Deo, et nulli alio sacerdoti, quia nullus sacerdos habet potestatem remittendi aliqua peccata nec absolvendi quemquam a peccato.

ᵃ W. Whyte ⎫
Huge Pey ⎪
W. Calys ⎬ preistes
Tho. Pert ⎪
W. Calys ⎭   Th. Pert (*both words deleted*) / J. Waddon
Ryc. Bellward / W. Baxter /
Th. Burel. W. Everden. J. Grey
W. Bate.
J. Warden.
J. Fowlyn.
J. Pert
Edmund Archer.
written in the margin in a different hand.

[188] Seething, south-east Norfolk.

(p. 244 / fo. 44v) Item quod quilibet bonus Christianus est sacerdos.

Item quod solus consensus amoris inter virum et mulierem, absque aliquo verborum contractu et sine solennizacione in ecclesia, sufficit pro sacramento matrimonii.

Item quod nulle peregrinaciones deberent fieri aliquibus sanctis, nisi tantum pauperibus.

Item quod nullus honor est exhibendus aliquibus imaginibus crucifixi, Beate Marie nec alicuius alterius sancti, nec maior reverencia est exhibenda crucifixo in ecclesia quam furcis super quas latrones suspenduntur.

Item quod licitum est subtrahere et detinere decimas et oblaciones ab ecclesiis et curatis, et dare eas pauperibus.

Item quod licitum est cuilibet creature facere et exercere quecumque opera corporalia diebus Dominicis et aliis festis sanctificandis ex precepto Ecclesie.

Item quod aqua benedicta et panis benedictus sunt nisi trupha et multum peiores propter coniuraciones et incantaciones quas sacerdotes faciunt super eos.

Quibus quidem articulis prescriptis per prefatum reverendum patrem dicto Thome Mone sic, ut premittitur, iudicialiter obiectis,[a] idem Thomas fatebatur et recognovit expresse in iudicio tunc ibidem se omnes articulos prescriptos[b] infra diocesim Norwicensem tenuisse, credidisse et affirmasse. Qua quidem confessione per ipsum Thomam iudicialiter facta, prefatus reverendus pater intimavit eidem Thome et dixit quod dicti articuli, per ipsum Thomam sic iudicialiter confessati, continent in se nonnullas hereses et errores quamplures fidei orthodoxe et determinacioni sancte Romane Ecclesie repugnantes. Quo audito, prefatus Thomas Mone asseruit se velle extunc dictas hereses ac errores ac generaliter omnem heresim re et verbo dimittere et abiurare, ac puro corde redire ad Ecclesie unitatem. Et, hiis dictis, prefatus reverendus pater prefixit eidem Thome diem Lune proximum extunc sequentem, videlicet vicesimum primum diem dicti mensis Augusti,[c] ad abiurandas hereses huiusmodi et errores in capella palacii predicti.

Presentibus tunc ibidem discretis viris magistris Hugone Acton et Roberto Aylmer, notariis publicis, necnon Willelmo Bamburgh et Roberto Bennys, capellanis, et me, J. Excestr.

Die vero Lune, xxj mensis Augusti predicti, Anno Domini, indiccione pontificatuque predictis, in capella palacii prescripti, in mei, Johannis Excestr, notarii prescripti, et testium infrascriptorum

---

[a] p *deleted.*   [b] ac omnes hereses et errores *deleted.*   [c] h *deleted.*

[presencia], coram prefato reverendo patre,*a* domino Willelmo Norwicensi episcopo, iudicialiter sedente, assistentibus sibi tunc ibidem venerabili et religioso viro, fratre Willelmo*b* Worstede, priore ecclesie Cathedralis Norwicensis, sacre pagine professore, ac magistris Willelmo Bernham et Thoma Ludham, in decretis bacallariis, adductus fuit ad iudicium prefatus Thomas Mone. Cui prefatus reverendus pater recitavit totum processum coram ipso per prefatum Thomam*c* et contra ipsum in dicto negocio habitum. Et interrogavit idem pater ab eodem Thoma si fuerit plenarie*d* deliberatus pariter et determinatus ad abiurandas dictas hereses et errores ac omnem heresim iuxta formam in quodam cirographo, super ipsius Thome abiuracione in Anglicano ideomate concepto*e* et indentato, scriptam. Cuius quidem cirographi tenorem, coram eodem Thoma publice perlectum, idem Thomas asseruit se audivisse et plenarie intellexisse. Et prefatus Thomas respondebat, dicens se velle libenter sub eadem forma in dicto cirographo indentato conscripta omnes errores et hereses abiurare. Et quia idem Thomas asseruit se fore laicum et legere nescientem, ipse constituit magistrum Johannem Wylly, notarium publicum, tunc ibidem presentem, organum vocis sue ad*f* legendam dictam abiuracionem nomine et vice ipsius Thome; promittens se ratum, gratum, firmum et stabile habiturum totum et quicquid*g* (p. 245 / fo. 45r)*h* per prefatum magistrum Johannem Wylly nomine suo dictum sive lectum fuerit in hac parte. Et deinde idem magister Johannes Wylly, organum vocis dicti Thome Mone in se assumens, totum tenorem abiuracionis ipsius Thome de verbo ad verbum publice perlegit. Et interim prefatus Thomas Mone, tenens manum eius dexteram super librum evangeliorum, iuravit ad ea se omnia et singula in dicto cirographo indentato contenta ac per prefatum Johannem Wylly, organum vocis ipsius Thome in hac parte gerentem, perlecta iuxta omnem vim, formam et effectum eiusdem cirographi imperpetuum inviolabiliter observaturum. Cuius quidem cirographi tenor sequitur et est talis.

In the name of God, tofore you, the worshipful fadir in Crist, William be the grace of God bisshop of Norwich, Y, Thomas Mone of Lodne of your diocese, your subject, knowyng, felyng and undirstandyng that before this tyme Y have be right hoomly and

---

a patre *repeated*.   *b* Willelmo *repeated*.
c hi *deleted*.   *d* informatus *deleted*.
e MS. conceptam.   *f* se *deleted*.
    g per prefatum magistrum Johannem Wylly *in bottom right-hand corner of page*.
    h Thomas Mone, ii (*i.e., folio 2 of the trial of Thomas Mone*) *in top right-hand corner of page*.

prive with many heretikes, knowyng thaym for heretikes, and thaym Y have receyved and herberwed in myn hous, and thaym Y have conceled, conforted, supported, may[n]tened and favered with al my poar—whiche heretikes names be these, Sir William White, Sir Huwe Pye, Sir William Caleys, Sir Thomas Pert, prestes, John Waddon, Richard Belward, William Baxter, wright, Thomas Borell, glover, William Everden, John Grey, William Bate of Sethyng, William Wardon, John Fowlyn, John Pert and Edmond Archer and many otheres—whiche ofte tymes have kept, holde, and continued scoles of heresie yn prive chambres and places of myne, yn the whiche scoles Y have herd, conceyved, lerned and reported the errours and heresies whiche be writen and contened in these indentures, that is to say,

Fyrst that the sacrament of Baptem doone in watir in forme customed in the Churche is but a trufle and not to be pondred, for all Cristis puple is sufficiently baptized in the blood of Crist, and so Cristis puple nedeth noon other baptem.

Also that the sacrament of Confirmacion doon be a bisshop is of noon availe ne necessarie to be had, for as muche as whanne a child hath discrecion and can and wile understande the woord of God, it is sufficiently confermed be the Holy Gost and nedeth noon other confirmacion.

Also that confession shuld be maad only to God, and to noon other[a] prest, for no prest hath poar to remitte synne ne to assoyle a man of ony synne.

Also that every good Cristene man is a prest.

Also that oonly consent of love betuxe man and woman, withoute contract of wordes and withoute solennizacion in churche, is sufficient for the sacrament of matrimon.

Also that no pilgrimage oweth be doo to oony seyntes, but oonly to the pore puple.

Also that no worship shulde (p. 246 / fo. 45v) be do to ony ymages of the crucifix, of Our Lady Seynt Marie ne of noon other seyntes, ne no more reverence shuld be do to the crucifix in the churche than to the galwes whyche theves be hanged on.

Also that it is leful to withdrawe and withholde tithes and offrynges from prestes and curates, and yeve hem to the pore puple.

Also that it is leful to do all bodely werkes on Sonedays and all other festival days whiche be commaunded of the Churche to be had holy.

Also that holy water and holy bred ben but trufes and muche the werse for the conjuraciones and charmes whiche the prestes do therover.

[a] seynt *deleted*.

Also that all maner of preyer oonly shuld be maade to God, and to noo other seyntes.

Because of whiche and many other errours and heresies Y am called tofore you, worshipful fadir, whiche have cure of my soule. And be you fully informed that the said myn affermyng, belevyng and holdyng be opin errours and heresies and contrarious to the determinacion of the Churche of Roome, wherfore Y willyng folwe and suwe the doctrine of holy Churche, and departe from all maner of errour and heresie, and turne with good will and herte to the oonhed of the Churche. Considerand that holy Churche spereth not hir bosom to hym that will turne agayne, ne God will not the deth of a synner but rather that he be turned and lyve, with a pure herte Y confesse, deteste and despise my said errours and heresies, and these opinions Y confesse heretikous and erroneous and to the faith of the Churche of Roome and all universal holy Churche repugnant. And for as muche as be the said thinges that Y so held, beleved and affermed Y shewed meself corrupt and unfaithful, that from hensforth Y shewe me uncorrupt and faithful, the faith and doctrine of holy Churche truly to kepe Y promitte. And all maner of errour and heresie, doctrine and opinion ageyn the feith of holy Churche and determinacion of the Churche of Roome—and namely the opinions before rehersed—Y abjure and forswere, and swere be these holy gospels be me bodely touched that from hensforth Y shal never holde errour ne heresie ne fals doctrine ageyn the feith of holy Churche and determinacion of the Churche of Roome. Ne no suche thynges Y shal obstinatly defende. Ne ony persone holdyng or techyng suche maner of thinges Y shal obstinatly defende be me or ony other persone opinly or prively. Y shal never aftyr this tyme (p. 247 / fo. 46r)*a* be no recettour, fautour, consellour or defensour of heretikes or*b* of ony persone suspect of heresie. Ne Y shal never trowe to thaym. Ner*c* wittyngly Y shal felaship with ne be hoomly with thaym, ne gyve thaym consell, yeftes, sokour, favour ne confort. Yf Y knowe ony heretikes or*d* of heresie ony persones suspect or of thaym fautours, confortours or defensours,*e* or of ony persones makyng prive conventicules or assembles, or holdyng of ony divers or synguler opinions from the commune doctrine of the Churche, Y shal late you, worshipful fadir, or your vicar general in your absence or the diocesanes of suche persones have soone and redy knowyng. So help me God atte holy doom and these holy gospels.

In wittenesse of whiche thinges Y subscribe here with myn owyn hand a crosse +. And to this partie indented to remayne in your

---

a Thomas Mone, iii *in top right-hand corner of page.*
b MS. of.   *c* be ho *deleted.*
d MS. of.   *e* of heretikes *deleted.*

registre Y sette my signet. And that other partie indented Y receyve
undir your seel to abyde with me unto my lyves ende. Yoven at
Norwich in the chapell of your palayce the xxj day of the moneth
of August the yer of our Lord a thousand four hundred and thretty.

Quo quidem sic prestito, ut prefertur, in testimonium quod prefatus Thomas Mone dictum iuramentum ratum habuit et gratum,
ipsemet Thomas manu sua propria signum crucis huiusmodi + in
dicto cirographo indentato subscripsit, ac uni parti eiusdem cirographi penes registrum dicti reverendi patris remansure sigillum
suum apposuit in iudicio tunc ibidem. Et tunc prefatus reverendus
pater intimavit dicto Thome Mone periculum sibi venturum si
postea in heresim fuerit relapsus,*a* dicens eidem Thome hec verba vel
consimilia in effectu. 'Thoma, abstineas te amodo ab omni specie
heresis iuxta*b* exigenciam abiuracionis tue hic coram nobis facte. Et
scias indubie quod si ab hac hora in antea relapsus fueris in heresim,
tunc auctoritas ecclesiastica te merito incorrigibilem pronunciabit.
Et tunc, secundum iura istius regni, iudicium secularis potestatis te
condempnabit propter tuam incorrigibilitatem temerariam huiusmodi*c* merito comburendum.' Et tunc prefatus Thomas iuravit ad
sancta evangelia tunc ibidem per ipsum corporaliter tacta de agendo
debite penitenciam quam prefatus reverendus pater sibi pro suis
commissis prescriptis decreverit iniungendam. Quam penitenciam
prefatus reverendus pater misit in suspenso et voluit deferri, ut
asseruit, propter senectutem et debilitatem dicti Thome. Et tunc
prefatus reverendus pater ipsum Thomam a sentencia excommunicacionis, qua premissorum occasione extitit alligatus, absolvebat in
debita iuris forma.

Presentibus tunc ibidem domino Willelmo Bamburgh, capellano,
Thoma Rodelond, capellano, ac Willelmo Steynwar et Hugone
Bryket, testibus ad premissa vocatis specialiter et rogatis. J. Excestr.

[36]

(p. 237 / fo. 40r) **Johannes Fynche de Colcestr'**[189]

In Dei nomine, Amen. Per presens publicum instrumentum cunctis
appareat evidenter quod Anno ab Incarnacione Domini secundum

---

a de *deleted.*   *b* *An illegible word deleted.*   *c* huiusmodi *interlined.*

189 Colchester.

cursum et computacionem Ecclesie Anglicane Millesimo Quadringentesimo Tricesimo, indiccione octava,[190] pontificatus sanctissimi in Christo patris et domini nostri, domini Martini divina[a]
providencia pape huius nominis quinti, anno terciodecimo, mensis
Septembris die vicesima, in camera principali palacii[b] reverendi in
Christo patris et domini, domini[c] Willelmi Dei gracia Norwicensis
episcopi[d] in civitate Norwic' situati, in mei, Johannis Excestr,
clerici, notarii subscripti et dicti reverendi patris in huiusmodi
negocio actorum scribe, ac Johannis Poleyn et Thome Walsham,
clerici, testium ad infrascripta vocatorum specialiter et rogatorum
[presencia], coram dicto reverendo patre iudicialiter sedente,
assistentibus eidem tunc ibidem venerabili ac religioso viro, fratre
Willelmo Worstede, priore ecclesie Cathedralis Norwicensis, in sacra
pagina professore, ac magistro Willelmo Ascogh, in sacra theologia
licenciato, Johannes Fynche, tyler, nuper commorans in vico vulg-
ariter nuncupato Crowche Stre de Colcestr'[191] Londoniensis diocesis,
qui[e] nuper in villa[f] Gippewici[192] Norwicensis diocesis propter suspicionem heresis et heretice pravitatis, de qua fuit notatus, captus
extitit et incarceratus, adductus fuit in vinculis, super dicto crimine
heresis personaliter responsurus. Qui quidem Johannes, ad sacra
Dei evangelia eius manu dextera tacta iuratus de veritate materiam
fidei concernente quam sciverit et noverit dictura, coram dicto
reverendo patre omnes et singulos errores[g] et hereses in subscriptis articulis contentos et specificatos se tenuisse, credidisse et
affirmasse fatebatur publice et recognovit. Qui quidem articuli sub-
scribuntur sub hac forma.

Inprimis quod sacramentum Baptismi, factum in aqua in forma
in ecclesiis communiter usitata, non est necessarium nec valet ad
incrementum glorie in celo, quia omnes infantes sunt sufficienter
baptizati in sanguine passionis Christi, et sic non indigent aliquo
alio baptismo.

Item quod omnis confessio soli Deo est facienda, et nulli alio
sacerdoti, quia nullus sacerdos habet potestatem absolvendi quemquam ab aliquo peccato.

Item quod nullus sacerdos ad missam habet potestatem conficiendi corpus Christi in sacramento altaris sub specie panis et vini.

Item quod solus consensus amoris inter virum et mulierem sufficit

---

[a] p'p' *deleted.*   [b] palacii *interlined.*
[c] dm' *deleted.*   [d] infra pa *deleted.*
[e] qui *interlined.*   [f] d *deleted.*   [g] MS. *erroreres.*

---

[190] Eighth according to the Bedan indiction, though ninth according to the
Greek indiction (see p. 32, n. 2).
[191] Crouch Street, Colchester.   [192] Ipswich.

pro sacramento matrimonii perfecti, sine aliquo contractu per verba et sine solennizacione in ecclesia.

Item quod non licet homini iurare in aliquo casu.

Item quod quilibet homo potest licite facere et exercere quecumque opera corporalia, excepto solum peccato, diebus Dominicis ac omnibus aliis diebus festivis, quos presbiteri in ecclesiis precipiunt sanctificari per ordinacionem Ecclesie.

Item quod omnis homo tenetur subtrahere et detinere omnimodas decimas et oblaciones a curatis et presbiteris, et dare illas pauperibus.

Item quod nemo obligatur nec tenetur ieiunare tempore Quadragesimali, diebus Quatuor Temporum, sextis feriis nec sanctorum vigiliis, que presbiteri precipiunt ieiunari.

Item quod omnes oraciones soli Deo sunt faciende, et nullis aliis sanctis.

Item quod peregrinaciones nullo modo sunt faciende, nisi tantum pauperibus.

Item quod nullus honor est exhibendus aliquibus ymaginibus in ecclesiis.

Quos quidem errores et hereses prescriptos prefatus Johannes Fynche asseruit iudicialiter coram dicto (p. 238 / fo. 40v) reverendo patre se tenuisse, credidisse et affirmasse a festo Natalis Domini Anno Domini Millesimo CCCC^{mo} Vicesimo Septimo. Pro quibus quidem heresibus et erroribus prescriptis idem Johannes Fynche asseruit iudicialiter se conventum fuisse ad iudicium coram magistro David Pryce,[193] commissario domini Londoniensis episcopi, in ecclesia Sancti Nicholai Colcestr'[194] procedente iudicialiter contra ipsum Johannem Fynche, notatum et diffamatum vehementer de heresi, circa festum Sancti Michaelis Anno Domini Millesimo CCCC^{mo} Vicesimo Octavo.[195] Coram quo quidem magistro David Price, commissario predicto, dictus Johannes Fynche, personaliter comparens et per dictum commissarium iudicialiter impetitus de heresibus et erroribus quos^a ipse Johannes prius, ut asseruit, tenuit et credidit, eosdem hereses et errores sic per ipsum tentos, creditos et affirmatos ab omni tempore expresse negavit. Ac super librum missalem per ipsum corporaliter tactum iuravit, licet falso, quod ipse nunquam tenuit, credidit nec affirmavit aliquos hereses vel errores. Et tamen, ut asseruit, contrarium fuit verum. Et insuper

---

^a p *deleted*.

[193] Emden, *BRUO*, i, pp. 549–50, David ap Rees. His proceedings against John Fynche were not recorded in the register of William Gray, bishop of London 1426–31, nor are they known to survive in any other records.
[194] The parish church of St Nicholas, Colchester.
[195] 29 December 1428.

prefatus Johannes Fynche coram dicto reverendo patre fatebatur
iudicialiter et recognovit quod post tempus quo idem Johannes
Fynche se sic falso periuravit super librum missalem coram dicto
commissario, ut prefertur, ipse Johannes Fynche diversis temporibus
audivit, didicit et reportavit ac tenuit, credidit et affirmavit dictos
hereses et errores quos ipse iuravit, licet falso, ut premittitur, se
nunquam tenuisse, credidisse nec affirmasse.

Quibus sic prehabitis, prefatus reverendus pater declaravit dicto
Johanni Fynche quod in dictis articulis, per ipsum Johannem coram
eodem patre sic iudicialiter confessatis, continentur nonnulle
hereses et errores quamplures fidei catholice et determinacioni
Ecclesie Romane contrarii et repugnantes. Ideoque prefatus
Johannes Fynche voluit,[a] ut asseruit, eosdem hereses et errores
prescriptos ac quoscumque alios re et verbo extunc pro perpetuo
dimittere et abiurare, ac puro corde ad Ecclesie unitatem redire. Et
tunc,[b] forma sive tenore abiuracionis ipsius Johannis Fynche in
ideomate Anglicano concepto et in quodam cirographo[c] indentato
scripto ac coram eodem Johanne de verbo ad verbum publice[d]
perlecto et per ipsum Johannem Fynche, ut asseruit, plenarie intellecto, placuit eidem Johanni, ut asseruit, sub eadem forma omnes
errores et hereses abiurare, asserens tamen se fore et esse laicum et
nescire legere ipsam abiuracionem propria in persona. Ideoque ipse
Johannes Fynche rogavit et requisivit instanter magistrum Johannem
Wylly, notarium publicum, tunc ibidem presentem, ad legendam
abiuracionem suam vice et nomine suis. Cui quidem magistro
Johanni Wylly idem Johannes Fynche commisit organum vocis sue.
Ipsumque organum vocis sue in hac patre constituit et ordinavit.
Promisit insuper idem Johannes Fynche se ratum, gratum et firmum
pro perpetuo habiturum totum et quicquid per prefatum magistrum
Johannem Wylly actum, lectum sive factum fuerit nomine suo in
hac parte. Qui quidem magister Johannes Wylly, organum vocis
ipsius Johannis Fynche in se assumens, tenorem abiuracionis ipsius
J. Fynche voce intelligibili perlegit iudicialiter tunc ibidem. Et
interim prefatus Johannes Fynche, tenens manum suam dexteram
super librum evangeliorum, iuravit ad ea se omnia et singula per
prefatum magistrum Johannem Wylly in dicto cirografo[e] deducta
et perlecta, quatenus personam ipsius Johannis Fynche concernunt,
iuxta tenorem eiusdem cirografi pro perpetuo inviolabiliter observaturum. Cuius quidem cirografi indentati tenor sequitur et est
talis.[f]

[a] *MS.* volens. [b] abiuracione sua *deleted.*
[c] sr *deleted.* [d] inte *deleted.*
[e] perlect *deleted.*
[f] in the name of God *in bottom right-hand corner of page.*

(p. 239 / fo. 41r)[a] In the name of God, tofore you, the worshipful fadir in Crist, William be the grace of God bysshop of Norwich, Y, John Fynche, tyler, duellyng in the parissh of Crowche Churche[196] in Colcestre, late taken in the toun of Gipeswiche of your diocese for suspecion of heresie and enprisoned, your subject, felyng and undirstandyng that Y have be familier and conversaunt with heretikes— that is to say with Laurence Tyler, Ducheman, and with John Laborere, hys man, and with otheres—of whos doctrines Y have hard, lerned, conceyved and reported alle the errours and heresies whiche be writen and contened in this indenture, whiche Y have holde, beleved and affermed,

First that the sacrament of Baptem doon in watir in the comune forme custumed of the Churche is nother necessarie ne vailable to encresse of blisse, for every chyld is sufficiently baptized in the blood of Cristis passion and nedeth noon other baptem.

Also that confession oweth be maade only to God, and to noon other prest, for no prest hath poar to assoile a man of ony synne.

Also that oonly consent of love betuxe man and woman is sufficiant for the sacrament of perfit matrimon, withoute ony contract of wordes and withoute ony solennizacion in churche.

Also that it is not leful a man to swere in ony caas.

Also that every man may lefully doo all bodely werkis, save oonly synne, on Sondays and all other festival day[s] whyche prestis commaunde to be kept holy be ordinance of the Churche.

Also that every man is bounde to withdrawe and withholde all tithes and offeryngges from curates and prestes, and yeve thaym to pore puple.

Also that no man is bounde to faste in Lenton tyme, the Ymbren Days, Fridays ne vigiles of seyntes, whiche prestes commaunde to be fasted.

Also that all preyer oweth be made oonly to God, and noon other seyntes.

Also that no pilgrimage oweth be do ne maad, but oonly to the pore puple.

Also that no maner of worship ne reverence oweth to be do to ony ymages.

Whiche errours and heresies Y herd, conceyved, reported, held and affermed from the feste of Cristemesse in the yer of our Lord a thousand four hundred twente and sevene. And for the whiche

---

[a] J. Fynche, ii (i.e., folio 2 of the trial of John Fynche) in top right-hand corner of page.

---

[196] The parish of St Mary at the Walls, sometimes known as Crouch Church because the church of the Crutched Friars lay within it.

heresies and errours (p. 240 / fo. 41v) Y, John Fynche, was convened judicially before Master David Pryce, commissarie of my lord of London, sittyng judicially in Seynt Nicholas Churche of Colcestre and procedyng ageyn me, noted and defamed hugely of heresie, abowte the feste of Seint Michael the Archangel the yer of our Lord a thousand four hundred twenty and aggte. Before which Mayster David Price Y, judicially apeched and articuled to of the heresies and errours whiche in trouthe Y held, beleved and affermed before that tyme, denyed and swore untrewly on the messe book be me bodyly touched that Y never held, beleved*a* ne*b* affermed noon heresies. And so untrewely and falsly Y purged me of all errours and heresies before the same Maister David. And aftir the said tyme that Y so foresware me falsly on the messe book Y have sundry tymes herd, lerned, reported, holde, beleved and affermed the said heresies and errours whiche Y swore untrewely that Y was not gylty of. Because of whiche and many other errours and heresies Y am called tofore you, worshipful fadir, whiche have cure of my soule. And be you fully enformed that the said myn affermyng, belevyng and holdyng be opin errours and heresies and contrarious to the determinacion of the Churche of Rome, wherfor Y willyng folwe and sue the doctrine of holy Churche, and departe from all mener of errour and heresie, and turne with good will and herte to the oonhed of the Churche. Considerand that holy Churche spereth not hyr bosom to hym that will turne agayn, ne God will not the deth of a synner but rather that he be turned and lyve, with a pure herte Y confesse, deteste and despise my said errours and heresies, and the said opinions Y confesse hereticous and erroneous and to the faith of the Churche of Rome and all universall holy Churche repugnant. And for as muche as be the said thinges that Y so held, beleved and affermed Y shewed meself corrupt and unfaithful, that from hensforth Y shewe me uncorrupt and faithful, the faith and doctrine of holy Churche truly to kepe Y promitte. And all maner of errour and heresie, doctrine and opinion ageyn the faith of holy Churche and determinacion of the Churche of Rome—and namely the opinions before rehersed—(p. 241 / fo. 42r)*c* Y abjure and forswere, and swere be these holy gospels be me bodely touched that from hensforth Y shal never holde errour ne heresie ne fals doctrine ageyn the faith of holy Churche and determinacion of the Churche of Rome. Ne non suche thinges Y shal obstinatly defende. Ne no persone holdyng or techyng suche maner of thynges Y shal obstinatly defende be me or ony other persone opinly or prively. Y shal never aftir this tyme be no recettour, fautour, consellour or defen-

---

a and *deleted.*   *b* ne *interlined.*
c J. Fynche, iii *in top right-hand corner of page.*

sour of heretikes or of ony persone suspect of heresie. Ne Y shal[a]
trowe to thaym. Ne wittyngly Y shal felaship with thaym, ne be
hoomly with thaym, ne gyve thaym consell, yeftes, sokour, favour
ne confort. Yf Y knowe ony heretikes or of heresie ony persones suspect or of thaym fautours, confortours, consellours[b] or defensours,
or of ony personys makyng prive conventicules or assembles, or
holdyng ony divers or singuler opinions from the commune doctrine
of the Churche, Y shal late you, worshipful fadir, or your vicar
general in your absence or the diocesanes of suche persones have
sone and redy knowyng. So help me God atte holy doom and these
holy gospels.

In wittenesse of whiche thinges Y subscribe here with myn owyn
hand a crosse +. And to this partie indented to remayne in your
registre Y sette my sygnet. And that other partie indented Y
receyve undir the seel of office of your vicar generall to abide with
me unto my lyves ende. Yoven at Norwich in the chapell of your
palaice the xx day of the moneth of Septembr the yer of our Lord
a thousand four hundred and thretty.

Quo quidem iuramento sic prestito, ut prefertur, prefatus Johannes
Fynch in testimonium quod illud iuramentum ratum habuit et
gratum, ipse manu sua propria[c] tale crucis signum + in dicto cirographo indentato subscripsit. Ac uni parti eiusdem cirographi,
penes registrum dicti reverendi patris remansure, sigillum suum
apposuit in iudicio tunc ibidem. Et deinde prefatus pater intimavit
dicto Johanni periculum sibi venturum si imposterum in dictum
crimen heresis fuerit relapsus, dicens eidem hec verba in effectu.
'Johannes, ab hac hora in antea abstineas te ab omni specie heresis
iuxta effectum abiuracionis tue. Quia indubie, si deinceps relapsus
fueris in eandem, propter tuam incorrigibilitatem in hac parte
sancta Ecclesia[d] te[e] extunc derelinquet. Et,[f] secundum iura regni,[g]
te[h] comburendum potestatis[i] secularis iudicium condempnabit.'
Quibus sic peractis, prefatus Johannes Fynche iuravit ad sacra
evangelia per ipsum corporaliter tacta de agendo debite penitenciam quam prefatus reverendus pater sibi pro suis commissis in hac
parte duxerit iniungendam. Et deinde prefatus reverendus pater
absolvebat ipsum Johannem Fynche a sentencia excommunicacionis, qua premissorum occasione extitit alligatus. Ac sibi iniunxit
penitenciam pro suis commissis sub eo qui sequitur tenore verborum.

---

[a] never *deleted*.   [b] and *deleted*.
[c] s *deleted*.   [d] te *deleted*.
[e] te *interlined*.   [f] Et *interlined*.
[g] p *deleted*.   [h] te *interlined*.   [i] iudic' *deleted*.

(p. 242 / fo. 42v)[a] In Dei nomine, Amen. Quia nos, Willelmus permissione divina Norwicensis episcopus, contra te, Johannem Fynche, nuper in villa Gippewic' nostre diocesis propter suspicionem heresis arestatum, subditum nostrum et subiectum, ad anime tue correccionem ex officio nostro legitime procedere intendentes, per tuam propriam confessionem coram nobis iudicialiter factam invenimus te infra dictam nostram diocesim nonnullas hereses et errores quamplures fidei orthodoxe et determinacioni universalis Ecclesie repugnantes—de quibus in quodam cirographo super tua abiuracione concepto et indentato, cuius una pars in archivis nostris noscitur remanere, ad quam nos referrimus et pro hic inserta haberi volumus, plenior fit mencio—tenuisse, credidisse et affirmasse, et per hoc in excommunicacionis sentenciam incidisse; nunc autem, usus consilio saniori, petis misericordiam et sponte redis ad Ecclesie unitatem; idcirco, inprimis abiurata per te omni heresi et recepta per nos a te secundum ritum Ecclesie iuratoria caucione de parendo mandatis Ecclesie, te absolvimus ab omni excommunicacionis vinculo quo tenebaris astrictus. Et quoniam per predicta que teniusti, credidisti et affirmasti in Deum et sanctam matrem Ecclesiam temere deliquisti, tibi pro pena penitenciali tres fustigaciones coram solenni processione ecclesie nostre Cathedralis Norwicensis tribus diebus Dominicis, et totidem fustigaciones circa publicum mercatum civitatis Norwic' tribus diebus principalibus mercati ibidem, capite et pedibus denudatis, corpore curtello solomodo induto, cum cereo cere ponderis unius libre[b] tuis[c] manibus deferendo et proxima Dominica post huiusmodi penitenciam peractam coram principali imagine Sanctissime Trinitatis[197] offerendo humiliter et devote, et[d] quod per tres annos proximos et immediate iam futuros singulis quartis feriis in Capite Ieiunii et singulis quintis feriis in Cena Domini coram nobis aut nostro locumtenente in ecclesia nostra Cathedrali Norwic' cum aliis penitentibus personaliter te presentes acturus publicam penitenciam pro commissis,[e] iniungimus iudicialiter in hiis scriptis.

Acta sunt hec prout suprascribuntur et recitantur sub Anno Domini, indiccione, pontificatu, mense, die et loco prescriptis; presentibus tunc ibidem testibus prenominatis. J. Excestr.

Memorandum quod feria iiij[ta] in Capite Ieiunii Anno Domini Millesimo CCCC[mo] XXX[o] [198] dictus Johannes Fyche non com-

[a] Johannes Fynche *in top left-hand corner of page.*
[b] suis *deleted.*   [c] tuis *interlined.*
[d] Penitencia solennis iij annis *in margin.*   [e] tibi *repeated.*

---

[197] An image in Norwich Cathedral (see Blomefield, *Norfolk*, iv, p. 30).
[198] 14 February 1431.

paruit in ecclesia Cathedrali Norwic' cum aliis penitentibus iuxta iniunxionem predictam.*a*

[37]

(p. 243 / fo. 43r) **Johannes Wroxham de Lodne,**[199] **sowter**

In Dei nomine, Amen. Per presens publicum instrumentum cunctis appareat evidenter quod Anno ab Incarnacione Domini secundum cursum et computacionem Ecclesie Anglicane Millesimo CCCC*mo* Tricesimo, indiccione octava,[200] pontificatus sanctissimi in Christo patris et domini nostri, domini Martini divina providencia pape quinti, anno terciodecimo, mense Septembris die vicesima secunda, in quodam claustro infra palacium reverendi in Christo patris et domini, domini Willelmi Dei gracia Norwicensis episcopi, in civitate Norwici situatum, in mei,*b* Johannis Excestre, notarii publici ac dicti reverendi patris actorum scribe, ac Johannis Wylly, notarii publici, Johannis Poleyn et Thome Walsham, clerici, testium ad infrascriptum negocium rogatorum specialiter et requisitorum, [presencia], coram dicto reverendo patre, domino Willelmo Norwicensi episcopo, iudicialiter sedente, comparuit personaliter Johannes Wroxham de Lodne Norwicensis diocesis, suter; de crimine heretice pravitatis dictus vehementer suspectus. Qui quidem Johannes Wroxham, de crimine heresis per ipsum, ut dicebatur, infra diocesim Norwicensem tente, credite et affirmate per prefatum reverendum patrem allocutus et iudicialiter impetitus, fatebatur et recognovit iudicialiter*c* tunc ibidem se infra diocesim Norwicensem tenuisse credidisse et affirmasse omnes hereses et errores subscriptos, qui sequuntur seriatim sub hac forma.

Inprimis quod sacramentum Baptismi, factum in aqua in forma in ecclesiis communiter usitata, parum vel nichil est ponderandum.

Item quod omnis confessio facienda est soli Deo, et nulli alio sacerdoti.

Item quod solus mutuus consensus amoris inter virum et mulierem sufficit pro sacramento matrimonii, absque contractu per verba et sine solennizacione in ecclesia.

---

a Johannes Wroxham *in bottom right-hand corner of page.*
b noti *deleted.*   *c* cor *deleted.*

[199] Loddon, south-east Norfolk.
[200] Eighth according to the Bedan indiction, though ninth according to the Greek indiction (see p. 32, n. 2).

Item quod licitum est cuilibet creature exercere quecumque opera corporalia, preter peccata, omnibus diebus festivis indictis per Ecclesiam, exceptis duntaxat diebus Dominicis.

Item quod nullus honor est exhibendus aliquibus ymaginibus in ecclesiis vel extra.

Item quod omnes oraciones soli Deo sunt faciende, et non aliquibus aliis sanctis.

Item quod peregrinaciones nullo modo sunt faciende, nisi tantum pauperibus.

Item quod nullo modo licet iurare.

Item quod nemo tenetur ieiunare diebus Quadragesimalibus, diebus Quatuor Temporum, sextis feriis nec vigiliis sanctorum indictis per Ecclesiam.

Item quod omnes campane in ecclesiis sunt[a] cornua Antechristi, et solum ordinate per cupiditatem presbiterorum.

Quibus quidem articulis per prefatum Johannem Wroxham coram dicto patre recognitis iudicialiter et confessatis, prefatus reverendus pater intimando dixit dicto Johanni Wroxham quod in dictis articulis, per ipsum sic confessatis, continentur nonnulle hereses et errores quamplures fidei orthodoxe et determinacioni[b] Romane Ecclesie repugnantes. Quo audito, prefatus Johannes Wroxham voluit, ut asseruit, eosdem hereses et errores ac eciam omnem heresim extunc re et verbo dimittere pro perpetuo et abiurare, ac redire puro corde ad Ecclesie unitatem. Et, tenens manum suam dexteram super librum evangeliorum, ad ea iuravit iudicialiter tunc ibidem quod ab hac hora in futurum ipse nunquam tenebit, credet nec affirmabit aliquas hereses vel errores nec aliquam heresim nec aliquam opinionem vel doctrinam fidei catholice et determinacioni Ecclesie Romane contrariam vel repugnantem, nec aliquos hereticos vel personam de heresi suspectam recipiet, supportabit vel sustentabit, nec eis prebebit consilium, auxilium vel favorem per se vel aliam mediam personam directe vel indirecte, publice vel occulte, sub pena mortis. Quo iuramento per ipsum Johannem Wroxham (p. 242[c] / fo. 43v) prestito, ut prefertur, prefatus reverendus pater intimavit dicto Johanni Wroxham penam sibi infligendam si in dictum crimen[d] heresis residivaverit in futurum, dicens eidem hec verba vel consimilia in effectu. 'Johannes, abstineas te amodo ab omni specie heresis iuxta effectum abiuracionis tue predicte. Quia tibi notifico quod, si ab hac hora in antea relapsus fueris in heresim sic quod pro relapso in heresim poteris legitime convinci,[e] extunc sancta mater Ecclesia propter tuam incorrigibilita-

---

[a] ca deleted.
[c] Sic, see p. 2 and Table 1 (p. 3).
[d] r deleted.

[b] ecclesie deleted.
[e] st deleted.

tem indubie te dimittet. Et tunc iudicium potestatis secularis, secundum iura istius regni, condempnabit te pro tua*a* incorrigibilitate temeraria merito comburendum.' Et tunc prefatus Johannes iuravit ad sacra evangelia, per ipsum corporaliter tacta, de agendo debite penitenciam quam prefatus reverendus pater sibi pro suis commissis in hac parte decreverit iniungendam. Quibus sic peractis, prefatus reverendus pater ipsum Johannem Wroxham a sentencia excommunicacionis, qua premissorum occasione extitit alligatus, canonice absolvebat. Ac sibi pro suis commissis iniunxit penitenciam infrascriptam: videlicet,*b* duas*c* fustigaciones circa cimiterium ecclesie parochialis de Lodne coram solenni processione eiusdem*d* duobus*e* diebus Dominicis, et totidem fustigaciones circa publicum mercatum de Lodne aliis*f* duobus*g* diebus, capite et pedibus denudatis, corpore curtello induto, et cereum cere ponderis j libre suis manibus deferendo et offerendo summo altari dicte ecclesie de Lodne post penitenciam huiusmodi peractam humiliter et devote.

Acta sunt hec et cetera, presentibus testibus prenominatis et ceteris. J. Excestr.*h*

[38]

(p. 287 / fo. 67r)*i* **Ricardus Clerk**

Ricardus Clerk de Sethyng[201] Norwicensis diocesis, citatus responsurus personaliter de et super crimine heretice pravitatis die Sabbati, videlicet nono die mensis Decembris Anno Domini Millesimo CCCCmo Tricesimo, coram magistro Willelmo Bernham, in decretis bacallario, reverendi in Christo patris et domini, domini Willelmi Dei gracia Norwicensis episcopi, vicario in spiritualibus generali, in capella palacii dicti patris in civitate Norwici situati iudicialiter sedente, comparuit personaliter. Cui prefatus vicarius in spiritualibus generalis, iudex in ea parte, dixit, obiecit et proposuit articulando articulos ac hereses et*j* errores subscriptos.

Inprimis quod ipse Ricardus habuit sepius suspectam communi-

---

a temeritate *deleted.*
c duas *interlined.*
e duobus *interlined.*
g duobus *interlined.*
b tres *deleted.*
d tribus *deleted.*
f tribus *deleted.*
h Thomas Mone *in bottom right-hand corner of page.*
i Sibilla, uxor Johannis Godesell, parchemen maker, fatebatur coram dicto patre *at top of page, the first five words being deleted.*
j err *deleted.*

---

201 Seething, south-east Norfolk.

cacionem*a* et conversacionem cum hereticis, et quod recepit hereticos in domos suas et eos supportabat, sustentabat et concelabat ac
eisdem in eorum opinionibus prebuit consilium, auxilium et favorem.

Item quod*b* ipse Ricardus infra diocesim Norwicensem tenuit,
credidit et asseruit hereses et errores ac opiniones fidei catholice et
determinacioni Ecclesie Romane contrarias et repugnantes: videlicet, contra sacramentum Baptismi factum in aqua, contra Con-
firmacionem, contra sacramenta Confessionis et Penitencie, Matrimonii, Ordinis et Extreme Unccionis et Eucaristie sacramentum,
item contra decimas et oblaciones, ac contra peregrinaciones et*c*
ymaginum adoraciones, et contra observaciones ieiuniorum*d* ac
sanctificacionem Sabbatorum, ac contra ordinem presbiteratus, ac
contra continenciam presbiterorum et monialium.

Contra fidem orthodoxam ac determinacionem Ecclesie Romane
omnia premissa negavit. Et produxit Nicholaum Bunne, Willelmum*e*
Noble, Johannem Ferant, Johannem Rendham, Johannem Cok,
parochianos de Sythyng. Et purgavit se de omnibus et singulis
erroribus et heresibus ac opinionibus prescriptis.

Presentibus tunc ibidem magistris Hugone Acton, Roberto Aylmer
et Johanne Cok, notariis publicis.

(Pro commissis iniunxit quod ieiunet in pane et aqua omnibus
vigiliis Beate Marie et in pane et cervisia omnibus*f* sextis feriis per
septennium, et quod semel in Capite Ieunii se presentet coram
domino et in Cena Domini proxim'.)*g*

[39]

(p. 288 / fo. 67v) **Thomas White de Bedyngham**202

Thomas Whyte de Bedyngham, citatus super crimine heretice*h*
pravitatis responsurus die ix° Decembris Anno Domini M° CCCC°

a on' *deleted.*
c An illegible letter *deleted.*
e Bunne Willelmus *deleted.*

b tu *deleted.*
d indictorum *deleted.*
f Dominic' dii *deleted.*

g The bracketed paragraph is at the foot of the page, detached from the other
contents of the page. It seems unlikely that it refers to Richard Clerk since he
successfully purged himself. Of those whose trials appear on the preceding page of
the manuscript and on the following one, it could refer to Katherine Wryght (see
pp. 193–4). But this, too, seems unlikely since there is space after the record of her
trial for it to have been written there. *h* pravat *deleted.*

202 Bedingham, south Norfolk.

XXX⁰ coram magistro Willelmo Bernham, dicti reverendi patris
vicario in spiritualibus generali, in capella palacii Norwici iudicialiter
sedente, comparuit personaliter. Et obiect' sibi quod ipse habuit
communicacionem et conversacionem cum hereticis, et quod ipse
tenuit nonnullas opiniones contra sacramenta Baptismi, Confirmacionis, Penitencie, Eucaristie, Ordinis, Matrimonii et Extreme
Unxionis ac contra decimas [et] oblacciones ac contra observacionem
ieiuniorum et contra sanctificacionem Sabbatorum indictas per
Ecclesiam* necnon contra peregrinaciones et adoraciones ymaginum
contra fidem catholicam et determinacionem Ecclesie Romane,
die nona Decembris Anno Domini M⁰ CCCC⁰ XXX⁰ comparuit. Et
negavit premissa sibi obiecta. Et* habuit ex prefixione magistri
Willelmi Bernham,* dicti patris vicarii in spiritualibus generalis, ad
purgandum se cum vij manu in capella palacii Norwici die Mercurii
proximo post festum Sancte Lucie Virginis.

Quibus die et loco, videlicet xx^mo die mensis Decembris Anno
Domini prescripto, coram prefato magistro Willelmo Bernham,
dicti reverendi patris vicario in spiritualibus generali, in dicta
capella palacii iudicialiter sedente, comparuit prefatus Thomas
White. Et produxit compurgatores suos: videlicet, Johannem Caly,
Ricardum White de Witton,²⁰³ Johannem Borle, Ricardum Borle
de Topcroft,²⁰⁴ Johannem White de eadem et Johannem Prathell.
Et purgavit se solenniter.

Presentibus tunc ibidem Johanne Yarnemuth, Simone Thornham
et Thoma Walsham, cleric', testibus et ceteris. J. Excestr.

[40]

Katerina Wryght, uxor Rogeri Wryght de Shotesham²⁰⁵

Die Mercurii, videlicet xx⁰ die Decembris Anno Domini M⁰ CCCC⁰
XXX⁰, indiccione nona, pontificatus domini Martini pape v^ti anno
xiiij⁰, coram discreto viro, magistro Willelmo Bernham, in decretis
bacallario, reverendi in Christo patris et cetera, Willelmi Dei gracia
Norwicensis episcopi, vicario in spiritualibus generali, in capella
palacii Norwic' iudicialiter sedente, comparuit personaliter dicta

---

a MS. ecclesias.   *b* cum vii ma *in margin.*   *c* j *crossed out.*

²⁰³ Probably Witton near Blofield, east Norfolk; possibly Witton near
North Walsham, north-east Norfolk.
²⁰⁴ Topcroft, south Norfolk.   ²⁰⁵ Shotesham, south Norfolk.

Katerina. Notata et vehementer suspecta de crimine heretice pravitatis et impetita iudicialiter de dicto crimine, fatebatur et recognovit iudicialiter tunc ibidem se tenuisse credidisse, asseruisse et affirmasse nonnullas opiniones sive conclusiones contra fidem orthodoxam et determinacionem Ecclesie Romane et in specie sacramenta Ecclesie: videlicet,

Contra*a* sacramenta Baptismat', Confirmacionis, Confessionis, Eucaristie, Matrimonii.

Ac contra observacionem ieiuniorum et sanctificacionem dierum et temporum indictorum per Ecclesiam.

Et contra decimas et oblaciones faciendas ecclesiis vel curatis.

Item fatebatur se tenuisse quod precepta Ecclesie non sunt observanda, nec censure ecclesiastice timende.

Et quod omnis oracio soli Deo est facienda,*b* et nullis aliis sanctis.

Et quod nullo modo licet iurare.

Et quod nullus honor est exhibendus aliquibus ymaginibus in ecclesiis nec alibi.

Et quod peregrinaciones nullo modo sunt faciende, nisi tantum pauperibus.

Quibus per ipsam Katerinam sic iudicialiter confessatis, ipsa Katerina iuravit ad sacra evangelia per ipsam tacta quod ab hac hora in antea ipsa nunquam tenebit, credet nec affirmabit predictas hereses nec aliquas alias hereses vel errores nec opinionem aliquam contra fidem Ecclesie et determinacionem Ecclesie Romane, nec hereticos vel personas aliquas de heresi suspectas supportabit, sustentabit, concelabit vel defendet per se nec per mediam personam, nec eisdem prebebit consilium, auxilium vel favorem sub pena iuris. Quam penam dictus iudex declaravit eidem Katerine iudicialiter tunc ibidem, dicens eidem sub hac forma: 'Katerina, credas pro firmo quod si post istud tempus in*c* heresis crimen fueris relapsa ita quod legitime possis convinci iudicialiter in hac parte, tradi debes potestatis iudicio secularis.'

Presentibus tunc ibidem Johanne Yarnemuth, Simone Thornham ac Thoma Walsham, cleric' Norwicensis diocesis, ac aliis pluribus testibus et ceteris. J. Excestr.

[41]

(p. 328 / fo. 89v) **Nomina personarum comparencium coram priore[206] ecclesie Cathedralis Norwic' quarta feria in Capite**

---

a bapt *deleted.*   *b* n *deleted.*   *c* dictum crimen *deleted.*

[206] William de Worsted (see p. 32, n. 8).

Ieiunii Anno Domini Millesimo CCCC^{mo} Tricesimo²⁰⁷ in eadem ecclesia Cathedrali iuxta iniunxiones^a reverendi in Christo patris et domini, domini Willelmi Dei gracia Norwicensis episcopi, propter hereses et errores quas et quos tenuerunt, crediderunt et affirmarunt per confessiones suas proprias coram dicto patre iudicialiter factas, acturarum^b in hac parte solennem penitenciam pro commissis, sunt hec:

Isti comparent per assignacionem penitenciariorum pro aliis causis.

[...]ice pravitat' [...]accem' dm'.^c

Johannes Skylan	Johannes Dawe ⎱
Ricardus Grace de Beccles²⁰⁹	Katerina, uxor ⎰ de Pulham²⁰⁸ eius
Johannes Reve de Beccles	Jacobus Godestone ⎱
Ricardus Knobbyng de Beccles	Margareta, uxor ⎰ de Possewyk²¹⁰ eius
Johannes Eldon de Beccles	Johannes Mannyng de M'ton²¹¹
Willelmus Hardy de Mundham²¹³	Johannes Cullyng de Gerveston²¹²
Willelmus Bate de Sethyng²¹⁴	
Johanna, uxor Johannis Weston de Norwico	
Katerina Hobbes, uxor Thome Pert	

[42]

(p.235 / fo. 38r) **Robertus Gryggys de Martham**²¹⁵

In Dei nomine, Amen. Per presens publicum instrumentum cunctis appareat evidenter quod Anno ab Incarnacione Domini

---

^a *For the injunctions, see pp.: 110 (John Reve), 119 (Richard Knobbyng), 124 (Richard Grade), 138 (John Eldon), 151 (John Skylan), 156 (William Hardy) and 163 (William Bate).* ^b sol *deleted.*
^c *Because the edge of the page has worn away, the letters which precede* ice (= heretice?) *and* accem' *have been lost as have, presumably, some other words.*

---

²⁰⁷ 14 February 1431.
²⁰⁸ Pulham, south Norfolk.
²⁰⁹ Beccles, north-east Suffolk.
²¹⁰ Postwick, near Norwich.
²¹¹ The place is unidentifiable.
²¹² Garveston, mid Norfolk.
²¹³ Mundham, south-east Norfolk.
²¹⁴ Seething, south-east Norfolk.
²¹⁵ Martham, east Norfolk.

secundum cursum et computacionem Ecclesie Anglicane Millesimo CCCC° Tricesimo, indiccione nona, pontificatus sanctissimi in Christo patris et domini nostri, domini Martini divina providencia pape quinti, anno quartodecimo, mense Februarii die decimaseptima, in capella palacii episcopalis Norwic' in civitate Norwic' situati, in mei, Johannis Excestr, clerici, publici auctoritate apostolica notarii, ac Thome Walsham, Willelmi Fraunceys et domini Johannis Blytheburgh, capellani, testium ad^a subscripta vocatorum specialiter et rogatorum, [presencia], coram reverende discrecionis viro, magistro Willelmo Bernham, in decretis bacallario, reverendi in Christo patris et domini, domini Willelmi Dei gracia Norwicensis episcopi, vicario in spiritualibus generali, pro tribunali ad iura reddenda—ut michi, notario predicto, tunc apparebat—sedente, comparuit personaliter Robertus Grygges de Martham Norwicensis diocesis, capenter; de heresi et heretica pravitate notatus, ut dicebatur, et multipliciter diffamatus ac ea occasione personaliter responsurus coram dicto vicario generali ad dictos diem et locum evocatus, et per prefatum vicarium generalem de heresi et heretica pravitate per ipsum^b Robertum infra diocesim Norwicensem tenta, credita et affirmata [impetitus]. Qui quidem Robertus Grigges tunc ibidem fatebatur iudicialiter et recognovit se infra diocesim Norwicensem tenuisse, credidisse et affirmasse omnes et singulos hereses et errores subscriptos.

Inprimis videlicet quod sacramentum Baptismi, factum in aqua per aliquem presbiterum in forma in ecclesiis fieri communiter usitata, parum vel nichil est ponderandum dummodo parentes infancium sint Christiani.

Item quod sacramentum Confirmacionis ministratum per aliquem episcopum nichil confert ad salutem.

Item quod omnis confessio soli Deo est facienda, et nulli alio sacerdoti, quia per peccata Deus offenditur et non sacerdos, et nullus sacerdos habet potestatem absolvendi quemquam a peccatis, sed solus Deus remittit peccata.

Item quod nullus sacerdos habet potestatem conficiendi corpus [Christi] sub specie panis et vini in sacramento altaris ad missam, sed post verba sacramentalia quantumcumque rite a presbitero prolata purus panis materialis remanet in altari.

Item quod solus consensus mutui amoris inter virum et mulierem sufficit pro sacramento matrimonii, absque aliquo contractu per verba seu solennizacione in ecclesia.

Item quod nemo tenetur ieiunare tempore Quadragesimali, diebus Quatuor Temporum, sextis feriis, vigiliis Apostolorum nec aliquibus aliis diebus vel temporibus indictis per Ecclesiam.

    ^{a} ad *interlined*. ^{b} in *deleted*.

Item quod peregrinaciones nullo modo sunt faciende, nisi tantum pauperibus.

Item quod nullus honor est exhibendus aliquibus ymaginibus in ecclesiis.

Item quod nullo modo licet iurare.

Item quod non est peccatum contravenire preceptis Ecclesie.

Item quod licitum est cuilibet subtrahere decimas et oblaciones ab ecclesiis et curatis, dumtamen hoc fiat prudenter.

Item quod panis benedictus et aqua benedicta sunt nisi truphe, et panis et*a* aqua huiusmodi efficiuntur peiores propter coniuraciones et carecteres quos presbiteri faciunt super eos.

Item quod papa est Antechristus, et episcopi ac alii ecclesiarum*b* prelati sunt discipuli Antechristi.

Quibus quidem articulis per prefatum Robertum Grigges coram dicto vicario generali, ut premittitur, (p. 236 / fo. 38v) iudicialiter confessatis, prefatus vicarius generalis asseruit et intimavit dicto Roberto Grygges quod*c* dicti articuli per ipsum sic, ut premittitur, confessati continent in se nonnullas hereses et errores quamplures fidei catholice et determinacioni Ecclesie Romane contrarias et repugnantes. Et hiis dictis, prefatus Robertus asseruit se velle dictos hereses et errores ac quoscumque alios hereses et errores extunc re et verbo pro perpetuo dimittere et abiurare, ac puro corde redire ad Ecclesie unitatem. Et deinde idem Robertus, manum suam dexteram tenens super librum evangeliorum, iuravit ad ea quod ab hac hora in antea ipse nunquam tenebit, credet nec affirmabit dictos errores vel hereses nec aliquam aliam heresim vel hereses nec opinionem vel doctrinam fidei catholice et determinacioni sancte Romane Ecclesie contrarias et repugnantes, nec aliquos hereticos vel aliquas personas de heresi suspectas recipiet vel supportabit, nec talibus personis prebebit consilium, auxilium vel favorem publice vel occulte. Quibus sic peractis, dictus vicarius generalis asseruit dicto Roberto quod si in posterum relapsus fuerit in heresim sic quod possit inde legitime convinci, propter ipsius incorrigibilitatem debet relinqui iudicio seculari, ignis supplicio comburendus. Et subsequenter idem Robertus, tactis evangeliis prescriptis, iuravit ad ea de bene et fideliter agendo penitenciam quam dictus vicarius generalis pro suis commissis suprascriptis sibi duxerit iniungendam. Et tunc idem vicarius in spiritualibus ipsum Robertum Grygges a sentencia excommunicacionis, qua premissorum occasione extitit alligatus, absolvit in debita iuris forma. Et pro suis commissis prescriptis iniunxit sibi tres fustigaciones circa cimiterium ecclesie parochialis de Martham coram solenni processione eiusdem tribus diebus Dominicis proximis facienda, capite et pedibus denudatis,

---

a q *deleted.*   *b* p's' *deleted.*   *c* n *deleted.*

corpore camisia et femoralibus duntaxat induto, candelam cere precii j^d suis manibus deferendo et offerendo summo altari dicte ecclesie proxima Dominica post ipsam penitenciam peractam.^a

[43]

(p. 248 / fo. 46v) **Isabella Chapleyn de Martham**²¹⁶

In Dei nomine, Amen. Per presens publicum instrumentum cunctis appareat evidenter quod Anno ab Incarnacione Domini secundum cursum et computacionem Ecclesie Anglicane Millesimo CCCC^o XXX°, indiccione nona, pontificatus sanctissimi in Christo patris et domini nostri, domini Martini divina providencia pape quinti,^b [anno] quartodecimo,²¹⁷ mensis^c Marcii die secunda, in capella palacii episcopalis in civitate Norwic' situati, in mei, Johannis Excestr, clerici, publici auctoritate apostolica notarii, et testium subscriptorum presencia,^d coram reverende discrecionis viro magistro Willelmo Bernham, in decretis bacallario, reverendi in Christo patris et domini, domini Willelmi Dei gracia Norwicensis episcopi, vicario in spiritualibus generali, pro tribunali sedente, comparuit^e in iudicio Isabella Chapleyn de Martham Norwicensis diocesis, de crimine heresis et heretice pravitatis multipliciter notata. Cui quidem Isabelle Chapleyn prefatus vicarius in spiritualibus, iudex in hac parte, ex officio suo ad anime^f correccionem dicte Isabelle, ut asseruit, procedens, proposuit et obiecit omnes et singulos articulos subscriptos.

Inprimis quod prefata Isabella tenuit, credidit et affirmavit omnes hereses subscriptos: videlicet, quod sacramenta Baptismi et Confirmacionis, ministrata in forma communiter usitata in ecclesiis, parum vel modicum sunt ponderanda si parentes pueri baptizandi vel confirmandi sunt Christiani.

Item quod omnis confessio facienda est soli Deo, et nulli sacerdoti,

---

^a Johannes Fynche *in bottom right-hand corner of page.*
^b mei *deleted.*   ^c ffe *deleted.*
^d add *deleted.*   ^e a *deleted.*
^f sue *deleted.*

---

²¹⁶ Martham, east Norfolk.
²¹⁷ Martin V died on 20 February 1431: Eugenius IV was elected on 3 March and crowned on 11 March 1431 (*Handbook of Dates*, ed. C. R. Cheney (London, 1945), p. 38). But even after the election and coronation of Eugenius IV, all the dates in the manuscript that use a pontifical year (the last datable to a day is 14 March 1431) continue to use a year of Martin V's pontificate.

quia nullus sacerdos habet potestatem absolvendi quemquam a peccatis.

Item quod nullus sacerdos habet potestatem conficiendi Christi corpus in sacramento altaris,[a] et quod post verba sacramentalia, a quocumque presbitero in missa quantumcumque rite prolata, remanet in altari purus panis materialis.

Item quod solus mutuus consensus amoris inter virum et mulierem sufficit pro sacramento matrimonii, absque verborum prolacione seu solennizacione in ecclesia.

Item quod censure ecclesiastice nullo modo sunt ponderande.

Item quod licitum est cuilibet creature subtrahere decimas et oblaciones ab ecclesiis et curatis.

Item quod quilibet potest licite exercere quecumque opera corporalia preter peccata omnibus diebus Dominicis et aliis festivis indictis per Ecclesiam.

Item quod[b] nemo tenetur ieiunare tempore Quadragesimali, diebus iiij^{or} Temporum, sextis feriis, vigiliis sanctorum et aliis diebus indictis per Ecclesiam, sed omnibus talibus diebus et temporibus quilibet potest licite edere carnes et omnimoda cibaria indifferenter.

Item quod nullus honor est exhibendus aliquibus ymaginibus crucifixi vel alicuius alterius sancti.

Item quod panis benedictus et aqua benedicta sunt nisi trufe et peiores propter carecteres et coniuraciones quos presbiteri faciunt super eisdem.

Item quod nullo modo licet iurare.

Quos quidem articulos prescriptos per prefatum vicarium generalem dicte Isabelle iudicialiter obiectos eadem Isabella fatebatur et recognovit iudicialiter se tenuisse, credidisse et affirmasse. Et tunc dictus iudex intimavit eidem Isabelle quod dicti articuli, sic per ipsam iudicialiter confessati, continent in se nonnullas hereses et errores quamplures sancte Romane Ecclesie repugnantes. Et deinde dicta Isabella asseruit se velle dictos hereses et errores omnes et singulos ac quoscumque alios hereses et errores pro perpetuo re et verbo dimittere et abiurare, ac ut filia Ecclesie puro corde redire ad Ecclesie unitatem.[c] (p. 249 / fo. 47r)[d] Et deinde eadem Isabella Chapleyn, tenens manum suam dexteram super librum evangeliorum, iuravit ad ea quod ab hac hora in ante ipsa nunquam tenebit, credet nec affirmabit dictos errores nec hereses nec aliquos eorundem nec heresim vel hereses nec doctrinam vel opinionem aliquam fidei catholice et determinacioni sancte Ecclesie Romane contrarias vel repugnantes, nec aliquos hereticos vel personas de heresi suspectas

---

[a] s' *deleted.*
[b] quilibet potest licite *deleted.*
[c] et deinde *in bottom right-hand corner of page.*
[d] Isabella Chapleyn *in top right-hand corner of page.*

recipiet, supportabit, concelabit vel defendet, nec talibus personis prebebit consilium, auxilium vel favorem publice vel occulte. Quibus sic peractis, dictus vicarius generalis denunciavit dicte Isabelle Chapleyn quod si imposterum relapsa fuerit in heresim et convinci poterit evidenter de relapsu in heresim, propter ipsius incorrigibilitatem in hac parte relinqui debet seculari iudicio comburenda. Et, hiis peractis, ipsa Isabella ut supra iuravit ad sacra evangelia de agendo penitenciam sibi pro suis commissis iniungendam. Et tunc dictus vicarius in spiritualibus ipsam a sentencia excommunicacionis, qua premissorum [occasione] extitit alligata, absolvit in forma iuris. Et sibi pro suis commissis prescriptis iniunxit vj fustigaciones circa cimiterium ecclesie parochialis de Martham vj diebus Dominicis coram solenni processione eiusdem, pedibus denudatis, capite flameola velato ac corpore curtello induto, cum candela cere valoris unius oboli, et totidem fustigaciones circa mercatum de Lodne[218] pari forma. Tamen propter senectutem, miseriam et impotenciam ipsius Isabelle dictus iudex remisit sibi omnem penitenciam predictam preter tres fustigaciones circa ecclesiam parochialem de Martham.

Presentibus tunc ibidem magistris Roberto Aylmer, Johanne Cok, Hugone Acton et Johanne Crakall, publicis auctoritate apostolica notariis. J. Excestr.

[44]

(p. 261 / fo. 53r) **Robertus Tolle de Thirnyng**[219]

Anno Domini Millesimo CCCC^{mo} ^a Tricesimo, indiccione nona, pontificatus domini Martini pape quinti anno quartodecimo, mensis Marcii die quinta, in capella palacii Norwic', in mei, Johannis Excestr, clerici, notarii publici, et testium subscriptorum presencia, coram reverende discrecionis viro magistro Willelmo Bernham, in decretis bacallario, reverendi in Christo patris et domini, domini Willelmi Dei gracia Norwicensis episcopi, vicario in spiritualibus generali, iudicialiter sedente, Robertus Tolle de Thirnyng Norwicensis diocesis, notatus et diffamatus de crimine heresis et lollardie ac ea occasione[b] auctoritate dicti reverendi patris arestatus et sub custodia carcerali[c] in palacio Norwic' aliquamdiu detentus,

---

a XX *deleted.*   *b* s *deleted.*   *c* a *deleted.*

218 Loddon, south-east Norfolk.
219 Thurning, north Norfolk.

productus fuit ad iudicium super dicto crimine personaliter responsurus. Cui prefatus vicarius in spiritualibus proposuit et obiecit sub hac forma.

In Dei nomine, Amen. Nos, Willelmus Bernham, in decretis bacallarius, reverendi in Christo patris et domini, domini Willelmi Dei gracia Norwicensis episcopi, vicarius in spiritualibus generalis, contra te, Robertum Tolle de Thirnyng Norwicensis diocesis, dicti reverendi patris et nostrum eius nomine subditum et subiectum, dicimus, proponimus*a* ac tibi obicimus articulos subscriptos coniunctim et divisim et quamlibet particulam eorundem ad anime tue correccionem et omnem alium iuris effectum qui ex infrascriptis vel eorum aliquo sequi poterit vel debebit.

Inprimis videlicet tibi dicimus, proponimus, obiicimus et articulamur quod tu infra diocesim Norwicensem animo deliberato tenuisti, credidisti et affirmasti quod nullus sacerdos habet potestatem conficiendi corpus Christi in sacramento altaris ad missam, sed quod post verba sacramentalia a quocumque presbitero rite prolata remanet in altari purus panis materialis,*b* cui nullus honor est exhibendus.

Item quod omnis confessio soli Deo est facienda.

Item quod licitum est cuilibet*c* creature subtrahere decimas et oblaciones ab ecclesiis et curatis.

Item quod nullus honor est exhibendus aliquibus ymaginibus in ecclesiis nec extra.

Quos quidem articulos omnes et singulos prefatus Robertus expresse negavit. Unde dictus iudex assignavit sibi diem Veneris proximum post festum Sancti Gregorii ad purgandum se in capella predicta cum septima manu de vicinis suis.

Presentibus tunc ibidem magistro Roberto Woler,*d* vicario ecclesie de North Elmham,[220] Willelmo Bamburgh et Johanne Irmynglond, presbiteris.

Quibus die[221] et loco, coram prefato vicario generali iudicialiter sedente, dictus Robertus Tolle comparuit personaliter. Et produxit compurgatores suos: videlicet, Edm' Mason de Stodey,[222] Simonem Ev'ard de Bryston,[223] Thomam Norton de eadem, Robertum Gent de Thirnyng, Willelmum Goter de eadem et Johannem Groom de Thyrnyng. Et purgavit se solemniter.

Presentibus tunc ibidem dominis Johanne Irmynglond et Johanne

---

a obiicimus *deleted.*   *b* cun *deleted.*
c cre' *deleted.*   *d* r *follows* Woler.

---

[220] North Elmham, mid-Norfolk.   [221] 16 March 1431.
[222] Stody, north Norfolk.   [223] Briston, north Norfolk.

Blytheburgh, capellanis, ac Willelmo Fraunceys et Johanne Braunche,[224] armigero, et aliis quampluribus. J. Excestr.

[45]

(p. 259 / fo. 52r) **Johannes Spyr de Bungey[225]**

Anno Domini Millesimo CCCC[mo] Tricesimo, indiccione nona, pontificatus domini Martini divina providencia pape quinti anno quartodecimo, mensis Marcii die terciadecima, in ecclesia parochiali Sancti Stephani Norwic', in mei, Johannis Excestr, clerici, notarii publici, et testium subscriptorum presencia, coram reverende discrecionis viro magistro Willelmo Bernham, in decretis bacallario, reverendi in Christo patris et domini, domini Willelmi Dei gracia Norwicensis episcopi, vicario in spiritualibus generali, iudicialiter sedente, comparuit personaliter Johannes Spyr de Bungeye Norwicensis diocesis, notatus et diffamatus de crimine heresis et lollardie. Cui quidem Johanni Spyr prefatus vicarius in spiritualibus, ex officio suo ad meram anime ipsius Johannis correccionem procedere intendens, ut asseruit, proposuit[a] iudicialiter et obiecit omnes articulos subscriptos sub hac forma.

In Dei nomine, Amen. Nos, Willelmus Bernham, in decretis bacallarius, reverendi in Christo patris et domini, domini Willelmi Dei gracia Norwicensis episcopi, vicarius in spiritualibus generalis, contra te, Johannem Spyr de Bungeye Norwicensis diocesis, dicti reverendi patris et nostrum subditum et subiectum, ex officio nostro dicimus, proponimus ac tibi obicimus articulos subscriptos coniunctim et divisim, et quamlibet particulam eorundem, ad anime tue correccionem et omnem alium iuris effectum qui ex infrascriptis vel eorum aliquo sequi poterit vel debebit.

Item tibi proponimus, dicimus, obiicimus et articulamur quod infra diocesim Norwicensem animo deliberato tu tenuisti, credidisti et affirmasti quod confessio vocalis alteri sacerdoti facienda non est, nisi soli Deo.

Item tibi dicimus, obiicimus et articulamur quod tu tenuisti, credidisti et affirmasti quod nullus sacerdos habet potestatem conficiendi corpus Christi ad missam sub specie panis et vini in sacramento altaris, sed post verba sacramentalia, ab aliquo presbitero

[a] et ob *deleted.*

---

[224] See Blomefield, *Norfolk*, ix, pp. 187, 402, 441–2, and x, p. 469.
[225] Bungay, north-east Suffolk.

quantumcumque rite prolata, purus panis materialis et vinum materiale tantum remanent in altari.

Item tibi dicimus, obiicimus et articulamur quod tu tenuisti, credidisti et affirmasti quod decime et oblaciones subtrahende sunt ab ecclesiis et curatis.

Item quod tu tenuisti, credidisti et affirmasti quod censure ecclesiastice nullo modo sunt timende.

Item quod tu tenuisti, credidisti et affirmasti quod non est orandum alicui sancto, nisi soli Deo.

Item quod tu tenuisti, credidisti et affirmasti quod nullo modo licet iurare.

Quibus quidem articulis suprascriptis, per prefatum vicarium in spiritualibus dicto Johanni Spyr iudicialiter obiectis, idem Johannes Spyr fatebatur et recognovit iudicialiter se tenuisse, credidisse et affirmasse. Et, hiis factis, dictus vicarius generalis asseruit et declaravit dicto Johanni Spyr quod dicti articuli per ipsum, ut premittitur, iudicialiter confessati continent in se errores et hereses quamplures fidei catholice et determinacioni Ecclesie Romane repugnantes. (p. 260 / fo. 52v) Et ideo dictus vicarius in spiritualibus quesivit ab eodem Johanne Spyr an voluerit dictos hereses et errores per ipsum, ut premittitur, iudicialiter confessatos defendere et tenere necne. Cui prefatus Johannes respondebat, dicens se velle omnes hereses et errores in prescriptis articulis specificatos ac generaliter omnem heresim re et verbo dimittere pro perpetuo et abiurare, ac puro corde redire ad Ecclesie unitatem. Et subsequenter tunc ibidem idem Johannes, tenens manum suam de[x]teram super librum [evangeliorum], iudicialiter iuravit ad ea quod ab hac hora in antea ipse nunquam tenebit, credet nec affirmabit hereses nec errores in dictis articulis contentos nec aliquam*a* heresim nec aliquam doctrinam vel opinionem fidei catholice et determinacioni Ecclesie Romane*b* contrariam vel repugnantem, nec aliquos hereticos nec aliquam personam de heresi suspectam recipiet, supportabit, sustentabit, defendet vel concelabit, nec talibus personis prebebit consilium, auxilium vel favorem publice nec occulte. Quo iuramento sic per ipsum Johannem Spyre sic prestito iudicialiter, ut prefertur, dictus vicarius in spiritualibus declaravit et dixit dicto Johanni Spyr in iudicio tunc ibidem quod si ipse Johannes S. de cetero in futurum relapsus fuerit in heresim et convictus legitime de heresi, tunc propter ipsius incorrigibilitatem in ea parte relinqui debet seculari iudicio comburendus. Et deinde, prestito per eundem Johannem Spyr iuramento ad sacra evangelia per ipsum corporaliter tacta de agendo debite penitenciam quam vicarius in spiritualibus

---

a hereses *deleted.*   *b* Ecclesie *repeated.*

H

predictus*a* sibi pro suis commissis duxerit iniungendam, prefatus vicarius in spiritualibus ipsum Johannem Spyr absolvit a sentencia excommunicacionis, qua premissorum occasione extitit alligatus. Et pro commissis sius s[u]p[ra]scriptis iniunxit sibi duas fustigaciones circa ecclesiam parochialem de Bungey et totidem circa mercatum publicum eiusdem ville, circa ecclesiam videlicet duabus Dominicis diebus coram solenni processione eiusdem et circa publicum mercatum dicte ville duabus diebus publici mercati ibidem, capite et pedibus denudatis, corpore camisia et femoralibus duntaxat induto, cereum cere ponderis unius libre suis manibus deferendo et post penitenciam suam huiusmodi peractam offerendo summo altari ecclesie parochialis predicte.

Presentibus tunc ibidem magistris Johanne Mosburgh, rectore ecclesie parochialis de Shipdam[226] Norwicensis diocesis, ac Hugone Acton, notariis publicis, necnon Willelmo Fraunceys ac Thoma Walsham, clericis, testibus ad premissa vocatis specialiter et rogatis. J. Excestr.*b*

[46]

(p. 250 / fo. 47v) **Willelmus Masse de Ersham**[227]

Die xiiij mensis Marcii Anno Domini M⁰ CCCC⁰ Tricesimo, indiccione nona, pontificatus sanctissimi in Christo patris et domini, domini Martini divina providencia pape huius nominis quinti, anno xiiij⁰,*c* in capella palacii reverendi in Christo patris et domini, domini Willelmi Dei gracia Norwicensis episcopi, in civitate Norwic' situati, coram reverende discrecionis viro magistro Willelmo Bernham, in decretis bacallario, dicti reverendi patris vicario in spiritualibus generali, in mei, Johannis Excestr, clerici, publici auctoritate apostolica notarii, et testium subscriptorum presencia, comparuit personaliter Willelmus Masse de Ersham Norwicensis [diocesis], notatus et vehementer suspectus, ut dicebatur, de heresi.*d* Cui quidem Willelmo Masse prefatus vicarius in spiritualibus generalis, iudex presidens, tunc ibidem proposuit iudicialiter et obiecit quod ipse Willelmus Masse omnes et singulos hereses et errores in subscriptis articulis specificatos et conscriptos in diocesi Norwicensi tenuit, credidit et affirmavit.

---

a vicarius in spiritualibus *repeated.*
b Robertus Tolle *in bottom right-hand corner of page.*
c cor *deleted.*   *d* q *deleted.*

---

[226] Shipdham, mid-Norfolk.   [227] Earsham, south-east Norfolk.

Inprimis videlicet quod sacramentum Baptismi, factum in aqua secundum formam in Ecclesia communiter usitatam, parum vel nichil est ponderandum.

Item quod omnis confessio facienda est soli Deo, et nulli alio sacerdoti.

(Item quod nullus sacerdos habet potestatem conficiendi corpus Christi in sacramento altaris, sed quod in sacramento altaris post verba sacramentalia a sacerdote rite prolata [remanent] panis materialis et vinum materiale.)*a*

Item quod solus mutuus consensus inter virum et mulierem sufficit pro sacramento matrimonii, absque aliquo contractu per verba seu solennizacione in ecclesia.

Item quod quilibet fidelis homo est sacerdos.

Item quod nullus honor*b* est exhibendus aliquibus ymaginibus factis per manus hominis.

Item quod nulle peregrinaciones sunt faciende, nisi*c* cum propriis bonis.

Item quod licitum est subtrahere et detinere decimas et oblaciones ab ecclesiis et prelatis.

Quos quidem articulos prescriptos, ac omnes hereses et errores in eisdem contentos et specificatos, prefatus Willelmus Masse fatebatur et recognovit iudicialiter coram dicto vicario in spiritualibus se tenuisse et credidisse. Et deinde prefatus iudex asseruit eidem Willelmo Masse quod dicti articuli continent in se nonnullas hereses et errores quamplures determinacioni Ecclesie Romane contrarias et repugnantes. Et, hiis dictis, dictus W. Masse asseruit se velle extunc suprascriptos hereses et errores ac omnem heresim pro perpetuo re*d* et verbo dimittere et abiurare, ac puro corde redire ad Ecclesie unitatem. Et deinde idem Willelmus Masse, tenens manum suam dexteram ad librum evangeliorum, iuravit ad ea quod ab hac hora in antea ipse nunquam tenebit, credet nec affirmabit dictos*e* errores nec hereses nec aliquam aliam heresim seu opinionem vel doctrinam aliquam fidei catholice*f* (p. 251 / fo. 48r)*g* et determinacioni Ecclesie Romane*h* contrarios vel repugna[n]tes; nec aliquos hereticos nec aliquas personas de heresi suspectas in domos

---

a The bracketed words form, in the manuscript, a two-line paragraph in which the first half of each line has been deleted.

b MS. hornor.

c pauperibus deleted.

d vl deleted.

e dictos interlined.

f Presentibus:
    magistro Johanne Midelton
           Roberto Goverton

Absolutus est, et pro commissis:
iij fustigaciones circa ecclesiam
et totidem circa mercatum Norwic'
cum cereo j libre

written at foot of page.

g Willelmus Masse in top right-hand corner of page.

h contrari follows Romane.

suas recipiet, supportabit, concelabit vel defendet; nec talibus personis scienter se associabit vel prebebit consilium, auxilium vel favorem per se vel mediam personam publice nec occulte; et si habuerit noticiam de hereticis vel aliqua persona de heresi suspecta, quod quamcito comode poterit prefatum reverendum patrem si[ve] ipsius vicarium in spiritualibus generalem de personis et nominibus eorundem effectualiter cerciorabit. Quibus sic peractis, prefatus vicarius in spiritualibus ipsi Willelmo Masse asseruit et intimavit quod si ipse in posterum relapsus fuerit in heresim et inde poterit legitime convinci, propter ipsius incorrigibilitatem in hac parte relinqui debet iudicio seculari, ignis supplicio comburendus. Et subsequenter idem Robertus ad sacra evangelia prescripta iuravit ad ea de bene et fideliter agendo penitenciam quam dictus vicarius in spiritualibus sibi pro suis commissis prescriptis decreverit iniungendam. Quo iuramento sic prestito, idem vicarius in spiritualibus iniunxit eidem Willelmo pro commissis tres fustigaciones circa ecclesiam suam parochialem de Ersham et totidem circa mercatum Norwic', capite et pedibus denudatis, cum cereo cere ponderis j libre, quem cereum proxima Dominica post penitenciam huiusmodi peractam iudex iniunxit per ipsum Willelmum Masse offerri summo altari ecclesie de Ersham.

Presentibus in premissis omnibus et singulis magistro Johanne Midelton, in artibus magistro, ac Roberto Goverton, rectore de Ersham, Johanne Blytheburgh, capellano, ac Thoma Walsham, clerico, et me, Johanne Excestr, notario publico, actorum scriba.

[47]

(p. 252 / fo. 48v)*a* **Johannes Goodwyn de Ersham**228

Die xiiij mensis Marcii Anno Domini Millesimo CCCC⁰ XXX⁰, indiccione nona, pontificatus sanctissimi in Christo patris et domini nostri, domini Martini divina providencia pape huius nominis

a et determinacioni Ecclesie Romane contrarios vel repugnantes; nec aliquos hereticos vel personas aliquas de heresi suspectas recipiet, concelabit nec supportabit; nec talibus personis se scienter associabit; nec talibus personis prebebit consilium, auxilium vel favorem per se nec per mediam personam publice nec occulte; et si habuerit noticiam de aliquibus hereticis vel de personis de heresi suspectis, quod quamcito comode poterit dictum dominum Norwicensem episcopum seu ipsius vicarium in spiritualibus generalem de nominibus eorundem reddet effectualiter cerciorem. Quo iuramento sic prestito, prefatus iudex *at top of page, deleted.*

---

228 Earsham, south-east Norfolk.

quinti, anno quartodecimo, in capella palacii reverendi in Christo patris et domini, domini Willelmi Dei gracia Norwicensis episcopi, in civitate Norwici situati, in mei, Johannis Excestr, clerici Exoniensis diocesis, publici auctoritate apostolica notarii, et testium subscriptorum presencia, coram reverende discrecionis viro magistro Willelmo Bernham, in decretis bacallario, dicti reverendi patris, domini Norwicensis episcopi, vicario in spiritualibus generali, iudicialiter sedente, comparuit personaliter Johannes Goodwyn de Ersham Norwicensis diocesis, notatus de crimine heresis et heretice pravitatis. Cui prefatus vicarius in spiritualibus, iudex in hac parte, ex officio suo, ut asseruit, ad correccionem meram ipsius Johannis[a] procedere intendens, proposuit iudicialiter et obiecit articulos subscriptos, dicens:

Inprimis quod ipse Johannes Goodwyn habuit sepius familiaritatem et communicaciones privatas cum hereticis et personis suspectis de heresi, et quod hereticorum scolas et opiniones exercuit et frequentavit. Ad istum articulum iste[b] Johannes impetitus dixit iudicialiter quod ipse habuit [communicacionem] secretam cum Johanne Waddon, heretico condempnato, ex cuius doctrina idem Johannes Godwyn concepit et didicit articulos subscriptos.

Inprimis quod omnes oblaciones sunt subtrahende.

Item quod nullus honor est exhibendus aliquibus ymaginibus in ecclesiis.

Item quod peregrinaciones nullo modo sunt faciende.

Quos quidem articulos prefatus[c] Johannes Goodwyn asseruit se tenuisse, credidisse et affirmasse. Et deinde idem iudex[d] quesivit a[e] dicto Johanne an voluerit dictos articulos, ac hereses et errores in eis contentos, defendere vel[f] pro perpetuo dimittere et abiurare. Idem Johannes asseruit se velle dictos articulos, ac omnes hereses et errores in eisdem contentos, et[g] eciam omnem heresim[h] re et verbo cum puro corde dimittere pro perpetuo et abiurare. Et tunc idem Johannes, tenens manum suam dexteram super librum evangeliorum, iuravit ad ea quod ab hac hora in antea ipse nunquam tenebit, credet nec affirmabit dictos hereses (p. 253 / fo. 49r)[i] vel errores nec aliquam heresim nec aliquam doctrinam seu opinionem fidei catholice et determinacioni Ecclesie Romane contrariam, nec aliquos hereticos nec aliquam personam de heresi suspectam recipiet, sustentabit, supportabit, concelabit nec defendet, nec talibus personis prebebit consilium, auxilium vel favorem per se nec per mediam personam publice vel occulte. Quibus sic peractis, iudex

---

[a] MS. Johannes, *the last two letters being partly rubbed out.*
[b] iuratus asse *deleted.* [c] prefatus *repeated.*
[d] declaravit *deleted.* [e] quesivit a *interlined.*
[f] prop' *deleted.* [g] mas *deleted.*
[h] d *deleted.* [i] Johannes Goodwyn *in top right-hand corner of page*

declaravit dicto Johanni quod si in posterum relapsus fuerit in heresim vel fuerit convictus de heresi, propter ipsius incorrigibilitatem in hac parte relinqui debet*a* seculari iudicio comburendus. Et deinde, prestito per eundem Johannem iuramento ad sacra evangelia de agendo fideliter penitenciam sibi pro suis commissis iniungendam, et hoc iuramento prestito, iudex*b* iniunxit sibi pro commissis unam fustigacionem circa ecclesiam suam parochialem, cum cereo cere ponderis dimidie libre offerendo coram summo altari post penitenciam peractam huiusmodi. Et deinde iudex predictus ipsum Johannem absolvit a sentencia excommunicacionis qua premissorum occasione extitit alligatus.

Presentibus tunc ibidem magistro Johanne Midelton, in artibus magistro, ac Roberto Goverton, rectore ecclesie de Ersham, et me, J. Excestr.

[48]

Henricus Lachecold

Die xiiij mensis Marcii Anno Domini Millesimo CCCC° XXX, indiccione nona, pontificatus sanctissimi in Christo patris et domini, domini Martini divina providencia pape quinti, anno xiiij°, in capella palacii*c* reverendi in Christo patris et domini, domini Willelmi Dei gracia Norwicensis episcopi, in civitate Norwic' situati, in mei, Johannis Excestr, clerici, notarii publici, et testium infrascriptorum presencia, coram reverende discrecionis viro magistro Willelmo Bernham, in decretis bacallario, dicti reverendi patris domini Norwicensis episcopi vicario in spiritualibus generali, iudicialiter sedente, comparuit personaliter Henricus Lachecold de Ersham²²⁹ Norwicensis diocesis, diffamatus de crimine heresis et heretice pravitatis.

Cui prefatus vicarius in spiritualibus generalis, ex officio suo procedens, ut asseruit, ad meram anime ipsius Henrici correccionem, proposuit iudicialiter et obiecit,*d* dicens quod ipse Henricus habuit communicacionem secretam cum hereticis, et eorum scolas frequentavit sepius et continuavit. Qui quidem Henricus, iuratus ad sacra evangelia de veritate dicenda, respondebat dicens quod

---

a iudicio *deleted.*　　　　　　　　*b* iudex *repeated.*
c nor *deleted.*　　　　　　　　　*d* s articulos subscriptos et *deleted.*

²²⁹ Earsham, south-east Norfolk.

nunquam habuit familiarem communicacionem cum aliquo heretico de sciencia sua nisi tantum cum domino Willelmo Whyte,
heretico condempnato, qui quidem Willelmus Whyte in domo istius
Henrici Lacchecold*a* dixit, asseruit,*b* docuit et affirmavit quod
omnes presbiteri sunt falsi, item quod omnes oblaciones sunt subtrahende, item quod peregrinaciones*c* nullo modo sunt faciende.

Quibus coram dicto iudice, ut prefertur, iudicialiter confessatis,
prefatus iudex asseruit (p. 254 / fo. 49v) dicto Henrico quod dicti
articuli, quos ipse asseruit se credidisse et affirmasse, sapiunt
heresim manifestam fidei catholice et determinacioni sacrosancte
Romane Ecclesie contrariam et repugnantem. Quo audito, prefatus
Henricus voluit, ut asseruit, dictos articulos ac contenta in eisdem,
in quantum sunt fidei catholice et determinacioni Ecclesie Romane
repugnancia,*d* re et verbo dimittere pro perpetuo et abiurare, ac
puro corde redire ad Ecclesie unitatem. Et tunc idem Henricus,
tenens manum suam dexteram super librum evangeliorum, iuravit
iudicialiter ad ea quod ipse nunquam de cetero*e* tenebit, credet nec
affirmabit dictos hereses vel errores, nec aliquam aliam heresim
nec doctrinam seu opinionem aliquam fidei catholice et determinacioni Ecclesie Romane contrariam, nec aliquos hereticos nec aliquam
personam de heresi suspectam recipiet, supportabit, sustentabit,
concelabit vel defendet, nec talibus personis prebebit consilium,*f*
auxilium vel favorem per se vel per mediam personam publice nec
occulte. Quibus sic peractis, dictus iudex declaravit dicto Henrico
iudicialiter tunc ibidem quod si ipse Henricus de cetero in futurum
relapsus fuerit in heresim et convictus legitime in hac parte, tunc
propter ipsius incorrigibilitatem relinqui debet seculari iudicio
comburendus. Et deinde, prestito per eundem Henricum iuramento
ad sacra evangelia de agendo penitenciam sibi pro suis commissis
iniungendam, dictus vicarius in spiritualibus absolvit ipsum Henricum a sentencia excommunicacionis qua premissorum occasione
extitit alligatus. Et pro commissis iniunxit sibi ij fustigaciones circa
ecclesiam suam parochialem de Ersham coram solenni processione
eiusdem, capite et pedibus denudatis, corpore camisia et femoralibus
duntaxat induto, cum cereo cere ponderis dimidie libre suis manibus
deferendo et offerendo summo altari dicte ecclesie post huiusmodi
penitenciam peractam.

Presentibus tunc ibidem magistro Johanne Midelton, in artibus
magistro, ac Roberto Goverton, rectore ecclesie parochialis de
Ersham predicte, ac Willelmo Fraunceys et Thoma Walsham,
clericis. J. Excestr.

---

a ut asseruit *deleted*.   *b* et *deleted*.
c ni *deleted*.   *d* pur *deleted*.
e ipse nunquam *repeated*.   *f* ax *deleted*.

[49]

Henricus Goode de Ersham[230]

Henricus Goode de Ersham, diffamatus de crimine heresis et heretice pravitatis, die xiiij mensis Marcii anno Domini[a] et[b] pontificatus[c] proxime suprascripto, coram reverende discrecionis viro magistro Willelmo Bernham, reverendi in Christo patris et domini, domini Willelmi Dei gracia Norwicensis episcopi, vicario in spiritualibus generali, in capella palacii dicti reverendi patris in Norwico situati iudicialiter sedente, comparuit. Et negavit omnem heresim sibi obiectam. Et quia, facta publica proclamacione coram nonnullis vicinis suis tunc ibidem presentibus,[d] nichil compertum est contra eum per inquisicionem, dictus iudex assignavit sibi diem Veneris proximum post festum Sancti Benedicti Abbatis, videlicet xxiij diem Marcii predicti ad purgandum se cum vij manu de vicinis suis in eodem loco.

Presentibus tunc ibidem magistro Johanne Midelton, in artibus magistro, ac Roberto Goverton, rectore de Ersham.

Quibus die et loco, coram dicto vicario generali, comparuit. Et produxit compurgatores: videlicet, Johannem Sherhawe, Johannem Wade, Ricardum Fyton, Johannem Horn, Johannem Wylyam et Johannem Terry de Ersham. Et purgavit se solenniter.

Presentibus tunc ibidem magistr' Roberto Aylmer et Thoma Walsham et ceteris.[e]

[50]

(p. 255 / fo. 50r) Ricardus Horn de Ersham[231]

Die xiiij mensis Marcii Anno Domini Millesimo CCCC° XXX, indiccione nona, pontificatus sanctissimi in Christo patris et domini

---

[a] suprascript' *deleted*.   [b] et *interlined*.
[c] mens *deleted*.   [d] et quia *repeated*.
[e] Ricardus Horn

Johannes Spyr de Bungey (*all four words deleted*)
in bottom right-hand corner of page.

---

[230] Earsham, south-east Norfolk.   [231] Earsham, south-east Norfolk.

nostri, domini Martini divina providencia pape quinti, anno quartodecimo, in capella palacii reverendi in Christo patris et domini,
domini Willelmi Dei gracia Norwicensis episcopi, in civitate Norwic'
situati, in mei, Johannis Excestr, clerici, notarii publici, et testium
subscriptorum presencia, coram reverende discrecionis viro magistro
Willelmo Bernham, in decretis bacallario, dicti reverendi patris
vicario in spiritualibus generali, iudicialiter sedente, Ricardus Horn
de Ersham Norwicensis diocesis, diffamatus de crimine heresis et
heretice pravitatis et ea occasione sub custodia carcerali dicti patris
aliquamdiu detentus, productus fuit ad iudicium super dicto crimine
personaliter responsurus. Qui quidem Ricardus, per prefatum
vicarium in spiritualibus allocutus iudicialiter et impetitus de nonnullis articulis errores et hereses quamplures fidei catholice et
determinacioni Ecclesie Romane contrarias et repugnantes in se
continentibus, quos, ut dicebatur, tenuit,[a] eosdem articulos omnes
et singulos et generaliter omnem heresim ab[b] omni tempore constanter negavit. Et quia nichil probatum nec compertum erat contra
ipsum Ricardum in specie, facta publica proclamacione in iudicio
tunc ibidem coram nonnullis vicinis suis et nullo dicto contra
eundem, datus erat sibi dies Veneris proximus post festum Sancti
Benedicti Abbatis, videlicet xxiij dies Marcii predicti ad purgandum
se cum septima manu de vicinis suis in capella predicta.

Presentibus tunc ibidem magistris Johanne Midelton, in artibus
magistro, ac Roberto Goverton, rectore ecclesie parochialis de
Ersham predicte, ac Willelmo Fraunceys et Thoma Washam,
clericis, et aliis quampluribus testibus. J. Excestr.

Quibus die et loco, coram dicto vicario in spiritualibus generali
iudicialiter sedente, comparuit dictus Ricardus Horn personaliter.
Et produxit compurgatores suos subscriptos: videlicet, Johannem
Terry de Ersham, Johannem Soyham de eadem, Johannem Horn
de eadem, Ricardum Fyton de eadem, Johannem Wade de eadem
et Johannem Sherawe de eadem. Et purgavit se ab omni tempore.

Presentibus tunc ibidem magistris Hugone Acton, Roberto
Aylmer et Johanne Walpool, notariis publicis,[c] ac Thoma Walsham,
clerico. J. Excestr.

---

[a] quos, ut dicebatur, tenuit *interlined.*
[b] ipso *deleted.*   [c] notariis publicis *interlined.*

[51]

(p. 256 / fo. 50v) **Johannes Belward de Ersham,**[232] **senior**

Anno Domini Millesimo Quadringentesimo Tricesimo, indiccione nona, pontificatus sanctissimi in Christo patris et domini nostri, domini Martini divina providencia pape quinti, anno quartodecimo, mensis Marcii die quartadecima, in capella palacii reverendi in Christo patris et domini, domini Willelmi Dei gracia Norwicensis episcopi, in civitate Norwic' situati, in mei, Johannis Excestr, clerici, notarii publici, et testium subscriptorum presencia, coram reverende discrecionis viro magistro Willelmo Bernham, in decretis bacallario, dicti reverendi patris vicario in spiritualibus generali, iudicialiter sedente, Johannes Belward de Ersham Norwicensis diocesis, senior, diffamatus multipliciter de crimine heresis et heretice pravitatis et ea occasione sub custodia carcerali per dictum vicarium generalem aliquamdiu detentus, productus fuit ad iudicium super dicto crimine personaliter responsurus, videlicet super articulis quibus Willelmus Masse extitit impetitus.[a] Qui quidem Johannes Belward, per prefatum vicarium generalem de et super premissis et[b] nonnullis articulis errores et hereses quamplures fidei catholice et determinacioni sancte Romane Ecclesie repugnantes in se continentibus—quos prefatus Johannes, ut dicebatur, tenuit, credidit et affirmavit—allocutus, interrogatus et iudicialiter impetitus, eosdem articulos omnes et singulos ac omnes hereses et errores in eis contentos et[c] generaliter omnem heresim ab omni tempore constanter negavit. Et quia nichil effectuale compertum erat vel detectum contra eundem, facta publica proclamacione coram nonnullis vicinis suis tunc ibidem presentibus si quis voluerit contra ipsum Johannem dicere, proponere[d] vel allegare quominus[e] eidem purgacio indici non debeat in hac parte, et nullo dicto contra eundem, iudex assignavit sibi diem Veneris proximum post festum Sancti Benedicti Abbatis proximum, videlicet xxiij[m] diem mensis Marcii prescripti ad purgandum se cum vij manu in eodem loco.

Presentibus tunc ibidem magistro Johanne Midelton, in artibus magistro, ac Roberto Goverton, rectore ecclesie parochialis de Ersham predicte, ac Willelmo Fraunceys et Thoma Walsham, testibus, et aliis quampluribus in multitudine numerosa.

[a] videlicet super articulis quibus Willelmus Masse extitit impetitus *interlined. For the articles, see p. 205.* [b] premissis et *interlined.*
[c] in specie *deleted.* [d] voluerit *repeated.* [e] idem *deleted.*

---

[232] Earsham, south-east Norfolk.

Quibus die et loco, coram dicto vicario generali iudicialiter sedente, comparuit dictus Johannes Belward iudicialiter. Et produxit compurgatores: videlicet, Nicholaum Cuckok, Johannem Goodwyn, Henricum Bucke, Henricum Paston, Thomam Katesson et Johannem Ayldr, seniorem, de Ersham. Et purgavit se solenniter.

Presentibus tunc ibidem magistris Roberto Aylmer et Hugone Acton, notariis publicis, ac Thoma Walsham predicto. J. Excestr.*a*

[52]

(p. 257 / fo. 51r) **Johannes Belward de Ersham,[233] junior**

Anno Domini Millesimo CCCCmo XXXo, indiccione nona, pontificatus sanctissimi in Christo patris et domini nostri, domini Martini divina providencia pape quinti, anno quartodecimo, mensis Marcii die xiiij,*b* in capella palacii reverendi in Christo patris et domini, domini Willelmi Dei gracia Norwicensis episcopi, in civitate Norwic' situati, in mei, Johannis Excestr, clerici, notarii publici, et testium infrascriptorum presencia, coram reverende discrecionis viro magistro Willelmo Bernham, in decretis bacallario, dicti reverendi patris vicario in spiritualibus generali, iudicialiter sedente, Johannes Belward de Ersham Norwicensis diocesis, junior, diffamatus multipliciter de crimine heresis et heretice pravitatis et ea occasione sub custodia carcerali in dicto palacio per prefatum vicarium generalem aliquamdiu detentus, productus fuit ad iudicium super dicto crimine personaliter responsurus. Qui quidem Johannes Belward, junior, per prefatum vicarium generalem iudicialiter sedentem de et super nonnullis articulis errores et hereses quamplures fidei catholice et determinacioni sancte Romane Ecclesie contrarias et repugnantes in se continentibus—quos et quas, ut dicebatur, prefatus Johannes Belward, junior, tenuit, credidit et affirmavit—allocutus, interrogatus iudicialiter et impetitus, eosdem articulos omnes et singulos ac omnes hereses in eis contentas ac generaliter omnem heresim ab omni tempore constanter negavit. Et quia nichil compertum vel detectum extitit contra eundem, facta proclamacione publica coram rectore de Ersham subscripto ac coram parochianis dicte ecclesie de Ersham ac aliis vicinis suis quampluribus tunc ibidem

---

a Johannes Belward, junior *in bottom right-hand corner of page.*
b mensis Marcii die xiiij *interlined.*

---

233 Earsham, south-east Norfolk.

presentibus si qui voluerint contra ipsum Johannem quicquam proponere, dicere vel allegare quominus purgacio sibi debeat indici, et
nullo dicto contra eundem, idem vicarius in spiritualibus generalis
assignavit eidem Johanni diem Veneris proximum post festum
Sancti Benedicti Abbatis proximum, videlicet vicesimum tercium
diem dicti mensis Marcii ad purgandum se ab omni heresi in capella
palacii predicta.

Presentibus tunc ibidem magistro Johanne Midelton, in artibus
magistro, ac Roberto Goverton, rectore dicte ecclesie de Ersham,
necnon Thoma Walsham et Willelmo Frlaunceys, clericis, testibus
ad premissa vocatis specialiter et rogatis.

Quibus die et loco, coram dicto vicario generali iudicialiter
sedente, comparuit personaliter dictus Johannes Belward, junior.
Et produxit compurgatores suos subscriptos: Nicholaum Cukkok,
Johannem Goodwyn, Henricum Bucke, Henricum Paston, Thomam
Catesson et Johannem Ayldr de Ersham. Et purgavit se ab omni
tempore.

Presentibus tunc ibidem magistris Roberto Aylmer et Hugone
Acton, notariis publicis, ac Thoma Walsham prescripto. J. Excestr.

[53]

(p. 258 / fo. 51v) **Robertus Shirwynd, Willelmus Shirwynd**

Anno Domini Millesimo CCCC^mo Tricesimo, indiccione nona,
pontificatus domini Martini pape quinti anno quartodecimo,[234]
coram reverende discrecionis viro magistro Willelmo Bernham, in
decretis bacallario, reverendi in Christo patris et domini,[a] domini
Willelmi Dei gracia Norwicensis episcopi, vicario in spiritualibus
generali, in capella palacii Norwic' iudicialiter sedente, comparue-
runt personaliter Robertus Shirwynd de Harleston,[235] bocher, ac

[a] nostri *deleted*.

---

[234] The outside dates for the trial are 21 November 1430 (when the year 14
Martin V began) and 24 March 1431 (when *Annus Domini* 1430 ended), even
though the year 14 Martin V had ended before the latter date (see p. 198, n. 17).
But several factors suggest that it took place on 14 March 1431: in the manuscript it follows several trials that took place on that day; it, like they, was
held in the Bishop's Palace in Norwich; and the two witnesses, John Midelton
and Robert Goverton, also witnessed the trials that took place on 14 March,
but very few others (see pp. 206–14).
[235] Probably Harleston, south Norfolk; possibly Harleston, cast Suffolk.

Willelmus Shirwynd de eadem, notati aliqualiter de lollardria et heresi. Qui quidem Robertus et Willelmus de omni heresi et lollardria se canonice purgarunt in forma eisdem per prefatum vicarium generalem indicta.

Presentibus tunc ibidem magistris Johanne Midelton, in artibus magistro, ac Roberto Goverton, rectore ecclesie parochialis de Ersham, et ceteris. J. Excestr.

[54]

Johannes Terry de Ersham²³⁶
habet unum librum de heresi

Johannes Ayltr de Ersham

Johannes Wade de Ersham

Die et loco prescriptis isti tres purgarunt se coram dicto vicario generali, presentibus prescriptis.

[55]

(p. 262 / fo. 53v) **Thomas Herde de Shipmedwe²³⁷**

Anno Domini Millesimo CCCC⁰ XXX, indiccione nona, pontificatus domini Martini pape quinti anno*ᵃ* quartodecimo,²³⁸ in capella palacii reverendi in Christo patris et domini, domini Willelmi Dei gracia Norwicensis episcopi, in civitate Norwic' situati, in mei, Johannis Excestr, clerici, notarii publici, et testium subscriptorum presencia, coram reverende discrecionis viro magistro Willelmo Bernham, in decretis bacallario, dicti reverendi patris vicario in spiritualibus generali, iudicialiter sedente, Thomas Herde de Shipmedwe, tayllour, diffamatus multipliciter de crimine heresis et heretice pravitatis, productus fuit ad iudicium super dicto crimine personaliter responsurus. Qui quidem Thomas Herde, per prefatum vicarium generalem de et super nonnullis articulis hereses et errores

---

ᵃ nona *deleted*.

---

²³⁶ Earsham, south-east Norfolk.   ²³⁷ Shipmeadow, north-east Suffolk.
²³⁸ See p. 214, n. 234; except that in the manuscript the trial of Thomas Herde does not follow those that took place on 14 March 1431, and it must have been held before 23 March 1431, when Thomas Herde purged himself (see p. 216).

quamplures fidei catholice et determinacioni Ecclesie Romane contrarios et repugnantes continentibus—quos prefatus Thomas, ut dicebatur, tenuit, credidit et affirmavit—allocutus, interrogatus et iudicialiter impetitus, eosdem articulos omnes et singulos ac omnes hereses et errores in eis contentos et generaliter omnem heresim ab omni tempore constanter negavit. Et quia nichil per inquisicionem nec quovis alio modo compertum est vel detectum fuit contra ipsum Thomam in specie, facta publica proclamacione tunc ibidem coram multitudine populi numerosa si qui voluerint contra ipsum Thomam*a* dicere, proponere vel allegare quominus purgacio canonica sibi indici debeat de premissis, et nullo dicto in hac parte, iudex assignabit eidem Thome diem Veneris proximum post festum Sancti Benedicti Abbatis ad purgandum se in capella predicta cum septima manu de vicinis suis.

Presentibus tunc ibidem magistro Johanne Midelton, Roberto Goverton, rectore ecclesie de Ersham, ac Willelmo Fraunceys et Thoma Walsham.

Quibus die et loco, videlicet xxiij⁰ die mensis et anni predictorum,[239] coram dicto vicario in spiritualibus iudicialiter sedente, comparuit personaliter dictus Thomas Herde. Et produxit compurgatores suos: videlicet, Johannem Caryon de Barsham,[240] Willelmum Caryon de eadem, Johannem Smyth de eadem, Michaelem Doraunt de Shipmedwe, Willelmum Chapman de eadem, Henricum Hundegate de eadem, Willelmum Carable de Barsham et Robertum Fokeneld de eadem.*b* Quibus preconizatis et personaliter comparentibus, facta proclamacione si qui voluerint contra purgacionem ipsius Thome dicere, proponere vel allegare, et nullo dicto, iudex predictus admisit purgacionem*c* ipsius Thome in forma iuris.

Presentibus tunc ibidem magistris Roberto Aylmer, Hugone Acton, Thoma Walsham, clerico, ac pluribus aliis. J. Excestr.

---

a purgacionem *deleted.*   *b* p. *deleted.*   *c* su' *deleted.*

[239] 23 March 1431.
[240] Barsham, north-east Suffolk.

APPENDIX[1]

Deliberatio gaole castri domini regis Norwici facta coram prefatis Willelmo Westbury, Johanne Fray et Ricardo Weltden, justiciariis domini regis ad gaolam illam de prisonibus in ea existentibus deliberandam assignatis apud Thetford die Lune[2] in vigilia Sancti Petri in Cathedra anno regni regis Henrici sexti post conquestum Anglie septimo

Johannes[a] Skylly de Flixton[3] in comitatu Suff', millere, Johannes Godeshill de Dychyngham[4] in comitatu Norff', parchemyn-makere, Simon Mansthope de Ilketeshale[5] in comitatu Suff', laborer, et Thomas Pell de Netesherde[6] in comitatu Norff', soutere, alias capti per indicamentum factum coram[b] justiciariis domini regis de pace in predicto comitatu Norff' de eo quod ipsi simul cum aliis ignotis falsiter et proditorie custodierunt scolas heresis apud Ersham[7] et alibi in diversis locis in comitatu Norff' et ibidem docuerunt diversas opiniones heresis et lollardrie ac male fidei contra fidem catholicam—continuando de die in diem, videlicet a festo Sancti Michaelis Archangeli[8] anno regni regis Henrici sexti post conquestum tercio usque festum Pasche[9] anno eiusdem regis sexto—pervertendo diversos homines et mulieres a dicta fide catholica ad artem lollardrie, dicendo Johanni Tuk et ipsum et alios diversos homines et mulieres docendo apud Ersham predictam die Sabbati[10] proximo post festum Sancti Petri in Cathedra anno regni regis Henrici supradicti sexto quod nullus sacerdos habet potestatem conficiendi corpus Christi set quod post prolacionem verborum sacramentalium remanet panis materialis, et quod nullus ieiunaret set licitum fuit omni die carnes manducare absque peccato, et quod ymagines sanctorum nullo modo sunt adorande, et alias opiniones hereticas tenent contra fidem catholicam; et[c] de eo quod predictus Thomas Pell die Martis[11] proximo ante festum Sancti Jacobi Apostoli anno

---

[a] Norff' *in margin:* Hundredum de Ersham et Disse (*i.e.,* Earsham *and* Diss) *in margin of MS. A.*
[b] *MS. A* indicati sunt coram.
[c] Hundredum de Tunsted (*i.e.,* Tunstead) *in margin of MS. A.*

---

[1] Public Record Office, JUST/3/207, m. 3r. Some of the material was also recorded in JUST/3/219/5, m. 149r (subsequently referred to as MS. A); what the latter adds is mentioned in the footnotes.

[2] 21 February 1429.

[3] Flixton, north-east Suffolk.

[4] Ditchingham, south-east Norfolk.

[5] Ilketshall, north-east Suffolk.

[6] Neatishead, east Norfolk.

[7] Earsham, south-east Norfolk.

[8] 29 September 1424.

[9] 4 April 1428.

[10] 27 February 1428.

[11] 20 July 1428.

regni regis Henrici sexti post conquestum sexto apud Netisherde docuit quod quis non deberet dare honorem alicui ymagini, set si quis alicui ymagini honorem dat seipsum peccato subicit, et alias quamplures opiniones erronias et lollardrie ibidem adtunc et pluries docuit et tenuit contra fidem catholicam et doctrinam sacrosancte Ecclesie.

Johannes[a] Skilly de Bergh[12] in comitatu Norff', husbondman, et Willelmus Wardon de Lodon[13] in predicto comitatu Norff', husbondman,[b] alias capti per indicamentum factum coram[c] prefatis justiciariis domini regis de pace de eo quod ipsi nocte diei Mercurii[14] proxim' post festum Purificacionis Beate Marie Virginis anno regni regis Henrici sexti post conquestum quinto vi et armis ex malicia precogitata intraverunt cimiterium ecclesie Sancti Andree de Trows apud Trows[15] in comitatu predicto, et ymaginem Sancti Andree Apostoli precii ijs ibidem inventam felonice ceperunt et asportaverunt, et usque villam de Bergh iuxta Lodon[16] eandem ymaginem predictam nocte diei Mercurii et anno supradictis cariaverunt,[d] et ibidem predictam ymaginem falsiter et proditorie combusserunt; et quod predicti Johannes et Willelmus sunt communes heretici et lollardi, dicendo et docendo Johannem Tuk et alios quamplures homines apud Bergh predictam die Veneris[17] proximo post festum Sancti Valentini Martiris et aliis diebus anno regni regis supradicti sexto quod Eucaristia altaris non est corpus Christi set panis sanctificatus tantum, et quod sacramentum Baptismi secundum formam usitatam in Ecclesia est nichil vel modicum ponderandum, et quod confessio vocalis facta sacerdoti est invalida; et quod alias opiniones contra fidem catholicam tenent.

Que quidem indicamenta Thomas Derham, unus predictorum justiciariorum domini regis de pace in predicto comitatu Norff', modo hic recordatur.

Et modo coram justiciariis hic venerunt predicti Johannes Skylly de Flixton, Johannes Godeshill, Simon, Thomas, Johannes Skilly de Bergh et Willelmus in propriis personis suis in custodia vicecomitis et per ipsum vicecomitem ducti. Et visis indicamentis predictis per justiciarios hic quia videtur eisdem justiciariis hic

---

[a] [Hundredum de] Hensted (*i.e.*, Henstead) *in margin of MS. A.*
[b] *MS. A* laborer.
[c] *MS. A* indicati sunt coram.
[d] *MS.* intraverunt: *MS. A* cariaverunt.

---

[12] Probably Bergh Apton, south-east Norfolk.
[13] Loddon, south-east Norfolk.
[14] 5 February 1427.
[15] St Andrew's parish church, Trowse, near Norwich.
[16] Bergh Apton, near Loddon, south-east Norfolk.
[17] 19 February 1428.

quod indicamenta, licet proditorie et felonice supponantur per-
petrari, nimis*a* valida et in lege insufficiencia existunt ad predictos
Johannem Skylly de Flixton, Johannem Godeshill, Simonem,
Thomam, Johannem Skylly de Bergh et Willelmum hic de prodi-
cione vel felonia super eisdem indicamentis aliqualiter alloquendos,
immo quod iidem Johannes Skilly de Flixton, Johannes Godeshill,
Simon, Thomas, Johannes Skilly de Bergh et Willelmus pretextu
eorundem indicamentorum reverendo in Christo patri Willelmo,
permissione divina Norwicensi episcopo, loci predicti ordinario,
iuxta formam statuti contra hereticos et lollardos*b* anno regni
domini Henrici nuper regis Anglie, patris domini regis nunc, secundo
apud Leycestre[18] nuper editi et provisi, sunt omnino liberandi et
super articulis in predictis indicamentis expressatis per ipsum episcopum examinandi, ideo precatus est vicecomes quod predictos
Johannem Skilly de Flixton, Johannem Godeshill, Simonem,
Thomam, Johannem Skilly de Bergh et Willelmum Wardon prefato
episcopo iuxta formam statuti predicti liberet iudicialiter.

a Sic.
b liberati ordinario ad examinandum in fide et ceter' *in margin.*

---

[18] *Statutum contra Lollardos*, passed by the Leicester Parliament of April 1414
(*The Statutes of the Realm* (London, 1810–28), ii, pp. 181–4).

INDEX

Abbot, George, archbp of Canterbury (1611–33), 5

Abraham, John, of Colchester, cordwainer, 28, 45, 152

Abraham, John, of Woodchurch, 45

abstinence; *see* fasting

Acle (Ocle), Norfolk, 43

Acton, Hugh, notary public, 65, 68, 94, 150–1, 156, 174, 177, 192, 200, 204, 211, 213–14, 216

Adam, 91

Aiscough; *see* Ascogh

Alnwick, William, bp of Norwich (1426–36) and of Lincoln (1436–49), 22, 48–9

—'accursed', 45

—'Caiaphas', 18, 46–7

—conduct of the trials, *passim*

—investigation of, into heresy in Bury St Edmunds, 8, 99

—*see also* Norwich, bishop of

Ambrose, St, 11, 14, 148

Andrew, St, image of, 218

Antichrist

—bells and, 19, 81, 190

—bishops, prelates and, 17, 53, 57, 61, 67, 86, 108, 112, 116, 122, 127, 135, 170, 197

—cross of Christ and, 13, 154, 166

—friars and, 17, 61, 67

—pope and, 11, 17, 53, 57, 61, 67, 86, 108, 112, 116, 122, 127, 135, 141, 147, 170, 197

—priests and, 108, 112, 122, 127, 135, 170

archbishops, 45

Archer, Edmund, of Loddon, cordwainer, 25–6, 75–6, 100, 140, 157, 163–8, 176, 179

Arteys, Thomas, rector of Wreningham, 40

Arundel, Thomas, archbp of Canterbury (1396–7 and 1399–1414), 17

Ascogh (Aiscough, Ayscogh), William, bp of Salisbury (1438–50), 9, 32, 39, 43, 51, 69, 79–81, 90, 102, 114, 120, 125, 132–3, 139, 145, 151, 175, 182

Augustine (Augustyn), St, 11, 14, 148

Ave Maria; *see* Hail Mary

Ayldr, John, of Earsham, 213–14

—*see also* Ayltr

Aylesham, John, 94

Aylesham, John, rector of Beeston, 39, 94

Aylmer (Aylmere), Robert, notary public, procurator of the Norwich Consistory Court, 54, 59, 62–3, 65, 68, 77, 92, 98, 119, 124, 130, 138, 150, 156, 177, 192, 200, 210–11, 213–14, 216

Ayltr, John, of Earsham, 215

—*see also* Ayldr

Ayscogh; *see* Ascogh

Bacon, family of, 76

Baker, *alias* Ussher, John, of Tunstall, carpenter, 40, 68–70, 72

Bamburgh, William, priest, 70, 119, 124, 138, 151, 163, 173, 177, 181, 201

baptism, 10–11, 20, 46, 52, 56, 60, 64, 66, 81, 86, 94–5, 107, 111, 115, 121, 126, 131, 134, 140, 146, 153, 157, 159, 165, 169, 176, 179, 182, 185, 189, 192–4, 196, 198, 205, 218

Barrow (Berwe), Suffolk, 101

Barsham, Suffolk, 216

Barton, Richard, Franciscan friar, 81

Basle, Council of (1431–49), 8

Bate, William, of Seething, tailor, 140, 146, 157–63, 176, 179, 195

Bath and Wells, bp of, 20

Baxter, Margery, of Martham, 13–15, 17–18, 20, 22, 26, 28, 41–51, 72

Baxter, Thomas, parish chaplain of South Creake, 89–90

Baxter, William, of Martham, wright, 26, 28, 39, 41, 43–4, 46–8, 50, 72, 86, 176, 179